The Sourdough and the Queen

ⓝ METHUEN

Toronto New York London Sydney Auckland

The Sourdough and the Queen

THE MANY LIVES OF

KLONDIKE JOE

BOYLE

LEONARD W. TAYLOR

CANADIAN CATALOGUING IN PUBLICATION DATA

Taylor, Leonard W.
   The sourdough and the queen

Bibliography: p.
ISBN 0-458-96810-2

1. Boyle, Joe, 1867-1923. 2. Gold miners–Yukon
Territory–Biography. 3. Adventure and adventurers–
Canada–Biography. I. Title.

FC4022.1.B6T3   971.9′102′0924   C83-098724-X
F1093.B6T3

Printed and bound in Canada by
T. H. Best Printing Company Limited

1   2   3   4   5   83   88   87   86   85   84

Contents

Acknowledgments

It is impossible to name all who have assisted in the preparation of this book, and it would be unwise to attempt it because some would surely be left out. The author is indebted to the many who have helped and who have provided, and still are providing, useful information about Joe Boyle, his life, and his times.

Having said that does not remove the necessity to be more specific in a number of cases. I am particularly indebted to Flora Boyle Frisch, Boyle's eighty-nine-year-old daughter and last surviving heir. Her help and encouragement have extended across a dozen years, even as she has contended with personal problems and met them with all the Boyle courage and resolution.

Others whose assistance has been invaluable include Deputy Director Brian Trainor and Research Assistant G.J. Slater of the Northern Ireland Records Office. I was helped in no small measure by the late Marion Braham, private secretary to Joe Boyle, Junior in his capacity as head of the Shell legal department in London, England. James Boyle was a warm host and a mine of information at the Boyle ancestral home. I have found useful material in the National Archives in Ottawa and the Yukon government offices in Whitehorse. My son Christopher did useful research for me in Rumania.

Also assisting and encouraging me have been the members of the Oxford Historical Society, especially its president, my old comrade Edwin Bennett, and Mrs. Susan Start, secretary of the Boyle Repatriation Committee.

All who have helped have been, I am sure, moved by a desire to see that Klondike Joe Boyle is finally accorded his proper place in Canadian history as a genuine, larger-than-life hero of a nation that all too often mourns that it has no heroes.

Introduction

More than one Yukoner has been called the King of the Klondike, starting with Alex MacDonald, who won and lost a fortune in a couple of years and then vanished from history. But only one man truly qualifies for the title—Joseph Whiteside Boyle.

Klondike Joe Boyle's singular right to the crown he never suggested was his lies in his association with two of the most important decades of the history of the territory. For nineteen years—from the time of his arrival in Dawson City in the summer of 1897 to his final departure in June 1916—Joe Boyle was part and parcel of the Klondike, someone to be reckoned with in the disposition of things in that region, even when he was several thousand miles away, as was the case from 1904 to 1909. On the Klondike diggings, in Dawson directing his various other businesses and participating in civic and social activities, and around the financial and political capitals of the English-speaking western world, he was known and respected as one of the most important citizens of the fabled land of gold.

Unlike most gold seekers who came early and left almost as precipitately as they had rushed to the Yukon, Boyle stayed on. However, merely having been there for a long period is no answer to the question of why he became a leader. He rose to wealth and power because he had vision, and because he was blessed with physical and mental courage and a determination to succeed that no contemporary surpassed. In the opinion of not a few of his contemporaries, his success was the product of sheer bullheaded obstinacy, a tenacity in the political and economic infighting that wore down all but the most resolute of those who opposed him.

More than any of his Yukon associates, Boyle fashioned the Klondike and directed its destiny. His almost immediate move into concession development, with machines replacing human hands in the extraction of gold, was an early pointer to the future of the region. His introduction of huge dredges, and his development of hydro resources to power them and to light the homes and business places of the region, put another distinctive Boyle trademark on the region.

Few of his achievements survived him. The Empire, of which he was so proud to be a Canadian member, has vanished. Many of his prized causes seem lost. The temperance banner he waved so long and hard is no longer seen in a territory where the annual per capita consumption of alcohol is among the highest in Canada.

In his later years, to the amazement of his Canadian friends, he was hailed as the "Saviour of Rumania" by many Rumanians, including the beautiful queen of that country who was his last and greatest love. But the Rumania he saved from Bolshevism is now a reluctant member of the Soviet bloc, whose keystone he sought to destroy.

Long the Unknown Canadian, Joe Boyle has received belated recognition by the recent transferral of his last remains to a burial place in the Woodstock, Ontario cemetery where his parents and other members of his family are interred in a plot just a few feet away.

This project, ably carried forward by the Oxford Historical Society at the request of Boyle's lone surviving heir, his daughter Flora, put an overdue spotlight on the amazing story of the man.

The Department of National Defence, through Defence Minister Gilles Lamontagne, provided vital assistance in the move. Canadians in many parts of the nation contributed funds to meet the costs of the venture.

Restless Joe Boyle, whose life took him to many faraway places, now fittingly rests among his kin in the soil of the land of which he always was so proud.

From the Shadow of the Slemish

The Irish Boyles are a lively, widely flung tribe, usually spirited and tenacious, not infrequently talented, and sometimes blessed with unusual wisdom, courage, and enterprise. There are Boyles, O'Boyles, and other variations. Some spellings designate racial, cultural, and religious affiliations. Plain Boyles are more likely to be Anglo-Irish and Protestant, their association with Ireland dating back to the first Elizabeth.

Most Boyles like to think they spring from Richard, the English adventurer who landed in Ireland in the Armada Year of 1588 with little more than the clothes he wore, but armed with a burning desire to succeed, a useful instinct to survive, and a rare administrative ability. This early Boyle climbed a dangerous ladder of preferment over the fallen Sir Walter Raleigh, to whose estates near Cork he fell heir, and reached the ducal pinnacle as Earl of Cork.

He had other qualities, too. History remembers that he was a kind host to Raleigh when the aging favourite of the dead Queen set out on his last, desperate voyage to find the South American Eldorado that alone could save his head from the chopping block of James I of England and James VI of Scotland.

From that line established in Cork came Robert Boyle, the great chemist and physicist, and it may well have been the source of another family of Boyles who settled at The Burnside, Upper Buckna, near Broughshane, County Antrim, at the end of the seventeenth century. The Burnside stands today, still tenanted by Boyles, a small residence even with recent additions, but proof that the size of homes is not a guide to the quality of those who spring from them.

The first Burnside Boyles were several of the seven brothers that family tradition holds "came out of the west" to fight for the Dutch William III. In 1690 they performed resolutely at the Boyne, the watershed battle at which his rebellious son-in-law wrote *finis* to the hopes of James II and provided a vital date for Irish tribal conflict to this day.

Subsequent Boyle settlement in Antrim was one result of the Orange victory. Since about 1720 there have been Boyles at Upper Buckna, on an eighteen-acre holding situated almost within the shadow of Slemish Mountain, a blunt peak once the core of an ancient volcano, that stands amid the rolling Antrim fields like a stubby forefinger pointing the way to heaven. Around it the good St. Patrick tended his flocks as a slave boy spirited from his English home by Irish pirates.

The Boyles, in addition to their eighteen fertile acres, shared and still hold grazing rights with four other families on some six hundred acres of nearby hillside. The original Burnside— little more than a large two-room cottage with outbuildings until the turn of this century—was for most of the years of Boyle tenancy fronted by a huge sycamore tree that was a valley landmark and a family legend.

For two centuries the sycamore was a mute witness to the ebb and flow of family life, and to the periodic turmoil that afflicts this too-often-unhappy land. It was in the thick of the 1798 rising that Protestant Wolfe Tone, leading a strange combination of Catholics and Presbyterians against the English adherents of the Anglican state church, won a temporary success in Antrim. The Boyles were on the losing side in that moment of eclipse, and high on the list of loyalists to be dealt with by the rebels.

One night soon after the rebels gained their brief ascendancy, an armed band marched to The Burnside and pounded on the cottage door. It was a wild night, with the wind howling down the glen and snatching at the flaring torches of the mob whose leaders dragged Charles, the eighty-year-old head of the Boyle family, from his bed, marched him outside his home, and forced the patriarch to dig what they planned to be his own grave. The noise of the mob and the cries of the victims carried down the glen, awakening neighbors who flocked to the scene. From over the hill behind The Burnside came the Montgomerys, an Irish Catholic family whom Charles Boyle had befriended with no regard for the scorn and whisperings of his Protestant associates.

Fortunately for the intended victim of the lynching mob, the Montgomerys were not overawed by the events. They boldly pleaded for the life of their friend and finally won agreement that it should be spared. The rebels, careless of his age, tied the old man to the sycamore and flogged him into unconsciousness. As they left, and as shaken relatives carried him into the house, the ancient Boyle revived. He looked back, shook his fist at his assailants and told them, "I'll live to see you all hanged," a prophecy that came true for many.

Having cast the bread of tolerance on Irish waters to the good end of saving his own life, Charles Boyle survived for another decade to help raise a brood of three female and seven male grandchildren. All but two of the grandsons emigrated to North America, most of them settling in Canada.

Twenty years before the mass migration brought about by the Potato Famine, the Buckna Boyles joined the swelling tide of Irish who were crossing the Atlantic. They settled in what is now Ontario, but was then an almost-empty Upper Canada, a colony still suffering the trauma of a recent war with the United States. The oldest Boyle son, who inherited the family acreage by custom, remained in Ireland. One of his sons emigrated to the United States and lived long enough in Wilmington, Delaware to sire an American-born son before returning to Ireland in 1876.

Among the brothers settling in Upper Canada was David Boyle, whose importance to this story was the fathering in 1839 of a first-born son who, following Boyle tradition, was named Charles. This Charles Boyle lived eighty busy and not undistinguished years. He was also the father of one of the most unusual and exciting Boyles in the family's history.

Charles Boyle had an inherited feeling for animals and a natural ability to look after them. His interest found an outlet in the breeding, training, and racing of thoroughbred horses, a rewarding business in an age when the horse was the most important means of transportation. It was the motive power for armies, dragging their cannon and supply wagons, providing mobility for the cavalry, and giving proof of status to commissioned members of the army who rode instead of walked. Thus horse breeding, encouraged by government subsidy, offered a form of assured income that other businesses lacked in the days of *laissez faire* economics.

Charles Boyle's early success in racing led him and his partner Charles Littlefield to the U.S. circuits where, then as now, the purses were bigger. In this more competitive field they held their own but, for reasons that are obscure, Boyle sold out his interest and returned to Canada. A likely explanation is his marriage to Martha Bain of Hamilton, Ontario, which took place soon after.

The new Mrs. Boyle was born in Dumfries, Scotland, but there is some mystery about her family. Boyles who have tried to trace their Scottish background have been unable to confirm any Dumfries connection. Rumour, which may be fact, is that the family name was Whiteside but that it was changed when a member became a deserter from the British army, creating a family disgrace that led to a decision to emigrate.

In Canada, racing luck continued fair for Charles and Martha Boyle. His reputation grew steadily. He became official timer for the Ontario Jockey Club, the colonial counterpart of the original, and reached a pinnacle in 1883 when he led in his own horse, Rhody Pringle, as winner of the Queen's Plate. Now well into its second century, the Queen's Plate is the oldest continuously run race on the continent and remains the most important race of the year in Canada.

The Boyle family expanded with the upswing in their racing fortunes. In the course of a single decade four children, three sons and a daughter, were born to the Boyles in Toronto. After David, Charles, and Joseph came Susan, the fourth and final child. Joseph had the distinction of being a Confederation baby, for he was born on 6 November 1867. His second name, at the insistence of his mother, was Whiteside. Neither his birth nor those of his brothers and sister are registered, because there was no official compulsory registration of births in Ontario until 1870. Normally, birth dates were recorded at christening time in church registers. Charles Boyle was a staunch Anglican and his wife a faithful Presbyterian, so it is likely that there was a christening. Thus far, no church in the Toronto district at which such a ceremony might have taken place has yielded any clue.

The Boyles soon afterwards moved to a farm in nearby Newmarket. Even there the family head was close to the racing scene. It was an ideal arrangement for Charles but a less welcome one for Martha, who found herself burdened not only with responsibility for a young, active quartet of children but also with the management of a staff of farmhands.

Possibly because this was an onerous, wearing task, the family in 1872 moved west to Woodstock, a small town some eighty-five miles from Toronto on the main railway line through Western Ontario. The Boyles lived in several houses in the town but their horses were quartered on farmland about three miles to the east along the Governor's Road, now called No. 2 Highway. Later the family purchased several business lots on the eastern limits of what was, for many years, a slow-growth community. Until the Second World War Woodstock remained content to be the county seat and hub of a rich agricultural region. The young Boyles flourished in this charming backwater, which offered much for the active body, if rather less for the questing mind. Small streams yielded trout and there were vast fields and forests in which the Boyles could work off their high spirits.

Charles Boyle, shuttling between home, farm, and the race tracks in Toronto and Hamilton, was only periodically in Woodstock. When he made trips out to the farm, young Joe was his frequent companion. This led to the boy's brief enrolment in the Bond's Corners one-room school, not far from the farm.

One day the father insisted on a report of his son's progress at school. The boy, silent at first, finally replied that he was doing well, and was actually second in his class. "How many in your class?" the father persisted. Joe—as Charles Boyle liked to tell the story—was silent for a long minute before he confessed, "Two: me and Peter Duncan."

Eventually, all the Boyle children attended Beale Street school. It was practical, no-nonsense schooling, the main virtue of which was to teach students how to read, write, and spell. It reflected life in the no-nonsense Boyle home with its emphasis on hard work, excellence, and honesty. Charles Boyle was known to be sturdy, whole-hearted, fearless, and energetic— qualities that his youngest son inherited in full measure. The father, it was said in his obituary, was "intolerant only of humbug and pharisaism, for these things his contempt was unlimited." These virtues shaped the development of the Boyle children—and at times were almost too much for them to emulate.

No doubt in reaction, young Joe played hooky from time to time. His impulsiveness on one occasion almost ended the Joe Boyle saga before it began. More than forty years after the event, which occurred in the late 1870s, Professor W. S. W. McLay of McMaster University told how close Joe Boyle came to drowning on a frozen pond near the railway tracks. Skating on rubber ice was a dangerous and exciting pastime. On this occasion most of the skaters steered clear of the thin spot, but Joe boldly challenged it and plunged through into head-deep water. A boy named Joe Spice came to the rescue, sliding out on his belly and extending a shinny stick to his freezing companion. Boyle, McLay recalled, was literally as cool as a cucumber.

Most decisions about education were made by Martha Boyle, although her husband shared her respect for learning. Between them they hoped to direct their sons into the three great professions: the law, medicine, and the church; but it was a hope never realized. Their greatest miscalculation may have been a belief that Joe would be the preacher. It was parental ambition that took him into Woodstock College, an institution that was to become famous as an all-male school specializing in preparing young men for the Baptist ministry; but it was co-educational during the years Joe and his sister Susan attended the college. He was there from 1883 to 1884, when he graduated; she attended the school from 1884 to 1887.

Charles Boyle, realizing that none of his sons was likely to follow their parents' designs for them, did not press them. He was determined, however, to keep them away from horse racing and the inevitable gambling that was part of it. He solemnly warned them off the track, then frustrated his own advice by continuing to be a success in the racing game. The Boyle stable, concentrating more of its effort in the New York area, soon boasted two homes, one of them situated in rented premises in New Jersey. There the young Boyles rubbed shoulders with trainers and owners and absorbed the atmosphere of the business their father had warned them against.

Restless Joe Boyle headed for New York in the summer of 1884. He may have taken a roundabout route, for in later years he told stories about a brief experience he had as a member of the Chicago fire department. Family members have disputed the claim, saying that Boyle was jesting. Whatever his route, Joe Boyle soon turned up in New York, where he worked with

7

his father. He learned how to handle horses and treat their ailments, from an expert who seldom needed the services of a veterinarian and who mixed his own special nostrums for his horses.

At times Joe stayed in New York with his older brothers, who had rooms in the Kelsey House on Lower Broadway. They were worried about Joe, who had become introspective and who vanished for hours at a time, returning without explanation for his absence other than a story of having been looking at the ships in the harbour. The lure of the sea in this twilight of the tall sailing ships was anything but fiction. Joe Boyle, like many of his age, was thrilled at the sight of a clipper under full sail heading for the rim of the world. The tales of the sailors opened a new world of excitement and skipped over the brutish hardships of their life at sea.

Joe Boyle, born with a full share of Irish romanticism, must have been an easy recruit for W. A. Smith, master of the barque *Wallace,* who engaged the young man in conversation and was impressed by his intelligence and enthusiasm. The *Wallace* flew the red duster, for she was built in Windsor, Nova Scotia in 1882 by J. B. North. This wooden ship, of 1,618 tons gross register, was owned by Shaw and Co. The Boyles were Loyalists, so the *Wallace*'s Anglo-Canadian background had a special appeal for young Joe.

One autumn afternoon in 1884, a few days after Joe talked with Captain Smith, his brothers Dave and Charles returned to the Kelsey House, expecting to find him waiting for them. Instead they saw a note on the table that read: "I've gone to sea. Don't worry about me. Joe."

Joseph Whiteside Boyle, in what was to be only the first of many impulsive departures, was off to distant horizons, the faraway places that beckoned him all the days of his life. He was a raw, excited, delighted seventeen-year-old deckhand, bound for India.

Home is the Sailor

The realities of life before the mast soon replaced the romantic notions that had drawn Joe Boyle to sea. There was much hard work, continual discomfort, appalling crudity, and real dangers in his new trade. It was still an age in which men went down to the sea in vessels little-improved for centuries, guided by imperfect instruments of navigation and moved by winds that were often fickle or overpowering.

For three years Boyle met the demands of his trade with courage and good humour, so busy growing up that he neglected to write to his family and ease the distress of his parents and brothers. In the lobby of the Kelsey House, in fact, the word spread that he had been lost at sea.

As the *Wallace* sailed south the vessel paused briefly at St. Helena, a meeting place and watering halt in the days of sail. This gave Joe an opportunity to ponder the story and the fate of the Little Corsican whose spirit still dominated the island, although he had been dead some sixty-five years.

At Capetown the country boy from rural Ontario glimpsed the beauty of South Africa and heard, for the first time but hardly the last, of the mineral riches that lay within it. It was an education far beyond the capacity of the Woodstock College curriculum to offer.

The first refining of the Boyle mettle began not long after the *Wallace* headed into the Indian Ocean. What had been a routine voyage was transformed into a tense life-and-death drama. Oppressive heat, a falling barometer, and a curious sky colour made the older hands look at one another and shake their heads. The weather's change could be felt more than seen, and a deep uneasiness spread through the crew that Joe could detect but not understand. Then, after a period of brief, frightening, flat calm, the storm struck. The *Wallace* rolled and tossed, sails flapping, cordage screaming, and timbers groaning, as if the vessel was in agony and feared the worst. For hours the ship was thrown around under a black sky full of rain and wild wind. Without a rag of sail it was hard to keep the ship running downwind in a blow that came from a half-dozen compass points at the same time. The crew could only hang on and, where the habit had not been abandoned, pray.

For a time Joe found it exciting, the most stimulating experience of his life. His adrenal glands responded in the hour of danger, but his real awareness of what might happen only dawned when, in one of the vessel's cataclysmic plunges, the mainmast snapped and trailed over the port side in a tangled mare's nest of ropes. And as the crew attempted to clear the wreckage they heard the ominous cry: "Water in the hold!"

Pumps were rigged and the crew fought desperately to keep the battered ship afloat. It was exhausting labour, because the first onslaught was followed by a succession of storms that permitted no time for rest or food. Captain Smith was fully engaged in trying to keep his vessel from turning broadside and capsizing, so directing the crew fell to the lesser officers. The fight to survive went on, not for hours, but for days, and was almost lost as weary men began to abandon the pumps, convinced that it was useless to struggle any longer against the inevitable.

In this moment of crisis it was the teen-age youth from

10

Canada who rallied them, and almost drove them back to their duty. As Joe Boyle's captain wondered at his enterprise, the youngster took command of the lifesaving pumping operations. Finally the storm ended. There was much water in the hold; the pumps didn't stop until the ship, under jury rig, staggered into port in India.

It was a traumatic experience, a turning point in the life of Joe Boyle. It convinced him that no cause was lost as long as men could be led into continuing to fight for it. Captain Smith recognized the leadership potential of the young man he had recruited on the New York waterfront and he determined to develop it.

The *Wallace* continued in the Eastern seas for some time, each new port introducing Joe to new wonders. The captain personally instructed the young sailor in navigation and seamanship, and found him quick and eager to learn. This preferential treatment might have created difficulties for Joe among his shipmates, but his wisdom, his personal attractiveness and openness, and his pleasing, unassuming manner of speech, with its touch of Irish blarney, enabled him to avoid the problem.

Most of all, young Boyle earned his shipmates' respect by his conduct and his courage. A half-year or more after the ship arrived in India it anchored in the Hooghly River, waiting to discharge a Calcutta-destined cargo. It was a warm evening and some of the crew were on deck, a few skylarking as young men do. In the horseplay one man tripped while running, twisted sideways over the bulwarks, and plunged into the murky water. There was laughter at first and no inclination to help until it became apparent that the man overboard was finding it difficult to keep afloat. Then the suddenly alarmed shipmates noticed a black fin cutting the water and heading toward the wildly splashing swimmer.

"Shark!" someone shouted. "Swing out a boat!" said another. Joe Boyle couldn't wait for the lowering of the boat. He seized a sheath knife from a companion and dived from the rail.

11

Fending off the shark, he kicked and fought and kept the sailor afloat and unharmed until the boat reached them. There was no inclination on anyone's part to be jealous of young Joe after that.

Life at sea and in port provided many opportunities for good times. Joe's natural ear for music and his baritone voice made him popular when the sailors got around to singing, as they frequently did. He had never studied music or taken any lessons, but he could play almost any stringed instrument on sight. He had a prodigious memory for tunes and lyrics, and an ability to improvise on them that delighted his companions.

These were gifts that all could share. Joe turned them to good account, organizing concerts for his shipmates and the crews of other vessels during cargo waits in distant ports. Booze and brothels would do for some until their money or their interest ran out, but almost all of them found pleasure in the concerts and Joe enjoyed their applause. He carefully laid aside the money they contributed when the hat was passed, realizing that there was profit as well as pleasure in the field of entertainment, and positive rewards for wise promotion.

Music was hardly enough to keep the bored young sailors out of trouble. And they were, for the most part, young, as an examination of any old ship's roster will show. They lived in a rough, tough age that mixed sentimentality and brutality in surprising combinations, and were ready customers for the boxing shows that the young entrepreneur introduced. Boxing was only one of many sports in which Joe was proficient. He preferred football above all other games although he was most skilled in baseball and, at the college, had done some boxing. He rode a horse with energy, if not with style.

It was an easy switch from Boyle the troubadour to Boyle the promoter, and on occasion, the boxer. He matched the contestants, rented the hall, set up the ring, advertised the bouts, and sold the tickets. Not infrequently he wagered the gate receipts on his estimate of the best bet of the card, and more often than not he doubled his profits, risking only the outlay of the hall rental if his judgment was faulty.

Boyle's final year as a sailor is one of uncertain record. It is clear that as his fortunes rose, those of the *Wallace* declined. Cargoes booked by chance in Eastern ports dropped in size and frequency. The waits in out-of-the-way ports became longer and it was obvious the *Wallace* was losing money. Captain Smith decided that it was time to go home, but Joe Boyle signed on with a ship bound for England whose master managed to run it aground off the coast of southern Ireland. So it was that Joe Boyle visited the homeland of his forefathers for a few brief weeks. He made no effort to visit County Antrim; instead, he went to work as a guide to holidayers visiting the Cork area.

Where he went and what he did in the final months at sea are a lost story. He reappeared one autumn day in 1887 when a small cargo schooner named the *Susan* dropped anchor in New York harbour with Joseph Whiteside Boyle as first mate and part-owner. The legend it would be nice to believe is that Joe won his share in the vessel by subduing a mutiny aboard her. The truth more likely is that his ready cash was the convincing argument. The schooner itself is a dim memory and can hardly be identified, for Lloyd's registry has many that fit the description.

Donning modish clothes purchased in England, the prodigal son strode from the docks to the Kelsey House, pausing to speak to an astonished desk clerk to make sure that his brothers still had rooms there. Dave Boyle was sleeping late that morning, and thought he was dreaming when a healthy apparition of his missing brother burst into the room. It was a taller, wider, handsomer, tanned young man than Dave could remember, but it was Joe right enough.

Dave's first reaction was to send a telegram to his parents in Woodstock. Appalled to find that Joe had walked through the roughest section of dockland with all his money in his pockets,

Dave insisted that his brother deposit most of his resources in the nearest bank. He admired Joe's clothes, but found his sailor-made haircut unforgivable. Dave turned Joe over to his own barber, then left to prepare a homecoming party at the Kelsey House.

Joe, trimmed to current style, took his time going back to the hotel and found all the guests assembled when he returned. It was a mixed group, most of them permanent hotel residents. Notable among them was an attractive young woman whom Dave introduced to Joe as Mildred Raynor, currently staying at the hotel. What Dave neglected to tell his brother was that he had been cultivating his friendship with Millie and that, despite her status as a newly divorced young woman with a small son, he was thinking of asking her to marry him.

In his usual forthright manner Joe concentrated his attention on Millie. He soon persuaded her to have dinner with him, something she agreed to without regard for an earlier promise to dine with Dave.

She would never forget that first meeting. As an old woman she spoke of that dinner date and how Joe Boyle had found out the colour of her dress so that his flowers would be a perfect match for a special evening which, he said, just "had to be perfect." After dinner Joe and Millie attended a Gilbert and Sullivan production of *Ruddigore,* a somewhat disappointing successor to *The Mikado* in New York. If there were short-comings in the work Joe and Millie could not find them through the wonder of their immediate mutual attraction. Three days later they were married. A second telegram to Charles and Martha Boyle informed them that their youngest son had become a husband and the father of an inherited son, before the age of majority. Dave Boyle said nothing to betray his anguish, but it was a blow from which he never quite recovered.

Marriage settled one thing for Joe: it ended his life at sea, for his bride had no intention of being married to a husband whose appearances would be spasmodic and uncertain.

Joe had left the *Susan* with a commission from its captain to pick up cargo as quickly as possible—any cargo, to any port in the world, as long as it was legitimate. Now he was permanently drydocked with a slightly older, bewitchingly feminine partner with expensive tastes, and a stepson to keep as well. Joe sold his share in the *Susan* and turned his attention to the immediate problem of maintaining a family. There was little time to waste, for Millie's alimony had terminated with her second marriage. For a start, he decided to invest in a feed grain and livery stable. In those days of horse-drawn vehicles it was easy for a well-managed feed business to return a profit. The returns were heartening, providing an income with some prospect of keeping pace with Millie Boyle's champagne tastes. Her love of furs—not her only extravagance—earned her the pet name of "Mink." The young Boyles were flying high, with only one dark cloud on their horizon: Charles and Martha Boyle could not bring themselves to accept Millie, whose divorce shocked their Victorian sensibilities. Joe was welcomed at the second home his parents had acquired at Eatontown, New Jersey, but the latchstring was never left out for his wife.

Eatontown was more than a place to renew family relationships. There, Joe met his father's racing friends, who were potential customers of his stable and feed grain business. The rising young businessman met them on equal terms. He dressed well, was wiser than his years, and they enjoyed his fund of engagingly told real-life stories. Joe, to put it simply, had the gift of gab. He spoke so well, in fact, that the Boyle Stable veterinarian, Dr. Stanley Harcourt, urged Joe to study law. He had been impressed by the young man's incisiveness and the clarity of his ideas and speech. "If he sticks with the law," he told Charles Boyle, "your son will be the greatest criminal lawyer in America." The old man smiled with pleasure, undoubtedly recalling the hopes he and his wife had had for their sons.

Joe was almost persuaded. He began a law course at night school and clearly was fascinated. He acquired an interest in the law and in litigation that never left him. It would be said he was far too fond of litigation and seemed to enjoy it. But, as quickly became apparent, Joe had to put first things first: he had to earn enough to pay the bills and keep his wife in some of the luxury she desired. They also now had two homes to maintain, for they had acquired a summer place in Red Bank, New Jersey, in addition to their home on 93rd Street.

Wrestling with books was no substitute for the restless young animal inside the skin of Joe Boyle. Even the physical attraction of the woman he had married palled after a while. He got back into boxing, then became the manager of a boxing club in Hoboken where, in 1891, he met Frank P. Slavin, a veteran topflight pro fighter, who both tutored the fine amateur and counselled him on other subjects.

Slavin, a native of Maitland, New South Wales, was thirty years of age, just past the peak of a notable and well-publicized career during which he had earned the titles of The Sydney Slasher and The Sydney Cornstalk. With dozens of tough fights on his record, Slavin was hard on the trail of the world heavyweight title, which was clearly slipping from the grip of an aging and careless champion, John L. Sullivan, the celebrated Boston Strong Boy. Sullivan, presumably because he knew his fate, was ignoring all the clamouring contenders, and finding spending money as an actor of questionable talents in spectacles such as *Kind Hearts and Willing Hands*.

Joe Boyle, who had matured into a two-hundred-pound, six-footer of unusual physical strength, sparred often enough with Slavin to realize that this scarred veteran from the Australian goldfields could be the next world champion if Sullivan could be coaxed into a title bout. Slavin, a survivor of the almost-vanished bare-knuckle days, ran his own training camp and paid the rent by charging spectators twenty-five cents to see him work out.

Boyle's position close to a potential champion opened up still another avenue of interest. Joe Eagan, sports editor of the *New York World*, offered him a job as a boxing and racing writer, a part-time role that he quickly accepted. Much of the sports talk revolved around how Sullivan could be lured from the stage into the ring, and there was endless argument about the qualifications and rights of prospective contenders.

Sullivan, unquestionably spurred more by the need for money than a suddenly discovered sense of the fitness of the act, reluctantly agreed to defend his title. He now had a field of contenders to consider and, like any modern champion, he was intent on selecting the least dangerous.

Publicly, Sullivan professed to see little merit in any of them. He scornfully dubbed the slim former bank clerk James J. Corbett with the derisive title of Dancing Master. He regarded Australian Jim Fitzsimmons, actually a middleweight, as a physical freak. There were few kind words for dirty-tongued Charlie Mitchell, even fewer for Peter Jackson, a talented black, or for the formidable Sydney Slasher. Slavin had his own private feud with Jackson; to any who cared to listen, he alleged that Jackson had run out of a fight with him in Australia.

To the champion the least formidable opponent appeared to be Corbett. He directed his attention to ensuring that the former banker won the chance to be mauled by the Boston bruiser. Sullivan gave the selection an air of open opportunity by laying down a set of conditions. One was that each contender post a side bet of $10,000 with an immediate $2,500 binding deposit. Slavin, with only a short time to raise the money, was unable to do so.

Early in 1892 it was announced that Sullivan would fight Corbett the following September in New Orleans. Newspaper controversy raged. Boyle was caustic. That spring two of the disappointed contenders, Slavin and Jackson, left for London to settle an old argument. They were billed to appear on 30 May in the main bout at the opening of the new National Sporting Club. Angry Joe Boyle sailed with them.

Edward, Prince of Wales, was among the spectators on that occasion, flanked by the pride of English nobility and sports-loving gentry. That evening was a memorable date in English boxing history, for the spectators witnessed what the boxing writers declared was one of the great bouts of the decade. For a full ten rounds the outcome was in doubt, until Jackson was declared winner when Slavin was unable to answer the bell. He had started impressively but had floundered badly as the bout progressed. Later he said he had made it a custom to lace his water bottle with a touch of brandy, and this proved his downfall. Someone, by accident or design, provided a mixture that was more brandy than water. John Barleycorn, sighed Slavin, was the winner, for he had taken all the tone from his leg muscles. Prior to the fight he had had nothing good to say about Jackson. After it he was a permanent admirer.

The delighted prince was so taken with the program that he asked some of the contestants to stage a private sparring exhibition for him. Among the performers were some talented amateurs, one of them a big Canadian named Joe Boyle. The exhibition must have been something special, too, for in conversation with Boyle a quarter of a century later, the still-beautiful Danish princess who had married the future Edward VII recalled her husband's pleased comments.

Disheartened by his loss, Slavin temporarily retired and elected to remain in Britain, but Boyle was back in America in plenty of time to attend the Sullivan-Corbett title match on 7 September. The Eastern sports notables travelled to New Orleans in a special train, partying all the way. They included bridge-jumping Steve Brodie, Colonel F. C. Lewes, manager of the mighty Erhart racing stable, and many such others.

Few of them thought that Corbett had a chance of defeating the crumbling Sullivan. Even Boyle, sure that the champion was ready to be taken by the right man, doubted that Gentleman Jim filled the bill. It was hard to find Corbett money, as Brodie, commissioned to handle the betting for some of the visitors, discovered. He had to offer four to one, a grave miscalculation; Corbett, the disdained jab-and-run master, won almost every round. He toyed with the badly conditioned Sullivan and finally knocked him out in the twenty-first round, winning the $25,000 purse and the $10,000 side bet on which

Sullivan had insisted. Boyle was irate at what he could only regard as the theft of the title from his friend Slavin. Boyle's subjective bitterness was too much for Eagan, who relieved him of his writing assignment.

Joe's meanderings contrasted with the orderly pattern of his parents' life. Charles Boyle, now training the powerful Seagram Stable of Waterloo, Ontario, had charge of one of the great racing establishments on the continent. It annually wintered more than three hundred thoroughbreds on an expensive racing farm layout on the edge of Waterloo, not far from the long-established distillery owned by the Seagrams. A quarter-mile covered training track permitted winter conditioning so that the Boyle-trained horses returned to competition in the spring in much better shape than much of the competition.

At Eatontown the Boyle home continued to be a popular rendezvous for the sporting set, in whose company Joe Boyle found congenial spirits and many with kindred interests. Among those he met was a neighbour, Michael Murray, a professional gambler whose life style demonstrated his success in a business that was, in those days, both legitimate and respectable. Murray liked Boyle and placed his own private riding stable at Joe's disposal, enabling him to put some polish on a riding style more vigorous than classic.

It has been said that, for those with the means to indulge themselves, the 1890s have never been surpassed for gracious living. The Boyles were on the fringe of the jet set of that day, but even the businesses into which Joe had ventured were barely enough to enable them to maintain the pace. Thanks to the managerial help of his brother Charles, the feed grain and livery business continued to flourish.

Dave, the quiet brother, was closer to the racing scene. His main interest was a poolroom, but his love of the track found him more often than not engaged in speculation that demonstrated how seldom Lady Luck favoured him. Then, in 1893, things changed. Early in that year Dave became the owner of a handsome, unraced colt that he named *Destruction*. Its con-

the responsibilities of running the farm.* Her feelings remained a secret entrusted only to a few female members of the family, strictly enjoined never to tell her husband or sons.

---

*The Firs, after a post–Second World War experience as a low-rental apartment block, was sold to an international fast-food chain and torn down in the summer of 1973 to make way for a hamburger stand.

THREE

Westward

The successful professional gambler must be a cold fish, equipped with the capacity of a computer and the quick striking power of a rattlesnake on the hunt. Infinite patience and hard self-discipline are vital. On those terms, and much as he welcomed a gamble, Joe Boyle seemed an unlikely prospect to join the ranks of those who prefer to lay the odds rather than play them. But join them he did, thanks to his financial needs and the persuasiveness of Mike Murray.

To Murray, the physical attractiveness and mental qualities of Joe Boyle were strong recommendations to make him a junior partner in the Murray enterprise. The only fault he could detect was Boyle's willingness to use credit. Boyle was a lifelong believer in lending and borrowing—it was easy for him to ask for credit, and difficult for him to refuse it. Credit, in fact, was a useful and desirable fact of life on which he always relied. It wasn't something he was concerned about specifically when he became a bookmaker. The somewhat extravagant lifestyle of his wife and the financing of two homes provided the spur to this new activity.

Millie's prediliction for spending might have been even worse had she not been slowed somewhat by a series of pregnancies that resulted in the births of eight children in seven deliveries over a period of just nine years. Her first child after her marriage to Boyle was premature and died at once. On 15 December 1890 she mothered a son who became Joseph Boyle, Junior. A set of twin sons died soon after birth. A daughter, christened Macushla, succumbed to scarlet fever at the age of six months. Flora Alexander Boyle, the eldest of the three daughters who would survive, appeared on 24 May 1894. She was followed by Susan and the last child, Charlotte, whose birth came under stressful circumstances in 1897.

Often pregnant but always as active as her condition would allow, Millie loved clothes and parties, and enjoyed life on the fringe of the celebrity circle to which her husband's activities and businesses gave her access. It was a realm inhabited by the likes of Diamond Jim Brady and others more notorious than famous. Whether this lifestyle satisfied Joe Boyle is doubtful; his tastes were simpler, although he looked and felt good in evening clothes. But his mother's Presbyterian background bestowed a legacy dictating that hedonism would never suit him.

Some of the financial pressures were eased by his bookmaking income, but ingrained in him was his father's advice to steer clear of racetrack gambling. Despite Joe's respect for Murray as an honest bookmaker, he was never comfortable in the bookie trade, and decided he would have to retire from it as gracefully as possible. The way out was effective in design, but expensive.

Murray had cautioned him against extending credit to a number of patrons of dubious honesty. Boyle deliberately took their wagers and these poor risks, as Murray had warned, welshed. Confessing his blunder, Joe pleaded that he was ill-suited to the business. He said he would pay the losses and quit, which he did. Thus he was able to get out without losing Murray's friendship, which the Boyles valued.

Boyle was about to change his life in other directions as well. Since the death of the infant Macushla he had been drinking, something he had never done and to which he said he was opposed. Obviously, personal stresses at home and in business were part of the problem. In any event, in an episode that some say never occurred, but which Boyle himself related to Irish relatives, the situation erupted in a drinking bout. He and a young boxer started off on a tour of watering holes and managed to locate a goodly number. Long after midnight they found themselves in a police precinct station, charged with a variety of offences, including being drunk and disorderly, stealing a hansom cab, and threatening the cabbie. Reliable Mike Murray was summoned. As they sat awaiting his arrival Boyle turned to his companion and said, "It's obvious I can't drink like a gentleman, and since I can't hold my liquor I shall never drink again."

The young boxer snorted his disbelief. "You'll get so virtuous you'll be giving up smoking next."

"A good idea," Boyle replied. "I'm giving up drinking and while I'm at it I'll give up smoking, too." With that he handed his friend a handsome cigar holder, which had been Slavin's gift to him. "Keep it," he said. "I'll have no further use for it." In a world fraught with broken resolutions, it is only fair to add there is no evidence that Joe Boyle ever smoked or drank again.

Those resolutions appear to have been taken in concert with some slow-growing new ones to reach for the top of the business ladder. The playboy days ended—a change that accentuated his domestic problems. His ambitions were large, and his knowledge of the feed and grain supply business was behind what became a master plan to establish a national chain of grain elevators—a project of such dimensions as to alarm Millie. The venture would require large infusions of capital— someone else's money—and it was up to Boyle to charm this support from New Yorkers.

Concentration on this great project demanded most of his time, and he saw little of his wife and children. The more he worked, the shakier his marriage became. It all came tumbling down one evening in the autumn of 1896, after Joe had warned

Millie that he would be bringing home some important businessmen for a planning conference and that he wanted the house quiet for a change—as quiet as a graveyard.

As Boyle and his associates drove up to the house on 93rd Street, they noticed some strange movement in the shrubbery, which turned out to be two white-robed ghosts bobbing up and down. He was later told that it was Millie and Flora's nurse, Anna Rupp, who were demonstrating in pantomime just how quiet it would be that evening. Far from amused, Boyle became angry; what might have been a reprimand to his wife developed into a dispute so prolonged and bitter that both partners finally realized, and agreed, that the marriage was irretrievably broken.

Moving with all the swiftness that he could when his mind was made up, Boyle liquidated all his assets in a matter of weeks, settling three-quarters of the proceeds on Millie. A legal separation was agreed upon, but Boyle's demand that it be accomplished immediately was held up when it became clear that both parents wanted custody of the children, Joe, Flora, and Susan. Then, in the middle of another dispute, Millie added yet another complication: she announced that she was pregnant once more. The revelation, surprising to her husband, provided the solution to the deadlock. Joe assumed custody of his son and his daughter Flora. It was agreed that Millie would take Susan and the unborn child, who would be named Charlotte, and who would be a stranger to Joe Boyle. Divorce would have been easier for Millie, who had been that route before, but it was too painful a process for her husband, so none was sought. Boyle insisted, and Millie agreed, that there would be no further claim for alimony and no future communication between the divided halves of the family.

Joe Junior was sent immediately to his grandparents at The Firs in Woodstock, and two-and-a-half-year-old Flora remained briefly with her mother. She has no recollection of the parting; when she was older, her Uncle Dave told her of her departure. Millie, dreading to be alone in the house when Joe came for the child, sent a telegram to Dave, asking him to be present when

Flora left. Dave, who had taken Joe Junior to Woodstock, was absent from The Firs and did not receive the message in time; there was no reply. Millie in her distress asked Diamond Jim Brady to be there with her as the final family links were severed, and that Broadway notable came to her rescue. Flora arrived in Woodstock on 15 December 1896, in time to attend her brother's birthday party.

Her father, having put his life in New York completely behind him, was at home until after Christmas. "Father," Flora insists, "would have left us as soon as Christmas ended but, I was told, I acted so badly that he delayed his departure until some time in January."

And it was around Christmas and after, Flora says, that her father first began to talk about going away to Alaska and the Yukon. What he had in mind immediately, however, was a tour with Slavin staging professional boxing shows, a sort of Slavin against the world, with Boyle as promoter and manager.

The times were out of joint for boxers, it seemed. Visiting Montreal, they found the ground very stony indeed, and were locked out of the Summer Gardens they had hoped to use for a program. Toronto was no more kindly. The city authorities refused to grant them a permit for a program to be put on in mid-February, 1897. It was all very discouraging, as they thought about it in the Boyle Woodstock home to which they retreated. Boyle arranged exhibitions in nearby Brantford, Guelph, and St. Thomas, but these provided little more than walking-around money. Slavin also told of their attempt to organize a bowling club for a brewery in Rochester, with similar lack of success.

It was, in any event, a brief hiatus, for Joe Boyle had his eyes set on a western destination, thousands of miles from Ontario. It is not difficult to believe that he had heard the call of the Yukon. He may have learned about the 1896 gold strike in the Klondike in some detail from a news story that was leaked to the press that year, after North West Mounted Police Inspector Charles Constantine sent a report from the Yukon to Ottawa

27

about the gold strike. The press magnified Constantine's August 1896 estimate that $2.5 million in gold would be recovered in 1897 to a $20 million figure. Also, Boyle's father, through his racing connections, knew a number of prominent men with links to Ottawa who probably were aware that something was up.

Boyle, desperately endeavouring to arrange some profitable action for Slavin, was heartened late in March by an offer from a San Francisco promoter to put Slavin in a headliner there against someone named Johnson. The purse has been variously reported as being $500 and $5,000. Whatever it was, acceptance was speedy and Boyle and Slavin soon were trekking west, a forward step to the Yukon. As they departed, Boyle handed his father most of the money he had, asking his father to keep it until he sent for it.

Their great expectations came to a grinding halt on their April Fool's Day arrival at the Golden Gate. The prospective Slavin opponent, they were told, was the same Johnson who had refused to fight Slavin back east, and he had done so once again. For weeks there was little to do. Boyle found bouts difficult to arrange. With time to burn, they used some of it spinning yarns with old-timers about the California diggings, and the transition that had taken place there.

The grubstake that Boyle and Slavin required had to be found in the boxing ring, and that is where they located it. Slavin quickly accepted a bout to fight Joe Butler, a fighter unknown to him. The terms were attractive enough: a purse of $1,000, win or lose. Slavin, confident that he could handle any unknown, regardless of his lack of training and his far-from-fighting trim, persuaded Boyle to bet the purse on a Slavin victory.

It wasn't the first time Slavin had been wrong, and it wouldn't be the last. Butler pummelled his aging opponent into a painful defeat. Slavin claimed that he had broken a bone in his hand, and later had a tendency to say he had been jobbed by ring officials who disqualified him. The purse money was gone and so, it seemed, was Boyle. He was nowhere to be seen as Slavin sat beaten and bewildered in an empty dressing room. Suddenly Boyle returned, waving two steamboat tickets for a trip north. He confessed that he had sent a telegram to Woodstock for his money, suspecting that Slavin might not win.

In company with a lightweight boxer named Frank Raphael, who had been on the same card as Slavin in San Francisco, the two wanderers disembarked from the SS *City of Pueblo,* in Victoria, British Columbia on 17 June. Whether they had come directly or not is not known, although they had been more than two weeks en route. They arrived in time for the official celebrations marking the Diamond Jubilee anniversary of Queen Victoria's ascent to the throne, and patriotic Victoria was *en fête.*

The local press noted the presence in the city of these boxing notables, providing Manager Boyle with an opening into the celebration program. Local talent was scarce but elements of the British Navy were stationed in Esquimalt and boxing had long been part of the entertainment program for the services. It was easy to arrange for Slavin and Raphael to meet the fleet champions in a program presented in the Victoria Theatre on 22 June. Only a handful attended, for there was a great deal of free entertainment and only a few dozen were prepared to pay to see the boxers.

"Alaska-bound" Boyle and Slavin, as they had been described in the newspapers, had strong evidence of the gold prospects in the Yukon. On the day they arrived in Victoria the SS *City of Topeka* had sailed for Dyea, Alaska, with Canadian Gold Commissioner William Fawcett on board, bound for the Klondike. A few days later the *Victoria Colonist* sent the gold fever chart a few notches higher by reprinting a portion of surveyor William Ogilvie's report of the previous November, telling of the unbelievable scenes on the creeks. Another story told of a Victoria hotel holding $60,000 in gold dust and nuggets in its safe for a recent arrival from the Yukon. All this was in addition to a demand voiced by the Victoria Board of Trade that the city take action to get in on the gold rush trade.

Four routes into the Yukon were known: over the Taku, via the Chilkoot and White passes, and by way of the Stikine River. Thirty years later Slavin told how two Victoria men— one a Captain Moore and the other a Jewish merchant whose name he could not recall—agreed to sponsor a Boyle-led expedition to mark out a commercially usable route over the almost-unexplored White Pass.

With Raphael agreeing to go along, a decision was made to get north as quickly as possible. No passage to Dyea being immediately available, they took ship for Juneau which, the map indicated, was relatively close to the White Pass region. "Relatively" proved an indeterminate description, for on their arrival in Juneau they found themselves marooned in a new, rough frontier community where everyone seemed to be armed and where the sheriff was incapable of halting a nightly quota of one or two murders. Many of the lawless were stranded gold seekers who were dead-ended in Juneau and unable to get away. The law officer was a surly rascal whom even Boyle could not charm. He threatened to arrest Boyle and Slavin when they applied for permission to put on a boxing exhibition. It was clear they were not welcome in Dyea.

They had to escape the way they had arrived—by sea—a need that led them to take passage on a dangerously overloaded, unseaworthy tub that almost foundered during the relatively short journey to Skagway, the takeoff point for the Yukon. Skagway, they found, had little more to offer than Dyea, for it contained only a store, a sawmill, a few small cabins, and some tents. This sorry-looking settlement was destined to mushroom into a wild frontier community notorious in gold rush history. A few weeks later Boyle wrote to his parents, telling them that when he and Slavin stepped ashore they had only fifty cents between them, which they promptly spent for a shared cup of very poor coffee. "But," he added, "we were as happy and contented as if our fortunes were already made."

For a brief time they were undistinguished additions to the ragged battalion of gold seekers, most of them unprepared for what lay ahead but already concerned enough to be lightening their packs for the testing climb over the Chilkoot. One day, as they walked around sizing up the situation, Boyle spotted a banjo that had been discarded by some wearied, songless adventurer. He picked it up, quickly tuned it, and began to play. Soon a small crowd had gathered, and within minutes Boyle had them singing and jigging. Slavin passed the hat, and the take was more than enough to quiet the rumblings of their empty bellies. It was a lucky instrument, one that Boyle carried to the Klondike, where it was enjoyed by his family and associates for fifteen years, until it finally was given away about 1912.

Finally outfitted with the supplies promised by their Victoria backers, Boyle and Slavin began preparations for the assault on the White Pass, a passage some one thousand feet lower than the famed Chilkoot barrier. This attraction disguised the fact that it was on a considerably longer route over the coastal mountains to the freshwater embarkation point on Lake Bennett, from which the Dawson flotillas set sail.

From the swelling ranks of Skagway's stranded gold seekers Boyle, Slavin, and Raphael enlisted a platoon of volunteers. The recruiting task wasn't as difficult as it might have been, for the rumour was that surveyors had found a route to Lake Bennett and the track was well marked. It was even suggested it would be a summer-picnic stroll to the height of land. Compared to the Chilkoot and its backbreaking climb it was a cinch, they were told.

Sometime late in July—the records conflict and it could have been 20 July or a week later—Boyle, Slavin, and Raphael set off with a column of fourteen men and twenty-five pack horses, with several tons of baggage and supplies. The rigours of the passage quickly dispelled the easy hopes of a summer stroll to the pass. The real truth became obvious almost as soon as the column lost sight of Skagway and moved along the narrow banks of the river of the same name. The "surveyed" trail was almost invisible, a broken thread they had to spend hours trying to tie together. On several occasions narrowing river banks forced them to look for easier going on the other side. They wasted hours searching for fords. The horses grew tired and balky, and the sweaty column moved in a cloud of camp-following flies and mosquitoes.

Some miles above Skagway they were obliged to leave the narrow valley, where the river swung east and away from their summit goal. The trail signs took them across rocky and often slippery sidehills, and they moved slowly into level patches, slashing out a path through the undergrowth. At times they floundered into muskeg that further strained their tired pack animals. Boyle and his associates drove the weary men hard, ignoring constant grumbling and talk of turning back. The "morning walk" to the summit took three long, difficult days, and at the top, where they could glimpse Lake Bennett on the distant horizon, the surveyed trail ended.

It was time to take stock of things. The tired travellers made camp, rested, and argued. After a meeting, six of the men said they had had enough and were returning to Skagway. Eight others agreed to stick it out, although the evidence was clear that the worst still lay ahead. Boyle was placed in complete command of the expedition. He was the captain, a name he retained for a long time in the northern wilderness, and he made command decisions with a minimum of further argument.

Announcing his plan of action, Boyle said that he would proceed alone, with a light pack, to find and mark the best route to Lake Bennett. Slavin, his second-in-command, would be in charge of improving and widening the trail from Skagway to the summit. In a crisis, Joe Boyle was at his best. Off he went—alone, strong, and confident. Meanwhile, Slavin hurried back to Skagway, where he recruited twenty men willing to take a chance on the venture now that the route to the summit of the pass was clear.

Boyle, unencumbered by the baggage train, pressed ahead steadily, reaching Lake Bennett in three days and leaving behind him a trail clearly marked with piled stones and notched trees. It was no small feat, for he had crossed thirty miles of wilderness from the summit of the pass to the shores of the lake, twice the distance from Skagway to the summit. The ultimate trail served thousands who headed for the gold fields. It was a good, easy trail in summer, but could become a bitter killer, a "Death Horse Trail" fatal to pack animals and humans when the weather turned cold or rainy.

Returning to rejoin his companions, Captain Joe found the trail-improvement program moving quickly under Slavin's direction. Early in August the party reached Lake Bennett. They had marked out a route along which, not many months later, the Whitehorse and Yukon narrow-gauge railway line would be built. Boyle and Slavin claimed that it never varied twenty feet either way from the passage they had indicated, and no one disputed that proud statement.

At Lake Bennett the White Pass travellers found themselves in company with several hundred others preparing to move into the Yukon, although the summer season was far advanced and the gold strike was almost a year old. Under the direction of a North West Mounted Police detachment, many were cutting timber and sawing logs to fashion crude boats and sturdy rafts that would—they hoped—carry them the 350-or-more water miles to the Klondike.

A few travellers were also returning from the Klondike, among them a San Francisco newspaperman who told wondrous stories of the riches there for the taking. "Tell them we've opened the White Pass for them," Slavin shouted to the departing reporter. It was clear that thousands more would be coming their way.

Boyle and Slavin wasted little time admiring the hard work of the boatbuilders. They had an ace to play. In the several tons of pack hauled over the pass were the components of a twenty-four-foot collapsible boat. It may have been one from the

Hamilton, Ontario, firm that specialized in making these craft, a number of which went west with the gold rush groups. They made a quick departure and left no record of difficulties they encountered on the voyage. The rapids that doomed so many—the dark, forbidding Miles Canyon—went by unrecorded, although there undoubtedly were some exciting moments in the swift, white water. Nor did they record the date of their arrival in Dawson toward the end of August 1897.

There was no shortage of work in Dawson. Claim owners were paying handsomely for pick-and-shovel labourers and Boyle and Slavin quickly joined their ranks. Boyle's first mining experience was on Eldorado Claim 13, and he was sentimental enough to keep his first sizable nugget and have it made into a stickpin for his cravat.

Necessity drove like the devil, for Boyle wanted to learn quickly the secrets of placer mining in the Yukon permafrost. They had arrived in Dawson slightly better-off than they were in Skagway. Boyle would later testify that he had twenty-two dollars in his pocket when they reached Dawson. He carried with him some other things much more to the point: a magnificent physique, a keen questing mind, unusual intelligence, courage, and the ability to seize the main chance.

He had lingered just long enough in San Francisco to learn that the best way to mine placer gold is by using hydraulics to wash out the metals. Oldtimers there had told him that the pan, rocker, and sluice of the Klondike would yield to hydraulics, the pressure hoses playing on the gold-bearing deposits. It had happened in California and Boyle was certain it would happen again in the Klondike. "From the very start," a *Dawson Daily News* feature story of 1899 noted, "he argued that hydraulic mining was the only method and set to work to get blocks of ground." It was a breathtakingly ambitious project. Merely obtaining a single claim was next to impossible unless one had a good deal of money to invest. Putting together a gold empire using mechanized mining on a twenty-two-dollar grubstake would have appeared impossible—to anyone but Joe Boyle.

FOUR

The Land of Gold

The Dawson City to which Joe Boyle and Frank Slavin travelled, in the vanguard of an army of thirty thousand that would arrive by the end of 1898, was a ragged community created by and for the gold seekers. Its claim to be a "city" was puffery. Its site near the junction of the Yukon and Klondike rivers, on land subject to flooding in springs of high runoff, was a questionable choice. Its appearance was unimpressive, for it was a nondescript collection of tents, shacks, and half-built log houses, clouded with dust in dry weather and fouled with mud in wet.

For all that, it was something else: the shining goal of the anxious thousands who pressed towards it in seven thousand boats of multitudinous shapes and designs, sharing only a mad willingness to risk everything, including life, to glimpse it. The difficulties of the journey were so overwhelming that, for many, just reaching Dawson was enough. Only half of those who got there ever bothered to look for gold. Many spent a few hours at journey's end, turned around, and went home.

For the first several years Dawson's population rose and fell with the tidelike pressure of miners passing to and from the diggings ten to twenty miles away. Most of them, even in 1897, went as employees of those fortunate enough to hold claims, for there was little left to stake for the latecomers. The rapidity with which the choicest prospects were gobbled up has been attested to by Staff Sergeant M. H. E. Hayne of the North West Mounted Police, who was given leave to go prospecting less than three weeks after the initial strike in August 1896.

In the early months the Mounties were permitted to stake claims, though the privilege was later cancelled. Hayne reached Bonanza Creek early in September. The discovery had been made on 17 August and the first claim filed on 24 August. Although the news of the strike was only a few days old, Hayne found the entire area staked, including almost all the richest of the many fabulously rewarding claims. The discomfited policeman left empty-handed, and in the strange way of the Yukon he unwittingly helped some strangers find a fortune as he retreated from the creeks. As he came out of Bonanza he met a party heading in, and advised them not to waste their time. Some just ignored him and continued. Several others were persuaded but reluctant to return, so they left the trail and walked into an unlikely looking gully where, more in desperation than hope, they started digging. The claims, duly staked, yielded them $132,000 in four months and eventually were sold to an American syndicate for $2 million.

There were many such stories to ponder in this grubby fairyland. German-born Andrew Hunker, for example, a gold-seeker from British Columbia, was at Forty-Mile Creek, a post seventy-two miles downriver from Dawson, when news of the strike arrived. He hurried to Bonanza only to find that he had been forestalled. Hunker wandered away, located a creek tributary to the Klondike River, found his fortune, and left his name on the watercourse. Then there was the tale of luckless Swede Anderson, who became very drunk at a party at Forty-Mile Creek and awoke with a giant hangover, only to find he had spent all his money buying a "worthless" claim from a couple of associates. They laughed when he begged them to cancel the deal. With nothing else to do, Anderson journeyed to the Klondike to inspect his "white elephant." It was a corner of Eldorado, a small creek that was a tributary of the Klondike River, which in turn joined the much larger Yukon River. Eldorado earned its name by becoming one of the richest gold-yielding tributaries. The shaft that Anderson sank on it yielded $300,000 in two seasons.

The stories Joe Boyle heard taught him that the Klondike had a tendency to reward the most trusting, and to mock the most experienced. Veteran creek miners had laughed at greenhorns staking hillsides. They knew from diggings in Australia, California, and elsewhere that gold was only to be found in creek bottoms and was more likely to appear in quantity below the original strike than above it. What they didn't know was that, ages before, the Klondike hillsides had been creek bottoms. Many of those hillsides were repositories of ancient treasures, and on some of the streams, Bonanza among them, the higher the ground was worked the richer were the returns.

Some of the veterans were victims of the incredulity arising from their experience. They flatly refused to believe that the rich finds were anything more than freak occurrences, and they were happy to sell claims for a few hundred dollars because they were sure the pockets would disappear. They laughed at novices who proposed to dig through a heavy layer of frozen muck to look for gold-bearing gravel not evident in the summer-thawed mess. And they were wrong once again.

The gold rush was awash with eccentrics. Gold seekers walked around Dawson babbling, unwilling to look for the substance that filled their every thought as long as they could find someone to listen to them talk about it. Some who struck it rich gave away nuggets to those who would listen to their story. Others, penniless and hungry, stumbled around with the gold glint in their eyes, ignoring the fish in the river and the game in the forest that could have stilled the loud protests of rumbling bellies.

Fortunately for Boyle and Slavin, they struck up a friendship with one of the most amazing characters among the many whose stories provide the colours for the Klondike rainbow. Their new friend was William C. (Swiftwater Bill) Gates, a short, noisy, flamboyant American, who had arrived in the Yukon a penniless roustabout. He had become wealthy when, in partnership with George Wilson and five others, he had acquired a one-hundred-foot portion of No. 13 Eldorado. This part-claim—a "lay" in Klondike terminology—was tested with seven shafts, but the syndicate reported that only one had shown any traces of gold. Despite this they agreed, with some apparent reluctance, to carry through an option deal with the vendor, J. B. Hollingshead, to purchase the property for $45,000. Hollingshead's satisfaction was marred when the partners paid him off in six weeks.

Gates and his mining associates were restless, questioning men who challenged accepted views by working their property through the long winter months. During the winter of 1897-98, although panning only two pans of gravel daily, they recovered $6,584.

Gates wasn't particularly avaricious, but he needed all the gold he could get to meet a well-developed taste for good liquor, good food, and not-so-good ladies of the night. He had a gaudy taste in apparel and could pursue a vendetta like an avenging fury. One of his heartthrobs was a handsome young courtesan named Gussie Lamont. When their relationship cooled and Gussie began looking elsewhere, Gates took his revenge by frustrating Gussie's yearning for fresh eggs in the winter. It was a costly way to find satisfaction but Swiftwater Bill bought up all the eggs in the town, paying one dollar each for nearly one thousand of them.

It was on No. 13 Eldorado that Swiftwater Bill introduced Joe Boyle to the mysteries of placer mining. And it was in Dawson, in the Monte Carlo saloon Gates had acquired in partnership with Jack Smith, that Boyle became acquainted with another side of life in the gold fields, that in which the winners celebrated their victories and dispersed much of their newly acquired wealth at the bar and the gambling tables.

However, Joe Boyle and Frank Slavin had few idle moments to spend in the Monte Carlo. Their first concern was to build a log cabin on the hillside behind Dawson, which they made their base for several years as they became established. From this squatter's roost they moved over the gold fields, acquiring between them, in various and unrecorded ways, the ownership of four claims.

Within a few weeks Boyle had laid the foundations for a great design to develop the mining area. He quickly noted how the staking had followed the rivers and creeks of the Klondike, whose waters were the lifeblood of a business in which production could almost be halted in a dry summer. His excitement was aroused by the sight of wide, timbered river valleys that remained unstaked because most of the property was too far from the water. It could be a realm ruled by machinery in the large concession concept he pursued almost from the first day of his arrival.

Dreaming and planning added savour to the hard daily routine of life on the creeks, for he and his partner had to wash enough gold to meet the realities of existence in a land where earning enough to eat was an achievement. A modest dinner of tough moosemeat, canned vegetables, a slice of bread, and a cup of tea cost $3.50, and there was more gold in the restaurant business than there was in most claims. One proprietor made a fortune and retired from the proceeds of a winter's work; another banked $30,000 in a single season by selling soup at one dollar a plate in a waterfront tent.

The potpourri of wealth and poverty, joy and misery, and avarice had the potential for an explosion of lawlessness and violence that could have matched any in the most sordid records of frontier mining communities. The Yukon situation was unique because through the early years, four-fifths of those who swarmed to it were foreigners, the majority coming from the United States. Many would have preferred to see the Stars and Stripes flying where the Union Jack waved. Fortunately for the Yukon, the Canadian government's providential dispatch of the North West Mounted Police in 1895 met the challenge of this most difficult situation, ensuring that justice in the Anglo-Canadian tradition prevailed and that the Yukon remained part of Canada.

Having acted with foresight and wisdom in the first instance, the Canadian government temporarily lost interest in this remote corner of the land. It ignored pleas by Inspector Constantine late in 1896 and early in 1897 for sixty more men, a steamer for river patrol duties, and the establishment of a Dawson gold assay office. And when the politicians finally woke to the truth of the Klondike reports, they hurried into some ill-considered moves that only accentuated the administrative problems of the territory, outraging miners with a Cabinet order that reduced creek claims to one-hundred-foot frontages, reserving alternate claims for the Crown, and imposed a 20 percent royalty on all claims producing more than five hundred dollars daily.

Angry miners organized a mass meeting that named a three-man committee to go to Ottawa to protest. The Cabinet moved to head off the posse with another order-in-council reducing royalties to 10 percent, increasing creek frontages to 250 feet, and permitting staking in ten-block sections, with the Crown taking alternate sections instead of single claims. Each miner was still required to buy a free miner certificate for ten dollars—a bargain, for it licensed him to hunt and dig gold, shoot game, fish, cut timber, and construct buildings. Claim registration was by swearing out an explicit affidavit of discovery and paying a fifteen-dollar fee.

Joe Boyle was one with the miners in their reaction to the ill-advised government actions, but he played no role in the ensuing protest movement. He had other concerns. As his understanding of placer mining broadened, he began to appreciate the shortcomings of hand methods by which, experts were saying, only 25 percent of the actual gold was being recovered. That meant that 75 percent was still there for anyone who could devise a more efficient mining system.

The Yukon had demanded special techniques from the very beginning, for much of the rich gravel was solidly encased in permafrost. Heavy overlays of black muck thawed and froze with the changing seasons. They had to be removed before the gravels could be touched, except in the cases where the gold had worked to the surface in creek beds or been exposed in open hillside gravel. The thickness of the permafrost belt varied. On Eldorado one shaft passed through frozen ground at 60 feet. Another was halted by running water at 200 feet. On the plateau between Bonanza and the Klondike the frost line ended at 175 feet. Regardless of depth, summer heat thawed only the top six or eight feet. Where moss or some other covering existed, the thawing might be a matter of inches.

Joe Boyle learned that these natural conditions imposed their own limitations. Conventional mining could not escape the need for winter shaft and tunnel excavation, with fires burned steadily below ground to thaw the gravels and permit them to be lifted to the surface for processing when winter ice on the creeks melted. It was hard, dangerous, and boring work that cried out for machinery to replace hand methods.

Boyle also learned that on one stretch of the upper Klondike River a British engineer named Robert Anderson was seeking timber and mineral rights for a five-mile tract of the river and Hunker Creek as a hydraulic mining concession. Anderson's basic concept was the one Boyle had worked out for himself, although his design took him several steps farther than Anderson planned to go. His vision of the future Yukon was a world of mining machines operated by a few skilled crews of men, replacing the thousands of individuals grubbing in the dirt with their bare hands. He intended to use the river both to clean surface waste and to power the machines. After a few weeks of consideration the problem was not one of decision-making but of action.

As his ideas developed, Joe talked privately with the new Gold Commissioner, William Ogilvie, of his plan to lay claim to a large tract of the Klondike River, a project presented primarily as a timber rights proposal. His talks with the commissioner convinced him that the place to settle his problem was Ottawa, and that the man to deal with was the new Minister of the Interior, Clifford Sifton.

In any event it was time to go, for in August Inspector Constantine warned the Klondikers that "the outlook for grub is not assuring," and alerted Ottawa to the possibility that the region would suffer a famine in the coming winter. Not many took Constantine's advice to depart, but Boyle was among the few who did, if for a different reason. He found a companion for his upriver journey to Whitehorse in Swiftwater Bill Gates, who wanted to get outside to spend some of his gold. Gates found an excuse in his need to round up a new, larger corps of women to work in the Monte Carlo in 1898.

On 24 September, in balmy weather, Boyle and Gates started upriver in the handy collapsible boat that had taken Boyle down the Yukon only a couple of months earlier. Poling and paddling their way along, they were making good progress when the weather changed dramatically. The temperature dropped, pack ice began to form, and after several attempts to repair the ice-damaged boat they abandoned it and moved on by foot. The journey became a struggle for survival. Swiftwater Bill was not the nimblest of partners, and almost brought them to disaster when he fell through thin ice and had to be rescued by his more powerful friend.

Boyle's physical strength and steel will and Gates's wiry tenacity pulled them through to Carmack's Post, a wayside centre some 250 miles from Dawson. There they fell in with a group of stranded travellers, including four men carrying U.S. mail, and a number of others heading down to Dawson. Among them was Jack London, an author who had nearly a month to study these unusual men and who probably fashioned one of his leading characters in *Burning Daylight* on Joe Boyle himself.

Despite the obvious dangers Boyle and Gates were anxious to get on, and found several who agreed with them. They held a meeting, elected Boyle captain, and made a pact to travel together, pooling their rations and resources. It was a daring decision, even foolhardy under the bitter winter conditions. Their goal was Haines Mission, at the end of what was known as the Dalton Trail, a route blazed by a man of the same name who operated a wayside inn near the Chilkoot Pass. The one-hundred-mile journey might have been made in four days in good weather, but it took the eight men twenty-five days from their 29 October departure in a temperature of 25 degrees below zero Fahrenheit. Several horses they had acquired to move baggage proved unequal to the task and had to be shot only a few miles along. Food was rationed and there were moments of sheer despair when some of the men in the party would have laid down to die; but Boyle would have none of that. He drove them like a chain gang, encouraging those who responded to exhortation and praise, and spurring others on with insults. On 23 November the party staggered into Haines Mission at the mouth of the Chilkat River, and all agreed that it had been a close call.

They were more fortunate thereafter, finding a passage almost at once on the SS *City of Seattle,* which landed them in Seattle on 29 November. On arrival they had some $12,000 in gold, and memories of an ordeal they would never forget. The following day they had a final meeting over dinner in Seattle's Tortoni Hotel. There they presented Captain Boyle with a gold watch, which the *Seattle Post-Intelligencer* reported was inscribed: *"Presented to Mr. J.W. Boyle in token of the expedition from Dawson City N.W.T. to Chilkat, Alaska in token of their appreciation of his most excellent management thereof."*

"Every man of the party," said the *Dawson Daily News* in an 1899 feature story, "except Boyle himself, declares till this day that but for his able management not a man would have reached the coast alive."

The U.S. mail he had helped to get through reached Washington before Joe arrived in Woodstock. The mail told of the grave concerns of famine in Alaska, and Washington acted

43

more promptly than Ottawa usually did. Joe returned to The Firs to find a message for him from the U.S. War Department, asking him to visit Washington and discuss leading a relief expedition to Alaska.

Impressed as he was by the speed of the American response, Boyle was appalled to learn that they wanted him to haul in supplies by using a column of reindeer—a notion so bizarre that he rejected the proposal. As a result, no one ever found out whether reindeer could have alleviated the famine. In the end, by tight rationing, the Yukon and Alaska came through the winter without serious discomfort.

After a brief period of recuperation in Woodstock the energetic Boyle continued on to Ottawa and Montreal. Just whom he saw and where he went is uncertain. Boyle worked quickly, and alone for the most part. Early in the New Year of 1898 Slavin joined Boyle in the East, having departed Dawson in mid-December. On 1 December 1897, and obviously in an arrangement with Boyle, Slavin had filed a claim in Dawson City to a large concession in the Klondike valley, in the names of himself and his partner.

There have been two views of Joe Boyle's movement into the Klondike. One is that he stumbled into the adventure by chance, as he and Slavin were barnstorming their way across the continent. The other is that he was aware of what was happening in the Yukon and was determined to see for himself. The chronology of the vital year 1897 suggests that more than chance was involved. The lengthy stay in San Francisco gave him an opportunity to learn about the gold rush experience there and to pick up the reports that were slowly filtering down from the Klondike. Whatever happened, the fact is that Boyle was short of cash—a condition not unknown to him even in his best years—and had to work his way to the scene of the action.

The impressive statistics are the brief stay in the Klondike from late August to 24 September 1897, during which he learned mining operations, scouted the area, and in consort with Slavin designed the concession plan that his partner put into operation as Boyle was starting east from Seattle. It is not difficult to conclude that Boyle had known where he was going, and that he had a very good idea, when he reached Dawson, of how he would go about winning the riches of the region. His success, as always, stemmed from his ability to make quick summations and rapid decisions, and then put them into action with a minimum of delay.

Boyle's search for backing in Eastern Canada led inevitably to Clifford Sifton, the Minister of the Interior in the Laurier government, and an important politician whom Boyle might have met on the Yukon trail on his way out a few weeks earlier. Sifton, anxious to inspect the new treasure house of the nation, had reached Skagway early in October with a party of civil servants destined for Dawson. The storms that so plagued Boyle on his way out prevented Sifton from proceeding inland and he returned to Ottawa. Frustrated in his desire for a first-hand view of the diggings, he would have been delighted to hear of them from someone so lately returned from the Yukon.

Boyle's introduction to the minister may have come through an Ottawa lawyer-politician, Harold B. McGiverin, who would have a great deal to do with Boyle in the years ahead. However it happened, it was to Sifton, on 5 February 1898, that Boyle addressed an application for a hydraulic grant on the Klondike River, with James J. Guerin joining Boyle and Slavin in the venture. The arrangement with Guerin appears to have been made very quickly. Boyle's solicitation of financial support in Montreal, then the financial centre of Canada, was not surprising, and adding the name of a well-known Liberal to an application to the minister of a Liberal government was nothing more than good sense.

Patience was not one of Boyle's virtues, but he was wise enough in the ways of officialdom to know that ministerial approval would require some time. He settled in at the Russell Hotel in Ottawa and prepared to wait in warm comfort. As his stay lengthened from days into weeks, Boyle relieved some of his boredom by talking with people he met in the capital and with the other guests in the hotel. Among the latter, he became acquainted with an unusual Englishman who gave his name as Arthur Newton Christian Treadgold.

Treadgold was yet another of the almost-unbelievable characters who would attach themselves to the Klondike like limpets to a rock, and one of the few who, like Boyle, played a vital role in its development. He was born in 1863, the youngest of five children of a Lincolnshire family. Through his mother he was directly descended from Sir Isaac Newton, the great physicist for whom he was named, and from whom he appeared to inherit unusual talents and a high degree of intelligence.

Although his physical frame was slight, he was strong and wiry, and a simple country upbringing had provided him with suppleness and dexterity that enabled him to excel in games. Like many men of small stature he was ambitious, courageous, and stubborn to a marked degree. An excellent student, Treadgold had earned a scholarship at Hertford College, Oxford, where he upgraded his sports skills as well as his learning, and finally won a degree in 1886. He added an M.A. three years later.

Treadgold's future seemed assured when he became a schoolmaster at Bath College, where his proficiency in cricket earned him the nickname "Treader." Within months he became senior classical master, and it was whispered that he would be the next headmaster if he would agree to take holy orders. However, the entire direction of Treadgold's life altered early in 1897 when he was introduced to a Miss Grace Henderson at a family party. A Toronto girl attending school in England, she happened to be a sister-in-law of Inspector Charles Constantine. She had learned from her sister of the amazing gold discovery in the Yukon and of the riches waiting there for anyone bold enough to attempt to recover them. Treadgold listened intently to the party talk, examined Miss Henderson on specific points, and said no more.

Without a word to anyone in explanation he left Bath College and journeyed to London, where he took a short course in geology at the London Geological College. "On Jan. 2, 1898," he wrote later, "off I went aboard the old *Etruria,* bound for New York."

Treadgold possessed one sterling attribute for the goldseeker. He was secretive. He could also make quick decisions and put them into effect without delay, two other useful qualities. The secretiveness surfaced first; when he arrived in North America he announced that he was a writer, having prepared his cover by obtaining commissions from the *Manchester Guardian* and the *Mining Journal* to send them articles about the Canadian West and the Klondike. It was a shrewd move. The articles would help pay his way, and his appointments would give him easier access to important people likely to be flattered by this personal attention from prestigious British journals.

Soon after arriving in Ottawa the peppery young Englishman fell in with H.B. McGiverin, who smoothed Treadgold's path to an interview with Sifton. The minister in turn helped him meet the prime minister. This progression provided him with additional credentials and took him to an interview with the president of the Canadian Pacific Railway, who was so enchanted with his visitor that he gave him a permanent pass to travel on the CPR.

The charm and erudition that appealed to politicians and businessmen quickly won Joe Boyle's confidence, and as they idled in Ottawa he and Treadgold found mutual pleasure in talk and exchanging ideas. The Englishman brought a new dimension from the world of the intellect to the miner, and Boyle offered the practical experience of the doer to the thinker who wanted to enter Boyle's sphere of action. They had some common interests as well (both genuinely enjoyed music) and in manner they were not dissimilar. They spoke persuasively, were quick to act, and could exercise a winning charm that attracted people at first sight.

In a practical way the relationship offered more to Treadgold than to Boyle, for he was learning about the gold mining business from someone who had dug the metal and learned the special secrets of Klondike mining. Treadgold, in later years, would tell people that Boyle was his pupil and learned the mining trade from him, but clearly, the roles were reversed: there was nothing he could teach Joe Boyle in 1898 and much he could learn from him.

Although they had much in common, there were some fundamental differences in character. Treadgold was careless of detail and upon occasion could be careless about facts; Boyle was the opposite. Treadgold could charm men, but he lacked the ability to command them and win their devotion. Boyle was a born leader who had demonstrated in the most difficult circumstances that he could lead and drive, and hold the confidence of his associates.

The weeks of waiting lengthened into months and Boyle's impatience increased as it became evident that all was not well with his plans. On 18 April 1898, he wrote a sharply worded letter to Guerin charging that their deal, verbally arranged through a Guerin agent, was about to collapse. He also charged that Guerin was about to withdraw his financial support, and insisted that the Montreal financier complete a formal agreement within seventy-two hours or accept cancellation of the arrangement. Four days later, after a highly acrimonious telephone conversation with Boyle, Guerin replied, ending the deal with a modest thirty stiff words.

That same day Boyle sent a letter to Sifton renewing the application for the concession in the names of Slavin and Boyle alone, stating that the Guerin group was no longer part of it. He pointed out that he and his partner had been waiting for word from Sifton since the spring opening of Parliament. The delay, Boyle wrote, had cost him and his partner "a whole winter's work" on their claims and it was vital that they get back to the Klondike by May. Slavin started back, but his partner remained in Ottawa.

In the new application Boyle defined the limits of the concession as starting

> at a point on the said Klondike River known as the Upper Ferry, and continuing in a straight line parallel with the general course of the Klondike River upstream ... about nine miles to a point at the mouth of Hunker Creek, and extending from the peak of the hill on one side to a peak of the hill on the other side of the said Klondike River, excluding claims that may be staked on the mouths of Bonanza, Quigley, Bear or Hunker.

The applicants offered to pay an annual rental of one hundred dollars per running mile, erect suitable cabins, and construct ditches for drainage and the carrying of water for hydraulic mining. Boyle further guaranteed to construct a mining plant and to place equipment to work the claims within three years of the approval of the application. Although agreeing to pay the royalty on production (happily just reduced to 10 percent), Boyle asked for relief from the tax on the first $20,000 extracted to help meet some of the development expenditure.

Slavin's application in Dawson in November had been in terms similar to that made by Boyle in Ottawa, except that it spoke of the land as extending for nine miles upstream and from "rim to rim" of the Klondike valley. It was a distinction with a major difference. Slavin's application could be interpreted as asking for a narrow band along the river, about nine square miles in all. Boyle's original application, and a later amendment speaking of from "summit to summit," was a bid for nearly forty square miles. At this distance in time from the event it is impossible to know whether Slavin erred or if the original thought was altered in Ottawa by other circumstances brought to Boyle's attention.

The request that reached the minister was a bid for a small empire of unknown potential. It might turn out to be largely barren land—no one could know, not even the applicants, whose knowledge of the tract was minimal. Perhaps fortunately for the applicants, few in Ottawa took them seriously and no one could imagine that one mining dredge, six years later, would extract in a day more than enough gold to pay the proposed river rental for a half-dozen years.

It may be, as members of the Boyle family have insisted, that the politicians thought that Boyle was overreaching himself, that he was even a little mad for launching a program so vast and expensive that it was bound to miscarry. Failure to meet the self-imposed conditions would mean forfeiture of everything, and the conditions were such that it left the partners potential victims of power plays by the unscrupulous.

Perhaps these considerations caused Guerin and his associates to withdraw. It could be, too, that someone in Ottawa wanted them out of the picture for other reasons. The undercurrents in the Klondike exploitation story run deep and have never been fully plumbed. Documents that have survived offer tantalizing hints of political deals and more, but it is unlikely that the complete story will ever be known.

FIVE

The Long Delay

Although in his first interview with Sifton Boyle had been assured that his request would receive speedy approval, after almost seven months in Ottawa he began to realize that political "speed" had little relationship to the normal understanding of the word.

Treadgold interviewed Sifton in May to get material for a story on "the resources of the West and the conditions of mining in British Columbia and the Yukon." He was anxious to go west, and headed out soon after his Sifton meeting, armed with an assignment from Boyle to take a look at the Klondike concession, for there were rumours that trespassers were moving in. It was odd, in a way, for the logical guardian should have been his partner Slavin.

In mid-June, when it was clear that procrastination would continue, Boyle took the train to Vancouver and boarded the first ship he could find among the swollen fleet of ships of every kind now engaged in hauling gold rush passengers.

Skagway, he found, was almost unrecognizable. It had been transformed into a boom town, a jumping-off point for thousands, including some of the oiliest scum on the Yukon trail. This dirty, wild, reckless community, in a few short months, had become controlled by a hoodlum mayor, "Soapy" Smith, whose cutthroat followers preyed on travellers, stealing their money and slitting their throats if they resisted. What the bandits missed, the barkeepers, the whores, and the crooked gamblers managed to snatch. In this reign of terror Joe Boyle moved unafraid and unchallenged. It was obvious that he could take care of himself and that there were easier victims to rob than Captain Joe, the man who had opened the White Pass.

Boyle was not in Skagway for long, but he paused briefly to save a life and acquire a retainer in the process. The bully boys of Skagway thought little enough of their temporary guests when they were white, but they reserved their deepest scorn for the native Indians. They had little to steal and their skin was dark, and they did not speak or understand the white man's language or his ways.

One of these unfortunates had offended the bartender who employed him, and that worthy was in the process of beating the native into insensibility, and probably to death, when Joe Boyle walked into the establishment. He glanced scornfully at a small group of disinterested customers and, seizing the bartender by the arms, threw him into a corner. He helped the Indian out of the bar, tended his hurts, and learned that the man he had rescued came from the Dawson area, where he was called Indian Charlie.

Charlie refused to leave his protector and was by his side when Boyle finally arrived back in Dawson on 7 July. Treadgold reported that he had inspected the concession, found that a man named Stewart had moved in a gang of men to harvest the timber, and had served notice on Stewart to cease trespassing, without result.

Yukon trees grow slowly, and in the gold rush they were a precious, vital commodity. The local timber provided the material for shelter, mine shoring, corduroy roads over muskeg, boards for rockers and sluices, and fuel for the miner's fires. They were a resource that could not be renewed in the lifetime of the users, and they were a rich claim to be tapped by sawmill operators, of which Boyle planned to be one. Stealing his timber was stealing his money—something Joe Boyle wouldn't countenance. His irritation grew when he found that a Crown timber agent named MacFarlane had authorized the cutting.

One important asset, provided by Sifton, was a letter authorizing Boyle to take certain actions, outlining his rights, and ordering that, in case of dispute over timber cutting, the felled timber was to be held until further instructions were sent from Ottawa. Boyle deposited the letter with Major J. M. Walsh, a Mounted Police officer now commissioner of the territory, but nothing happened. An appeal to another Crown agent, John S. Willison, got Boyle an order to Stewart to desist, which the wood poacher ignored, sending his cutting crew back on the concession in defiance. Boyle found them there and a noisy confrontation erupted.

The jousting continued, with Boyle making the next move. He posted official "No Trespassing" signs provided by Willison, which Stewart's men seemed unable to see. What Boyle began to suspect was a plot thickened when Walsh refused to issue an order confirming Sifton's instructions, saying he had lost the letter. Willison consulted a lawyer named Wade, who said he thought Stewart might be within his rights in making off with the timber Boyle claimed. At that point Boyle decided there had been enough talk. Recruiting a gang of men, he marched them to the concession with orders to expel any intruders unless they had written permits from Crown timber agents. He then notified all the agents that he would hold them personally responsible for loss or damage.

These actions produced some results. Walsh found the letter and sent instructions to Gold Commissioner Fawcett and others, outlining Boyle's rights. Walsh, a most inadequate official, as his removal a few weeks later over a personal scandal proved, had waited too long. Boyle concluded that the situation could only be remedied in Ottawa. Leaving the protection of the concession and the direction of work on their claims to Slavin, he started back for the East on 13 July, only six days after he had reached Dawson.

Early in August he outlined his complaints to Sifton on letterhead of the legal firm of McCraken, Henderson and McGiverin, also requesting the immediate granting of a timber licence. "Bonanza . . . and Hunker . . . are absolutely dependent on this timber," he wrote. Sifton, who was under rising political pressure over his handling of the Yukon, was inclined to temporize. He conceded that the trespassing must end, but urged Boyle to work out a settlement with Stewart. (A year later the minister was informed that the problem had been settled, "although it had been hard work to keep it out of court.")

Treadgold stayed in the Klondike for four months before returning to Ottawa, where he talked with Sifton, Laurier, and others, expounding a theory of mine development by consolidation of claims. He was given assurances that a charter would be available for large-scale hydraulic mining. His path then led him to England, where he hoped to attract rich supporters for his venture. The Treader was persuasive and the freshly mined gold he offered as evidence was a convincing argument. He quickly raised $250,000, and among the group of financial backers were two former schoolmates, William Trask and Malcolm Orr Ewing. They were important to Treadgold, for it was in their names, not his own, that he filed a formal application for a charter of water and mineral rights early in 1899.

The application was sent directly to Sifton, whose relationship with Treadgold, as revealed in his correspondence, had developed well beyond the official. The minister should have been dealing with the applicant at arm's length, but Treadgold's letters to Sifton suggest a joint-venture position on a man-to-man basis.

Although he used front men in the application, Treadgold inserted a significant paragraph by which any Klondike claim that lapsed through nonpayment of royalties—a not-infrequent condition—would be registered in Treadgold's name, not in that of the company he was forming. His bold plan was designed to consolidate the entire mining area in a single company. There were no anti-trust laws to worry about in 1898.

Back in Dawson, Joe Boyle toiled doubly hard in the waning months of 1898 to make up for the time spent in Ottawa. In addition to gold claims that now were steady producers, the wood found on their concession was making Boyle and Slavin wealthy men. Through the last winter of the waning century they provided cordwood for the stoves of the Klondike, "dry, green or mixed," they told the public in newspaper advertisements.

As these enterprises flourished, Boyle acquired the finest of Yukon status symbols: a dog team second to none, one that gained local fame and may well have been the model for Jack London's dog team stories. Legend has it that Cronja, the Boyle team lead dog, is the canine hero of London's great novel, *White Fang.*

Cronja's role as a fictional canine hero may be doubtful, but there is no disputing his actual position as boss dog and leader of Koolikee, Craw, and Killidee, the other members of the Boyle pack. This quartet functioned with rare harmony and efficiency, providing their owner with reliable transportation through the long Yukon winter. Reliability was important to Boyle after his experience with late-season boating a year earlier, for he planned to go outside by dog team in the winter of 1898-99.

Once again Swiftwater Bill was to accompany him, as well as Indian Charlie and others. This was a well-supplied, thoroughly experienced group capable of speed and safety. The men had their pictures taken before moving out, proud in their fur garments, snowshoes at the ready, and the dogs couchant at their feet. Boyle, slimmed down by hard work, had grown a mustache and looked handsome, even a bit foreign. Swiftwater

Bill added a note of levity by parading in a gaudily striped tie that ought to have stopped all traffic on the Arctic trails.

It was a swift, easy passage, as Boyle had predicted it would be. His dog team performed beautifully and he almost regretted his decision to send them back to Dawson from Skagway in care of Indian Charlie. What a sight they would have made on the staid streets of Woodstock. Charlie settled that issue by refusing to return to face the wrath of his chief, who had warned him not to make the trip or help the white men get to Skagway. He insisted on accompanying Boyle. That meant the dogs had to go, too, for Boyle was loathe to sell them. So the whole entourage sailed south, a subject of interest and conversation all the way.

In December 1898 young Flora Boyle was playing in the lane that led to the back door of The Firs when she saw two strangers walking towards her. The tall, fur-clad man with the mustache, she realized with a shriek of delight, was her father, and she soon learned that his companion was Indian Charlie. After the homecoming greetings, Flora was permitted to accompany her father and Charlie to the railway station several miles distant, where she was entranced to be introduced to four handsome dogs.

Boyle decided to give Woodstonians a treat by letting them see a real northern dog team. He hitched up his dogs to their Yukon sled, piled on the luggage, and sat Flora on top of it all. Like a small queen she rode through the centre of town, Joe Boyle urging the straining dogs on with appropriate whip-cracking and trail commands.

The homecoming was a pleasant interlude and an older Woodstock resident can still recall the Boyle dog team getting a workout along Dundas Street with their owner in command. However, business drew Boyle to Ottawa and elsewhere, and the dogs could not accompany him there. They were left at The Firs in the charge of Indian Charlie, whose fears were calmed by Boyle's promise to return as quickly as possible.

Charlie was uncomfortable and unhappy in his strange

surroundings, and nothing the Boyles could do for him made him accept his isolation. When he ventured into town, the male hangers-on in the saloons and barber shops made fun of him and told him his master would never come back for him. Ladies glanced at him with scorn, his alien face offending their sensibilities. As the days lengthened into weeks, Charlie began to believe that Captain Joe had deserted him. One morning he failed to appear for breakfast, and the Boyles found that he had departed, taking only the clothes he wore and the two five-dollar gold pieces he always carried.

Alerted in Ottawa, where he was again experiencing a long, frustrating wait, Joe Boyle found an outlet for his dampened energies in directing a hunt for Charlie. Police forces across the continent were notified and a reward was posted, but the hue-and-cry returned nothing. Later that spring, when he arrived back in Dawson, Joe Boyle learned that Indian Charlie had beaten him home by several weeks, although no one knew how he managed the four-thousand-mile journey on a ten-dollar stake. Charlie, overcome with guilt at having abandoned his dog team and failed his master, fled to the hills. Boyle never saw him again.

In Woodstock the dogs languished without a skilled handler to exercise them. They began to roam the neighborhood, terrorizing animals and chickens. With increasing frequency, owners brought their mutilated fowl to The Firs, demanding compensation, and Charlie Boyle, grumbling more and more, paid for the depredations. Finally one day, a very angry farmer drove up with a small cart loaded with several dozen dead chickens. The head of the household looked grim, paid the damages, and summoned one of the farm hands. Charles Boyle was judge and jury in a very brief trial that ended in a series of shots, terminating the story of the Boyle dog team.

In the spring of 1899 Joe Boyle went back to Dawson and to a partnership with Frank Slavin that was beginning to come unravelled. Slavin had done some prospecting and had staked more than a dozen claims on Quartz Creek, beyond the height of land to the south of the rich Klondike tributaries. But his administrative duties in the partnership were taking second place to his enjoyment in the boxing ring. He was back in training, the undisputed heavyweight king of the region, enjoying the notoriety of the role and the relatively easy money it yielded. So, for a variety of reasons including the boxing activity, the partnership was ended in the summer of 1899. Slavin received $20,000 for his concession interest in seventeen jointly owned claims elsewhere. These included claims on Gold Bottom, Quartz, Sulphur, Boulder, Hunker, and Meadows creeks. Prior to the dissolution of the partnership the partners had commissioned surveyor T. D. Green to prepare a blueprint of their largely unexplored concession. He completed the work in the autumn of 1899, and Commissioner William Ogilvie approved the plan on 19 December 1899.

Boyle reported Slavin's withdrawal from the partnership to Sifton in a letter dated 9 June 1899, which asked that the hydraulic concession approval be made out to Boyle alone. The petitioner made it plain that the long delay in approval was deeply disturbing to him.

In view of the fact that it is now eighteen months since our original application was made to Fawcett and over a year since you informed me positively that we would receive the grant I think it only fair that the matter should be closed as speedily as possible.

It will also be necessary for me to have the renewal of the Timber Licences from Sept. 1st 1899, for Berths 25 and 26 on the Klondike River. . . .

The timber rights were vital, for Boyle was now operating two sawmills—the Arctic and the James William—and his firms cut more than one million feet of logs in 1899. In addition he had built a two-hundred-foot wharf along the waterfront with a one-hundred-foot warehouse and lumber dock, and had purchased several valuable pieces of Dawson real estate. Although the great gold rush was in its last days, there were many enterprises to be launched, geared to the long-term operation of the mines.

There were fewer people around, it was easy to see. Many of the footloose and the unsuccessful departed in that summer of 1899, most of them to follow the gold dream to Nome, Alaska, where, it was said, fortunes could be picked up on the beaches. The rush became a frenzy as some of the stories were confirmed. In one week of August more than eight thousand people left Dawson forever. The town's newspapers hurled invective on all who spread the Nome reports, predicting that the alleged strike would be a flash-in-the-pan, but the exodus continued.

Even as his Klondike application dangled, Boyle worked on another plan of concession exploitation, this one in partnership with Swiftwater Bill Gates. Both men now owned property along the Quartz and their plan outlined a large hydraulic operation that, said the *Dawson Daily News,* would develop properties "thoroughly proven and rich." By the late fall of 1899 they had moved heavy hydraulic equipment to the mouth of the river, intending to haul it to the mining site on the winter ice.

By the autumn of 1899, Joe Boyle had become a citizen of substance in the Yukon, as the special mining edition of the *Dawson Daily News* noted in the fall of that year:

Although Mr. Boyle has worked hard and incessantly, his work has had no ill effects for there is no finer specimen of physical manhood in the world today—his magnificent physique, great strength and happy, sympathetic nature, coupled with a total abstinence from the use of liquor and tobacco, make him an ideal character for this rigorous climate.

Mr. Boyle has always taken a lively interest in public matters. During the fall of '98 the front street of Dawson had become impassable for teams. Getting the teamsters together Mr. Boyle, in one day, laid a slab road from the A.C. corner to the Fairview. ... [H]e is at present, in connection with Alex McDonald, setting on foot a movement among business men and mine owners to establish a hospital tax for the maintenance of St. Mary's Hospital.

He is a member of the board of trade and chairman of the committee on legislation. Mr. Boyle has, by his strong personality, determination and downright honesty, won for himself the respect and esteem of all who have come into contact with him.

Although he was constantly on the move during most of his years in the Klondike, and frequently absent when important issues were being debated, Boyle was present to chair a protest meeting on 25 September 1899, when Klondikers protested the announced transfer of North West Mounted Police superintendent Sam B. Steele, one who was, as they put it, "always the miners' friend." These protests could not alter the decision, but the friends of Sam Steele made Boyle the head of a group to raise money for a departure gift. Boyle collected gold from many claims, the gifts totalling more than $2,000. Appropriately, he thought, it should be bestowed in the form of a gold brick. But after it had been cast the committee began to have doubts about the ethical considerations and what his superiors might think if Steele were to leave his post with such a memento. Boyle provided a solution: give the gold brick to Mrs. Steele. Her husband was presented with a handsomely inscribed paperweight that just happened to be solid gold and worth several hundred dollars.

It was a happy interlude, lightening more pressing matters. Poachers were still stealing timber, and Boyle was still on tenterhooks over the mysterious delay in approval of his hydraulic concession. He would have been much more concerned had he known about the manipulating that was going on behind his back. The origin of much of the difficulty lay with Slavin who, in June 1898, before Boyle returned from Ottawa, had agreed to sell part of the Slavin interest in the concession to Treadgold and accepted five hundred dollars as a down payment. Boyle was angered by this action, which may have led to the eventual dissolution of the partnership, but the Slavin-Treadgold deal appears to have fallen through when the latter failed to make subsequent payments when due. The Treader's default did not subsequently prevent him from suggesting that he really owned 25 percent of the concession but had been cheated out of it.

From such reports have arisen claims that Treadgold and Boyle were equal partners from the start, and that Boyle robbed the little Englishman of his rights. Recent documentary evidence available in the Sifton files demonstrates that if there was a villain it was Treadgold who, it is now clear, hoped to squeeze Boyle out by depriving him of the water that Treadgold would come to control if his syndicate's application was approved.

There was a real genius in Treadgold's effort to corner the water resources of the Klondike, for the entire mining operation depended on the water flow that would separate the gold from the gravel dross. Hydraulic mining, with huge hoses pouring water on the soil, would shift thousands of tons of waste material in such a way that it was bound to interfere with, or halt, the work of the hand miners. Eventually, Treadgold hoped, this could irritate most of the individual miners into selling. He reported privately to Sifton:

I found considerable difficulty likely to occur on the question of dumping grounds because nearly every one of the gulches on the left side of Hunker and Bonanza are turning out rich for at least three claims from the mouth. I set to work, and in other names, bought creek claims at convenient intervals. I have invested 219,000 dollars in this way and when I have got three more claims on the Lower Bonanza there will be no need of expropriation and no chance for blackmailers.

The output is safe to be more than maintained this year and maintained next, but I think that by the end of 1901 you may reduce your royalty (and your expenses, too) for the Klondike, because by then the Yankees on Eldorado and Upper Bonanza will have cleared out and the low grade gravels can begin to be treated if we get the water going right.

Treadgold's personal correspondence, which might have thrown more light on the real position of the minister in these convoluted schemings, was destroyed in the London blitz of 1940, but the small amount now public can lead only to one conclusion: Sifton was in on the deal.

The little Englishman, in any event, was working harder digging up capital than he ever toiled to extract the gold he sought. He was in Chicago on 27 September 1899, reporting to Sifton: "I shall not leave Chicago 1—until I have proven to them that 5,000,000 will be well invested on the terms which I hope you will see your way to grant use; 2—they trust me with their interest as much as I them with my information."

In yet another letter, this fast-moving correspondent urged Sifton, "keep me free and strong and the enterprise is a gainer. That is why I want the concession made out to mere nominees of my own; the enterprise is still at the stage at which orders must come only from you." Treadgold's front men, Trask and Ewing, were not similarly informed and never seem to have been aware of the actual situation. If Joe Boyle had known, he might have understood why a minister of the interior would have occasion to delay approval of the Boyle application.

Klondike suspicions of Sifton were long-standing. At a public meeting in Dawson on 2 June 1902, lawyer C. M. Woodworth charged that it had been proven the real owners of the first of the concessions, Anderson's, were applicants named McLaggan and Sutherland, and Clifford Sifton. It is a fact that the Anderson concession was approved with a minimum of difficulty, apparently establishing a policy as early as 1898 that where property was considered to be too wide to prospect for pay dirt in the conventional way it could be mined hydraulically. Gold Commissioner Fawcett, in fact, urged that such areas be opened up.

Boyle remained busy despite his annoyance at the delays. In May 1900, he joined with Thomas Adair, W. C. (Swiftwater Bill) Gates, Humboldt Gates, H. F. Peters, and J. T. Cleyworth to petition for the right to divert two hundred inches of water from Quartz Creek for five years.

The long wait ended 5 November 1900, two years and nine months after the application to Sifton in Ottawa, and three years after Slavin's Dawson application to Gold Commissioner Fawcett. Joe Boyle had his concession. It may not have been solely on merit, though. He had friends at court, not the least of them the Honourable James Sutherland, the government whip and a minister without portfolio who was from Woodstock, and who knew the Boyle family intimately.

The Cabinet's acceptance of Sifton's recommendations to grant the Boyle application opened the door for other actions that Sifton desired. In May 1901 it was announced that the government had approved the Treadgold application with all its water-diversion clauses, and the Treader's sole rights to the ownership of lapsed claims. Treadgold, as czar of the water supply, was effective ruler of the Klondike. Or so he thought.

The tortured phraseology of the order baffled Gold Commissioner E. C. Senkler, who was unable to interpret what was meant by the right given the syndicate to work abandoned claims. Protesting miners asked whether Treadgold had won immediate, uncontested control of all such claims, or whether they could be restaked by anyone provided that the syndicate had not recorded them. Senkler, stung by the uproar, reacted cautiously, closing all claims to relocation until Ottawa clarified its instructions—a remedy that favoured Treadgold more than anyone else, for it prevented others from forestalling his grabbing tactics.

As the miners more clearly understood the sweeping nature of the Treadgold concession, their anger mounted and Ottawa was assailed with protests. The politicians, dimly understanding that they had blundered once more, procrastinated, but finally advised Senkler to reopen the claims and treat everyone alike.

Changing direction once again, the government, on 13 February 1902, closed all claims to relocation, retroactive to 1 January. The timing could not have been worse, for Dawson was filled with those whom winter had left idle, with plenty of time on their hands and not much else to do but demonstrate. Yukon Liberals formally complained to the Liberal government in Ottawa. When Duff Pattullo, a future premier of British Columbia, tried to soothe a public meeting he was howled down and forced to concede that the clauses were restrictive and unfair. Another public meeting named a four-man committee to proceed to Ottawa and make a formal protest to Laurier and Sifton. But when the hat was passed, only enough money was contributed to send two of them, a failure that led government supporters to charge that most of the protesting was hot air.

Ottawa was impressed, just the same. After meeting the delegates the government ordered all abandoned claims thrown open, and the Yukoners returned to Dawson to report that Sifton had been sternly rebuked in Cabinet. On 21 April 1902, four days after its action reopening the claims to all miners, the Cabinet cancelled the original concession to Treadgold and substituted more restrictive arrangements. As usual, actions that would have answered the first complaints had been so long delayed that they were now inadequate to calm the protesters. They organized another mammoth public meeting and demanded an end to all concessions, naming them as belonging to Treadgold, Anderson, Milne, Boyd, Ray and Bronson, Matson, Slavin and Gates, and the Millers. The coupling of Gates and Slavin indicates that Boyle had withdrawn from the Quartz Creek venture, trading his interest in that for Slavin's claims and share of the Klondike concession.

The danger was acute for concessionaires, for the outcry appeared likely to wipe out all of them. And Joe Boyle, who was in London, England, all that winter and spring, had difficulty defending his hard-won interests from a distance of seven thousand miles.

In the winter of 1901-02 Treadgold and Boyle were both in England, where the latter was under pressure to make a deal with the Treadgold syndicate, all duly reported to Sifton by Treadgold. On 15 January 1902, he had written to warn the minister that a very dissatisfied Joe Boyle was "too much piqued to realize what an advantage it would be in the working of his lease to be able possibly to get some water from the water company." But he advised Sifton "that all the water which we can find in Rock Creek is ours to take, provided we fulfill our obligations to you with it, and that nobody can get back from you as much as a spoonful. . . ."

The acrimonious sparring continued through that summer, with Boyle remaining obdurate. In July Sifton received another letter from Treadgold in which he spoke of a very generous offer to Boyle that "the fellow flatly refused. . . ."

How he proposes to get out of the hole I cannot think. Probably by fooling with the holders of the Rock Creek grants; both his hydraulic lease in the Klondike River and his timber berths are so hopelessly involved and at your mercy as well that it is difficult to see how he could refuse such a splendid offer. . . .

But refuse Boyle did, despite his problems in financing the concession development and despite the attacks on the concessionaires while Boyle was still overseas.

The latter controversy ignited a federal territorial election that was most bitterly fought and in which, to the surprise of many, Commissioner James Hamilton Ross, the Liberal candidate, defeated Joseph A. Clarke, the candidate of the dissidents, by 2,944 to 2,065 votes. One reason undoubtedly was that many of the protesters were Americans, ineligible to vote although they comprised more than half the territory's population. But there were other more compelling reasons. Following an investigation of fraud charges, George Black, a future Yukon MP, reported many illegalities. He found that one poll, which supported Ross by 161 to 15, had a register of only 35 eligible voters.

Boyle was fortunate to miss all this, for he might have been tarred by the suspicions merely because he was thought to have political connections. The late Thomas Ainsworth, a curator of the Vancouver Museum and in his younger days a Boyle employee, said that many Yukoners felt that Boyle got his concession because he was "a good Liberal."

The fate of the concessions still dangled, despite the government victory. Administrative changes set up a territorial council having limited powers, which was composed mainly of dissidents whose first action was to appoint a committee to act against Treadgold. The motion was ruled inadmissible because it contravened Ottawa instructions, and this attempt to muzzle the critics only created more anger. Finally, in May 1903, Laurier gave way and appointed a royal commission to investigate the mining situation. This conventional Canadian way of putting things aside aroused even more protests, with claims that the appointment of Judge B. M. Britton, a former Liberal MP, as chairman was the start of a whitewash.

The Britton commission's hearing in Dawson in August 1903 attracted large crowds to daily sittings that continued for five weeks. Only the largest concessionaires were scrutinized. At the time of the probe, forty-four concessions had been granted, of which twenty-nine were still extant, though, in all, five hundred applications for concessions had been filed.

Boyle and Slavin were among the many to testify. Treadgold was there, too, his secret scheming against Boyle still unknown to the latter. In fact, the two of them, in company with several others, departed on a two-week exploration trip to the north fork of the Klondike, some twenty-two miles from the gold area but a junction where the possibility for generating electricity from the river was reported to be ideal.

They were absent when one lawyer, in argument before the commission, related how Boyle and Slavin had become rich men in the gold fields. The main complaints against them at the hearing were that they had not done the required exploratory work before filing for the concession and that the original application's terms had become altered from one asking for nine square miles to a claim for more than four times that amount of land.

Boyle's testimony shed some light on his situation. He said he had pulled out of the Quartz Creek syndicate although he still held some stock in it, that he was operating a ten-square-mile timber berth in the Quartz area, held a lease on Dawson waterfront property, and acted on Treadgold's behalf when the latter was away. He admitted that he had been unable to do the development work required by the terms of his lease, but several trips to London had failed to produce the necessary financing.

He had, however, obtained a loan of £7,500 from Sir Thomas Tancred, secured by timber leases and other properties, part of which had been used in the Quartz Creek machinery purchase. Failure to repay the loan led to court action by Tancred, in which Boyle was required in April 1904 to transfer timber leases to the British plaintiff and repay him a sum of money. Boyle's wisdom in quitting the Quartz scene was demonstrated in the same month, when the Slavin-Gates concession went into liquidation in a London meeting at which Tancred, a shareholder and principal, was present.

Boyle's plans had outrun his financial resources, but he had other problems as well. Determined rivals were still trying to poach his timber on the Klondike, a situation that led Boyle to hire his former partner Slavin to act as watchman. Slavin forcibly ejected some of the trespassers and was arrested and charged with assault against two of them. Charles Boyle, now established in the Klondike to help his brother with his growing interests, went surety of $250 to have Slavin released. He was exonerated when evidence showed that he had been hit on the head with a rock and that Mrs. Slavin had had to intervene to pull his assailants away from her dazed husband. Slavin then laid charges against the two men who had made the first complaint. They were convicted of assault and sentenced to four months at hard labour, chopping wood in the

Dawson jail. The severity of the sentence led to a public outcry in which councilman Joseph A. Clarke demanded a pardon for the convicted men and an overhaul of the legal system.

The Britton commissioners dragged things on for more than a year, finally reporting in July 1904 that they thought the Yukon would benefit from hydraulic concessions. It was an anticlimax, for the Cabinet a month earlier had cancelled the Treadgold concession at the request of the syndicate.

One of the witnesses at the Britton hearing had been Sigmund Rothschild of Detroit, president of the Detroit-Yukon Mining Company, an American firm working claims on the Williams concessions. Rothschild was prepared to make a deal with Boyle to participate in the development of Boyle's properties. The first public evidence of the new association came on 18 June when it was announced that Elmer Bremer of Detroit-Yukon would set up a steam shovel at the mouth of Bear Creek for Joe Boyle. Bremer moved into the original Boyle-Slavin cabin near Dawson and hung his shingle outside for all to see.

Boyle's enterprise was now launched with capital provided by a sharp-shooting, hardheaded group of American entrepreneurs. The arrangement provided the financial resources to permit the long-delayed, much-criticized work to be done on the concession, and may well have stopped Ottawa from cancelling the grant.

Treadgold, too, was moving into another operational phase. Balked by miner protests, he had persuaded his associates to abandon their concession, forestalling government action and relieving Ottawa of some embarrassment. His new design was the assembly of masses of mining territory by staking, lease, or purchase of claims. What had been lost was the control of water, which now would have to be found within the rules applying to all, but which might still be utilized for hydro power that would put the initial developer in a position of pre-eminence. The sortie to the North Forks of the Klondike

with Boyle to examine hydro-generating potential demonstrated what they had in mind.

The Boyle program required not only all the water available
in the Klondike River, but every additional drop available
adjacent to the concession. Treadgold's original lease had given
him a stranglehold on Boyle and provided a lever by which he
could remove Boyle from control. One of the key areas involved
Rock Creek, a tributary of the Klondike entering it from the
right bank above Hunker, beyond the Boyle limits.

Now, thanks to the Britton commission and his new Detroit
associates, Boyle was clear of the pressures that Treadgold
could apply through the water rights. Things were changing in
the Klondike. The way had been cleared for an era of machines,
and Joe Boyle expected to be very much a part of it.

But the Rothschild connection was made at a price, and how
steep that price was became apparent when Boyle returned to
the East yet again—this time not only to sort out financial
affairs but also to take part in one of the maddest Yukon
promotions of all time.

SIX

The Challenge

Although baser metals are far more important to it today, the Yukon remains the Land of Gold. It is a paradox of sorts, then, that one of its greatest ventures was a search for a few ounces of silver to be found some four thousand miles to the east.

The metal involved, a few years earlier, had been handcrafted into a sports trophy bearing the name of its donor, Lord Stanley, erstwhile Governor-General of Canada—a challenge cup for annual competition to determine the hockey champions of the nation. This rather ordinary-looking trophy became the Holy Grail for a hockey expedition mounted in the Yukon. And Joe Boyle found himself in the thick of the adventure.

Hockey had been taken to the Klondike by the Canadian gold seekers, who found an outlet for their energies, and some relief from the boredom of the long winter nights, on the frozen mining ponds and ice-locked rivers of the region. For a couple of early winters competition was on a pickup basis; it was only when the gold rush ebbed, with a dramatic outpouring from Dawson and the Klondike to Nome, Alaska in the summer of 1899, that the way was cleared for a more organized approach to winter ice sports.

The newly organized Dawson Athletic Club that year made

available a portion of level land in Dawson where, on 24 November 1899, soldiers of the Yukon Field Force laid out and flooded a rink. The enclosure was 180 feet long and 130 feet wide—unusual dimensions that made the rink too wide for hockey but ideal for skating. Maintaining the rink was a useful activity for the bored soldiers and a boon for the community. Pickup hockey teams, utilizing brief periods of daylight, proved popular and on weekends they attracted crowds of excited partisan spectators. The big game of the 1899-1900 winter matched a town side against a team of soldiers from the Field Force. The *Dawson Daily News* promoted the affair, which for a few days supplanted news of the difficult events in South Africa.

Increased activity in the winter of 1900-01 led to a call for organized competition for the season of 1901-02. It was sounded with the Dawson Athletic Club's announcement that it would build a modern clubhouse with a covered arena attached, complete with training quarters, dressing rooms and showers, lounges, a dining room, and other facilities more likely to be found in Toronto or Montreal than in the northwestern wilderness. Directors were named to operate the large wooden structure with its unusual three-storey twin towers. As might be expected, Joe Boyle was front and centre, chairman of the sports and gymnasium committee and a leading spirit in the enterprise.

As enthusiasm for the club rose, the directors voted to install an electric power plant, and placed that project in Boyle's hands. Before the end of October 1902, installation of the power plant boiler and dynamo had begun and the editor of the *Daily News,* praising the edifice, noted that "a water pipe has been laid . . . to the club building for piping water to the club tank. The pipe is in a box on the surface of the ground, and covered with manure." There was the Boyle touch, for sure. Coming from a family racing one of the biggest stables on the continent, Joe was all too familiar with the many uses that could be made of the permanent by-product of the stables.

The tank arrangement ensured that hot water would be available for rink flooding. Cold water would freeze before it spread, making the ice lumpy. Fine spray nozzles helped, but in the Yukon and other parts of Canada deep in the winter freeze, hot-water flooding was a necessity.

From this hurly-burly the Dawson Hockey League emerged, with H. S. Tobin as president, and Duff Pattullo an executive member. Pattullo was with the Civil Service team, but his ability wasn't quite up to the playing standards that would emerge.

The Klondikers voted to use the rules of the pre-eminent Ontario Hockey Association, with some slight modification of the offside rule. Few hockey fans can recall when hockey totally banned the forward pass, but in those days the rink was divided into halves and passing the puck forward to a teammate was illegal. The passer, however, was entitled to shoot the puck forward and make the man ahead of him eligible to retrieve it by skating his teammates "onside," which meant a quick dash up ice, passing the rest of his team. It was a system geared to argument, particularly in scrambles near the goal. Claims that goals were scored by "offside" men were common.

Only one official handled the game, and the difficulty for a single referee to spot all that was going on in front, beside, or behind him was obvious. Goal judges signalled legal scores by waving flags or handkerchiefs, and they had no protection from crowds that frequently menaced their safety and continually abused them verbally. A referee not only had to impose penalties; he had to make spot judgments of the severity of the offence and determine how long the offender should be benched.

Four teams immediately entered the new Dawson league: the Civil Service, the Police, the DAAA, and a citizen's team adopting the impressive name of the Eagles. They were amateurs in a time of strict amateurism, but voted to contribute 25 percent of all gate receipts to a pot to be split among the teams. Admission prices were one dollar reserved and twenty-five cents for standing, high by the price scale of the time.

The hockey league was launched with ceremony and excitement in the luxurious surroundings of the new building, which was astonishing in many ways. Fitness devotees could cavort in Joe Boyle's gym, said to be the equal of any in the nation, enjoy a meal, swap tall tales over a drink, and do just about everything but smoke. Boyle's anti-tobacco crusade had managed to isolate the tobacco users on the third floor of one of the towers.

Rival teams were busy packing their lineups. The Civil Service scored a coup when two proven performers, L. G. Bennett and Randy McLennan, were mysteriously transferred to Dawson from the recorder's office in Stewart. The DAAA entry announced that League President Tobin would be in goal for the team—about the equivalent of the president of the National Hockey League playing for the Montreal Canadiens. Boyle, who usually left Dawson for the winter, gave the DAAA a helping hand: Archie Martin, who suddenly transferred to the Association lineup, was found a job in the Boyle enterprises.

Within three weeks of its opening the league threatened to dissolve, when the Civil Service said it was withdrawing because the arena management was uncooperative, but the crisis was overcome and the Civil Service complainants went on to win the Yukon championships, ignoring a challenge from the Whitehorse Knights in the process.

From the success of the hockey venture came the odd notion that the top team in Canada might very well be playing in Dawson City. A number of the Klondikers had played with the best teams in Eastern Canada eight or ten years before, and they now had an opportunity to be on ice for half the year in Dawson, considerably more than hockey players in the East. They worked hard, lived hard, and were fit, tough, and supremely confident. And some of them were homesick, eager for a chance to visit the more civilized society the Yukon was trying so hard to emulate.

The father of the original notion of competing for the Stanley Cup does not appear to have been recorded, but chances are there was a collective father, fashioning a decision around a table during a post-game beer-drinking hour. Somehow the vagrant thoughts came into focus by March 1903, when Deputy Sheriff Jack Eilbeck wrote to J. F. Fairlamb of the New York Central Railway, inquiring about the availability and cost of a chartered railway coach for an extended hockey tour.

On 27 April Fairlamb responded, enclosing in his reply a letter from an official of the Pullman Company, makers and operators of sleeping cars on North American railways, who said the Yukoners could charter their own private Pullman for $45 a day for fewer than thirty days, and $40 per day for more than thirty days. In view of their small number he suggested that they might prefer a private car rather than the standard Pullman. The price included the services of a cook, a porter, and a dining room waiter. Food was not included, but Pullman would provide it at a markup of 20 percent above cost.

Clearly the tour was possible, so for six months Eilbeck pursued the matter quietly, perhaps to avoid upsetting the senior Civil Service officials, who might lose some of their best men for several months. He found that there was high interest in such a tour and that many eastern teams would be prepared to play the Yukoners. Eilbeck also learned that an all-star team, rather than the Civil Service champions alone, would be preferable.

He managed to keep a publicity damper on the proposal until 27 January 1904, when the *News* reprinted a story about the negotiations that had appeared in the *Toronto World*. "They do not seem to have a very strong team," the *World* commented, "but it is quite safe to say they will have a full house wherever they go."

Talk of a Stanley Cup challenge was now a year old and it was time to advance the cause or forget it. Some time in July 1904 Weldy Young wrote a long letter to P. D. Ross, editor of the *Ottawa Journal* and, along with Sheriff Sweetland of

Ottawa, custodian of the trophy. Ross made no announcement until 9 September, when he revealed that he had Young's letter, as well as one from officers of the Klondike Hockey Club, making the challenge official. The club communication included a postscript saying that "Mr. Joe Boyle will represent our club with full authority to enter into and arrange all eastern dates." It was Boyle's first public linking with the challenge.

Late in July, and as usual with no fanfare, Boyle had left the Yukon via Whitehorse and Skagway. The hockey club had selected the right man, for the Klondike knew by 16 August that a team from their area would probably tour the East the next winter. Prior to Ross's announcement Boyle wrote a letter to the Dawson hockey men informing them that the hockey series would go ahead, and warning them of a proviso that would materially affect the Klondike plans.

The proviso was that Ottawa approval depended on the challengers agreeing not to play any exhibition games prior to the challenge matches. This would substantially alter their training program, and make more difficult the financing of a tour that was estimated to cost $10,000.

Just the hint of the tour had brought in a flood of inquiries and invitations from clubs all across Canada. As the *Dawson Daily News* saw it, the Klondikers would not accept any lest they have the misfortune to lose to a few second-rate clubs in their games en route to Ottawa, and "lessen their potency as an attraction when the big game came off."

Boyle set about providing the challengers with a public presence. He named them the Yukon Nuggets and bespoke their virtues widely. He said the duration of the series hadn't been settled but it would be "for not fewer than four games and perhaps as many as six." Following the cup series, he added, the tour would begin in Montreal, followed by games in Toronto, New York, Brooklyn, Washington, and Pittsburgh; and possibly Detroit, Chicago, St. Paul, Minneapolis, Winnipeg, and Brandon.

The Klondike Hockey Club now had a manager who thought

big, and Dawson's reaction was enthusiastic. "Attempt will be made to bring North the Stanley Cup—Lightning men from the Yukon certain to defeat most eastern teams" blared one headline. Knowledgeable Eastern hockey men were not as optimistic. They wondered about the plan to "walk out" the 350 miles from Dawson to Whitehorse, and the difficulties of working out a transportation plan involving hiking, railways, and ocean steamers. The Stanley Cup challenge presented its own problems, for there were no playoffs, and there might be a number of official challenges in a single season. All of the games would have to be played on the home ice of the trophy holder. The officials, if not local, would be from close by, the bulk of the spectators would be supporting the champions, and the ice surface would almost certainly be an enclosure much different in size and shape from the one on which the challengers were accustomed to perform. There was no uniformity in arena sizes or shapes: some had square corners and some were rounded. (There is no uniform size in these particulars in North America to this day.)

The defending champions, the Ottawa Silver Seven, had reigned for several seasons and were heralded as the greatest team ever. Even today they are often referred to as the greatest team in the era of seven-man hockey.

The time came for the selection and preparation of the Nuggets. Weldy Young was the logical choice for captain and coach, and probably the best man to handle the behind-the-scenes bickering over player selections. It was important to make the public feel that there was open competition for the places on the select team. Some of the likely candidates were in training early. There was no ice in the DAAA rink, but Sureshot Kennedy and Hec Smith got in some early licks on a good sheet of ice near the mouth of Bear Creek, where Boyle had established a headquarters for his operations along the creeks. In Dawson the other candidates worked out daily in the DAAA gym, which Boyle had so carefully filled with dumbbells, climbing ladders, trapezes, vaulting horses, and horizontal bars to encourage the pursuit of fitness.

Despite the early freeze at Bear Creek there was little evidence that winter was about to descend on the Yukon and give its hockey players an early advantage in ice practice. Rising temperatures by the end of October aroused public discussion of the strange weather. Some learned folk said that the vagaries of the elements were the result of the artillery barrages in the Sino-Russian War, some six thousand miles away across the Pacific.

It was not until the night of 12 November, when the Yukon Hockey Club held an important meeting, that the cold descended. The temperature dropped to 14 degrees below zero Fahrenheit, and the YHC made arrangements for a series of exhibition games that would determine the makeup of the challengers. More than twenty players turned out for the trials, although they had been warned that five places had been filled, leaving no more than four open—in those days of seven-man teams no club carried more than one or two spares, and most players were expected to be on the ice for a full sixty minutes.

More trouble came when travellers reported the Whitehorse trail devoid of snow, which was bad news for those team members who planned to walk at least part of the way, with their luggage hauled by dog teams. A number of players decided to ride bicycles down the open Yukon trail. The thirty-day forecast was "clear and cold," and on 4 December, Frank Slavin, who had just walked to Dawson from Whitehorse, reported a total absence of snow on the hard-packed frozen dirt road.

The rising clamour of a coming federal election on 16 December held the Dawson spotlight so that the 9 December announcement of the team selection was buried inside the newspapers. There was disturbing news that Weldy Young, heavily involved in the election process, would not be able to leave with the team, but would follow a few days later.

The selectees included Albert Forrest, a nineteen-year-old

goaltender from Quebec, who would be sent out to face the finest sharpshooters in the hockey world. A number of survivors of the Trail of '98 were on the team: Quebec-born left-winger Norman Watt, Manitoba-born right-winger George (Sureshot) Kennedy, and centre Hector M. Smith, who still worked in the diggings. The territorial administration would lose Dr. D. R. McLennan, a native of Glengarry, Ontario, whose droopy mustache was the only facial adornment in the party; and J. K. Johnstone, point, another Ottawan who arrived in Dawson in 1901 and worked in the Post Office with Norman Watts, the YHC's secretary. The list of choices even included the name of a player who wasn't in the Yukon. Lorne Hannay had played in the Dawson league but had recently returned to his home in Brandon, Manitoba. He would join the Nuggets as they rode east on the train from Vancouver. His acquisition as cover point was considered a stroke of good fortune. It also demonstrated the looseness of the eligibility rules in Cup competition. The spare players were reduced to one—Joe Boyle's employee Archie Martin. He would not only play upon occasion but would be team trainer and equipment manager.

Managing by first-class mail was proving a problem for Boyle, but he got word back to Dawson on 12 December that he had obtained a brief delay in what would be a best-two-of-three series. It would open Friday, 13 January, and continue the following Monday and Wednesday. Boyle said he had consulted railway timetables and schedules of coastal steamers from Skagway before acceding to the dates. "Bring light training apparatus for use on the steamer and trains. Bring at least three sets of pulling machines, Indian clubs and dumbbells."

The Ottawa rink, he warned, was twenty-five feet longer than that in Dawson and would present a problem. He asked for the selection of a drill captain to maintain daily records of conditioning to be presented to him in Ottawa. He concluded: "I know many of the boys need no admonition but [I] insist that on leaving Dawson all players cut out liquor and tobacco."

Boyle reported that he was fighting to remove the right of

the referee to determine the length of a penalty, and he was asking that any player guilty of a deliberate foul be thrown out of the game. Joe was a professional in the tough mining business, but his comments reveal a lack of understanding that amateur sport was as professional in its outlook as plain business.

The great departure started in the half-light of seven o'clock Sunday morning, 18 December 1904, when the first flight of walkers moved off. Twenty-four hours later the cyclists followed them. There were just twenty-five days before the first game, and the players were four thousand miles away from the Ottawa arena.

As soon as they were out of sight it began to snow in the Klondike, but the players' nine-day trip along the winter trail kept them ahead of the white flakes. Christmas passed in Dawson with no news of the travellers, but two days later came word that Albert Forrest's bicycle had collapsed near the Yukon Crossing and that he was planning to go to Whitehorse by stage.

One by one the bicycles went down, but they lasted long enough for the cyclists to catch up with the walkers in the advance party. Amazingly, all nine of them, including Forrest, reached Whitehorse at the same time. Sureshot Kennedy's pedometer showed that they had walked 321 miles, an average of about 36 miles daily with heavy packs—no mean feat in a land where long hikes were commonplace.

At Whitehorse they sent a telegram to Ottawa. "All of us are very tired," they confessed; but they were also elated. The SS *Amur,* which was to carry them to Vancouver, was on schedule and they had two days in which to board her at the Skagway harbour. They could count on reaching Ottawa at least four days before the opening game. Their timetable gamble seemed to have paid off.

The weary hikers enjoyed a large dinner before going to bed in their Whitehorse hotel. As they drew the curtains they noticed that snow was beginning to fall. They had outraced it from Dawson to Whitehorse, and they felt pleased about that as well. When they opened the curtains the next day the snow had become a blizzard. It continued even more heavily through the whole day. Deep drifts on the narrow-gauge railway line over the White Pass halted the trains. There was no way to reach Skagway until the railway reopened, which it did on the third day. The worried Yukon Nuggets sent word to the *Amur* to wait, but they reached the dock to learn that the ship had sailed two hours earlier, twenty-four hours behind its scheduled departure time.

The *Amur* reached Vancouver on 31 December as scheduled, having made up the lost time en route. But the hockey team's movement schedule, so carefully designed by Joe Boyle from three thousand miles away, was shattered beyond recovery. Nothing could alter the fact that the Nuggets were stranded in Skagway for three days, with nothing to do but wait for the next ship.

Three days later they departed Skagway on the SS *Romano*, a U.S. vessel bound for Seattle. Another day was added to their travelling time because they had to head back by train to Vancouver to catch the CPR trans-continental.

To add to their frustration, the seas were so rough that they could not carry out the exercise program demanded by their absentee manager. Most of their activity came in rushing for the rail or the heads. Some just lay in their bunks and tossed, hardly caring whether they lived or drowned. Far from improving their condition, the sea voyage worsened it. On 6 January, now five days behind schedule, they were in Vancouver. Sports writers there, more charitable than usual, felt they were in "pretty good condition," although they refrained from saying in comparison with what.

Back in Dawson that same day, Weldy Young left by stage for Ottawa. He departed none too soon, for he had fudged his final assignment of preparing an electoral list for the upcoming territorial elections. A few minutes before he dashed off, Weldy deposited his lists with the territorial officials. A few days later they realized he had merely copied the electoral list used in the federal vote of 16 December, about which there had been charges of vast irregularities. It was a final farewell for Dawson's hockey hero. He never returned to the territory.

The CPR travellers dismounted at Ottawa on Wednesday, 11 January at 4:45 P.M. to learn that their pleas, dispatched en route by telegram, for a delay in the series opener had been rejected. They would play before a capacity crowd at Dey's Arena on Friday the thirteenth. And the Governor-General of Canada would grace the scene of this historic event.

Their arrival commanded attention on the front pages of the *Citizen* and *Journal.* "The spectacle of a team travelling 4,000 miles," said the *Citizen,* "and at an expense neighbouring around $6,000 . . . [is] something calculated to overawe anyone not aware of the popularity of Canada's great winter game."

Certainly Ottawa seemed excited. All the reserved seats had been sold out days before and crowds gathered to view the coveted Stanley Cup displayed in Bob Shillington's store window. Ottawa, it was plain, was ready for the series. There was some doubt about the readiness of Joe Boyle's men.

SEVEN

Moment of Truth

On the morning of 12 January, thirty-six hours before the opening of the Stanley Cup series, the paths of the Nuggets and their manager converged. Joe Boyle returned from Detroit on the night train in time to watch his charges go through their first and only ice practice in more than a month, a preparation for a championship series that is unique, and will remain so forever.

There was no time for discussion of strategy. It was makeshift and mend as they tried on new uniforms and tested new sticks, all ordered in Eastern Canada. They had brought their own skates in the vain hope that they might get a chance to use them. They were far from downhearted, though. Ottawans observing their practice were told that the challengers expected to get into shape in the opening game and improve enough after that to win the series and take the Stanley Cup to Dawson, where it would remain forever.

It would be a makeshift lineup, just the same. Weldy Young was missing, for the first game, at least. At the last minute G. L. Bennett, a useful veteran forward, had begged off. So, for the opening game it would be Forrest in goal; Johnstone, point; Hannay (picked up in Winnipeg), cover point; McLennan, rover; Kennedy, right wing; Watt, left wing; and H. Smith, centre.

Ottawa was honed to a fine pitch and would present its long-advertised lineup of trophy holders. There was no ban on pre-series play for them, and they had been confidently prepared by practice and exhibition games. It seems unlikely they had any doubts about the outcome of this series.

From the goal out, where D. W. Finnie held sway, the Cup holders were a picked team—conscripted, some said, by means that were not exactly in keeping with the spirit of amateurism. Jobs and money, the envious whispered, had been the tools by which this talented collection had been fashioned.

Certainly there was little that was amateurish about the play of people like Arthur Moore at cover, and slick Harvey Pulford on the point, who would be termed defence men today. And few had been able to match strides with their forwards, led by crafty winger and coach-captain Archie Smith, and featuring the peerless Frank McGee at centre, with H. L. Gilmore as the other winger, and doughty Harry (Rat) Westwick the tireless rover.

More than 2,500 payees packed Dey's Arena that Friday the thirteenth, an ominous date for an old sailor like Joe Boyle. (Some captains wouldn't put to sea on Friday, regardless of the date.) The fans had been sternly admonished not to smoke, which pleased Boyle. The press box was crowded, telegraphers at the ready. The whole place was awash with political, business, and social notables.

Attracting almost as much attention as the game was Canada's new Governor-General Earl Grey and his Lady, just arrived from London. Some officials were concerned that Grey and his party might not take to rugged colonial sports. Some had been known to sniff at such things. Earl Grey, who would donate a football trophy for Canadian teams, was made of different stuff. He was a widely travelled cosmopolite, a former administrator of Cecil Rhodes' colony of Rhodesia, and like Rhodes was an admirer of "manly" sports. As it turned out, he genuinely liked what he saw and, many years later, had occasion to mention his experiences in the Ottawa rink. Together at centre ice with a clutch of notables that included Joe Boyle, the earl officially launched the championship series.

Boyle looked back to the Yukon bench and was heartened by cries of encouragement from a cross-section of Klondike fans, among them his mining associate, Arthur Treadgold. And he looked closely at Referee Harlow Stiles, a Brockville man who had agreed to officiate when Boyle stubbornly fought efforts to have an Ottawan placed in charge of the game.

The change of referee was one of his few victories that night, he thought, as he sat at a desk three hours later vainly trying to compose the special story he had promised to write for the *Dawson Daily News*. Admitting defeat never was easy for Joe Boyle, but this one couldn't be shrugged off, or appealed to a higher court like a business lawsuit. "Score, Ottawa nine and Dawson two," he scrawled. That was prosaic enough, and hardly news, for the Klondikers had clustered around the telegraph office late that afternoon to get the running account tapped out from Dey's Arena. They knew the result only too well.

"As Boyle Saw the Game" ran the headline across the top of the *Dawson Daily News*'s front page on Saturday, 14 January. As Boyle saw it,

It was a great game and the score was no criterion of it, nor of the relative merits of the two teams.

It was a fast, rough game and Ottawa, in the first half, made four offside goals which Referee Stiles of Cornwall was not fast enough on his skates, nor with his eyes, to follow.

Still it had only been 3–1 at half time.

Ottawa was continually offside thus putting our boys to the dis- advantage which always belongs to the team playing a clean game, when larger liberties are allowed the other side.

Some of the play had been brutal. Boyle noted that when Ottawa's Moore had crosschecked Watt, the Yukoner had broken his stick over Moore's head in retaliation and drawn a fifteen-minute penalty.

The Yukon, Boyle continued, showed best in the first half, but lack of condition and the rigours of their twenty-four-day journey told in the second. But Boyle remained optimistic. "We all expect a great game Monday," he wrote. "We have a good chance to win the cup."

The rival *Dawson World,* relying on a special correspondent named MacKenzie, produced a considerably more lucid and informative account. He agreed that Dawson had held command for the first fifteen minutes of the opening thirty-minute half, deteriorating steadily thereafter. Dawson had started the big second-period fight, he noted, when Watt tripped Moore, who hit Watt in the mouth with his stick. The Yukoner then skated across the rink and poleaxed Moore, rendering the Ottawan unconscious for ten minutes. Both were sent off the ice for fifteen minutes when order was restored. Yukon goalie Albert Forrest, in a special despatch to the *World,* conceded it was a rough game and charged that six of the Ottawa goals were offside. Yukon rationalization found no place among the Eastern hockey writers. The *Toronto Telegram,* without mentioning the score, concluded that the whole problem was that "the Dawson team weren't there with the goods."

The erudite P. D. Ross, chief custodian of the Stanley Cup, smoothed off some of the rough edges.

How does the story of the match read when put this way? Up to the time the Ottawans were leading 3-1 it was anybody's game and the Yukon men had the most of the play. . . . It was only when the Yukoners tired and showed the effect of their long journey that Ottawa began to pile on the score. . . . Add also that for a major portion of the game Yukon were playing a man short, and sometimes two, and it looks a bit better.

Editor Ross was not about to suggest that people should stay away from the second game of the series on Monday; not at all. They had packed a record crowd into the rink on Friday the thirteenth and at least one more gate of the same size was needed. Ross laid it on with a trowel, though. "Some go so far as to say," he added, "that given equal conditions this is the best team that has come after the Stanley Cup for two or three years." He admitted the referee was wrong in not calling three offside scores but urged that he be retained to handle the second game.

Saturday was a lost cause for the battered Nuggets. Boyle let his walking wounded rest for twenty-four hours before calling them out to a Sunday practice. The roll call was a distressing moment, for it was clear that one or two would not be able to play in the second game, and that half the remainder would be playing hurt, in modern parlance. Boyle was about to spring a small surprise on that score. He was planning to enter Fred Fairburn on his lineup in place of Randy McLennan, who would not be playing. Fairburn, it turned out, had been quietly recruited in Winnipeg "just in case." He was ostensibly to play in the post-series tour, but the elastic rules of the Cup competition enabled him to appear in the big event.

"We've got the team and will show Ottawans the real thing tonight," Boyle said on Monday morning. That night the arena was jammed again. And once more the Nuggets raised brief hopes for their supporters. They rushed to the attack and quickly tested Goalie Finnie, seeking the early lead that had eluded them in the opener. It was a passing flurry. Rat Westwick scored for Ottawa after four-and-a-half minutes of play. The Silver Seven survived another Nugget onslaught and at 8:10 Westwick scored again. That was the cruncher. The challengers stopped skating and one of the worst debacles in Stanley Cup history was under way. It was 10–1 for Ottawa at the half and a horrifying 23–2 at the finish. The Silver Seven had rewritten the record book, with a special chapter for Frank McGee, the one-eyed centre, who scored fourteen times in a performance that will never be matched. McGee scored eight successive goals in the second half alone.

The irksome *Toronto Telegram* led eastern press denunciation of the Nuggets. The challengers, their reporter wrote, were the worst "consignment of hockey junk to come over the metals of the CPR." The *Ottawa Citizen* said that Goalie Forrest played a "really fine game" despite the twenty-three goals registered against him. "But for him the figures might have been doubled."

What did Joe Boyle write for the *Dawson Daily News?*

Nevertheless, it was a good game. There was one stage of it 15 minutes of the fastest and fiercest play without a score. Then Friday's game told on the Klondikers and they were "all in" and Ottawa scored at will. . . . [I]n short, our team was broken up and in no condition to play in such a game which was put up against them.

To all who witnessed the massacre the conclusion was inevitable that the Silver Seven were invincible. But invincibility is a transitory thing in athletics. They would lose the Cup before the year was out.

Boyle's post-season Grand Tour had been scheduled to begin on 19 January with a game at Kingston against the powerful Queen's University team. Surveying the survivors of the challenge matches, Boyle realized that the Nuggets would need some polishing. He sat at the telephone and endeavoured to talk some of Canada's best amateurs into joining him on the touring circuit. Cyclone Taylor, later a member of the Hockey Hall of Fame, and a hockey wanderer of supreme skill, was sitting in Toronto waiting for the Ontario Hockey Association to decide whether he could play for the Marlboros. Taylor listened to Boyle, but said no. Eventually he joined the immigration department and played in Ottawa.

At Kingston on 19 January the Queen's team learned that the Nuggets not only would not appear, but that they had departed from Ottawa by train for Nova Scotia. The Klondikers left twenty-four hours ahead of coach-captain Weldy Young's arrival in his former home town, where he was met by a group of old friends who, it was said, "kept his arm working like a pump handle." Weldy stayed a few hours, then set off once more on his stern chase, hoping to catch up in Amherst, Nova Scotia on Monday, 23 January.

The humiliation in Ottawa appeared to have little negative effect, because the Nuggets were offered as many games as they could handle. Amherst defeated the tourists 4–2 in the first game of the tour, and the Nuggets carried their bruised and aching muscles into Cape Breton, where they lost 4–0 in a game refereed by one of the host Victorias. They lost 3–2 to the Halifax Wanderers and an all-star team beat them 2–1 the following night. Beating the Nuggets had become a habit, and some teams were preening their feathers. Amherst sent in a challenge for the Stanley Cup that raised a few eyebrows in Ottawa.

There were post-game dinners and much hospitality, and Boyle quite charmed his hosts with his eloquence and wit, voicing more invitations to visit the Klondike for a challenge series. Dawson, he said, would put up a magnificent gold challenge cup, open to all comers, and would pay legitimate travelling expenses.

By this time the tourists had become conditioned and were starting to win. Weldy Young had joined the team, and Norman Watt, who had been injured in Ottawa, was back in uniform. They whipped a Cape Breton all-star team 5–2, and concluded their Maritimes visit with a 7–3 win over the Pictou County All Stars, a 4–4 tie and a 4–2 victory in Moncton, and a 2–0 victory in Fredericton.

Travel-weary by now, they lost in Three Rivers, and to the Montreal Montagnards. Queen's rubbed it in for that early disappointment, defeating the Nuggets 15–2. Two days later, Brockville bounced them 8–2. Clearly they were tired out, so Boyle took them back to the Russell House in Ottawa and set about lining up a Western Ontario tour in places close to his Woodstock home, and a swing through the United States.

By 21 February it appeared the Ontario tour was complete. Then it collapsed, when the Toronto Marlboros and St. Georges officials charged that the Nuggets were pros and were making a small fortune on their tour. Boyle made a formal denial of charges and offered to play the Nuggets against any Toronto team provided the gate receipts went to charity. But in the end all that happened was the cancellation of the Ontario tour. The irate Canadian hockey establishment agreed that the Nuggets could play a three-game series with the Pittsburgh Athletic Club, although Pittsburgh had previously been blacklisted for stealing Canadian players.

On 8, 10, and 11 March the Nuggets flew their standard in Pittsburgh, winning the first match 8–5, losing the second 4–3, and convincingly whipping the import-laden Burghers 6–1 in the third.

With spring coming, Boyle turned their railway coach westward. The Nuggets outraced the spring thaw to the Lakehead, where the tourists defeated the home side 8–4. Winnipeg Victorias halted them 8–1 in a game where the electricity failed, but the following night, 21 March, the Nuggets carried away a 9–1 victory in Brandon against the Manitoba champions.

They looked out on roads running with water the next morning. Spring had finally passed them as they journeyed west. Games in Regina, Calgary, Rossland, and Nelson were cancelled. The long tour, the first of its kind in hockey history, was over.

In Brandon the Nuggets and Joe Boyle parted company, having written an unusual chapter in the history of Canadian hockey. The players decided to return home individually, and the first of the wanderers to return to Dawson was young Albert Forrest, who walked in from Whitehorse in seven days. The irrepressible young goalie noted, with some pride, that he had returned with just as much money as he had left Dawson, for the split of tour receipts had covered all the expenses. Had those games in the West not been called off, the players could have returned with a profit.

It has long been popularly believed that Joe Boyle financed the tour. Clearly this was not the case, unless it is conceded that his not unskillful management of the venture had provided the gate receipts that enabled it to break even.

Joe Boyle and his Nuggets may not have won the Stanley Cup, but they helped bring about some important changes in the hockey rules. The Cup selection committee ruled that all future challengers must have established their credentials in games against established opposition, which eliminated teams such as Amherst and others who wanted to take up where the Nuggets had left off.

The pro–amateur dispute, which the Nuggets had helped exacerbate, ended a couple of years later with the formation of professional hockey leagues that not only "stole" most of the leading amateur teams in Eastern Canada but made off with the amateurs' most prized possession, the Stanley Cup itself.

Few things in which Joe Boyle became involved had results as long-lasting as his dabbling in the murky waters of hockey entrepreneurship.

EIGHT

The Battle of Sandwich

Joe Boyle's return to the East in July 1904 marked the beginning of a four-year exile from the Klondike. The exile was the result of the long-developing crisis arising from a shortage of development capital, and the unrelenting assault on all concessionaires.

The concession critics were determined to dismantle the whole system, despite the Britton report that Boyle and some others had done nothing wrong. This clearance at least relieved Joe of charges of fraud, but the same report noted his failure to do the annual $5,000 worth of work necessary on the concession, and pointedly remarked that placing machines on the property was not enough to discharge the obligation. Agitation continued in the newspapers and it was clear that the commission findings would not terminate it.

Boyle had considered selling out all through the spring of 1904 in a deal with the Detroit-Yukon syndicate. It all appeared to be settled on 27 June 1904, when Sigmund Rothschild and his associates offered Boyle and his lawyer H. B. McGiverin $750,000 for the concession. McGiverin was referred to as trustee, a position he had filled because of the Tancred litigation. Two months after the preliminary agreement, how-

91

ever, the Detroiters announced that the offer to purchase had been withdrawn. Boyle was in Ottawa by this time, and some concern about that development may have been responsible for his sudden, quiet exit from Dawson late in July.

Rothschild instead proposed that an incorporated joint stock company be formed into which the Detroiters would put $500,000 in cash, with thirty thousand shares issued, of which Boyle would receive ten thousand. In addition he would receive $250,000 as a royalty from gross gold production. The new company would be called the Canadian Klondike Mining Company (CKMC). Boyle's ten thousand shares would be paid off over a period of three years, an arrangement he could not control once agreeing to it, since he would be only a minority shareholder.

To accept the proposal meant that Boyle's dream would be realized only without his participation. He would be frozen out. Yet the proposal was accepted. It is not clear why Boyle agreed to an arrangement in which he lacked control. Obviously he was under some great pressures; it is difficult to believe that at the age of thirty-seven he was prepared to become a rural squire on the family's acres in Woodstock. Once his shares were purchased by the syndicate he would have no position in equity or employment. That he intended to quit the Yukon forever seems unlikely, for he still retained substantial business interests there that produced considerably more in profits than the $5,000 annually he was paying his brother Charles to manage them.

In any event, Boyle's sale to CKMC did not halt the attacks on him in the Dawson newspapers. But even those attacks had their strange side. They were devoted to things Boyle was alleged to have done, or not done, prior to the sale. The usual Dawson growling about selling out to foreigners, which might have been expected, did not appear.

Boyle was in Ottawa when the Britton Commission report was made public. It was publicly hinted that the government, as a result, would crack down hard on concessionaires who had failed to carry out the annual development work obligation. That possibility could have been the reason Boyle agreed to sell. It did—possibly to ease the Detroiters' concerns—lead Boyle to issue an affidavit claiming that he had done $25,000 worth of work since 1903. He carefully omitted any reference to the earlier years, when he had done almost none.

Life at The Firs was comfortable but dull for Boyle. He enjoyed the reunion with his children. From the early years of his success he had made it a point to take Joe Junior and Flora with him on his trips. Earlier, in 1902-03, they had gone to London, where they were introduced to a rising young Canadian named Max Aitken, an aggressive Maritimer who had made a reputation as secretary to John F. Stairs, a leading Maritimes banker. Aitken's transformation into a British press baron with a peerage was some distance down the road, but Boyle realized that Max was headed upward. Aitken never forgot the Boyles; his interest in them was responsible for his *Express* newspaper informing Britons of Boyle's hockey expedition for the Stanley Cup.

During his exile in the East, Boyle continued to move around. He travelled to Britain and spent considerable time in New York and Detroit, frequently spending the daytime with lawyers—so much so that Flora Boyle's best recollections of these years were the hours she waited for her father in the legal offices of his advisers.

In these years, Flora saw more of him than her brother did. Joe Junior had been firmly planted on the academic path, which for him became considerably longer than the one trodden by his father. He attended Woodstock College from 1905 to 1907, moved on to the Michigan School of Technology in Houghton, Michigan, and eventually to Columbia University in New York. He discovered that his real interest was the law, but his father insisted that he become an engineer competent to take over the Boyle operations in the Klondike. It was not the first time they differed about what young Joe should do with his life. This time the father won out.

There were other complications for the King of the Klondike in his personal relationships. His wife Millie, from whom he had been parted for eight years but from whom he had not been divorced, appeared in Woodstock in 1904 with the two younger daughters, Charlotte and Susan. She wanted money despite the separation agreement, which said she had no claim on Boyle after 1896. She spent several fruitless weeks living at the Oxford Hotel, but got nowhere.

The rebuff did not discourage her. In mid-September 1905 Ottawa newspapers reported that she and her daughters were in the nation's capital, where she was hoping to enter a suit for divorce, citing a theatre personality, Jessie Wyatt, as co-respondent. Boyle, the story went, had met Jessie Wyatt during his long 1897-98 wait in Ottawa. "Mr. Boyle," said the press report, "was greatly impressed with Miss Wyatt's attainments and induced her to go to Dawson."

The records show that Boyle did indeed arrive back in Dawson in July 1899 with a lady introduced as Mrs. J. W. Boyle. Her name appeared periodically in newspaper accounts of social events, so it is clear that she was no figment of Millie Boyle's imagination. Life in the Klondike proceeded by its own standards and no eyebrows were raised. That particular Mrs. Boyle shared a niche in the domestic life of the region occupied by quite a number of other "wives" whose real situation was uncertain, but remained unchallenged. Miss Wyatt, the temporary Mrs. Boyle, disappears from the Boyle story at the end of 1901, and her ultimate fate is unknown.

Millie may have had the goods on Joe, but she preferred to make her challenge elsewhere after she discovered that the divorce application would have to be processed in the Senate of Canada. The decision to delay did not stop Millie from her quest for some of the Klondike gold. Boyle finally was moved to offer her a substantial annual payment in settlement, presumably to obtain the divorce that it was clear he now desired, but Millie preferred to take her chances in an American court. The 1907 divorce hearing in Chicago demonstrated how wrong her decision had been. She was awarded fifty dollars a week alimony—far less than Boyle had offered.

Boyle was generous, even indulgent, with those he cared for. He had been giving his brother Dave a generous allowance, and was shocked when, during the difficulties with Millie, he discovered that Dave had secretly been providing money for her to pursue her hunt. Reasonably enough, Joe concluded that thanks to his brother's actions, he had been financing his own harassment. He ended Dave's allowance and treated him very coldly for a long time. Joe never permitted Dave to visit him in the Klondike.

Divorce, far from concluding Boyle's problem with the opposite sex, merely accentuated it, for now he was fair game for every matrimonially inclined admirer. Flora Boyle recalls quite a few of them, and says that she and her brother spent a good deal of time and energy trying to discourage the attentions of the most obvious. Boyle was rich, handsome, gregarious, and very much a man. He wasn't a woman chaser, but he *was* woman-chased.

For the most part, Boyle's restless energy was seeking an outlet, and there were many pleasant (if somewhat bizarre) episodes when the banked Boyle fires blazed. One of them was Boyle's assumption of the management of a broken-down touring circus, which was about to go into bankruptcy when it reached Woodstock. It was a challenge for Boyle the showman, who took over the derelict Lemon Brothers Circus, moved it through Western Ontario in a welter of publicity, and bade it farewell at the end of the touring season as a financially restored operation.

Boyle's reward was the enjoyment of doing what most people said couldn't be done. His legacy in this case was his composition of a song, "Lemon Brothers Had a Circus," which he sang lustily upon the appropriate occasions in the Boyle home, a memory that resides still with Flora Boyle.

Joe's interest in The Firs was only rarely exhibited, but when he did enter into its operations it was with all the vigour he put into other ventures. Raising and marketing well-bred pigs intrigued him, and he went heavily into this sideline, constructing special pens and laying out a good deal of money for stock he was certain would add substantially to the income of the estate. As usual, his drive and enthusiasm aroused criticism; there were more than a few who secretly felt that Boyle ought to stick to his specialty, mining gold. They never discovered whether they were right or wrong, for the Boyle piggery was destroyed by an outbreak of hog cholera, a development that seemed to cheer up Dave Boyle considerably. Despite this, Boyle never lost his enthusiasm for raising hogs—as his Irish relatives discovered years later.

These months of spasmodically enforced idleness were peripheral to Boyle's real concerns. He was watching the operations of the Detroit syndicate, in which he had such a large stake, with interest that grew to alarm. Originally the five Detroiters had agreed to place $100,000 apiece in cash in the syndicate treasury, to be used to develop the Klondike River property. Boyle discovered that the early reports that the deal would cost them little or no money were true, and that the $500,000 deposit in the treasury had been written off by selling the company some old machinery and two claims held near Boyle's property, along with other dubious assets.

Boyle's temporary retirement ended. It had been difficult enough to sell the company, and the realization that he probably had been bilked sent him charging into battle. He moved quietly, laying the ground for an action to expose the matter and recover his position with a minimum of publicity. He wisely engaged the services of Woodstock's leading lawyer, Wallace Nesbitt, a small-town expert who would soon demonstrate his skills on Boyle's behalf.

Preparation for the engagement took months and many meetings with Nesbitt, McGiverin, and others privy to the suit. Boyle was content to let the Rothschilds do all the running for a time. Early in 1906 they had been expansive in revealing their development plans to the Dawson press. They were operating one mammoth dredge and planning to operate another, but having some problems in getting it from the Marion Steam Shovel Company of Marion, Ohio, manufacturers of the monster earth gougers. This was despite the best efforts of Elmer Bremer, who had assumed Boyle's position as manager of the Klondike properties.

In midsummer of that year Sigmund Rothschild visited Dawson and enthralled the populace with tales of his company's plans for developments at Bear Creek and all along the river. These announcements attracted wide interest. Curiously enough, they failed to draw the criticism that might have been expected, for the war against the concessionaires was continuing on two fronts, in Dawson and in Ottawa.

In May 1906 the complainants appeared to have scored a major victory when the Minister of the Interior, Frank Oliver, who had succeeded Sifton in the portfolio, announced the cancellation of seven concessions, including the trailblazing Anderson grant and one that had been leased to Boyle on Quartz Creek. Some of the concession holders were given a few claims as a sop for their loss. Boyle was allowed to retain five on Quartz Creek. A public meeting in Dawson on 21 May drew attention to the fact that the Boyle concession had been exempted, and there were demands that it be cancelled as well.

Despite the feeling, the big dredge at Bear Creek kept working away and the Rothschilds announced on 25 July that it had made a record day's cleanup of more than $5,000. Rumours abounded, one of the juiciest being a report that the ubiquitous Arthur Treadgold was in New York discussing a merger with the Guggenheim interests.

Boyle had been in London as usual that year, in company with Treadgold, and this raised other speculation. Clement Buras, Yukon secretary of state in the territorial government, returned from London and spoke of meeting Boyle and Treadgold there. Not long after Buras's return, MPs in Ottawa were loudly complaining about the great extent of foreign holdings in the Yukon.

Through the long months, impatient but determined, Boyle planned and waited. Early in 1907 he moved, seizing an opportunity opened to him when the Rothschilds sold ten thousand shares of Canadian Klondike stock to the Guggenheims for $110,000. And the Guggenheims were reputedly dickering with Treadgold.

Entering an action in the Supreme Court of Ontario, Boyle claimed on behalf of himself and other shareholders that the sale left him as the largest shareholder and in effective control of the company, because the Rothschild claim to own twenty thousand shares was defective. The application was scheduled for October 1907 at Sandwich, Ontario, just across the river from Detroit, but was briefly delayed.

Principal witnesses for Boyle were his brother Charles, who was delighted to come out from Dawson after some six years in the Klondike; Dawson surveyor Charles Barwell; and Boyle's old friend and adversary (depending on circumstances), Arthur Newton Christian Treadgold.

The action finally commenced before Mr. Justice R. M. Riddell, an experienced jurist who completed the case in eight hours—a feat that drew comment because of the apparent complexity of the issues.

The Detroit case was that in 1905 Boyle had agreed to take ten thousand shares of the new Canadian Klondike Mining Company as part of the $750,000 sale price for his concession, with $500,000 to be withheld and used to pay off creditors for machinery used by Boyle and financed by them. Boyle's stock, they testified, was ultimately to be redeemed from him for cash from the mining profits, leaving him with no corporate interest.

Boyle's counsel asked the court to set aside the entire transaction because of the fraudulent conduct of the Rothschild group. Sigmund Rothschild escaped the embarrassment of this denunciation, having died a few weeks earlier, but the court did not spare his associates on that account.

Michael J. Murphy, a financier connected with the Detroit

Security Trust, presented a confident front that suddenly collapsed under the shrewd cross-examination of Wallace Nesbitt. Murphy reluctantly conceded that the machinery allegedly sold by the syndicate for $500,000, along with the two leases, was worth only $270,000—although it had been shown as worth the $500,000 allegedly placed to the company treasury by the Detroit partners. He and his associates claimed that the purchase of the machinery was part of the deal, a claim that Boyle vigorously denied.

Mr. Justice Riddell clearly was unimpressed by Murphy. Before retiring in disorder, Murphy conceded that the bill of sale, which the witness agreed was properly drawn, made no mention of any transfer of money for machinery. He feebly admitted that he had signed the agreement without reading it, an escape hatch also sought by Fred T. Moran, another member of the syndicate, in his testimony. The second claim of ignorance appeared to outrage the judge, who turned to Moran and asked: "Do you want me to believe that, Mr. Moran?" Moran, it was reported, turned red and responded, "No, Your Lordship, I will say I don't remember reading the document." Nesbitt commented on this convenient lack of memory, and pointed out that the agreement clearly called for a deposit of $500,000 in cash by the five Detroiters.

All this was very damaging, but Nesbitt and his associate counsel A. H. Clarke, K.C., of Windsor, weren't finished. As the spectators gasped, Nesbitt and Clarke called Otto Brenner of London, Ontario, to the stand. Brenner was employed by the syndicate and had been summoned by them but had not been called to give evidence. He provided the clincher when he testified that he had been present when the deal with Boyle was consummated, and that there had never been any discussion of the sale of machinery.

Boyle's case was further bolstered by the evidence of his brother Charles, by surveyor Barwell, and in a considerable way by the testimony of Treadgold, whose lucidity won the approval of the judge.

One of the best witnesses of all was Joe Boyle himself. He told the court how he had invaded the Klondike with little more than the clothes he wore and how he had succeeded where so many had failed. The judge expressed his amazement at the story and said he found it hard to believe that Boyle had been so impoverished. "You are overlooking one thing," Boyle responded. "When I went into the Yukon I took along Joseph Whiteside Boyle." "How very true, Mr. Boyle," the judge replied.

Mr. Justice Riddell wasted little time in returning his verdict. He found the Boyle witnesses, both in their words and demeanour, completely truthful and believable. "In the case of at least some of the witnesses for the defence," he added, "I fear that 'the wish was father to the thought.' At all events I prefer the evidence of those already named."

It was a preference demonstrated in the sweeping terms of the judgment. The court found that Boyle had not known of the claimed agreement to spend the $500,000 on machinery, and that it was not part of the agreement. The plaintiff, Mr. Justice Riddell ruled, was entitled to recover from "the fraud of the directors," who had tried to obtain $500,000 for machinery that Riddell finally decided was worth only $50,000. Holding the syndicate liable for breach of trust, he loaded them with all the court costs, permitting only a further adjudication to determine what amount, if any, they should receive for use of their machinery.

For Joe Boyle, it was a story to dine out on. He told it with relish to all who wanted to know what had happened, even regaling his delighted Irish relatives with the full account in such a way that they recalled it in detail sixty years later.

But it was far from over. The Detroiters went to court in their own country and obtained an injunction to restrain Boyle from interfering with CKMC assets or properties. They attempted to cover the $500,000 in dispute by depositing a mere $190,000 in a bank, and offering bills and various accounts they claimed covered the remainder of the money.

A company meeting was called in January 1908, at which Boyle claimed that he and some friends were the only paid-up shareholders, and were alone able to vote to appoint officers and conduct the business of the company. It was a rowdy affair, breaking up into two separate meetings at which the two sides held their own elections. There were comic-opera aspects to the whole muddle, but no one was laughing.

Boyle took the whole issue back to court when the Detroiters balked at paying the bill for court costs awarded to Boyle in the initial hearing. The costs claim included $1,350 for each of the two Charleses, Boyle and Barwell; $500 for Treadgold; a relatively modest $300 for Boyle; and a $1,000 expert-witness fee for Barwell.

The resumption of the court battle went on before Mr. Justice Riddell on 10 March 1908, and once more the judge came down very strongly on Boyle's side. He found that the court actions in Detroit had been an effort to avoid payment of the $500,000 and that the intention was that CKMC should never have control of the money. He termed the conduct of the defendants "dishonest" and added, "I do not think that the affairs of the Ontario company are safe in the hands of these persons in a foreign country, who cannot be reached personally by the Court, and who show by their conduct no desire to abide by the direction of the Court." Riddell ordered the appointment of a receiver to bring within the jurisdiction of the court all the assets of the company. Boyle was appointed receiver, and agreed to post a substantial bond.

The judge also ruled on the court costs, giving Barwell $1,510, Charles Boyle $650, Treadgold his $500, and Joe Boyle only $22.50. Boyle had been living in Detroit at the time, and this may have been enough to cover the ferry fare.

Boyle had won round two of the bitter fight, but it was not yet over, partly because he made a mistake and left an opening for still another attack. He had obtained a $300,000 bond to meet his receivership position, but the amount was challenged by the Detroiters. Once more they came before Mr. Justice

Riddell. To prove the even-handed justice of Canadian courts, the judge ruled that the bond was insufficient and gave Boyle fourteen days to put up a total bond of $450,000.

There was worse to follow. An Ontario Divisional Court hearing on 22 May revoked Boyle's appointment as receiver, upsetting the Riddell decision. The ruling appeared to put the Detroiters back in charge. Boyle was rocked by this development but he was far from whipped. He launched an appeal that had to wait a year to be heard. It went ahead on 5 April 1909, this time before Mr. Justice R. M. Meredith and the appellate court in Toronto, and to Boyle's consternation he was told there were "no substantial grounds" for taking the management out of the hands of the Detroit men. Other judges at the hearing concurred.

Boyle barely paused to draw breath. He filed two more actions, one against the CKMC and a second against the individual directors of the company. The case was set for 28 May 1909, once more in the Sandwich Court House where Boyle had scored so effectively two years before.

Everyone was settled down for another battle when, suddenly and dramatically, the Detroiters hoisted the white flag. Telling the Klondike that Boyle's long fight was over, the *Dawson Daily News* revealed that Boyle had arranged the outright purchase of the twenty thousand shares from the Detroiters, paying twenty dollars a share for them but yielding Boyle complete mastery of the company. The sellers would receive a mortgage, with the principal to be paid off in three yearly instalments. No interest would be charged. The real price was $355,000, for the vendors agreed to credit Boyle with $45,000 due him under a former arrangement.

It was sensational news in the Klondike and the rumour mongers were busy immediately, whispering that Treadgold was the man behind Boyle and that a major deal, with the Guggenheims or some other big operator, was in prospect.

Now Joe Boyle was a major shareholder of CKMC and he would return to take over the management of Canadian

Klondike from Fred Rothschild, son of the late Sigmund. The Rothschilds had introduced the large-scale dredging era, but Joe Boyle would be the man to play the leading role in the revolutionary story.

There were many things to tidy up but Boyle, as always, was at his best under pressure. He set out for the Yukon early in September and was reported at Whitehorse, heading down the river for Dawson on 18 September. He may have slipped away with barely a notice in July 1904, but his return would be something else.

NINE

Thunder on the Creeks

Ten years after the Dawson newspapers had reported the arrival in the Klondike of a spurious Mrs. J. W. Boyle, the King of the Klondike was back, this time with a legitimate wife on his arm.

Elma Louise Humphries had been the maiden name of the new Mrs. Joe Boyle. His marriage to her was a shocking surprise to his children and family. Even the date of the marriage is not certain, but it appears to have been in or near Detroit in the spring of 1909, not long before the end of the school term.

The presumption flows from the memories of Flora Boyle, who was attending school in Toronto and studying music at the Royal Conservatory of Music there. She was summoned from her classroom and informed that she would have to travel to Detroit immediately. Joe Boyle met her at the riverside railway station in Windsor and introduced her to her new mother. It was an unwanted surprise that marred their relationship from the start. To Flora her new relative was "Steppie," who struck Flora as "a nice, quiet little person who could have been happily married to a substantial business or professional man with whom she could have led a normal life."

But life with a Joe Boyle could never be normal in that sense. Flora knew that. Elma would have to find out.

Boyle tried to make the meeting as pleasant as possible with a gift. In her music studies Flora had enjoyed playing the harp. Her father had bought her one, and probably had boasted a little. When Elma asked her to play for them, however, Flora was inwardly incensed and not easily persuaded. The harp, like so many other things Boyle purchased, was stored in Detroit and eventually lost.

Boyle also had other news for his daughter. This time when Boyle returned to the Yukon, Flora would go along to make her home at Bear Creek. In the end it was a long, tiring journey for Elma and it did nothing to enhance the relationship between the two women.

Elma, it appeared, had met Boyle in the hotel where she was employed as manicurist and where he had taken rooms. Flora and others got the impression that Boyle had married to escape the attention of all the fortune seekers on his trail. Where women were concerned, Boyle clearly was impulsive—a romantic, some would say—but in this case he was more practical than romantic.

There would now be two Mrs. Boyles in the overcrowded family quarters at Bear Creek, for Charles Boyle had married a handsome, personable Pennsylvania widow, Nan Morgan, after the 1907 court case. He had taken her and her son by the earlier marriage, Ralph Morgan, back to the Klondike.

The housing problem was easily solved by an addition that doubled the size of the establishment. Bear Creek, CKMC headquarters, had become a small village, with quarters for company employees, a dining room common to all in which the Boyles had their meals, a gold room for refining and casting gold ingots, and other buildings for animals and machinery.

Bear Creek was remote, but Boyle spared little to make it homey and happy. He had a piano installed in the mess hall, where he was delighted to play and lead his employees in community singing, working over the old gold rush ballads, and the eye-misting Irish songs he loved. On warm summer evenings, when the sun disappeared for only a few seconds, Boyle helped carry the piano outside, and the carolling went on until midnight.

By the standards of the time, life at Bear Creek was comfortable. There was a lawn, flower beds, and a vegetable garden in which a variety of edibles grew quickly and to wonder-provoking sizes. Much food had to be imported, adding to the higher cost of living on the frontier—a condition that persists and is unlikely to alter—but game and fish were easy to obtain and native hunters kept the camps supplied.

The Yukon that Flora returned to was vastly different from the one she remembered. She could note the changes from her first visit at the turn of the century, when the vestiges of the great gold rush still were evident.

That first trip up the Pacific coast had been a memorable experience for her and Joe Junior. Their father had been particularly carefree on that occasion, looking after them like a mother, washing their hair, tidying their clothes, and laughing and singing with them. As the wood-burning engine chuffed its way along the remarkable narrow-gauge railway over the White Pass, he pointed out the landmarks to them. He urged them to listen to the engine. "Can't you hear what it's saying?" he would ask. "It's crying, 'give-me-four-foot, give-me-four-foot.'" The wood burners were fueled by logs cut in two- and four-foot lengths, and the slow panting of the engine as it crawled upward seemed to cry for the longer ones. Over the summit the sound of the train altered, and the beat picked up. "What's it saying now?" the father asked. "Can't you hear it? It's easy; just listen. It's 'two-foot'll-do, two-foot'll do.'"

That's when Flora first heard her father sing the lugubrious ballad she would frequently hear in the mess halls and social gatherings of the miners: "He's Sleeping in the Klondike Vale Tonight." It was, their father told them, the "meal ticket" song he and Frank Slavin had intoned at Skagway when they had arrived penniless and had to sing for their supper. But now the mining songs were drowned out by the clank of machines. Most of the characters of the gold rush days had departed— some to greater glory, the majority to anonymity. Even Swiftwater Bill Gates was said to be living penniless on the charity of his father in Oakland, California.

Among those remaining they found Martha Louise Purdy, a handsome, talented woman who had been on the Dawson dock to greet them when they first arrived eight years before. This remarkable Klondiker had walked in over the Trail of '98 carrying an unborn child, determined to establish a new life on the ruins of a foundered marriage. Her cheerful, engaging personality was matched by a business acumen that soon saw her established as proprietor of a successful sawmill.

In her autobiography she related that one of the first to befriend her in Dawson was Joe Boyle, and they remained lifelong friends. When the Boyle children first arrived in Dawson they learned that the home they had moved into was one prepared by Martha Purdy as more suitable accommodation than the one-room cabin built by Boyle and Slavin.

Homes were easy to find in Dawson after the turn of the century, for the great departure to Nome and the Alaska diggings had left hundreds of residences untenanted and available to anyone who wanted to walk in. By 1910 it was possible to buy a furnished cabin for three hundred dollars.

Boyle found that life in the Klondike had assumed a slower, smoother rhythm. It was a primmer community. The Louse Town whores, who had plied their trade across the Klondike from Dawson, had long ago departed. Life was relatively domesticated and the city a modest shell of its boom days. The Dawson hockey league had declined, and curling was now the major interest at the DAAA arena.

There was a continuing effort at a social life similar to that of the longer-settled areas of Edwardian Canada. Dawson may have been the last frontier of Canada, but it had pretensions to the lifestyle of world capitals. Women squeezed into imported gowns to adorn its social functions. The balls and parties were dim shadows of New York and London, but the champagne and caviar were the real thing, for they could be purchased with Yukon gold. But there was a difference. In Dawson's social whirl the handsome guest conversing knowledgeably about art or literature may well have been that undistinguished individual who had been delivering bread to the back door of the official residence of the commissioner that very afternoon.

The arrival of yet another Joe Boyle added to the confusion of an expanded Boyle household at Bear Creek—but this one was no relative. He was the son of British journalist John Baxter Boyle and Clara Wade, an opera singer of some repute. He was brought into the Yukon by his Canadian namesake to work in the company office. To avoid confusion he was called "English Joe."

Joe Boyle returned to the Klondike in time to meet another newcomer to the scene, a new bard of the gold rush. Robert W. Service spent only a few years in Dawson, but he became the acknowledged lyricist of its story. Service became a regular visitor to the Boyle home and the family came to know him well. In one of the amateur programs offered for the local populace Service stood in the stage wings while Flora recited "The Shooting of Dan McGrew." He was not impressed, which was fair enough, for Flora wasn't overwhelmed by Service. He had a reputation for being tight-fisted, and a Yukoner later recalled that Flora, helping take up a collection for some Dawson unfortunate, found donations excellent until she braced Service. He dropped two lead pencils into the pot.

For all the excitement Service generated elsewhere, he was, and remains among the survivors, a controversial figure in the Yukon. They disliked his stinginess and resented his not-too-well-disguised suggestions that beneath the façade, the moral standards of the region were somewhat lower than they might have been.

Some recalled him as a bard with marked inability to recite his own poems. His voice, said the late Thomas Ainsworth, a one-time Boyle dredge operator, lacked inflection and was devoid of dramatic quality so that by the time he had finished, listeners were left with the uncomfortable feeling that they had rated his works too highly. Service left Dawson in October 1910 and never returned. But he retained at least one Yukon fan. Joe Boyle memorized many Service poems and recited them with only a little urging on any suitable occasion.

In the decade prior to the First World War there was continuous rivalry along the Klondike creeks between the operations of the large gold mining companies. Bitter rivalries developed, none surpassing that between the Canadian Klondike Mining Company, now proudly Canadian at last, and the Guggenheim-backed Yukon Gold Corporation. In its early years YGC—the "Guggies," in local parlance—was commanded by Arthur Treadgold. In his term the rivalry, though sharp, was reasonably amicable. It did not prevent Treadgold from doing yeoman service for Boyle at the Battle of Sandwich.

Being in the East, Boyle had missed the startup of the first CKMC dredge, an event that had occurred on 13 August 1905, with the territorial commissioner pressing the button to start operations. This seven-and-a-half cubic-foot bucket dredge was driven by power from a turbo generator set up near Bear Creek, and the thunderous clank of the huge machine told the Klondike that the future was now, and was here to stay. Production topped expectations and the dredge paid for itself in little more than two months, although it had cost a stunning $200,000.

CKMC Dredge No. 1 remained the undisputed heavyweight producing champion for a year, when YGC countered with two Bucyrus dredges of about the same capacity as their rival's. Yukon Gold found the Bucyrus models thoroughly satisfactory; between 1906 and 1911 YGC had nine such dredges constructed, stationing eight of them in the Yukon and shipping the ninth to Iditarod, Alaska, after a trial run on Hunker Creek.

At the time that Boyle went into involuntary exile he was planning a super dredge, and shortly after his return to the

Klondike, he set himself the task of completing construction during the next mining season.

Securing financial backing and setting in motion the flow of materials to the Yukon took him east again, this time on a dramatic journey that served another purpose as well.

The very first shipment of Klondike gold in 1897 had gone to the United States and geography alone dictated that this was its logical destination. Boyle, the ultranationalist by 1909, was determined to alter that. In December of that year he travelled to Ottawa with $50,000 in Boyle gold specially ordered by the Canadian Mint to help Finance Minister Fielding keep a budget-speech promise to strike Canadian gold coins from Canadian gold.

Boyle's decision to assist had its business side. He complained that Yukon banks did little to help in the movement of gold. They charged a 2 percent-of-value fee, even though the metal could be shipped in the mail for half that amount. Even more annoying to Boyle was a bank surcharge on gold handled after the regular mining season closed. He resented the size of the first levy and the unfairness of the second.

As a result, porters on the platform of a Chicago railway station one winter's morning watched as three fur-clad people descended from a transcontinental train. The largest, a big male who looked about six feet square, deposited two large rawhide bags on the platform beside a pile of personal luggage. Two of the porters rushed up to earn a dollar. They seized the hide bags and found they could hardly move them. The large gentleman smiled, picked up the bags, and deposited them on the luggage trucks. "What's in them bags?" the amazed porters asked. "Just a few stones," said Klondike Boyle, waving Elma and Flora into a taxi.

The porters were still puzzling when they saw an even odder sight. The travellers suddenly climbed out of the far side of the taxi, the man hauling the two hide bags as the women wrestled with the other luggage. They jumped into a taxi parked parallel to the first and sped off. The preamble to this

110

had come two weeks earlier when Boyle had decided to beat the late gold shipment surcharge, estimating that the money saved would pay for the travelling expenses of himself, his wife, and his daughter in their trip east.

Under Boyle's friendly persuasion some Indian friends at Moosehide village fashioned two moosehide bags with shoulder straps, secured by a heavy chain and a padlock. Boyle packed his bags with some three hundred pounds of late gold output, and placed them under the driver's seat of the Royal Mail sled that carried passengers and mail to Whitehorse. Joe helped Flora into the front seat beside the driver, a man known as Top Hat. Boyle and his wife seated themselves behind the driver in company with a number of other passengers, all of them blanketed and robed in furs against the Arctic cold. Just before departure, Boyle arranged to have a picture taken of the group.

At a Mounted Police station a few steps along the trail the holiday atmosphere vanished when Boyle was informed that thieves would attempt to hijack the gold shipment. Top Hat agreed to advance the travel schedule, and from that point on a careful watch was maintained. Flora Boyle later recalled that they were served their New Year's dinner at Carmack Post, with the rawhide bags hauled into the primitive dining area where Flora rested her feet on them throughout the meal.

Nothing untoward happened until Boyle took alarm in the Chicago station where they had to change trains. His guard was never lowered until they reached Woodstock, where the women were to stay. Arrival at The Firs appeared to mark an end to this vigilance, but it was a brief respite. That evening, as the family reunion was in full swing, a terrified maid rushed into the house screaming that she had been stabbed by a prowler she had surprised in the garden. Boyle took the next train to Ottawa, where he delivered his shipment to the Mint, defying the bankers and all else.

Quickly leaving Ottawa for U.S. financial centres, Boyle began the mammoth task of organizing the construction of the super dredge, which duly appeared before the year was out.

111

CKMC No. 2 was thirty feet longer, ten feet wider, and nearly double the draught of its predecessor or any of its YGC rivals. It had a bucket capacity of 18 cubic feet, and could handle 16,000 cubic yards of gravel daily, compared with 5,000 cubic yards for the smaller machines. Boyle constructed this "Dreadnought Dredge" in a curious parallel to the naval arms race of the times, when the dreadnoughts all but made obsolescent the more lightly armoured and gunned conventional battleships.

Construction of CKMC No. 2 became a community event, arousing wide interest throughout the Klondike. As it began to soar above the Klondike about a mile below Bear Creek, the site became a focal point for Dawsonites on Sunday afternoons. The *Dawson Daily News,* no friend to Boyle in the past, was lyrical about his new creation:

Not in the history of man, counting far back into the unfathomable darkness before the days of Solomon when the gold of Ophir enchanted the world, has there ever been such a mammoth machine conceived or built by the hand of man to recover the golden wealth scattered in ages past in the secret pockets of Mother Earth.

Joe Boyle proudly announced that his new flagship would have a name—"The Canadian"—and would fly the Canadian red ensign, a thrust at the nationality of the owners of YGC.

The dredge was an impressive vessel, lying in the great excavation made to cradle it. More than 1,700 tons of steel parts had to be moved over the White Pass and down the Yukon River to Dawson to give it the rugged frame it needed. There were seventy-one earth-scooping buckets moving around a ninety-seven-foot digging ladder on a belt. The finished machine would be anchored to its operational area by a huge steel spud so long and heavy that Klondikers were wagering that it would never be lifted into position. As usual, the sceptics lost, for it seemed that in the Yukon nothing was beyond the ingenuity of men like Boyle.

The recounting of dredge statistics took up the best part of a column of solid type in an August edition of the *News,* but it was not until early November 1910 that the monster, cheered by a crowd of several hundred, churned into deafening action, permitting Yukoners to boast that they had the world's greatest mining dredge in production. The Canadian had only a brief opening run, for both CKMC units closed down on 13 December, No. 1 having operated for a record-shattering 233 consecutive days. Boyle's dredging initiative was extending the working season, normally one of about six months from an April start, in pursuit of almost year-round operations.

The Canadian had one major advantage over its predecessor: it was powered by hydroelectric energy from a new plant established at the North Forks of the Klondike. The power-generating site had been scouted years before by Boyle and Treadgold, and the latter, no longer a Guggenheim employee, had directed the plant construction for the newly organized Canadian Klondike Power Company. Formed in the spring of 1910, the company had James McDougall as its president, A. E. Nash as secretary, and J. W. Boyle as manager.

Diversion of water to the plant was achieved along a six-mile ditch twenty-eight feet in width that emptied into two seventy-two-inch conduits, each about a quarter-mile long, that carried the flow to the generators. Construction of this facility in the wilderness was another Yukon marvel and produced the customary crop of cynics. Old-timers said the diversion canal would freeze solid in the winter and asked how Joe Boyle could solve that problem.

Boyle's solution was the ingenious response of an engineer who had been taught in the hard school of frontier pragmatism. As winter approached, he permitted the canal to fill to the brim. When the frost had provided a solid ice cover about eighteen inches thick, Boyle lowered the water to its normal level, leaving several feet of air space between the natural roof and the water—an insulating device that halted any further freezing. For insurance he inserted electric heaters at the intake points and at intervals along the canal. To prevent summer collapse of the ditch banks from permafrost thaw, he covered the banks with brush. The protective measures functioned well and were proven in one particularly severe winter, when the power station functioned without interruption in a record-setting week of cold when the average temperature was –60° F.

North Forks power lighted much of the Klondike, servicing Dawson and smaller communities along a twenty-two-mile line. In Dawson the Dawson Electric Light and Power Company and the Dawson City Water and Power Company distributed the electricity. Substations on Bonanza and Hunker creeks extended the service to those areas. It was a lucrative monopoly that Boyle was careful to preserve. When a potential rival began to develop a coal deposit on Coal Creek to fuel a thermal plant, Boyle waited until the work was nearly complete, and then bought out the enterprise. Coal from the mine, moved over a narrow-gauge railway, heated many Dawson establishments, including the police barracks and the commissioner's residence.

The wide horizon of Boyle's activities contrasted to the narrow approach of his Guggenheim rivals, whose main interest was to extract gold. Boyle preferred natural means to thaw the gold-bearing gravel and used the artificial devices of steam points driven into the ground, or pipes carrying hot water, only when no other method would do.

Although in the first instance the thawing season was brief and in the second it was limited to the river area, Boyle improved on nature, introducing a massive plan of rechannelling the Klondike. He was fortunate: the day of the vocal environmentalist was a half-century away.

Treadgold too was a firm advocate of natural thawing methods but the Guggenheims, trapped in a sharp 1907 Wall Street decline, ordered a speedup in gold production that could only be achieved by artificial thawing. Treadgold fought the order to proceed on this basis, knowing that it would add 25 percent to the extraction cost; but in the end he followed Guggenheim's instructions. He was also angry because he had been led to believe that his plan for a hydro power plant with adequate water controls had been accepted. The Guggenheims had put up $4 million to back the enterprise, and he and Teddy Bredenberg had done extensive exploration and testing.

The Guggenheims pointed with great pride to the $11 million in dividends produced by their Klondike operations in the years 1908-09, in spite of the higher costs of heat treatment but Treadgold was not to be mollified. He retorted that he could have doubled that take with his methods.

His bitterness led him to resign as manager of the Klondike properties. He sold almost all his YGC holdings, retaining only a directorship. It was a move that included abundant balm for his wounded pride, for he later confessed he had cleared $4 million on the sale, an astonishing return for his small investment—an exploratory trip to the gold fields only a decade earlier. Treadgold departed with more than a large fortune. He took away all the leases acquired in his own name, and an unrivalled knowledge of the entire gold territory. Accompanying him, as well, was his continuing dream of the consolidation of Klondike gold operations into a single company—directed, of course, by A. N. C. Treadgold. Within three months he was investing his fortune, purchasing leases on Eldorado, Hunker, Sulphur, Quartz, Dominion, Last Chance, and other gold-producing areas.

By 1911 he had organized another consortium, the Granville Mining Company, with some of the best-known mining engineers in the world as his associates. They included a fast-rising young American Quaker named Herbert Hoover, who already had made a fortune in mining ventures, and A. Chester Beatty, a former Guggenheim associate who also had flown their restrictive coop. Granville was planned in a series of meetings in New York, but it was incorporated in London, with its head office at 8 Old Jewry Street. Francis Govett was chairman, and Hoover became a director.

Boyle appears to have rejected an invitation to participate—he was merger-minded only when he could be in charge and, as owner of CKMC as well as power, water, telephone, sawmill, and other interests in Dawson, he had a full plate for the moment. Nonetheless, his horizons were widening and he was thinking about investment in South African properties. A letter addressed to Boyle as an official of the Consolidated Gold Fields of South Africa—directed to 8 Old Jewry Street—also raises some questions now beyond answer.

There is other evidence that Boyle had some interest in the possibilities of gold mining in Siberia. There was a school of thought in the Yukon that believed that the Klondike outcroppings were only the surfacing of a continuous belt of gold-bearing rock and gravels, reaching from California through the continental west to Alaska and across to Siberia. In the pre-war years, Russian visitors periodically turned up to see Boyle. One of the most enthusiastic was a nobleman who watched with interest in the winter of 1913-14 when The Canadian worked through −70° F temperatures, as Boyle explained how a similar machine could be used in the somewhat less extreme temperatures of Siberia.

By that time CKMC had achieved a ten-month working year, which its Klondike rivals could not begin to match. The competitive advantages were great. The success of the mighty Canadian, far from satisfying Joe Boyle, stimulated an ambition to build two more super dredges, embodying all the modifications and improvements that the operations of the first two had indicated were necessary.

They would be impressive—and expensive—additions to the CKMC fleet, costing some $500,000 each. The need for capital financing was obvious. Financing could be found only outside the Klondike, and there was only one place to look. Boyle knew that in 1911, thanks to the new Granville organization, Treadgold had $8 million to invest. That was a source to be tapped, and it was controlled by someone he knew very well.

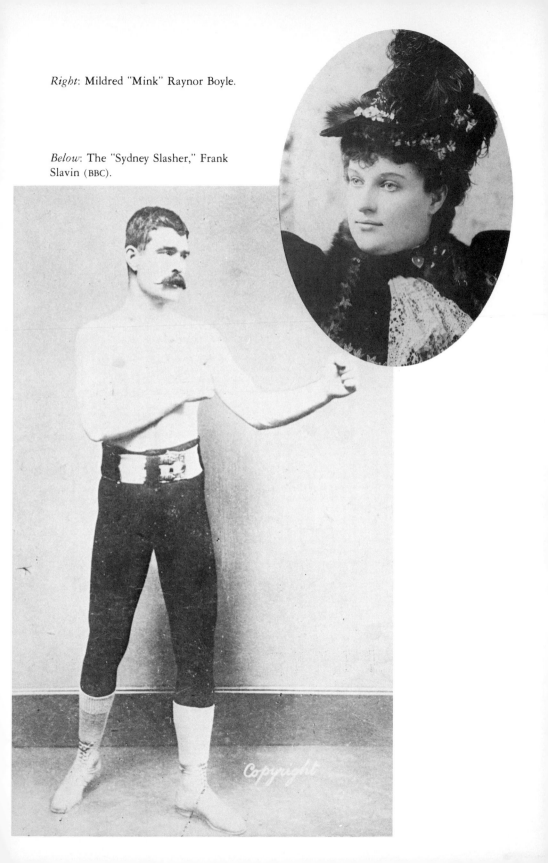

Right: Mildred "Mink" Raynor Boyle.

Below: The "Sydney Slasher," Frank Slavin (BBC).

The Yukon cabin built by Boyle and Slavin in 1898. Later occupied by J.H. Brener.

Top above: "The Denver," a Bear Creek café and postal station.

A trip outside in 1909. Flora and driver Top Hat sit above gold-filled bags. Behind are Joe and Elma, with Gus Bredenberg in rear.

The group preparing to trek "outside" in 1898 included Indian Charlie (far left), Boyle (far right) and Swiftwater Bill Gates (in short cravat).

Dawson Amateur Athletic Association in 1903 (Yukon Archives).

Yukon hockey team with Boyle (front row centre) outside Ottawa's Dey's Rink.

(Left to right) Charles Boyle Sr., Joe Jr. and Dave Boyle at The Firs circa 1900.

Flora and Joe, whose stickpin was made from the first Klondike nugget he mined.

Joe Jr. and Flora in 1902.

Above: Joe (at wheel) and Charles Boyle.

Right: Mining engineer Herbert Hoover circa 1900 (BBC).

Opposite: Joe Boyle (left) and Teddy Bredenberg at Bear Creek.

Dave Boyle (left), Martha Laperriere, Flora and Joe.

Susan Laperriere Boyle and Flora outside The Firs.

✤ TEN ✤

A Crucial Decision

Arthur Newton Christian Treadgold disembarked from a river
steamer at the Dawson dock at one o'clock on the morning of 6
September 1911. Among those waiting to shake his hand was
his old associate Joseph Whiteside Boyle. This time Treadgold
was not alone. He had a small entourage including Malcolm
Orr Ewing and, of all things, a young American-born wife, a
woman with literary pretensions. The journey to the Klondike
had involved stops at various points and several interviews had
been granted by Treadgold, one of them with a *Vancouver
Province* reporter who wrote that Treadgold was "the true
King of the Klondike" and that he was on his way to Dawson
to take over the Boyle concessions. Treadgold remained vocal
and visible for his first week in Dawson—until the day his wife
vanished, leaving word that she had decided to return to
civilization.

Her husband was not easily discomfited but she had managed
to accomplish it. Although widely sought by them, Treadgold
stayed out of the sight of reporters for the next three months.
They finally learned what had happened to him on 22
December when it was announced that he, Joe Boyle, and Teddy
Bredenberg had departed on a chartered sled to catch up with

the regular courier transport that was conveying Elma and Flora Boyle to the outside.

Boyle, anxious to obtain financing for his new dredges, had succumbed to the lure held out by Treadgold for an involvement with the Granville Mining Company. It was a fateful choice, for the results that flowed from it were catastrophic to both Boyle and Treadgold. Those wintering in Dawson heard little of Boyle until, on 20 March 1912, the Dawson papers reported that a message from Boyle in New York told of a giant merger and that the Boyle properties would be operated under the name of the Canadian Klondike Mining Company, with Boyle as manager, and with two new monster dredges to be constructed.

Boyle had proceeded to England for lengthy negotiations that capped months of talks. Granville desperately needed an association with a successful Klondike mining company, and Boyle required money to advance his dredging plans. These needs seemed to coincide, providing Boyle with the money and Granville with a source of income until their affairs could be set in revenue-producing order.

Under the agreement reached in London, Boyle was to be in control of operations north of the Dome, a height of land that directed one set of gold-bearing streams into the Klondike, and another group south into the Yukon River. Granville would be master of the latter territory. Included in the deal but not understood publicly at the time was the provision that Boyle would take full control of the North Forks power plant, which had been owned by Treadgold's Granville Power Company before it became the Canadian Klondike Power Company Limited.

As promoters of Granville, Treadgold, Herbert Hoover, and A. Chester Beatty were issued 1.2 million shares with a nominal value of £1 each. Convertible 6 percent debentures would raise an additional £1 million (about $5 million). Boyle got his loan in return for making over 29 percent of Canadian Klondike stock to Granville. The stock was for the properties that would be turned over to Boyle. In addition, debentures to be issued by Boyle could be turned into another 20 percent of the Boyle stock by Granville if desired.

The negotiations were long and contentious, but the verbal agreement reached persuaded Granville to advance Boyle the money. But when the detailed memorandum was presented for signature, Boyle objected in strong language to the written terms claiming that the verbal agreement had been so altered as to nullify, disguise, and quite misinterpret the whole tenor of the settlement. He refused to sign and abruptly departed for Canada, leaving the Granville directors in a panic. Boyle never did sign that particular agreement and refused to turn over securities alleged to have been promised to Granville. For some reason the Granville directors took no steps to enforce implementation of the agreement for several years, although Boyle did make regular payments of principal and interest on obligations that required Canadian Klondike to pay some $250,000 annually to Granville.

Two Americans who investigated the strange dealings of Granville have charged that Herbert Hoover was the villain of the piece. Their charges appeared in two books* published when Hoover was running for re-election as U.S. president in 1932. Despite rumours that the authors would be sued, nothing happened. Hoover, says Flora Boyle, was asked to institute proceedings but declined to act.

John Hamill alleged that Granville had been dreamed up by Treadgold, Hoover, and Beatty during a 1911 meeting at 71 Broadway, New York City. Subsequently, and presumably as a holding company for the shares they would receive from Granville, Hoover and Beatty registered in Delaware a firm called the Eastern Trading Company, which in the April 1911

---

*John Hamill, *The Strange Career of Mr. Hoover* (New York: Fargo, 1931); James J. O'Brien, *Hoover's Millions and How He Made Them* (privately printed, 1932).

edition of *Mining Magazine* was reported to be a syndicate with a capitalization of £200,000 and development claims in the Klondike.

Although the required prospectus was not provided, Granville was permitted to incorporate in London in August 1911. The company promoters were set out as Treadgold, Hoover, and Beatty. One of their first actions was to transfer $550,000 in shares to Hoover's Eastern Trading Company, allegedly for services in placing a $2.2 million debenture issue. Hoover, Hamill says, received an additional $150,000 in shares, as well.

Hamill charged that the property assembled by Treadgold for Granville was low grade, worth only twenty cents a yard in gold content when the break-even operating cost was thirty cents. The plan, he insisted, was to make Granville stock saleable by playing up the potential of the Boyle and Yukon Gold properties with which Granville had no connection.

Treadgold, to whom Granville had promised a large block of shares, never received them, Hamill added, and by the time the directors had finished what he labelled "a debenture flap trap game," only 190,000 shares were left to provide working capital. Boyle, Hamill found, was asked to give Granville $1.2 million in 6 percent bonds on the power company, plus $1.5 million in 6 percent first mortgage bonds, and $2.32 million in common stock in CKMC, according to Granville.

"This supposed argument on the face of it, is ridiculous," Hamill decided. "A remarkable feature is that it was not registered, as required by law, with the registrar of joint stock companies and Boyle apparently never paid the slightest attention to it." Hamill found that Granville made public announcement of a deal, rejected by Boyle, to help sell a $2.2 million mortgage debenture. Treadgold, he concluded, returned to London in 1913 determined to expose the whole fraudulent mess, but was bought off by the Granville directors who pulled out their claims on the Indian River watershed on the south side of the Dome and, again without a prospectus, set up the North West Corporation and financed it with a $7.5 million stock issue from which they offered Treadgold $1 million to develop the property. The Treader accepted, promising to produce an annual profit of $500,000.

To conclude this episode the venture never did get off the ground. By the end of 1915 the company closed down with liabilities of $70,000 and assets of $175. Hamill found that most of the money was siphoned off by North West with transfer of shares to Goldfields American Development, another mysterious new firm with which Hoover was associated.

The other examiner, James J. O'Brien, in a self-published book illustrated with pictures and photostats of Granville reports and documents, is even more scathing. "The Granville Mining Co.," he wrote, "was the rankest kind of swindle: the money that the stock and debentures were sold for went straight into the pockets of the promoters."

He showed that although Granville never received any assets from Boyle, it claimed in five successive annual statements to hold them and only finally admitted in 1917 that it never had held them. A dozen years later a Yukon mining commissioner made it plain that Granville had never held any mining property in the Yukon. Some of the annual statements appeared without the signatures of the officers, but the officers were available upon other occasions. A Granville statement of 11 October 1911, transferring 206,000 shares to Hoover's Eastern Trading Company, was signed by Hoover.

One safe conclusion is that the British officials responsible for the proper operations of companies in London were extremely negligent, or worse. Another is that Joe Boyle, in his anxiety to finance the purchase of the big dredges on which he was placing so much hope, had become involved in a very dubious enterprise. Unlike Hoover, who sold his shares and resigned his directorship in Granville, pocketing a handsome profit while alleging he could no longer work with the eccentric Treadgold, there was no such escape for Boyle, even if he had refused to sign the agreement.

The Golden Years

Recovery of his Klondike concession and the apparent consolidation of its financing in 1911-12 brought a golden summer for Joe Boyle, one that might have continued indefinitely but for mighty forces at home and abroad that would shape his future to unexpected ends.

The first few years of his return were among the happiest and most productive of his Yukon life. The CKMC operation became a showpiece of the region, attracting many interested people, some of them notable and others run-of-the-mill. All were met hospitably and departed impressed. Politicians, writers, schoolteachers and students, even visiting artists appearing in the Dawson theatre were among those who turned up at the Bear Creek head office.

Boyle sometimes invited the more illustrious to visit the gold refinery and storehouse to inspect the process and some of the larger and more unusual nuggets held out of the melting-down. Upon occasion he would invite guests to select a souvenir nugget as a special memento of the visit. Usually they chose small ones, but occasionally greed overcame good manners, as it did with an Australian singer who selected one of the larger nuggets on display, because, she insisted, it looked just like the map of her native Australia. Boyle dealt with the situation tactfully, agreeing that it did have some resemblance to the outline of Australia but expressing his regret that it was such a poor amalgam with a rather low gold content. His guest, he insisted, was entitled to do something better—which just happened to be considerably smaller than the one first selected.

Boyle was fond of children and in these years his annual picnics for them were notable events in Dawson. Bob Kunze, a Vancouverite who spent his childhood in the Klondike, was one of the fortunate picnic guests. He remembers that Boyle would draw his small steamer, the *Pilot,* up to the Dawson dock where it would be loaded with children and adults to be transported to a shallow Yukon River tributary such as the Sweet River. The water was very cold, but Boyle happily doffed his boots and socks, turned up his pant legs and waded around in the shallows splashing with the young fry, piggy-backing some of the smaller, more timid children. He usually loaded the CKMC piano on the ship and played and led sing-songs for his guests as they sailed home.

Boyle's affection extended in equal measure to animals, which added to the circus atmosphere at Bear Creek. The domestic establishment included two white Aberdeen terriers, gifts of Herbert Hoover; two lynx kittens; a black bear cub picked up by some Boyle surveyors; horses of various ages and types; and other four-footed domesticates, including a mule.

The pets were kept in a usually unlocked paddock, and as a result they had more time inside the house than in the paddock. All of them seemed to have an affinity for Boyle. One summer afternoon, as he napped after a substantial lunch, Flora went to his bedroom to awaken him. She found one of the lynx kittens sleeping at his feet and the other dozing on the floor beside the bed, next to the sleepy bear cub, while the Aberdeens lay on the bed, one on each side of Boyle's head. Boyle gave the menagerie a sleepy grin and remarked, "It's a good thing we don't have any chickens."

He unleashed his anger on anyone who mistreated animals.

A. E. Nash, the CKMC accountant, had a rare turn one warm afternoon as he sat talking business with Boyle. As they chatted there was a noise on the road. Boyle glanced outside, and suddenly leaped from his chair and dashed out the front door of the office. Nash looked out and saw a team of horses, which were in obvious distress, being mercilessly flogged. One of the animals clearly had the spring halt, a painful leg condition that caused the creature to lift its leg high in the air as a reaction to the pain of walking.

Boyle halted the wagon, hauled the driver off the seat and shook him like a small boy found guilty of a major misdemeanour. Then he removed the sick horse from its harness as he shouted to one of the office staff to send to his stable for a replacement. Boyle told the unnerved driver that he would attend to the sick horse and return the animal if the man agreed never to mistreat it again. Boyle personally doctored the animal with the skills he had learned from his father. The stranger never came back and his horse—named Fall Guy by the Boyles—swelled the collection of family pets.

His liking for animals led him on several occasions into situations where wild animals considered dangerous were involved. Late one fall, for example, some CKMC employees reported that four half-starved wolf cubs were living under the floor of the warehouse office. They suggested killing them, but Boyle vetoed that proposal. He calmly wrapped the squalling cubs in some old blankets and carried them into the building. He was sure that their mother was hunting and would return to feed them, so he put one puppy outside the door and let it howl.

Armed with a revolver, Boyle stood behind the door and when the mother wolf approached, he opened the door. The wolf, hearing the cries of the three other members of the litter, picked up the fourth and carried it into the room. Boyle gently closed the door. The wolf bitch snarled and for a brief moment appeared likely to attack. After regarding Boyle for a few moments she relaxed and suckled her pups. When she had finished, Boyle opened the door and she departed.

This ritual was maintained daily until the pups were strong and large enough to leave with their mother. Unfortunately, they had become domesticated and rejected the mother's every urging to depart. She finally left them and did not return. For months, until it was evident they were feeling the call of the wild, the cubs were a special part of the Boyle animal farm.

Unlike many of his contemporaries, Boyle had comradely feelings for the native Indians and treated them with a respect they reciprocated. One of his warmest admirers was Chief Isaacs, a Siwash who lived at the Indian village of Moosehide. The two men had known one another since 1897, and Boyle frequently visited the Moosehide village. Isaacs was a periodic visitor at Bear Creek, padding the twelve-and-one-half miles to the CKMC establishment to talk with Boyle. His admiration for the King of the Klondike was open and unbounded. He once even remarked to Flora, "Joe Boyle a good man. Joe Boyle all the same God, pretty soon Jesus Christ."

The religious note likely derived from the fact that Boyle had built a church in which the Moosehide residents could hold regular services. He laid down one condition: the church had to be open to all people, regardless of denomination. Boyle was critical of missionaries of different faiths who sometimes competed bitterly to sell their own brand of enlightenment to the Indians. He was determined that his gift chapel would be free of the Christian world's religious divisions.

Another odd friend was "Old" Smith, a brother of the notorious Randolph "Soapy" Smith. Soapy's thugs had terrified Skagway until an irate citizen shot down Soapy on the street in a two-way shootout fatal to both men. Old Smith suffered much because of his brother's notoriety. Touched by Old Smith's plight, Boyle offered him a mining lay (portion of a claim) on a corner of the concession. Old Smith worked diligently on the property, faithfully giving Boyle a share of the gold hard won by the old pan-and-rocker method. Boyle made it a point to visit Old Smith regularly, never failing to take along some special food and drink.

One day Smith's pick chunked into an oversize boulder in which he could see flakes of gold, unfortunately beyond recovery with his primitive tools. Boyle was enlarging the Bear Creek home at this time and had planned a large fireplace. Old Smith carefully chiselled off slabs of the rock until he had enough stone for Boyle to face the fireplace, a gift that created the only gold fireplace in the territory.

Joe Boyle had a host of Klondike tales, and was a great "yarner" in the true Irish tradition. Like most Klondikers he enjoyed a bit of exaggeration with a good tale. One of his best stories needed no embellishment: the tale of the Sidehill Gouger and his experience as a midwife. The role fell to him by chance, some time after he learned that the wife of a Yukon Gold Corporation employee, who lived over the hill from Bear Creek, was expecting a child. Her husband was a pipeline walker—an employee who continually walked over hill and dale inspecting the water-system piping. He was away from home for long periods and was concerned about his wife. Boyle told the worried husband to bring her to Bear Creek when the time came, and he would have her driven to the Dawson hospital.

Several weeks later Boyle spotted someone staggering down the hill several hundred yards away and clearly in trouble. Rightly suspecting that it was the pregnant woman, he ran to her as quickly as he could. By the time he reached her she had collapsed, and Boyle found himself with the task of delivering what turned out to be a lively male baby. He completed the job, placed the baby in the mother's arms, picked up the two of them, and carried them to the camp.

None of the principals seemed to suffer from this experience. The mother made a normal recovery and the infant turned into a sturdy-legged Yukoner whom Boyle christened the Sidehill Gouger, after the legendary Yukon animal with two short legs on one side so that it could walk up the side of a mountain in an upright position. The Sidehill Gouger became a Boyle favourite, and won a large share of the largesse and treats that Boyle carried around to distribute to young friends.

These were the kinds of stories that entranced his Irish relatives, whom he frequently had a chance to visit in County Antrim. His first visit to the family home took place in the winter of 1900-01, an event bright in the memory of the oldest Boyle in Antrim, Joe's cousin Charlotte, a daughter of Charles Boyle. She was only five years old when a husky stranger and his bearded father loomed up one day out of the mists.

Joe and his father got lost while looking for the cottage from which their ancestors had departed seventy years before, and they had to be rescued by Alec Boyle, who was then the occupant of The Burnside. Alec, who was not the first-born son, had taken control of The Burnside when his older brother Charles decided not to remain in Ireland, choosing instead to become a customs man and spend the rest of his life in England and Scotland.

Joe, fresh from talks with possible English backers, arrived stylishly clad in a frock coat and wearing a top hat, which stunned the Buckna natives. In Ireland frock coats and top hats were worn by the gentry and other important people at important events such as weddings and funerals. Boyle was clean-shaven in a land of beards, and wore an unheard-of centre-part in his hair. The novelty was such that children from the school at the corner a bare 150 yards from the Boyle home were permitted to leave early to glimpse the imposing visitor.

Joe and his father soon shucked their coats and settled down in front of an open hearth fire with the inevitable "cup of tay" as if they had lived all their lives in that blessed spot. Cousin Charlotte remembered him best just that way—her Canadian cousin with his shoes off, toes extended toward the warmth, talking and talking and asking questions.

His father, familiarizing himself with the spot about which he had been told so much, soon made friends with the neighbours. He cut himself a cane from the great sycamore tree, had it treated, and took it back to Woodstock where he carried it triumphantly into the bars and barbershops as proof of his journey and his patriarchal authority.

Joe Boyle kept the re-established family ties bright and shining for the rest of his life. He returned again in 1901 when he took his parents, Joe Junior, and Flora to England with him. Almost from the first Joe insisted on helping his Irish kin, taking a proprietary interest in the old family home. Charlotte recalled that he often turned up around Christmas, sometimes with no advance notice of his coming, and always laden with gifts and large hampers of food and provisions from Fortnum and Mason in London.

Boyle spoiled Charlotte outrageously, as he had a habit of doing with children; but she best remembered his thoughtfulness in finding and personally bringing an expensive, rare medicine to ease the suffering of her father Charles, who was seriously ill with tuberculosis.

Boyle's visits were occasions for the whole district. He arrived on one memorable day with the first gramophone to be heard in the region. Its cylindrical records and horn amplifier attracted the curious, and classes of schoolchildren came to see and hear it. Other gifts were more practical, such as the first hydraulic ram ever used at The Burnside. It was located in the low land between the Boyle home and the creek, and ended the toil of water-hauling for the Boyles.

After only a couple of visits Joe was determined to renovate the old homestead, and busily drew plans to provide it with a modern kitchen, a proper fireplace that would burn coal, and other improvements for which he paid. The flood of gifts hardly ceased after he left. One day a chicken incubator was delivered—another wondrous success copied by others. The Boyle creamery at The Burnside shone with the metalwork of a cream separator hauled in on another trip.

He talked at length of scientific farming, crop rotation, and the need for better stock. Alec noted his mild obsession with hog raising, reflected in a piggery that proved a success, in contrast to the disaster that had overtaken a similar effort at The Firs.

Guy McCulloch, a neighbor who still lived near The Burnside in the 1980s, had vivid memories of the large, amiable Canadian, and marvelled that he neither drank nor smoked, but had no trouble at all enjoying himself more than anyone.

There was, said McCulloch, a canopied bed on the ground floor of The Burnside in which Joe Boyle used to sleep. It had been his grandfather's bed and after his first night in it McCulloch heard Sarah, Charles's wife, ask Joe how he had slept. "Wonderfully," replied Boyle. "I would rather have slept in that bed than in Windsor Castle"—as right an answer as he could possibly have given, for Sarah simply glowed.

A mile or so down the burn from the Boyle ancestral home a flax mill gave dangerous employment to some of the men of the district. One day word came to The Burnside that a labourer named Rowan had been badly injured in the machinery. Joe Boyle hurried to the scene and found the victim lying on the ground with one arm torn off, bleeding so profusely that it seemed unlikely he would live. Joe took command, directing first-aid measures and shouting instructions to find a hire car to rush the injured man to the Ballymena hospital. A doctor arrived on the scene to find this stranger in full charge.

"Are you a relative, by any chance?" the doctor asked. "Yes, we're related through Adam. Now get this man to the hospital," Joe replied. That night he privately sent a five-pound note to Mrs. Rowan. The next day he started a whip-around among the neighbours to provide Rowan and his family with some financial help. The response was gratifying, the more so because the Rowans were Roman Catholics living in a largely Orange Protestant area.

This deep interest in the home of his forefathers unquestionably prompted Joe Boyle to preserve the small estate for the family. His assistance enabled Alec Boyle to purchase the property in 1907, after nearly two hundred years of tenancy, under new legislation making long-term acquisition of such lands possible for the first time. The purchase has now been completed by Boyles still in residence.

Charlotte Boyle might have become a Canadian, for Joe urged her to join him at Bear Creek after she had qualified herself to work in the office by completing a business course. Charlotte finished the course but balked at life in the wilderness on the frontiers of Canada. Sixty years later, she still wondered whether she made the right decision. Fresh in her memory was the poem Joe had sent her from the Yukon:

As ye journey through life you'll find plenty of strife
Without looking for bridges to cross.
Keep a stiff upper lip, and stand by your ship,
Calmly sort out the gold from the dross.
And if ever you find life too hard
And your spirits are falling too low,
If you need a good pard, buy a halfpenny card,
And send for your Big Cousin Joe.

TWELVE

Shadows of Discord

The orderly pattern of life at the Boyle Bear Creek household, which had emerged in the early years of Joe's return to the Klondike, began to crumble about 1912.

His success at that time might have satisfied most men, but Joe Boyle was different. He enjoyed riches, but only if they could be spent on something useful or enjoyable. His entrepreneurial achievements were the product of a restless ambition, a burning curiosity, and a thirst for action that the few orderly years at Bear Creek could not meet.

Part of his growing disenchantment sprang from the gnawing problem of family relationships. Domestic discord was never far below the surface when it involved Flora and Elma. Joe Boyle's new wife was a pleasant woman, who tried hard to be a good companion to an individual whose capacities and strivings were all too often beyond her comprehension. She was happy and satisfied with what Boyle had, hardly realizing that these were milestones, not the final destination, in the broadening road of the Boyle dream.

Boyle, who so charmed and won the hearts of children, could just as easily alienate some adults. People who knew him say there was no middle ground: you admired Joe Boyle or you disliked him. At home he was the true Edwardian father. He was sternly opposed to the budding relationship his sister Susan had begun with Adolph Pierre Laperriere, a French-Canadian lumberjack who had worked on the Boyle timber concessions. Laperriere had gone east to testify in a lawsuit, and had stayed at The Firs.

Boyle considered Adolph a fortune hunter, and warned him that he would gain no financial benefits by marrying Susan. Secretly he appears to have been appalled that the member of a stout Protestant family would marry a Roman Catholic. Despite Boyle's opinions, Susan and Adolph were married. Boyle predicted disaster for the union, a prophecy he helped guarantee by discharging Laperriere. The marriage, as predicted, foundered partly on these obstacles and partly through another Boyle anathema, alcohol. Adolph and his bride stayed on at The Firs with a daughter, christened Martha in the proper Boyle tradition, until the marriage broke up.

Forgetful of his own resentments when his parents had attempted to direct his youthful life, Boyle insisted that his namesake son become an engineer, although the young man had a strong desire to become a lawyer. Joe Junior's preparation for a career with CKMC was not entirely distasteful, for it eventually took him to New York, where his father's connections introduced him to people and events not usually the lot of postgraduate students at Columbia University.

Young Joe travelled abroad with his father and upon one occasion, in the course of a trans-Atlantic voyage, he met Elsie Janis, one of the brightest and most prominent theatrical stars of the time. Joe Junior had all of his father's charms. He was attracted and attractive to women, and was considerably more sophisticated than his father had been at the same point in his life. The affair with Miss Janis was going nicely and there is no telling where it might have ended when Joe Senior stepped in. Perhaps because of his earlier experiences—shades of Jessie Wyatt—he was not tolerant of theatrical people in his family relationships. There would be no actress in the Boyle family, he is reputed to have told his son. The romance was shattered, and at the final parting Miss Janis presented her pet dog Rowdy to young Joe as a remembrance of their association.

Flora had her own problems with paternal direction of her activities. Her musical training had advanced to the point where she was seriously considering making a career of music. Joe Boyle loved music but he hated the idea that any of his children would follow a music career professionally. He cast a permanent veto on the suggestion.

This merely prolonged Flora's life within the family, and no doubt helped accentuate her problems with Elma. This constant discord, she noted, appeared to alter Boyle. Where he had once been quick to get angry when the two wrangled, he now left the house and went for long, solitary walks to compose himself.

The breakdown in life at Bear Creek continued to worsen. Eventually, the relationship with his faithful older brother Charles, who had supported Boyle and preserved his Klondike interests in the tough years, became so bad that Charles, his wife Nan, and his stepson Ralph Morgan moved into Dawson. Charles took this breach quite hard but Nan, a woman of great good sense, was less concerned, and Ralph remained one of Boyle's stoutest enthusiasts.

There was some family nattering that Boyle developed instant enthusiasms and then forgot them. They recalled that while living in Detroit he had purchased a large yacht on the Rideau Lakes, had it sailed to Detroit, and anchored it in the Detroit River in front of a Grosse Isle property he had leased. When he departed he put the yacht in storage, where it languished for several years before it was auctioned off to pay the storage charges. The same fate befell the harp that Flora's father had bought for her.

In the spring of 1912, with the warm approval of her father, Flora took her grandmother to New York for extensive treatment and an operation for cataracts that threatened to blind her. They lived in a hotel for several months; on her eighteenth birthday Flora left the hotel to discover a brand-new automobile parked in front of the building, in the custody of a chauffeur, who said it was a birthday gift to her from her father.

Her excitement was intense until she was told that on no account would she be permitted to drive the car. That was a job for the chauffeur. When Flora and her grandmother returned to Woodstock the car was put into storage; it followed the same path to the auction floor as the yacht and the harp.

Back at The Firs, the aging Charles Boyle continued to operate a considerable stable of thoroughbreds, with the direction of the house and the farm left to his long-suffering wife Martha. One of his obstacles was the difficulty of getting horses ready for the opening of the racing season in Canada. It was inadvisable to do much with them outdoors in the middle of a Canadian winter and Charles Boyle longed for the days when, with the mighty Seagram Stable, he could start conditioning early in the enclosed quarter-mile training track.

Joe decided that what was good enough for the Seagrams was good enough for the Boyles. He sat down and drafted plans for a covered track at The Firs. The tanbark circle would have wooden walls and a stout roof, just like Seagram's, so he approached a number of Woodstock lumber yards for tenders on the supplies. When his notion of prices was not shared by the proprietors, his response might have been expected: he purchased an east-end lumber yard. "After a while," Flora recalled, "he wound up owning but not managing a lumber yard that no one seemed to control." Boyle's mill struggled along for some fifteen years before being sold in 1927 to meet long-standing debts.

The deteriorating relationships at Bear Creek reached a crisis the first week in September 1913, after a particularly bitter row between Flora and Elma. Boyle remonstrated with his daughter but only drew a hot response that she just wished she could get away, anywhere, to be free of it.

"Where would you like to go?" Boyle asked.

"Oh . . . to China," Flora flung back.

A few days later she was stunned, but far from displeased, to learn that arrangements had been made for her to visit China. Boyle had even provided her with an ideal companion, a family friend named Ida May Burkholder, a nurse on the staff of the Dawson hospital. There was barely time for farewells, for on 13 September the two women boarded the steamer *Whitehorse* for an enjoyable first leg of their travels, enlivened by the presence on board of a group of young geologists who had spent the summer in the Yukon.

Boyle had set up an itinerary that would take the two young women to Hong Kong for several months of sightseeing and study. They were to sail from Vancouver aboard the SS *Mont Eagle,* but Flora objected to sailing on such a small, indifferent vessel, and her Boyle temperament bubbled over. She refused to accept the booking and insisted that she and Ida May travel on the crack CPR liner *Empress of Russia* or not at all. This time Flora won the argument.

Ocean travel afforded them a leisurely, comfortable procession of days filled with entertainment and graced with dining room menus catering to the most finicky palates. After Hong Kong they moved on to Singapore aboard the SS *Derflinger,* a handsome German liner, for more relaxation and sightseeing, with the Raffles Hotel as a base. By this time they had decided on a leisurely voyage around the world. They were not concerned about events at Sarajevo at the time, but subsequent developments sent them rushing back to North America as quickly as they could. Ida May went back to the Yukon, but Flora settled in New York—for her the Klondike days had ended forever.

Back at Bear Creek, there was some blessed peace, even though Boyle had little time to enjoy it. Claim jumpers continued to squat on his property, but this was a relatively minor irritation, hardly to be compared to the difficulty of trying to live cheek-by-jowl with the hated Guggenheim Yukon Gold Company. After Treadgold had left YGC it had come under the direction of a much more aggressive, even hostile, management as far as CKMC was concerned. It now was managed by Chester Thomas, an uncle of a youngish American professor named Lowell Thomas, who made occasional visits to the Klondike.

The two mammoth dredging rivals found a great deal to quarrel over, for in a number of places their properties were contiguous and the landmarks poorly defined. And there was gold in abundance over which to fight.

A 1912 government report calculated a minimum of $169 million in gold had been extracted since 1897, an estimate likely far short of fact, since computation of results and recording of amounts taken out barely existed in the early days. The greatest production year had been 1902, when $22 million was produced, but the mining was still providing an average $4 million annually in what still was only $16-an-ounce gold, and seemed likely to maintain that flow indefinitely. Boyle, however, expected the totals to increase when his two new super dredges came into operation.

His difficulties with YGC were threefold. There was the natural rivalry of companies in the same business, aggravated by Boyle's proud Canadianism, demonstrated in what he said and in his flying the Canadian red ensign on his dredges. There was YGC resentment at being obliged to purchase from Boyle the electrical power needed to operate their dredges. Finally, in a region where dredges piled up mountains of tailings and spring floods wreaked havoc on landmarks, there were hot, vital arguments about property rights, some involving the extra-rich gravels at the point where Bonanza Creek runs into the Klondike River.

The Guggenheims were vocal and sometimes abusive. Their complaints about electrical supply found support in Dawson. When they said that Boyle could, and did, control power to suit his own purposes, the charges of inadequate service began to create a demand in Dawson and on the creeks that the territorial government take over the Boyle-owned utilities.

Nature stirred the pot some more in the spring of 1914 with

a flood that washed out overhanging banks and landmarks, particularly in the Ogilvie Bridge area where the rivals were working little more than a handshake apart.

An obvious invitation to litigation was accentuated by a heated personal encounter between Boyle and Thomas. Both were impressive physical specimens, Thomas perhaps a little larger than Boyle, and just about as formidable in a fist fight. But despite his great strength and his boxing skills Joe Boyle had long kept his hands to himself, even under great provocation. He hadn't done any boxing for nearly twelve years, since he and Slavin had put on an exhibition bout in Dawson on a holiday sports occasion. No one at Bear Creek could recall seeing him strike a blow in anger.

The argument on the diggings went on for some time, causing a crowd to collect to see what they expected to be the Klondike fight of the century. Boyle brought a sudden end to the debate when he seized a two-bladed axe and with one mighty swing severed the power cable to the YGC dredge.

There now was no prospect of trial by combat. It was to be an extended campaign in the law courts, which YGC launched on 21 November 1914, with a claim for damages for unlawful trespass. CKMC presented a counterclaim for damages created by illegal disposal of tailings on CKMC property by YGC.

Boyle mustered his troops and relied on the supple evidence of a coterie of young engineers, led by his own son. Mr. Justice McAulay, the presiding judge, declined to accept their testimony and ruled in favour of the case presented by the older witnesses of YGC. Boyle had argued that the 1897 survey in dispute was faulty but the Guggies won the debate and were awarded $11,700 in damages, while Boyle's counterclaims were dismissed.

By this time the Guns of August had already sounded and many felt it was a good time to forget the dispute. Nonetheless Boyle, as might have been expected, persisted through the appellate court, where he lost, and finally sent the problem to the Supreme Court of Canada, where in 1917—with Boyle far away and past caring—Chief Justice Fitzpatrick again upheld YGC with the comment that the "protracted litigation was out of all proportion to the importance of the subject matter involved." It was fortunate, in a way, that Boyle was unaware of the Ottawa decision, for it is likely that he would have appealed even further to the Judicial Committee of the Privy Council in London.

The dispute did not prevent the Boyle dredges from digging up their usual satisfactory amount of gold. What hurt was that Boyle's troubles appeared to increase as quickly as the output of gold. His property rights were under renewed assault, and questions were being raised about the probity of the Granville coterie that had loaned Boyle the money for his third and fourth dredges. The clamour to "nationalize" his utilities grew.

Boyle could hardly ignore the Granville criticisms, but he was more incensed about the move to seize his utilities than anything else. He pointed out that after his 15 February 1913 takeover of the Northern Light Power and Coal Company and its subsidiaries, the Dawson Electric and Power Company and Dawson Water and Power, he had reduced charges by 50 percent. He suspected a conspiracy against him, a deduction strengthened when he found that some of the people trying to jump his claims were agents of YGC.

The power company takeover had barely been completed when, on 3 May 1913, the Dawson power station burned to the ground under unexplained circumstances. Its destruction appeared to have been caused in part by the tardy arrival of members of the volunteer fire department. It was a Saturday night, and the firefighters had been "hard to locate," that being party night in the Yukon as elsewhere.

G. G. Hulme, manager of the power company until the Boyle takeover, said the fire was due to overloaded circuits. He charged that Boyle was selling power at twenty cents that cost only ten cents to produce, and that the water company was yielding a weekly profit of $1,500. Boyle contended that his original rate reduction had been well-meant but had proven

138

too sharp, and that he now required an additional $10,000 to operate profitably.

In the early fall the Dawson council accepted a Boyle proposal that he continue to furnish hydrant service without a price increase but that he be permitted to advance commercial light rates to yield the needed $10,000. The commercial users challenged the decision and after eight days of what in part was heavily stimulated public outcry, Boyle announced that he would shut down water services on 15 October and keep them closed until 15 May 1914. To add to the difficulties, Oscar Newhouse, a large shareholder in the original Northern Light and Power firm, challenged in court the legality of the sale of that company to Boyle on forty-three different counts. The case was put over until the summer of 1914, with Boyle agreeing to operate the utilities. It looked as if yet another Boyle court battle was coming.

Klondikers were further bemused by a report of the *London Financial Times,* circulated by the Dawson papers, telling of the formation of a new Canadian Klondike Mining Company with $8 million in share capital, of which Boyle was reputed to be receiving $3,825,000 worth. Granville, it was said, would retain shares worth $2,175,000. In addition, Granville would issue a $2 million convertible debenture of which the company would hold 80 percent, with the remainder left in the treasury. It noted that from 1 January to 19 July 1913, Canadian Klondike Mining Company had cleaned up 25,437 ounces of gold, and that profits for the year would exceed $1 million.

Klondike mine managers chewed on the figures, then turned to more pressing local concerns. High among their priorities was the spectre of unionism in the camps, where in the past despotic paternalism had reigned. Union agitation meant trouble and the disliked "Guggies" were the first to experience it. Early in 1914 one of their dredges was wrecked by a dynamite explosion.

It was time for close attention to business, so Joe Boyle, whose paternalism toward workers had been kindly and remained so, stayed on the scene at Bear Creek, where Joe Junior was demonstrating that he would become a useful addition to the operation.

There were lighter moments, too, in the pre-war years. On Christmas Eve, 1913, the Boyles played host to friends and company officials in a gala party complete with Santa Claus. It appears to have been a relatively easy and happy occasion, and the festivities continued for a week. Charles and Nan Boyle did not attend the partying. They had left the Yukon just before Christmas and were in Seattle awaiting the arrival of Joe and Elma, who planned to join them early in January. With Flora in the Orient, the family had become scattered; it would never be reunited.

Joe arrived in Seattle full of excitement, optimistically telling reporters how his dredges had cut production costs from ten cents a cubic yard of gravel to a mere six cents. This meant that a good deal of low-grade property that could not be worked previously was now within the range of the creek-devouring monsters.

The Boyles set off on visits to The Firs, Ottawa, New York, and London, and did not return to Dawson until 16 June 1914. Boyle returned to the Klondike anxious to talk about his expansion plans. He would install two new stripping machines to remove useless overlay on the gold-bearing gravels. On the way was a new pumping plant to be installed on Hunker Creek that would lift water from Rock Creek to the unexploited Dago Hill diggings. Accompanying Boyle was another personable young man, a friend of his son's, John Kennalley by name, who had accepted a position at Bear Creek.

There was litigation ahead, but things appeared to be settling down as Boyle started another campaign in the first of the minimum of eighteen years' production he now was predicting for his Klondike gold operations. But 1914 was the year that the world changed for Joe Boyle and everyone else—and it would never again be the same.

THIRTEEN

A Diligent Patriot

It seemed that the entire population of Dawson and the mining regions had assembled in the Dawson Amateur Athletic Association theatre that late afternoon of 4 August 1914. Everyone had gathered to hear the official pronouncement that a state of war existed with Germany, at what would be the equivalent of midnight in London.

Almost seventy years later, the memory of the occasion was fresh for the Reverend John A. Davies, then rector of Dawson's Anglican Church, who was among the hundreds in the building. In Woodstock, Ontario, at the age of ninety-six, he told how, on the stroke of that fateful hour, the Yukon Commissioner George Black rose to speak. The words were few but chilling in their finality. "The Mounties present immediately sprang to attention and everyone sang 'God Save the King.' It was an unforgettable occasion."

It was war by cabinet decision—and a cabinet in London, England, at that—but no more challenged in the Yukon than elsewhere in the Dominion. When Britain was at war, it followed that the Empire was at war. Those who could do so rushed to join the colours, responding to the tribal instincts that were part of their heritage. They worried, as did so many

141

in other places, that they might be too late to take part in a conflict sure to be over by Christmas.

While their employees schemed about getting away to don a uniform, the Klondike mining employers looked at ways to increase gold production. It took some time for them to realize the contradiction, for the first men to go were the most skilled and hard-working of the crews. Replacements would be difficult to find, less capable, largely inexperienced, and far from increasing it, unlikely to even maintain production.

The manpower shortage put a premium on the services of those who remained. These workers were told how vital their gold production was to the war effort. For the first time, they were beginning to understand their bargaining power, and to listen seriously to the seductive arguments of union organizers.

In the first burning moments of the war the Klondike responded magnificently with men and money. It seemed that the whole community was involved when the Dawson chapter of the Imperial Order of the Daughters of the Empire opened a hospital ship fund with a $2,500 donation from Joe Boyle and his CKMC employees. Boyle's interest in the war effort—Davies found him an enthusiastic and diligent patriot—at least distracted him from the management of his mining properties and other interests. The truth was that he not only wanted to support the war effort, he wanted to be a soldier. But at forty-six, he was too old to wear a uniform in combat.

Within days the Yukon's first volunteer, Howard Grestock, headed for Port Lévis, Quebec, hopeful of joining the proud Princess Patricia's Canadian Light Infantry. He departed in a shower of praise with Dr. Alfred Thompson, MP, who was off to Ottawa to help Parliament run the war.

Dr. Thompson had another, unpublicized assignment in hand. He had been commissioned by Boyle to offer Sam Hughes, the minister of militia and defence, a special Yukon corps for overseas service—raised, paid, and outfitted by Boyle. The secret became public on 2 September when the minister announced his acceptance of the offer. (The new contingent would be one of a half-dozen similar units raised privately by leading citizens.) Within four days recruiting officer Andrew Hart was enrolling men for the Dawson brigade. The sponsor quickly arranged for them to be taught the rudiments of army drill by Major Moodie of the Mounted Police, and persuaded George Brimston, captain of the Dawson Rifle Association, to be the musketry instructor.

Boyle, who over the years had been alternately hero or villain for the Dawson press and many of its readers, was now back in favour, more popular than ever before. Wrote the editor of the *Dawson Daily News:* "Unbounded credit is due to Joseph Whiteside Boyle for his more than generous contribution which makes it possible for Yukon to have a brigade in the great conflict. Mr. Boyle is a true Yukoner, a loyal Canadian and a sterling Britisher."

But Boyle's dedication to the cause was not shared by his son Joseph, who refused to join the colours. Junior Boyle was American-born, and he held the view of many of his countrymen that there was no place in the war for them. He wouldn't go with the Boyle detachment or any other unit, a position he maintained throughout the war. It was a decision with grave consequences, precipitating a bitter quarrel between father and son, and leaving a rift in their relationship that never healed.

Boyle's offer to the government specifically laid down that his unit would be a specialist force, equipped with and specially trained in the use of machine guns, still a new and controversial weapon. Veteran professionals of the British Army doubted that machine guns would ever replace controlled rapid fire by the crack riflemen of the army. Boyle had no claim to military experience but he knew something about weapons, and rather more about machine guns than many in the services. He was convinced the machine gun would dominate future battlefields, and the spectacle of a British army marching off to war trailing two machine guns for one thousand men saddened him. Boyle's brigade, he ruled, would be a fifty-man force equipped with its own transport, and armed with four machine guns as well as rifles and revolvers.

This enthusiasm for the automatic weapon had been acquired from another Boyle. Charles, the first Irish eldest son to spurn the Antrim patrimony, had become a customs officer in Glasgow and a sergeant in a territorial battalion, where he concentrated his interest on machine guns. He had introduced Joseph Boyle to them several years before, and later revealed that his Klondike relative had agreed to finance the purchase of a number of them for use by Ulster men in the 1913 crisis, which almost saw a mutiny in the British Army over Home Rule in the northern counties. This story has been confirmed by yet another Charles Boyle, son of the territorial sergeant and a retired teacher from Glasgow University, who was present when discussions on the subject took place. Joe Boyle may have been a Canadian, but under the skin he was an Ulsterman as well.

It is likely, too, that he had talked machine guns as well as mining with Raymond Brutinel, a French-born engineering entrepreneur and French army reservist officer. Brutinel, born in 1882, came to Canada in 1905 and prospected on the Peace, Pembina, McLeod, and other western rivers before joining a mining syndicate organized by G. T. Greenshields, a Grand Trunk Railway official. In August 1914 he was commissioned to create the First Canadian Machine Gun Corps, with the blessing and particular financial support of Sir Clifford Sifton.

The first two detachments recruited by Brutinel were known as the First and Second Clifford Batteries. Joining them eventually were three more: the Eaton, Borden, and Boyle units. The corps was provided with armoured cars for move-ment to vital battle areas, but had to wait until the spring of 1918 to demonstrate its worth by playing a major role in stemming the German breakthrough of Hough's Fifth Army in the final crisis of the long struggle.

Boyle's speedily recruited detachment shared the impatience

of recruits throughout the Empire at arriving in France and sharing in the fighting, still expected to be over quickly when they began their training in Dawson. The presence of these would-be soldiers, drilling in mufti and conditioning themselves in route marches, created great enthusiasm in Dawson. If they were to get out before the winter freeze they would need to be under way quickly, so Boyle scheduled their departure for 7 October on the steamer *Casca*. Dawson was intent on a real sendoff, and a mammoth public reception produced scenes of wild enthusiasm, during which the detachment was presented with a husky dog as a unit mascot. The recruits were lauded to the skies by just about every public figure in the Yukon. Joe Boyle spoke briefly and sincerely, and more than a few eyes were wet when he stopped. Everything was ready for departure—and then the word came that the *Casca* was unavailable.

Boyle was not to be foiled by a balky steamer. Three days later he led his contingent down to the Dawson docks for embarkation on the *Lightning*. Newspaper reporters told of the hundreds on the dock joining with the contingent to sing the new war song "Tipperary," about a peaceful place in rural Ireland. Joe Boyle was cheered to the echo, and there were more huzzas when Elma Boyle presented the unit with a certificate for silk colours that would be picked up in Vancouver.

At about 10 P.M. Jack, the unit mascot, led the troops aboard in a tumultuous torch-lit ceremony. "Give us your address," shouted someone in the crowd to Andy Hart, the erstwhile recruiting officer. "Berlin!" Andy roared back. The crowd went wild. Then, at midnight, it was time to depart. Hart lined up his stalwarts on the deck for a parting benediction, followed by the band playing "The King," with everyone standing ramrod stiff in the flickering shadows and an electric current coursing up and down countless spines. The Yukon had never before sent an army to battle.

With this pulse-stirring occasion over, it was back to the mundane for the Klondikers left at home. Joe Boyle's first task was to raise his big dredge, which had suddenly filled with water and sunk. The cause of this disaster was never determined.

Boyle worked hard during the next few months, but there was time to play, too. Curling was now his big interest, and he organized DAAA events, competed in them, and in the Patriotic Bonspiel on 7 January 1915 defeated Commissioner George Black's rink in the final. Boyle, a full-time devotee of the game, donated a handsome trophy for competition at the Woodstock Curling Club, where it remains a premier event trophy to this day.

Despite the socializing, Boyle worried about the lack of progress in the training and deployment of the Boyle brigade, and he corresponded frequently with Sam Hughes. The detachment had been attested and signed on at Victoria on 27 October 1914, then ferried across Georgia Strait to Vancouver's big military camp at Hastings Park. There it was stuck, seemingly forgotten, although technically the unit was part of the 29th Battalion of the Canadian Expeditionary Force. They were a forlorn outfit, with no spiritual home, condemned to hours of square bashing and route marching, dulling to the soul of Yukon individualists. They bombarded their patron with complaints and he grimly passed them on to Ottawa.

Joe Boyle saw for himself how fed up they were late in January after a precipitate departure from Dawson on what was vaguely reported to be "a big race to the outside on vital company business." The departure, some conjectured, had something to do with the report reaching Dawson of the annual meeting of Granville in London. It announced abrupt termination of the short-lived North West Corporation, but spoke optimistically of the money that would accrue to Granville from the profits of Boyle's concession where, in 1913, output had been valued at $1,299,333.

True to a promise made to his unhappy detachment members, Boyle stopped in Ottawa and took their complaints to the office of the defence minister. It brought one concrete result: official authorization on 18 February of Boyle's Yukon detachment with a strength of two officers, fifty-two other ranks, seventy-two horses and, best of all, four machine guns. But by 1 April there was still no sign of any movement from Vancouver. Two weeks later six of the enlisted men filed requests for discharges, alleging that enlistment promises made to them in Dawson had not been carried out. By this time they were considered a troublesome lot. An angry staff officer instructed, "Let them go." It was still the kind of war you could resign from if you were far enough distant from Flanders Fields.

Boyle was back in the Klondike by the end of April, barraging Hughes with complaints that his men were still being held back, and gilding the protest with praise for the gallantry of the Canadians who had held the line at Ypres, choking in the fumes of the first German gas attack. The story of the five battalions of Canucks who held off twenty battalions of German shock troops rang through the land. The Dominion thrilled with pride in their courage and agonized at their suffering.

Sam Hughes was in a good mood when Boyle's letter crossed his desk with its impatient message from a man almost as impetuous as the minister himself. "Send over, as a unit, without horses," he minuted on the letter margin. Staff officers winced and neatly filed away in their memory banks the name of this brash civilian who ignored protocol and went over their heads to get things done.

When he learned that his boys had arrived in England and were attached to the Eaton Motor Machine Gun Brigade, Boyle, fully placated, wrote Hughes on 19 June to thank him for his intervention. He told the minister that while in England six months earlier he had talked with two members of the Canadian provost staff in London—a Captain Shaw and a Sergeant Strang, both Manitobans and both anxious to be assigned to the Boyle unit. He urged their appointment to officer vacancies within the unit. In closing he wondered why, ten months after mobilization, he still had not been billed for the unit machine guns.

The reply came from a staff captain who, in the absence of the minister, coldly informed Boyle that nothing could be done about appointments to the unit because it had gone under British command. He might have informed Boyle that he had received no bill for machine guns because none had yet been provided, but decided not to mention the fact.

Transfers, discharges, and ordinary attrition had reduced the original detachment to just thirty-three by June 1916, when it was given a new establishment of four officers and fifty-five other ranks and designated a machine gun battery. Early in July of that year, brought up to strength, it was attached to the 4th Canadian Division and moved to France with it on 15 August. Four days later it was attached to the 1st Canadian Motor Machine Gun Brigade. The eager volunteers who had rushed to join up in Dawson had waited two years to reach the zone of hostilities; they had yet to hear a shot fired in anger.

After his return to Bear Creek in the spring of 1915 Boyle's preoccupation with his detachment waned, for there were more immediate matters to claim his attention. The doyen of Bear Creek, a lifelong foe of alcohol, found time to actively campaign against its use in the Yukon segment of a national wartime drive to bring in Prohibition.

Young Joe Boyle was very much in the Dawson news in June when he married Paris-born Susanne Jeannerette, "one of the most beautiful and charming young ladies of the North," according to one gushing writer. Another wedding of interest to the Boyles occurred when Ida May Burkholder, Flora Boyle's global tour companion, took Gustaf Edward Bredenberg, Teddy's uncle and resident manager of Treadgold's interests, as her husband.

Then there were the bad days. In August, as his crews attempted to right the overturned sunken dredge, the obstinate machine inexplicably toppled once more, killing the crew foreman and injuring three helpers. A few weeks later the plant generating steam power and heat for the Bear Creek establishment burned down for no apparent reason. Then came the November judgment in favour of the Guggenheims to add to the sense of frustration.

Through it all Boyle carried on doggedly, perhaps a bit desperately in view of reports of the war that suggested the unthinkable: a German victory in the field. The Yukon establishment rallied around. The Patriotic Fund went into a renewed drive for war funds, and Boyle, at the behest of his old associate Herbert Hoover, made a strong public plea for the Yukon to contribute to Belgian relief. At this time, Dawson also formed a British Empire Club with Mr. Justice McAulay Frederick T. Congdon, Joseph Boyle, and other local notables as patrons.

In the second half of the year Boyle was cheered by the report of New York mining consultant and engineer Henry J. Payne, who had extensively examined the CKMC operations in early summer. Payne found the Boyle enterprise flourishing and his glowing report was a boost, even if Boyle had commissioned the investigation himself. Payne obviously got around. In late October there was a letter from him in Moscow informing Boyle that the trip to Russia would take Payne to the Siberian gold fields in which Boyle was interested.

To the caged lion in his Bear Creek den, this was a deep pinprick. The stories appearing in the newspapers did nothing to settle him down. There was that headline trumpeting, "Sam Hughes Will Lead the Canadian March to Berlin." Hell, Sam Hughes was older than Joe Boyle, and a lot less fit. Other men were helping remake the world six thousand miles away, but Boyle was grubbing for gold on a remote frontier. The knowledge angered him; he realized that the world was changing, that events were out of control. The war that was to be over by Christmas was still going on; they had merely forgotten to say which year the war would end.

The CKMC dredges were anticipating a shutdown as the new year came in, briefer than usual because the crews were preparing No. 1 and No. 2 for renewed operations by 25 February 1916. But the dredges stood idle that winter, waiting for steel plates ordered the previous fall. Word came that the steamer bringing them to Alaska had gone down in a wild gale. Replacements came slowly; it was April before The Canadian lumbered into action on Hunker Creek.

At least the courts kept to their schedules, an unwelcome efficiency that brought another round in the YGC dispute about those controversial claims, this time near the Bear Creek area, involving claims staked by alleged squatters.

In June the Yukon bade farewell to a company of 130 men recruited for military service. Joe Boyle was on the dock when this contingent sailed away in command of George Black, soon to be an infantry captain. This, too, must have added to Boyle's longing to get overseas. Black was no youngster and here he was going off to war, while the only campaign Boyle was leading was far more mundane.

Social change was in the air and the Boyles were in the thick of it, campaigning for the Drys in a territorial fight to end the sale of alcohol. Elma assumed a role on the finance committee of the movement, and her husband was head of the organizing committee. His fight was conducted with a simple honesty and lack of malice that made him an effective advocate in what appeared to be a rather hopeless cause. The wet-dry struggle continued until 13 September when the Wets, to no one's surprise except for the paucity of their margin, won the plebiscite 874 to 871.

The closeness of the vote made the result a partial triumph for the Dry forces but Joe Boyle wasn't there to share in it. He was on his way to England to confer with British interests about a vast gold mining venture in Russia. "Heretofore," he told a Vancouver reporter, "the Russian government didn't allow foreign interests to develop mines in Siberia. All this is about to change and my mission to London is to confer with certain men regarding projects in hand for gold mining on the Lena River."

Vancouver, he added, ought to be very interested, for the first requirement in Russia would be 665,000 board feet of

British Columbia lumber to construct a dredge similar to his mighty Canadians at Bear Creek.

This would be a very quick trip, he told his friends, and Elma would not be going with him. Joe Junior would act as CKMC manager in his absence. He admitted that he was anxious to get overseas and visit the Boyle unit about whom he had received encouraging news from Colonel Sam B. Steele, the former Mountie who once had served in the Yukon. But he insisted that it was "urgent company business" that was taking him outside.

After a brief stop in Woodstock, Boyle hurried to New York to see Herbert Hoover, but on his arrival found that Hoover had departed for Europe. He took the first available passage and set off in pursuit. Boyle had told the press the truth, but not the whole truth by any means. For there was a curious development in Ottawa on 13 September 1916. On that day Boyle was gazetted as an honorary lieutenant colonel in the Canadian militia.

❧ FOURTEEN ❧

Farewell to the King

The London to which Joe Boyle proceeded in 1916 was a sober, grim city, vastly changed from his previous visits over a period of some sixteen years. The still-mounting bill for the Somme offensive that had wasted Kitchener's New Army on the barbed wire in front of German machine guns had cast a pall across the metropolis and shrouded the nation in mourning.

Even Britain's mighty navy seemed unable to cope with German Willie's rival fleet, which had fought to a draw and escaped at Jutland and now menaced Britain by threatening to push a U-boat blade across its marine jugular.

Boyle was still some distance from the war zone but at least he could now say he had been under fire, for German Zeppelins and airplanes were raiding London. Before year's end Joe Boyle finally had a uniform, turning his courtesy title into reality by purchasing outfits of the British pattern worn by Canadian officers. He assumed a few liberties in dress by using Boyle gold for his general service badges, and the gold-embroidered flashes at the sleeve tops carried the name Yukon.

In his military garb Boyle beat a path between Whitehall and Canadian Army headquarters, seeking an active duty assignment. He made friends with middle-echelon folk, but none was powerful enough or with sufficient authority to find him employment with the Canadian Expeditionary Force. He was permitted to talk about and see how the forestry units functioned, and how the light railway supply lines set up by the Canadians—reputed to be the most efficient on the western front—were operated. But there was no place for an unproven civilian with nothing to recommend him but desire.

Not even his friend Walter Long, the colonial secretary in the British government, could open the door. Boyle liked Long and admired his wife, a daughter of the ducal house of Cork, and so by birth a Boyle. And he was pleased when she addressed him as "cousin" in recognition of the legend that all the Boyles were related a few centuries back.

Not all of Boyle's time was spent on fruitless pleadings with the military, however. The Granville shareholders and creditors were becoming vocal. The pressure of his confused dealings with Granville prompted him to send for John Kennalley to come from Dawson to help him with the mining business problems.

Some of the other interests were more personal, for Boyle was close by when a German Zeppelin was shot down near Croydon. The next day he retrieved a piece of the twisted frame, which he later took home as a souvenir to show to curious Canadian visitors. Christmas afforded him an opportunity to visit his cousin Charles Boyle at The Clydebank and then continue on to the ancestral home in County Antrim. He also had a welcome reunion with members of the Boyle detachment, whose lot he sought to improve during his months in England. He wrote to the Vickers armament firm inquiring about an automatic two-pounder cannon the company had designed, a weapon that may well have been the forerunner of the pom-pom and other quick-firing, small-calibre cannon of another global war, a quarter-century later.

From Herbert Hoover, who was also in London, he learned details of the vast program of Belgian relief that was now under way. Hoover added that he had a job for Flora, and Boyle wrote to his daughter in New York, advising her to become inoculated and vaccinated and to prepare to go overseas to work with Hoover. Boyle enclosed a draft for fifty dollars in the letter. "He told me to sit tight, that I would hear from him again very soon, and that he was making arrangements to have money sent to me from Dawson every month." She never heard from him again, and in the confusion surrounding CKMC and Granville the monthly allowance never materialized.

Through nine months in Britain Boyle lived at The Savoy, an address of consequence. As time passed he seemed far more likely to get to the law courts than to the battlefront, and in preparation for litigation now threatened by some Granville directors he obtained the services of John Broad, senior member of the legal firm of Broad and Son.

Joe Boyle was persistent in offering his services to the war effort and he was becoming widely known in London. F. T. Congdon, KC, returned from Britain singing the praises of Colonel Joe Boyle, about whom he had not always been so complimentary. He told a Dawson reporter:

If I were to be asked who is the most prominently-mentioned man in England from Canada—that is, the Canadian whose energy and activity have won for him the highest esteem as an organizer, planner and adviser, I would give the honor to our own Joseph W. Boyle. . . .

Boyle, he predicted, would be knighted for his services before the year's end.

Some of those who cheered the loudest were the members of the Yukon infantry company raised by Captain George Black, who had arrived in England to be told they were to be broken up as reinforcements for Canadian regiments in France. Boyle couldn't talk himself into an active service posting, but somehow he persuaded Canadian authorities that the company should be turned into a specialist machine gun unit.

Ironically for a Canadian and Imperial patriot, it took the entry of the United States into the war for Boyle's talents to be used effectively. When Wilson declared war, Americans in London were able to publicly declare their support of the Allies.

One of the first organizations to emerge was the American Committee of Engineers (ACE) in London, a group of scientists and engineering experts pledged to devote their talents to advancing the Allied cause in special fields. Their interests ranged from pure science to psychological warfare and counter-intelligence.

Joe Boyle was one of the original members of ACE, which soon boasted fifty-nine active and eleven consulting members spread from the United States to Russia. Among the consultants were the Hoover brothers, Herbert and T. J., of Washington, D.C., and Palo Alto, California, respectively.

A permanent office was set up at 6 Copthall Avenue, EC2, with C. R. Purington as honorary secretary. One of their projects was a survey of British railways to determine the relative values of steel and composite ties. Another was an exposé of enemy interests in U.S. and Allied metal companies, with the purpose of discovering how to control and exploit them.

One of sixteen plans offered for sub-committees to consider was a project to assist Russian railways immediately behind the Russian front lines. This project was placed in the charge of J. W. Boyle, W. Poland, and I. N. Dessau. It was no accident that Boyle found himself in charge of the plan. He had operated light railways in the Klondike and had learned more about them during his months in England. Also, he had left Canada intending to visit Russia. Everything came together in a matter of days, when it was decided that Boyle would head an ACE mission to Russia to develop the project.

He had some excellent guidelines to study. Earlier in the year another Canadian, Sir George Bury, vice-president of Canadian Pacific Railways, had been summoned from Canada on short notice to join Lord Milner's mission to Russia. After three weeks in Petrograd, during which he witnessed the spring revolution that ended the three-hundred-year-old Romanov dynasty, Bury wrote a comprehensive report of his findings. He found much wrong with the Russian transportation system, but he was warm in his praise of Ways and Communications Minister Nikolai Nekrasov and other harassed senior officials.

Although this new mission was sponsored by a private American organization, Boyle saw that its members were partly Canadian. He enlisted the services of Lieutenant-Colonel J. A. MacDonell of the Canadian Army engineers and arranged for John Kennalley to travel with him as private secretary. None of the Canadians spoke Russian, but the Russian embassy in London solved that problem by offering the services of Vladimir Andreav, of the London office of the Department of Ways and Communications.

There was private advice for the mission on how to deal circumspectly with the Stevens Committee, recently sent from the United States to advise the Russians on how to improve their civilian rail services. This committee had much broader terms of reference. Its leader was John F. Stevens, planner and builder of the Panama Canal, who had worked on the Great Northern Railway. Overlapping investigations were a distinct possibility, but the presence of military titles in the ACE delegation would provide that mission with an edge in dealing with the military.

Ostensibly this was to be a relatively short-run mission, but from the start Boyle obviously thought otherwise. Before leaving London he had a meeting with General Richard Turner, VC, commander of Canadian troops in England, during which he suggested that as many as three hundred Canadian officers might be required to sort out the Russian tangle and get the front-line supply system working. Turner left Boyle with the impression that he would support any reasonable application for such assistance. Some of the troops would have to be fighting men, and Boyle perhaps hoped that they would include the Yukoners with their machine guns and some Vickers quick-firers.

Preparations for departure were clouded by the necessity of briefing the Boyle lawyers on the Granville matters, now certain to wind up in a court plea for the appointment of a receiver for the Boyle properties until the whole mess was untangled. Boyle was confident of the outcome. After a number of disappointing years, reports from Joe Junior showed improved dredging prospects, with production reaching two thousand ounces weekly by mid-June.

Young Joe, learning that his father was bound for Russia, pleaded for instructions, seeking power of attorney to arrange new placer groupings and deal with a possible strike of workers. Another strike had closed down Yukon Gold, whose 350 hired hands demanded a 25 percent wage boost. Boyle's men were still loyal but wavering. Joe Junior pointed out that $186,000 was owing in back wages and asked to have all production diverted to settlement of the arrears in order to avoid trouble. There was trouble on the domestic front too, and the young boss at Bear Creek demanded confirmation of his management and an order terminating periodic draft demands by his Uncle Charles.

The Granville application was listed for 20 June, but that was too late for Boyle. On Sunday morning, 17 June, the ACE mission left London by train for "a northern port," which now can safely be named as Aberdeen. Congdon was among a small group wishing them Godspeed. Boyle took a side trip on his own, rejoining his companions at the seaport after briefly leaving them for a wild dash across the Irish Sea to County Antrim. His Irish friends and relatives saw him for three or four hours before he departed, whispering that he was off to Russia.

The departure order from the Admiralty was so sudden that the mission was forced to leave under-strength. Colonel MacDonell reported sick but promised to join them as quickly as he could—a pledge he was unable to keep, for he became worse, was invalided home, and discharged.

Boyle was travel-weary but unable to sleep when he reached Aberdeen. The excited travellers arrived early for the 2 A.M.

sailing on 20 June. They left in a sizeable convoy shepherded by a lively flotilla of British destroyers, dashing about like a pack of terriers. The King of the Klondike was in the process of abdicating his throne for another realm, the proportions of which he couldn't have begun to imagine.

FIFTEEN

A Very Desperate Condition

The bright face of summer illuminated the wide streets of Petrograd that Monday morning, 25 June 1917, cheering a mixed procession of civilians and groups wearing weary-looking military garb. It was a time of travail but the city was quiet this day, as it had been all weekend, despite widespread predictions of civil disorder and worse.

It looked handsome enough to three men moving along its broad avenues. Although preoccupied with their own thoughts, some of the citizenry still stopped to gaze in astonishment at the largest of the trio of strangers. This rugged six-footer, seemingly almost as broad as he was tall, strode along in the khaki uniform of an Allied army, proudly wearing his rank badges, his ceremonial sword clinking. Rank badges and swords had vanished in the Revolution, which had ended Czarist rule, and officers in the Russian services were anxious not to be noticed. This man obviously didn't worry about the scrutiny.

Being looked at and talked about was nothing new to Joseph Boyle, late miner of Dawson. His uniform was spanking new, not many weeks out of the tailor's hands in London, made-to-measure as befitted a recently appointed lieutenant-colonel in the Canadian militia, albeit an honorary one.

159

His companions in this morning stroll were slighter physically. One was obviously a Russian, the other an attractive, fair-haired visitor of uncertain origin. He was a citizen of the United States. The Russian was interpreter Vladimir Andreav; the American, John Kennalley, for two years a valued member of Boyle's mining company headquarters staff in the Klondike. Acting as Boyle's secretary, he was needed to maintain some order in the flow of messages that Boyle was wont to originate daily.

Kennalley was excited by his arrival in Petrograd, and if he had any doubts about the mission on which his chief was embarked—which seemed in sober second thought the epitome of foolishness—he was wise enough to keep them to himself.

Boyle, with what assistance he could muster, had been charged with the immense task of straightening out the Russian military transportation system, which had failed so dismally that much of the blame for Russian defeats could be laid to the inability to bring arms, munitions, men, food, and supplies to the fighting troops. The railways had become so ramshackle that the vast stores of food in the countryside could not be moved to the large population centres. Boyle had been told that the overthrow of the Romanov dynasty had come about because the women of Petrograd rioted over a shortage of bread. The winter uprising had taken everyone by surprise, even the wily Lenin, leader of the Bolsheviks, who had been very slow to respond as he waited out his exile in Switzerland, writing speeches and tracts when the time for action arrived.

Petrograd, as St. Petersburg had been named in 1914, was a spectacular city and, to Boyle's surprise, a quiet one. He had been warned before departing Britain that there was real danger of an uprising that might turn into civil war. The defiant Bolsheviks had been in the streets a few days earlier, and had scheduled another larger demonstration on the weekend of 23–24 June. To the surprise of many the almost immobile provisional government had moved quickly to forbid the monster demonstration, announced by the Central and Petro-grad committees of the Bolshevik party.

Boyle quickly understood the plight of the provisional government, an ill-assorted collection of mediocrities thrown together a few hours after Czar Nicholas had abdicated. It had inherited a ponderous, old-fashioned bureaucracy and was unsure of its own philosophies. It was vacillating and uncertain, and all too aware that few members of the government saw eye-to-eye on anything except the necessity to survive. This rickety leadership had undergone a face-lifting in May to meet the rising challenge of the Bolsheviks, who had shown their scorn of the provisional assembly by forming their own unofficial but vocal assembly of worker and military unit delegates, which more and more appeared ready to fill the power vacuum created by the weakness of the government.

Boyle's letters of introduction—his briefcase was well-stocked with them—were to the ministers and civil service department heads of this uneasy, faltering regime. He might better have been directed to the likes of Stalin, Kamenev, and Muralov, who had returned to the capital in March; and most certainly to the small, bearded genius, Lenin. A month earlier, another unusual revolutionary named Trotsky had returned after infuriating holdups in the United States and Canada. Boyle, it turned out, had reached Russia during the intermission of the two-act revolutionary drama.

At the time of Boyle's arrival, however, the spotlighted figure was the orator-lawyer, hyperactive Alexander Kerensky, who claimed he had the situation in hand. For a time it looked as if he might be right, for Lenin and some of his followers fled into hiding in Finland.

First among those to whom Boyle was recommended was Sir George Buchanan, the British ambassador, and Boyle immediately paid his respects. Appearing in full regimentals, he confounded the British military attaché by remarking that he was in Russia to do what he could to help. The military staff received the impression that their unusual colonial visitor was talking about military activity, and it worried them that a fifty-year-old, inexperienced militia amateur should have such thoughts.

Boyle also had a letter to David R. Francis, U.S. ambassador in Petrograd. And Colonel Millard Hunsiker, a member of the American Committee of Engineers, had recommended Boyle to H. Custis Vezy, an expert in the light railway field who had been seasoned behind the lines in France. Boyle had other, less well-known strings to his bow. Yet another ACE associate, I. N. Dessau, furnished him with a letter to a Petrograd businessman, Frederick Gross, urging that Boyle be employed as a mining consultant and be sent to examine gold properties in Siberia when he had completed his railway assignment. This letter probably was the result of representations by ACE secretary C. R. Purington, who was associated with a British company that had large gold interests in the Lena district of Siberia.

The old-boy network had been around for a long time, and Boyle was quite prepared to use it when necessary. He approached the ambassadors on 28 June, after forty-eight hours of intensive briefing by Andreav. It was obvious that he attracted their attention, for Buchanan urged him to keep in touch and asked for a full report on his mission.

At the embassy Boyle also met General Frederick C. Poole, British control officer who soon would, at Russian request, assume command of British and Canadian forces in Northern Russia to guard that entrance against a German intervention. Boyle thought they had gotten along very well, but a member of Poole's staff had second thoughts about the Canadian. On 2 July the Imperial Munitions Board in Ottawa received a strange cable from Whitehall, reporting that a "Col Byrne" was in Petrograd, wearing a Canadian uniform, "who states he had been sent to work on the railways here by Americans in London but his real interest is to help."

The cable noted that the stranger had a letter of introduction from General Hermonius, head of the Russian supply mission in London. "Can you tell me confidentially whether he represents the Canadian government," asked the Whitehall questioner, "and under whose authority he is acting and what is the real object of his mission?" Several days later Ottawa replied that Boyle was an honorary colonel of militia and no one knew what he was doing in Russia. ACE hadn't bothered to tell official Whitehall what was going on. Their understanding of military protocol was minimal.

Unaware of these immediate reactions, Boyle plunged into a series of five major conferences between 28 June and 2 July, assisted by Andreav. Kennalley kept detailed minutes of the meetings, and they somewhat miraculously have been preserved. The meetings involved General A. A. Manikovski, assistant commissioner of war; his aide, General Sapojnikoff; General Kislikoff, assistant minister of ways and communications; M. Danilevski, director of railway administration on the civilian side of the house; and finally, Ways and Communications Minister N. V. Nekrasov.

Boyle had hoped to meet Kerensky, but the war minister was away at the front exhorting, in his usual dramatic fashion, disinterested Russian soldiers to fight bravely in the coming Kerensky offensive that would, he said, restore the military honour of the nation and deal a crushing blow to the Germans and Austrians.

The reports suggest that despite the language barrier Boyle got along very well with the Russians, who must have been impressed and heartened by his forceful, confident manner. To a man who had moved mountains and changed the course of Yukon rivers, nothing seemed impossible, and he radiated that confidence.

Manikovski was particularly encouraged and held a second long meeting with Boyle in which, Boyle reported, Manikovski had urged him and his companions to travel to Mogilev, where Stafka—the Russian military headquarters—was situated, to begin their investigations. The general explained that the government would have to give the assistant minister permis-

163

sion to authorize the trip. It was Boyle's first glimpse of a system so hidebound by rules that even a senior minister could not authorize a travel warrant, indicative of the sad fact that in the end very little authority was exercised by anyone.

Manikovski urged the ACE committee to work separately from the American Stevens Commission, which had recently arrived with instructions to assist in the transportation difficulties. Stevens, said Manikovski, could co-ordinate civil and military rail lines after Boyle had completed his survey.

Boyle's terms of reference had been explicit: to work on light railways behind the fighting front. Someone, he soon found, wanted to prevent that, for there were strong suggestions that he take charge of

the Mourmon [Murmansk] railway to Kola Bay and the line to Archangel. ... However, when I met the minister of ways and communications on Saturday morning he expressed a strong desire that I confine my activities to the military zone. ... I, of course, agreed to follow his wishes and the minister then asked me to proceed to Stafka. ...

The words in his report to ACE in London sound innocuous, but there was more to it than that. Twenty years later, Russian staff officers who had been present told Joe's daughter, Flora, what had happened. Boyle, they related, had rejected the northern assignment in terms so firm they never forgot them: "I shall never operate a railway built on the bones of prisoners forced, under terrible conditions, to build a railway with a right-of-way dotted with the graves of the workers." He had been in Petrograd for only three days, yet this amazing visitor was laying down the terms of his employment. "My mission," he continued, "is to the war front railways, and I shall accept no other."

As Boyle turned to walk out of the meeting a British officer rose and began to apologize for such steely words. He was quickly put in his place when Boyle cut him short: "I mean what I say, and I say what I mean. No one needs to apologize for me." The room was hushed. The minister was impressed, and told Boyle a few days later that at that moment he had been convinced that the big Canadian was his man.

Manikovski, Boyle wrote, said that while he understood Boyle represented ACE, he also had an indefinable feeling that he represented Canada. It was a compliment Boyle appreciated but was wise enough to disown. He asked that it be fully understood that he had no authority to represent any government, "although I had the assurance of high officials of both countries [the United States and Canada] that they wished to help Russia in every way they could." The interview wasn't quite over. Joe Boyle gently warned that he would have to be in charge wherever he went. "I told him that there should be but one head man and that any place I went this would be the case."

"When will your party be ready to travel to Mogilev?" he was asked. "Tonight," Boyle replied. The minister started. That would be a bit too soon, he demurred. "Would you be prepared to go Monday?"

By this time he had begun to realize that, perhaps more in hope than conviction, these government officials shared Kerensky's optimism about the success of the coming offensive. Their main concern, said the minister, was whether the Austrians and Germans would destroy the railway lines as they retreated, and hinder the Russian pursuit.

As promised, Boyle called on Stevens on 1 July, Canada's national holiday. Stevens, who had just been released from hospital, was amicable, Boyle reported, and agreed that any Americans coming to Russia should be military personnel. This would avoid any Russian criticism that the visitors were stealing jobs from their hosts.

Boyle's hurried departure from London had left many matters dangling and now, as he was preparing to travel to Stafka, some of them caught up with him in Petrograd. For one thing, there was the mass of litigation over CKMC's association with Granville Mining Company. Granville had lost the first round but Boyle's attorney, John Broad, wrote a warning that an appeal was imminent. Then there was Junior Boyle's clamouring for power-of-attorney and a clear definition of his duties and responsibilities. Boyle had scribbled the necessary document on the dock at Aberdeen and mailed it to Broad. Now his lawyer was telling him that something more formal and legally respectable was required. Seven weeks later he found time to send the needed power-of-attorney.

Before leaving Petrograd he spent several hours drafting a long memorandum to Manikovski. Allied ignorance of the suffering and sacrifice of the Russian armies and people was profound, Boyle told the war minister. To remedy this situation he advised Manikovski to establish a co-ordinated news department for the foreign office, war office, and admiralty, "ensuring that all news items . . . should collectively constitute an exposition of the facts of such a nature as to create a feeling of confidence in and sympathy towards Russia." In particular, he continued, cultivate a relationship with Associated Press by giving the agency regular access to departmental heads. "It would be essential that sufficient confidential relations be established to ensure the publication of any other items which . . . have a tendency to ensure the right impression. . . ." He noted that the French and the British had made similar arrangements and "the results were quickly apparent."

Joe Boyle was never comfortable with the press and tried to avoid reporters, but he was demonstrating a rare instinct for what, today, is called "management of the news media." AP, for its part, never quite managed to clear itself of charges that it was a wartime propaganda agency for the Allies. Boyle's remarks make it clear that this was the case.

On the afternoon of 2 July, with much of his desk work untended, Boyle, Kennalley, and Andreav set off for Mogilev by road, travelling in a large staff car, a cumbersome touring model that demonstrated its durability on the three-hundred-mile trip by depositing them at Stafka about 3 P.M. the following day. Their arrival had been expected, for they were quickly quartered in the Bristol Hotel and advised to take their meals at the foreign officers' mess. The headquarters was spread over several hundred acres of ground, utilizing private buildings and scores of private railway cars on a specially constructed siding as offices and living quarters. The environment was completely military. Boyle liked that and was pleased that he had a uniform to wear, although lieutenant-colonels were as thick as fleas on a village mongrel.

That same day Boyle prepared the way for his most important session by spending an hour with General Kislikoff, the assistant minister of ways and communications who had journeyed to Stafka to continue his observation of this unusual visitor. Andreav again served as interpreter, Kennalley sat with notebook at the ready, and soon they had moved on to a long interview with General Tickminev, director of light railways.

Kislikoff had surprised Boyle by remarking that he did not believe in light railways, despite the impressive performance reports from France, and preferred to run standard-gauge heavy lines as close to the front as possible. He had been in a sombre mood, impressing Boyle with the dangers and disasters that might lie ahead. In his ACE report, Boyle wrote that

He went on to say that the transport conditions ... were in a very dangerous state ... which might bring about a great disaster at any time ... that they had been obliged to notify all of the different railways ... that they might be called upon ... for equipment ... and that he fears to suggest what the result [might be] if this is done. ...

At the meeting with Tickminev, he heard about the inadequacy of the rail repair system, which forced tired men to work long hours in extreme cold, sharply reducing output because of the sickness that followed. Russia needed cars, locomotives, more track to complete unfinished lines, and masses of material and equipment.

Boyle already had learned of the thousands of tons of barbed wire supplied by the Allies that sat rusting in rear supply depots for lack of transport to move it forward, and he formed the firm opinion that the real immediate need was weapons and ammunition for the sadly equipped Russian foot soldiers.

Tickminev came armed with detailed needs for light locomotives, light railway trucks, and a monthly supply of steel track with fish plates. He was trying, he added, to operate one hundred lines of light railways, and provision of 150 locomotives, he told Boyle, would eliminate 80 percent of the horse transport, freeing hundreds of cars now engaged in hauling horse fodder and bedding to the forward areas.

It was an impressively sad tale, and Boyle was moved, but he had only started his probing. A long session with Engineer Mischka, civilian head of non-military lines, provided more doleful information, and by 5 July Boyle had quickly reached some early conclusions, which he embodied in a written report to the ACE in London:

I have recommended the abolition of the joint system and the turning over to the ministry of ways and communications of all railway battalions. These . . . consist largely of either skilled or semi-skilled workmen who could be distributed and used to very great advantage by putting the best of them in the repair shops and utilizing the others in the service in the ordinary way.

This, he added, would give the ministry complete control of all trunk lines up to a point where they joined the light railway system. Light railways, he advised, should be left in the hands of the sapper units, which were really railway battalions in the British establishment. "The assistant minister," he concluded, "has already made a recommendation that this plan be adopted."

The report was also significant for its mention of the fate of the small kingdom of Rumania. Prompted by its beautiful British-born Queen Marie, granddaughter of the mighty Queen Victoria, Rumania had belatedly and with some trepidation

168

entered the war on behalf of the Allies. After some deceptive early success its forces had been smashed and driven back into a small redoubt on its eastern borders, abutting the Russian province of Bessarabia.

One problem that confronts us is the feeding of a very large Rumanian civil population now herded into the corner of Rumania still within the Russo-Rumanian lines. Information received . . . today justifies the assumption that something will have to be done to relieve these people and their relief is as much the duty of America, England and the other Allied nations as it is of Russia. . . . [I]t is an absolute impossibility for Russia to handle the situation. I have telegraphed the British ambassador in Petrograd asking him for information. . . .

So, hardly realizing what he had done, Joe Boyle made the cause of Rumania his own. He in effect pledged his efforts to preserve the five million refugees of a stricken nation that had never been in his thoughts until a few hours earlier.

The decision made, Boyle went to work. He sent a fuller letter to Buchanan, offering the view that the only chance to save the Rumanians was to evacuate them or to set up a relief organization to feed and care for them that was similar to the one Herbert Hoover had arranged for Belgium. Hoover, he informed the ambassador, was a close friend of his and he was confident that the American would help succour the Rumanians. The International Red Cross, Boyle noted, had raised $100 million to help Belgium and was planning to assist Russia, and should be similarly anxious to help Rumania. The enlarging scope of his vision was demonstrated in his final remarks to Buchanan. Aiding Rumania, he suggested, would be self-serving for the Allies, because this relief would keep Rumania in the war—a small but important asset at a time when all was in the balance.

On 5 July, along with the other communications that must have taken hours to prepare, Boyle cabled General Turner in

London, reporting Russia's gratitude for any help Canada might be able to provide. He urged Turner to send him an associate, asking for a Colonel Griffin of the Canadian railway troops. Two weeks later Turner's reply arrived: Headquarters had no objection to such an appointment providing it was "without expense to Canada."

At this juncture Boyle lost the services of the very competent Andreav, who reluctantly answered a command to return at once to his office in London. Boyle was sorry to see him depart; he sent a letter to the British Embassy highly praising his young companion's work. Future interpreters, Boyle was told, would be available from the Stafka pool of linguists. Eventually he would be permitted to set up his own corps of interpreters.

The round of interviews continued, and each day concluded in a spate of report and letter writing. It was exhausting but highly exhilarating work—eighteen-hour days that Boyle tossed off with the flare of his youth. On 8 July, for the first time, he conversed at length with General A. Brusiloff, commander-in-chief of the Russian armies. Boyle had always wanted to be where the fighting was, and now he was moving toward the sound of the guns at last.

That same day, 8 July, accompanied by the faithful Kennalley and his new Russian interpreter, Colonel Nevelskoie, Boyle left Stafka in a private railway car. He had been in Russia for only twelve days, and he had been a very busy man. Now he would be even busier, for the car that carried him off to Tarnopol in the southwest was also bringing him closer to astonishing new adventures.

The Amateur is Blooded

At first the summer Russian offensive into Galicia had gone well. Using a plan drafted by the former Czar and his generals just before Christmas, 1916, the Russian high command sent 312 battalions of fighting men into action after a two-day barrage by some 1,300 guns on 2 July 1917.

This assault against the Austro-German forces over a forty-five-mile front quickly penetrated the first line of defences. The Seventh Army was particularly successful, and a substantial degree of success was reported from the Eleventh Army front. The left flank of the Russian front, running to the Black Sea between Odessa and the Rumanian port of Constanze, remained passive. It was manned by six broken Rumanian divisions, still licking the wounds from their disastrous defeats a few months earlier.

For a few brief hours the air was electric, and the optimism that Joe Boyle had noted seemed to rise. But the successes were transient. Troops scheduled to relieve those who had made the breakthrough failed to arrive. Supplies of food and ammunition failed to move forward, and within five days the advance had come to a standstill.

By the time Boyle's party reached Tarnopol it was obvious to the high command that the offensive was turning into a disaster, though immediately behind the Seventh Army lines this realization had not sunk in. Boyle found the communications headquarters there functioning well enough. He and his companions were quickly billeted in the comfort of a private railway car owned by the president of the railway company. In this temporary home Boyle laid plans for a series of visits to transportation units, scheduling nine conferences during an eight-day period at the rear area of the Seventh Army battlefront.

On 12 July he was closeted at Boczacz (pronounced *Boocash,* noted Boyle) with Major-General Narecki, the Seventh Army's chief transport officer. It was an uninspiring session. Narecki, whose troops were failing miserably to support their fighting countrymen, was singularly uninformative and downright stupid. His role, he said, was "to give instructions and not to worry about how well they were carried out."

Boyle motored over to the 9th and 18th railway battalions at Monastajicka, talked to their commanders, and was equally appalled. None of those he met had demonstrated a spark of initiative and were prepared only to try to do as ordered, and nothing more. They were totally lacking in drive and inspiration, and were bogged down in apathy. The following day he talked with officers of the 5th exploitation battalion at Podhaytse. They were cut from the same shoddy cloth. A better moment came when he visited the 92nd surgical hospital and was agreeably surprised to find it competently staffed and run by British volunteer nurses and doctors.

This first sortie into the field had been enlightening and depressing. He hurried back to Tarnopol for meetings with the officers of the 4th Siberian railway battalion and with Engineer Serafemurich, commander of a civilian construction train.

Fragmentary reports filtering back from the front were alarming, for they hinted at a Russian withdrawal. Boyle ignored the portents and set out for Kamenetz Podolsk, headquarters of the crumbling Seventh Army, halting to inspect the 19th railway battalion on the way before huddling with the headquarters staff. He reached Kamenetz Podolsk on 18 July, the date on which the war ministry in Petrograd looked anxiously at the battleflags on the maps and decided to remove General Brusiloff as supreme commander. Summoned to replace him was General Lavr Korniloff, who had been commanding the offensive in Galicia. Reinforcing failure with failure was becoming a standard practice. Forty-eight hours later Kerensky, who had insisted on this last reckless fling of the military dice, was made head of the provisional government, replacing Prince George Lvov.

Boyle knew nothing of these political moves; he was swamped in detail from the data accumulated during his hurried dashes around the rear areas. He had found discouraged, dispirited leaders. And, freed from the shackles of military terrorism of floggings and other punishments by the infamous Order No. 1 abolishing saluting, rank badges, and other traditional systems, lazy, insolent soldiers were clearly near revolt. The story was the same everywhere. Clever agitation by enemy agents and Bolshevik sympathizers was bringing into focus all the weaknesses of the Russian military system.

Behind the battlefront Boyle had found frighteningly inefficient operations, with few of the infrastructure facilities functioning. There was a shortage of personnel, a leadership vacuum. Some units were filled with old men and unskilled boys, totally unable to perform their minimal duties. Every stop brought more evidence of a long-standing shortage of tools, track, supply wagons, engines, and almost everything required to make a rail system function.

Communications were inadequate, in some cases nonexistent. Supply requisitions were lost or ignored. Not a single officer knew the establishment for horses in a railway battalion. One guessed it was 230, another opted for 460, and they finally agreed that it might be 180 two-horse teams. The animal lover from the Klondike was enraged to find out that horses were dying at the rate of 1 percent monthly, and that 700 had died in May. He decided to ask the U.S. government to send caterpillar tractors to relieve the overworked animals in the winter months.

One unit reported it had 460 cars available of the 900 in its table of organization, and of those, only 70 were serviceable. Boyle was shocked to discover that the average daily mileage for a locomotive was 60, and that it was no more than 2,000 miles monthly for those in good working order.

The journey to the front confirmed Kislikoff's fears of the desperate situation. Upon returning to Tarnopol on 18 July, Boyle decided to move immediately to inaugurate whatever changes could be made from that distance. Kennalley worked long hours typing out his chief's reports and messages, and his pleas to almost anyone he knew who could assist him, from individuals to national governments.

He asked Colonel B. M. Humble, of the Canadian Railway Troops in London, for details of the weight, cost, and establishment of a complete Canadian railway battalion, less only horses and arms. Humble was quick to reply. A week later Boyle learned that the weight was seventy-five tons, but the cost was unknown.

He appealed to ACE in London for small machine-shop equipment, lathes, drills, presses, nut and bolt machines, emery wheels, forge equipment, tools, rolling stock, and "anything for immediate delivery in any quantities." Pleased at having something definite to get its teeth into, the ACE headquarters cabled that it had found five lathes, ten drill presses, and other material that would be available within eight weeks. Welborne and Company, Whitehall, cabled that it had machine-shop equipment available immediately, and asked for specifications. Private firms in the United States offered assistance. Half the world, it seemed, might help. Only the Russians were unable to respond. Associates in Petrograd, exhorted to look around, reported that Russian stocks were exhausted.

Boyle, now assured that the needed equipment could be

supplied, sat down to figure out how to pay for it. He cabled ACE to find out if they could help.

Million dollars worth needed desperately now, ten millions more which will include rails and rolling stock for light railways quickly as possible. Nothing America can do will help as much as furnishing. Can arrangements be made American government to finance this without cutting into any other Russian credits?

If Boyle sounded desperate, it was a reflection of his concern about the disaster descending on the Russian Army, one that might take that unfortunate country out of the war and release several million men to fight against the Allies on the Western Front in France.

Returning from Kamenetz Podolsk, he and his associates had to depart hurriedly from overnight lodgings in Koseva under a curtain of German artillery fire. As they fell back, the signs of a disorderly retreat bordering on panic were obvious. A London *Times* war correspondent reported that at several places "everybody ran away." Everybody, that is but an armoured-car corps commanded by Royal Navy Commander Locker-Lampson, whose machines dashed back and forth between connecting roads to engage the advancing Austrians. They succeeded admirably, thanks in part to shortcomings in enemy initiative, and found the retreating Russians their worst foe, for they jumped on the British machines and destroyed three of them by overloading them as they attempted to flee. Locker-Lampson told the *Times* the only Russian regiment that fought well was a Finnish ski battalion.

Like thousands of others, Boyle's party was swept into Tarnopol by the panicking soldiery. There he found his railway car intact, but the Russian headquarters staff had decamped, leaving no one in charge. In a report prepared for Canadian authorities two years later, Boyle wrote:

The officers in charge had disappeared. The people were in a highly excitable condition, and what had been only confusion was rapidly developing into a riot. . . . With the assistance of two young Russian officers, and by assuming an authority I did not have, I got a "death battalion" to throw a cordon around the town, establish patrols and restore some semblance of order.

Boyle's example, and the courageous performance of the women of the Death Battalion (so called because they had sworn to fight to the death for Russia) halted the rout and provided Locker-Lampson's armoured cars and some Belgians in another armoured unit with a secure base from which to operate.

Tarnopol came under bombardment by German aircraft almost at once, with two raids in the first day. The planes, totally unopposed from the air, dropped bombs and strafed the town, with special attention to the railway station, from which many soldiers and civilians were to be evacuated.

Boyle turned his attention to the station where, aided by a Colonel Truscott, a British artilleryman in Russia as an observer, order was restored. The unexpected appearance of three British nursing sisters enabled Boyle to set up a first-aid station in the railyards where many who had been injured by the air raids were treated.

The fortunate appearance of the nurses reminded Boyle that the British 92nd hospital battalion at Podhaytse was now in grave danger and that three other Britons, two of whom were surgeons, were even more seriously threatened in an outpost at Zeleschiki. These overworked people had been sent to Podhaytse and told to prepare its ninety-bed facilities to handle three hundred patients; more than 1,200 wounded had been brought in on the first day. Boyle's appeal to Locker-Lampson to try a rescue brought welcome news that most of the staff had been brought away, although four were missing, including the threesome at Zeleschiki. The rescue had been touch-and-go, for the nurses refused to leave until all the patients had been evacuated. This had left them with no transport, and they had resigned themselves to capture when Locker-Lampson's four armoured cars rolled up.

The fate of the Zeleschiki staff prompted Boyle to telegraph Manikovski asking him to institute a search along the entire army front. His fear was not so much that they would be captured by the Germans, but that they might fall in with the disorganized rabble of the defeated army. The armoured-car officers had described a dreadful scene at Boczacz where Russians had assaulted and raped two Russian nursing sisters in scenes of indescribable brutality. Reports from many sectors indicated that the defeated troops were looting, raping, burning, and pillaging as they fell back.

After four days of activity in Tarnopol, during which the main elements of seven Russian divisions managed to pass through the centre on the way to a new defensive line thrown up by four cavalry divisions some miles to the east, Boyle decided it was time to go. He could no longer communicate with the outside world and there was much to do yet in his search for assistance for the Russians.

The Boyle party moved out by road, but their vehicle broke down at Volochysk and it seemed for a moment as if they would be stranded. Boyle, utilizing documents provided by Stafka, persuaded railway officials there to give him a private car attached to a hospital train. He loaded it with refugee women and children and wounded soldiers, and travelled to Mogilev via Kiev, reaching Stafka on Monday, 23 July. Tarnopol fell quietly to the Germans on 24 July.

Kennalley, who had worked long hours under great pressure in the Tarnopol crisis, fell ill with dysentery immediately upon his return to the Bristol Hotel, but recovered in time to take his place with Boyle in front of the Stafka troops and the new commander-in-chief General Korniloff on 8 August. Members of the Allied military missions were also present as Boyle was presented with the Military Order of Stanislaus. Kennalley, because he was a civilian, was awarded the Order of Anna, the highest award a civilian could receive as a first decoration. The ceremony was symbolic in Kennalley's case because the new order, from which the czarist insignia had been removed, had not yet been sent to Stafka. Colonel Nevelskoie presented it to him some days later. These were the first decorations conferred by Korniloff in his position as supreme commander.

The amateur soldier from Canada had been blooded, and more to the point for him, had demonstrated that age is no criterion when it comes to deciding who is capable of being a soldier.

The postscript to all this came twenty-four months later when Boyle's baptism by fire became a breakfast table subject at Buckingham Palace. Among those present was Dudley Field Malone, American lawyer, diplomat, and writer who was among the first to urge western diplomatic recognition of the Soviet Union. Field recalled that King George V had remarked to Boyle that the fall of Tarnopol was a major disaster. Colonel Boyle agreed, but added, "Well, Your Majesty, it wasn't taken while I was there." And he had the Order of Stanislaus to prove the point.

SEVENTEEN

On the Raw Edge

Supreme Headquarters, Boyle discovered on his return from Galicia, may not have had much experience in treating with Triumph but it met that other imposter, Disaster, with admirable and even surprising equanimity. The military machine continued to function. Paper was shuffled as usual, orders went out to units that Boyle knew very well would never receive them because they had ceased to exist. There would be a parallel to this mindless performance in a Berlin bunker a quarter-century later.

In this relatively normal atmosphere Joe Boyle found sixteen days in which to catch up on his report drafting, his letter writing, and his sleep.

On 28 July Boyle was a delegate at a major transportation conference at Stafka; the following day he met General Tickminev in a long meeting, during which he indicated that his work on behalf of ACE would terminate with the writing of his final report. Tickminev was concerned. Why not stay on and serve with the Russians? he suggested. He would be specially assigned to investigate the transportation system at the eastern edge of Rumania, where more than one million Russian soldiers were penned up. Boyle's acceptance was

immediate. On 1 August he forwarded a five-page memorandum to the Russian General Staff, urging immediate action to
meet a disaster he felt was close at hand.

Russia today faces a situation so tragic and appalling, with her fate so
closely linked with that of the nations allied with her ... that any
disaster which befalls her must bring disaster to them; so as to
constitute her troubles their troubles, and to render it obligatory
upon them, entirely aside for any sympathy for Russia, to use their
utmost endeavour to assist her in every way.

With Russia ... entirely disorganized ... with all known rules of
procedure abolished, it is difficult to suggest a remedy, and impossible
to predict the results of any attempt at restoring order.

Just the same, he said, an effort had to be made, and the best
hope lay in a successful prosecution of the war. He urged the
formation at Stafka of a council of Allied nations to help
reorganize and retrain the Russian armies, and advise their
home governments on the needs and priorities of supplies for
Russia. The problem, he pointed out, was the prospect of
importing huge quantities of supplies without the rolling stock
to move them from ports as far distant at Vladivostok.

The country is full of idle men who, while now during the hot
months when food is comparatively easy to get ... constitute simply
a horde of idle, contented human beings [who] will, when cold
weather arrives ... develop into a horde of desperate, starving men.
... With the carefully-planned and splendidly-circulated propaganda
which the Germans have throughout this country, it is difficult to
predict the results, but it is safe to say they will be disastrous. Nothing
appears more necessary than the immediate provision ... of camps
at which these men can be organized and trained.

Boyle conceded that his advice might be presumptuous but said
that he was forwarding his memorandum to the heads of Allied
missions and was prepared for any criticism that might arise.

I personally feel we are on the raw edge of things and that, while carefully safeguarding the interests which we represent and taking the utmost care to neither commit nor embarrass our countries or their official representatives, it is compulsory upon all of us ... to exercise every bit of initiative, energy and ability ... which will be of service to the cause in which already so many sacrifices have been made.

He proposed a small executive committee of Allied representatives sitting in Petrograd to act as liaison with the war department and the government generally. He stressed that "I have not been in any way authorized by either the British mission at Stafka, the British embassy, or any other authority, to broach this subject—having conceived the idea and taken the liberty and responsibility ... upon my own initiative."

Boyle arrived in Petrograd on 9 August, just five days before the provisional government moved the former Czar and his family from their suburban Tsarskoe Selo palace. Some reports claim that Boyle met the fallen monarch in that brief period when it might have been possible, but the truth may never be known. The number of guards around the Romanovs had been sharply increased, and access to them made much more difficult. Romantic tales that Boyle made a secret visit with a plan to rescue the imprisoned royal family have been told from time to time. The Czar, such stories insist, turned him down. It all seems unlikely. The only evidence that Boyle visited the Czar was verbal, a story told to Boyle's daughter Flora many years later by Prince Peter Troubetskoy, an officer in the Russian diplomatic service and a member of one of the most ancient ducal houses of the nation.

Boyle always expressed a scornful dislike of the last Russian autocrat, but probably obtained his impression of the ex-ruler from Russian associates who had served at the imperial court. One reason for Boyle's dislike was the fact that he had learned that Nicholas was a chain smoker. In any event, if he did meet the Czar, Boyle never made any public record of the fact.

On his return to Petrograd's Hotel Europe one of the first things he did was to forward the power-of-attorney for Joe Junior, which had been requested by solicitor John Broad. In it the deponent proudly described himself as a miner of Dawson, Yukon Territory.

He inquired after the missing nurses and hospital staff from Zeleschiki and was happy to be informed that they had escaped by making their way to Kiev. The nursing staff from Podhaytse had reached Petrograd and Boyle enjoyed a reunion with them as they exchanged stories of their adventures. The meeting led him to ask General Manikovski to ensure that special attention be given to nursing staff, particularly the female workers. He urged that special rail cars be made available for their use and that they be provided with armed guards. His representations to the government led Kerensky to tender formal thanks to the 92nd hospital battalion staff.

In a separate letter he asked Manikovski to have the government authorize him to procure neutral vessels to move extra supplies to Russia. The Belgian Relief Committee, he noted, had been able to get assistance in this way from shipowners who refused to charter their ships to the British government, "feeling that there was more danger from submarines if they were directly under charter from any of the warring nations."

"In compliance with your request," Boyle provided Sir George Buchanan with a six-page résumé of his activities and findings. His transportation proposals, he told the ambassador, had been accepted by the Russian government and should release 300,000 horses from the front, provide more heavy locomotives and cars, improve the railway repair services, and free up to 300,000 men for more important work. It would also "provide the army with adequate means for its maintenance, which it evidently has never had."

He warned Buchanan that some recent events had aroused his suspicions about the activities of some members of the

American Stevens committee, due to leave Petrograd on 24 August:

From responsible sources I have gained a good deal of information from which it is quite evident that individual members ... have been, and are, endeavouring to procure control of the entire railway systems of the country for private American interests; at the same time getting concessions and privileges in this country.

Boyle named the American corporations as U.S. Steel; the J. P. Morgan interests; his old foes, the Guggenheims; and the Lewisohns. These Americans, Boyle charged, were trying to gain operating and tariff control of all the railways without any government control of freight or passenger rates. In addition, they had asked for concessions including checkerboard pattern areas of one square mile of land to a depth of two miles on each side of the four-thousand-mile trans-Siberian railway.

The exploiters, he added, had made some progress in obtaining the support of senior Russian officials. Their actions, Boyle complained, were

an absolute betrayal of their country and its president ... and nothing ... could be more inimical to British interests than a successful carrying through of their plans. I am also quite sure nothing could be more inimical to the interests of Russia.

Boyle suggested to the British ambassador that his country send General "Condahl" to look after British interests in the Murmansk and Archangel routes, in which he had found the Americans to be unusually interested. General de Candolle was a British engineer who had been working in South America. He had been placed in charge of the Rumanian railways, succeeding Norton Griffiths, whose raids on German-occupied oil fields in the Ploesti region had drawn warm praise in the British press and in Parliament only eight months earlier. De

Candolle's presence in Rumania worried Boyle, for the engineer had been given the rank of brigadier-general; Boyle intended to be the boss in that area.

When Buchanan asked what Britain could do, Boyle told him to immediately procure three sets of equipment for railway battalions and obtain all the machines and machine tools available in Britain for quick shipment to Russia. Britain, he continued, should drop a requirement that the Russian mission in London buy only from manufacturers for a policy of buying wherever stores were available.

The British, he warned, should not consider the situation eased by American promises to supply up to 800 locomotives and 10,000 rail cars by the end of the year, for that would not begin to meet a crisis in which Russia found itself short nearly 4,500 locomotives and 115,000 cars.

Inability to make repairs caused large quantities of rail equipment to lay idle. "Unless something is done to release some of this rolling stock and get a larger percentage in running order, this government will not be able to tide over the winter. . . ."

Boyle blamed German agents for the frequent shipment of useless cargoes that slowed up the movement of vital supplies. He alleged that the agents were bribing station agents and rail officials to fill cars with wood, fruit, and furniture, proof of which were advertisements in the Petrograd newspapers offering wood specifically stated to have been "delivered by rail."

Turning to the problems of the coming winter, which would pose great difficulties for the movement of Russian artillery, Boyle proposed heavy sleds, supplied by North America, and recommended that a small staff of Canadians experienced in making snow roads and in loading heavy sleds be attached to the artillery department of the Russian armies in the frostbitten north.

He did not conceal his suspicions about the American railway mission from the many Americans in the ACE, although he absolved Stevens of blame. His high opinion of the mission's leader declined sharply soon afterwards when he was told that Stevens had been advising the U.S. ambassador that the only salvation for Russia was the aid offered by U.S. capitalists. Boyle immediately sent a telegram to Nekrasov, totally disagreeing. "Russia," he said, "can only be saved by Russians and the best others can do is help."

As he neared his fiftieth birthday Joe Boyle was demonstrating the depths of his many qualities. It was clear that he was much more than a man of action and courage. Decisive, incisive, with the power to dissect problems and the ability to make up his mind what to do about them, he was becoming a superior adviser at levels to which he had never aspired, a confidant and adviser to leaders of the world's largest country. This amazing transition continued for some time as his understanding of the situation grew and his tireless, inquisitive mind focused on seemingly insurmountable problems and found possible solutions.

A few days before leaving on his Rumanian assignment he issued a stream of letters, articles, and memoranda, all written in his readable longhand for translation into the printed word on Kennalley's typewriter. At the request of Nekrasov he drafted a 1,500-word memorandum on transportation and food problems. He minced no words. Let the government take control of all the railways, regardless of private owners. Impose cargo quotas based on a scale of priorities, he urged. Co-ordinate supply and distribution by having community committees list the entire population of their areas in age groups. Compile data on food production and future crop prospects "to give the location of the entire population and the visible and prospective food supplies" to feed them. This, he said, would permit rational planning of transportation needs and proper utilization of surplus stocks.

He found time to advocate one of his pet projects, one that

persisted despite the swine fever that had ruined his own efforts in Canada: encouraging the raising of pigs in areas of moderate weather and good grain supplies.

One of Boyle's new confidants in Russia was Leslie Urquhart, an economist with long experience in Russia. Like Boyle, he was a member of ACE and had been on assignment in Petrograd as a consultant to both the Czarist government and its successor. Urquhart was returning to London and on 21 August Boyle gave him a letter of introduction to his friend, Secretary of Colonial Affairs Walter Long. He also wrote to Long, urging him to consult Urquhart, whose qualifications included working with Russian industries employing forty thousand men. Urquhart's experience, Boyle pointed out to Long, was with a firm that produced more than half the copper, lead, and zinc mined in Russia.

In a separate letter, marked private and personal, and of the same date, he raised the subject of his military rank:

A question has been raised with me by some of the officials here, which is very difficult for me to deal with. They expressed the opinion that the work which I have in hand is of such importance that it is altogether desirable that I should have a higher rank.

... A general here receives attention and homage from almost everybody, whereas they look with a certain amount of familiarity ... upon a colonel and raise questions they otherwise would not think of. The Russians ... have promoted to the rank of major-general almost everybody who is in any sense considered as the head of a department, regardless of size and the British have followed the same course in connection with their mission. ...

The promotion would help him in his work and cost Canada nothing, he added, since he was not asking for pay or allowances. Would the secretary, he asked, take up the matter with Sir Sam Hughes, or with Sir George Perley, who represented the Canadian government in London?

186

Boyle then turned his attention to assisting Kennalley's search for shipping. He wrote to Lieutenant-Colonel W. Grant Morden, a Canadian officer in London dealing with wartime shipping, and outlined the problems. Canadian help in finding additional shipping, in addition to assisting Russia, might pay big future dividends for Canada, he suggested.

Looking at it from a mercenary standpoint, I would say that nothing Canada or Canadians can do would be of more benefit to Canada as, when this war is over, Canada is going to be a manufacturing country, and whether she likes it or not, will have to get out and compete with other countries for foreign trade, and there is not going to be any sort of market in the world to compare with the Russian market.

Boyle said there was no objection in his mind to any Allied country doing all it could to help Russia now with future trade in mind as long as there was open, honest competition to which the Russians did not object and from which they would benefit. The only objectionable thing, he concluded, was aid contingent on a preferred status in postwar years.

He had those scheming Americans in mind. More evidence of Yankee machinations had come to his attention. Agents of U.S. Steel, he discovered, working through the National City Bank of Petrograd, were buying up in advance the 1918 Russian wheat crop by making advances on production to the peasants. U.S. Steel, he wrote, was concurrently trying to obtain postwar contracts to sell steel to the Russian government.

A later letter to Walter Long informed the colonial secretary that the Russian government had accepted Boyle's advice about equipment for three British railway battalions and would soon be making an official application for this help. He asked Long to advance the project as much as possible. Canada, he added, could help

by furnishing a few men to act as a staff for me in case I take a permanent position with the Russian general staff; and by furnishing a number of train dispatchers to help improve efficiency ... in the military zone.

If money was easy with me, I would not hesitate whether it was one man or a hundred and if Canada ... would furnish them on that basis and no other I would pay for them myself.

But Boyle, who had departed for Russia with little money of his own, had not been able to obtain financial help for obvious reasons. Payments from Dawson were not reaching him in the middle of Russia, and he was unaware of the plight into which his mining operations had fallen as his interests were challenged in the law courts on both sides of the Atlantic.

He asked Long to intercede with Canadian officials and request them to foot the bills for his plans but added, "if it cannot be arranged other than their being financed outside of the government, telegraph me and I will [somehow, he seemed to say] manage to finance them."

In the same post went a letter to General Turner at Canadian military headquarters in London, with a summary of his activities to date. Explaining that he was now attached to the Russian general staff and about to leave for Rumania, he asked to be provided with a suitable staff of Canadian assistants, pointing out that the suggestion had been approved by General Barter, British mission chief at Stafka. He asked, in particular, for Lieutenant-Colonel Frank A. Reid, four other officers, three railway construction men, and one really good train dispatcher, a complement of ten in all.

Saying that he would, if absolutely necessary, finance the project himself, he rather wistfully noted that the British and Americans had full military missions in Russia, and that the French, Belgians, and Italians had troop formations there, so "perhaps if you take the matter up with the government they might look favorably upon the question of financing, with a very small expense attached, and send a few men here."

Boyle had suggested to Long that as many as one hundred men might be needed, but he made no such demand on Turner. Clearly, he was planning to move in on the Canadian establishment committee in a series of siege parallels.

The flood of correspondence hardly waned. Russian winters still worried him, and he asked Colonel Barney Hepburn of the Canadian forestry service in Britain to send details of snow ploughs that could be used to keep those dusty Russian dirt roads open in the winter. The next day he was investigating the possibility of obtaining wooden ships and wrote Herbert Hoover, at 120 Broadway, New York City, that he was well and busy, and asked for data on U.S. designs.

ACE did well for its member in Russia. It sent plans and specifications of two types of wooden ships, and reported that the United States could build fifty such vessels, of 3,500 tons, in twenty-four months, at a cost of only $575,000 each.

Finally Boyle, all but written out, was off, heading for a brief halt at Stafka before departing for Rumania. The fate of that impoverished little kingdom seemed to haunt him, and the prospect that several million unfortunate civilians might starve to death was in his dreams. On 26 August, as he was leaving, a cable arrived from London. In it Purington told Boyle that he was sending three copies of a pamphlet by Robinson Smith. It was titled "Rationing a Population."

EIGHTEEN

The Only Way to Go

In Russia during the First World War the finest way to travel was by train, and railway cars, when properly fitted out, could be luxurious travelling hotels for the privileged, as Joe Boyle had discovered in his railway billet at Tarnopol.

His early movements had been made by automobile, and Russian roads were no worse, and no better, than those in the Yukon; but travel by train had more advantages. In one's own private railway car, such travel was even better. Boyle, now the special representative of Ways and Communications Minister Nekrasov, was entitled to such preferment and was quickly fitted out with his own private car, one he could have hitched to any train proceeding in the direction he wished to travel.

Certainly the assignment of his own railway car weighed much higher in his view than the political crisis brewing at Stafka. Even today there is no positive evidence of what was intended in the abortive move to use the army to take over unruly Petrograd. It was generally regarded as an attempt by the Supreme Commander, Lieutenant-General Lavr Georgyvich Korniloff, to become the supreme authority in the state.

This conclusion is hardly borne out by the facts, which had

Korniloff making an ill-advised, badly supplied, and poorly prepared cavalry raid on Petrograd with a few thousand none-too-loyal mounted soldiers. The whole show foundered at Tsarskoie Selo, an end as certain as any that could have been expected. Kerensky quickly labelled it an "abortive conspiracy" and an attempted coup d'état. But there is good ground to believe that Korniloff moved with Kerensky's approval and believed he was acting in conjunction with the new premier.

The venture collapsed, and on 28 August Kerensky announced that he would personally assume command of the army, with General M. V. Alekseev as his chief of staff. The Bolsheviks made a propaganda victory out of the fiasco, and their histories say it was the resolute opposition of the workers and the soviets that crushed the revolt, and that it had been assisted by British soldiers in Russian uniforms using British armoured cars.

It all seems to have had little to do with Klondike Joe Boyle, who was wise enough to stay away from the army politicians. He said later that he was not at Stafka when the coup was attempted. Clearly he was mistaken, but his retrospective look may be explained by the fact that Korniloff was not replaced until 14 September, some five days after Boyle had departed on his first journey to Rumania.

The comparative luxury of his own railway car, with his own interpreter and servants, permitted him to relax while travelling. It is not certain who his interpreter was on this occasion, although it may well have been Colonel Nevelskoie. Within the next couple of months Boyle was able to assemble a small corps of interpreter-aides, including Lieutenant-Colonel Dmitri Tzegintzov, an officer of an Imperial Guards regiment at the Russian court; Prince Peter Troubetskoy from the Russian foreign service; Staff Captains Poritchinski and Count Tolstoi; and a Captain Galavin of the First Smolensk Guards Regiment. It was an impressive assembly, indicative of Boyle's stature in the eyes of both the army leaders and the government officials.

Proceeding by way of Kiev and Odessa, Joe Boyle reached Jassy on 12 September, after a halt to meet railway officials in Odessa and take public issue with the Stevens-Francis claims about the role of U.S. capitalism in the salvation of Russia, a subject that so aroused him that he gave a special, and rare, interview to reporters in Odessa.

A day in Jassy interviewing railway officials did little to remove his apprehension about the future of railway operations and the salvation of the Russian and Allied cause in that part of the world. Following the frustrating talk he sat down and wrote himself a long memorandum under the heading "Information Required," a document indicating that he would undertake a very exhaustive study of the unholy mess.

His preparations were thorough, but despite them the tour began disastrously. Boyle had arranged to meet General de Candolle at the important junction of Sokola. He arrived on time, but the British engineer-officer was late, which gave Boyle time to look around de Candolle's territory. Boyle found the rail lines in chaos. No traffic was moving, he wrote in his report, "because of a failure of foodstuffs to arrive from Russia—reasons therefor not known."

An all-pervading air of slackness and incompetence held sway. Boyle was angered, told de Candolle so, and said the British commander could not escape responsibility for it. A roaring argument followed in which Boyle blistered the ears of his military superior. Although humiliated, de Candolle made no official complaint, probably because the case would not stand investigation. But he did mention privately, along the old-boy network, how difficult this upstart colonial and military inferior had been, painting him as a troublesome interloper who would require future attention.

Without mentioning de Candolle by name Boyle, for his part, filed a highly critical report of his findings. Various departments, he noted, worked without any liaison; train schedules were ignored; and thanks to repair shop inefficiency, loaded trains sat idle for hours for lack of an engine to move them. This absence of planning and concern multiplied the discomforts of the wounded in the overcrowded hospital trains.

Boyle did more than write. He found damaged lines and insisted that they be repaired at once. He personally ordered up 15,000 cubic metres of fill to make usable a particularly bad stretch between Unghari and Bel'tsy. Imperiously he enforced a new scale of traffic priorities in which the movement of food came first, transfer of wounded second, and the forwarding of military stores and equipment third. There was no time for the niceties of consultation. Boyle gave the orders and the Russians and Rumanians, seemingly overawed by his presence, ceased their quarrelling and name-calling and sprang into action. And de Candolle never forgave this mortal insult.

Boyle had discovered 120 cars at Sokola Junction alone which had become a small village of the idle, and when he was told that rolling stock was in short supply, he replied, "Throw out those refugees using rail cars as home."

Scribbling on both sides of some old typing paper, he sent a message to Rumanian Interior Minister M. Constantinescu—a man he hadn't heard of until a few hours earlier—and started making recommendations and demanding action. Ask Russia for permission to select and purchase supplies in Russia, he urged. Let the Russians advance money for payment, and transport the supplies to Rumania on terms identical with the repayment provisions of the Russian Liberty Loan, he suggested. (He had anticipated lend-lease by a full quarter-century.) Find out where the food and supplies lay by polling the some five thousand Singer Sewing Machine Company agents scattered across Russia.

His thoughts now were on Rumania, but he hadn't forgotten his Russian employers. "Get a lake cargo steamer capable of running a cargo from an Eastern Canadian port to Archangel," he cabled Morden in London. He pleaded with I. W. Dudley, in Seattle, to find ships to haul cargo from Vancouver to

Vladivostok, and he specified Russian-Rumanian needs for massive numbers of tractors, clothing, underwear, socks, boots, and other wearing apparel.

Some of his efforts were beginning to bear fruit. Acting Railways Minister Liverosky wrote from Petrograd that the government had approved Boyle's plan for regulating rail traffic and had placed orders with British suppliers for telephonic equipment.

After a full week spent along the waterfront, it was time for him to return to Stafka, for he could accomplish more there than out in the remoteness of a front all-but-abandoned to its fate. The Rumanians pressed him to stay on. They finally yielded to his decision, but urged him to return as soon as possible, receiving as a parting gift their new friend's promise to try and find four light-draft steamers to increase the volume of waterborne freight on the Ismael-Lake Yalpool route in the Danube River delta.

Convinced by his Rumanian visit that his new assignment would be an important, long-term mission, Boyle returned to the Russian headquarters to step up his campaign for Canadian reinforcements. Now he asked for fourteen men, once more seeking Colonel Reid as an aide. His appeal was directed to General Turner, Walter Long, and Colonel Morden. To the last-named he wrote, "in case the question of finance looks like causing delay, advance amount necessary to cover, drawing on me at Dawson for the amount."

He quickly reached an understanding with General Rattell of the Russian General Staff for his own full attachment to Russian headquarters and agreement that all Canadian personnel loaned to Russia would be accredited to, and under the command of, Joe Boyle, their salaries paid by Canada (or failing that, by Boyle), and all other expenses met by Russia. Canada and Britain hadn't cared to use him, but the Russians leaped at the opportunity.

It was a period of great excitement and rising optimism for

Boyle. He made plans for the arrival, by early December at the latest, of his own special contingent, which would form the skeleton around which three railway battalions, organized and equipped on Anglo-Canadian lines, would be established.

His exuberance was tempered somewhat by a letter from faithful John Kennalley, who reported from London that Boyle's solicitor saw trouble ahead in the courts. Solicitor Broad urged Boyle to leave at once for the Yukon and prepare to defend himself and his property against a Granville assault that was shaping up as a fight to the finish. Broad said he doubted that the Yukon holdings could be touched before 1 December, just about the time Boyle hoped to welcome those long-awaited Canadian reinforcements he had been pleading so hard to get. There was never any doubt what his choice would be. The Yukon would have to wait.

As for those supplies Boyle had been requesting, none had been sent because, Kennalley pointed out, the Russian government had neglected to make the promised formal request for aid. ACE had found a three-thousand-ton ship available for charter, and supplies to fill it, when the shipment was applied for and approved. Boyle's achievements had so impressed his ACE associates that they had set up a special sub-committee to deal directly with his pleas for aid to Rumania.

In a separate letter Kennalley told of a strange interview with Lord Leitrim, private secretary to Walter Long,

who seemed *most* interested in the circumstances surrounding your going to Russia. At first he did not understand the exact circumstances under which you went, but when I explained . . . he seemed quite satisfied.

Leitrim said Long had spoken with someone about Boyle's promotion, but gave no details.

In the Boyle records there is a yellowing page of notepaper with the British Embassy seal, identified as the copy of a letter. It reads:

General Headquarters,
Russian Army,
27th September, 1917

I certify that Lieut Colonel J. W. Boyle, Canadian militia, is at present
employed by the Russian Government in the administration of
railways, and that his services cannot be spared at the present
moment from the urgent and important duties on which he is
engaged.

C. Barter
Lieut-General

Chief of the British Military Mission
with the Russian Armies in the Field

This document, it is now possible to discern, was the decisive
counter in defeating a behind-the-scenes attempt to remove
Joe Boyle from his advisory post to the Russian government, a
protracted bit of scheming that began with the 2 July query
from Petrograd to Ottawa, via Whitehall, about Boyle's status.
Lord Leitrim's odd cross-examination of Kennalley indicated
that official curiosity had not been allayed by Boyle's studious
reporting to the British ambassador in Petrograd.

As Whitehall saw it, this unauthorized intruder was playing
a role well beyond that of transportation specialist. He was
dealing with Russian and Rumanian ministers directly—and
very firmly—and even presuming to give advice to British
diplomats, as well as importuning his own countrymen with
ridiculous suggestions. Imagine: Boyle was seeking charter
shipping beyond the control of the shipping board, making
attempts to obtain scarce industrial supplies, and asking for
millions in extra aid outside approved allocations—almost in
defiance of them. The powers-that-be decided that something
had to be done.

Boyle's reports to Long, passed along the official chain of

command, rang alarm bells in the Foreign Office when it realized that the unknown Canadian was directly assisting the Russian ministry of ways and communications without the benefit of FO direction. This same upstart was in virtual control of the military zone railways from Petrograd to Odessa.

And it is a sure bet that de Candolle's unofficial bleatings had been heard. At the War Office a Major Casgrain wrote to Canadian headquarters that the Foreign Office considered Boyle's presence in Russia "a source of embarrassment." The War Office, for its part, he added,

recommend that Col. Boyle be called to London to state his views. Mr. Balfour is of the opinion that Colonel Boyle should either be placed under the orders of Gen. de Candolle, the railway expert sent to Russia by the War Office, or recalled.

Casgrain's letter is dated 29 September, but General Barter's letter is dated 27 September. Obviously the reaction anticipated the event. Barter, it is clear, was aware of what was coming and determined to prevent this unfair action towards a man he had come to admire.

The puzzle found no solution in Ottawa. Canadian officials there, and in London, considered the problem, then replied that since Boyle was not on active service, and not a member of the overseas forces or subject to their discipline, the only official who could order him home was the minister of militia. The War Office, the Canadians cannily suggested, might prefer to ask him to return voluntarily to ascertain the importance of his work and how his status might be regularized. It was a pretty game of "dodge 'em." Whitehall ignored the sly suggestion. It did not wish to involve the militia minister, it replied, and thought the invitation to return ought to come from General Turner. That's where the game ended, without resolution. Boyle, the old boxer, had escaped without their landing a blow.

Barter, impressed by one of Boyle's reports on the food and transportation crises, was moved to append his own brief memo, expanding on several points that had impressed him. Boyle, in that report, had noted that the peasants were hiding their grain, some in fear of future shortages, some to wait for higher prices, but far too many to use the grain in the manufacture of raw vodka, worth forty roubles per pood (a thirty-six-pound measure) compared to the much lower price offered for food grain. The government was reluctant to appropriate grain for fear of a vast peasant reaction.

Boyle, as his correspondence shows, was also trying to clothe the ragged Rumanian regiments. He appealed to Morden in London, to an old friend Alfred Thompson, MP, in Ottawa, and to others for uniforms, underwear, shirts, socks, boots, and greatcoats to equip 200,000 men, and urged shipments to Archangel within a month in view of the dire distress. He also appealed for desperately needed hospital, medical, and surgical supplies, condensed milk, rice, beef extracts, sugar, civilian clothes. It was all very noble—and all very hopeless, for the key to the solution lay in Petrograd and nothing, it seemed, could move the moribund Kerensky government. Back in London a despairing Andreav contemplated the prospect that nothing could be shipped to Boyle before February 1918, because of Petrograd's inertia.

Boyle's prime interest on a second dash to Rumania was to find a solution to the looming food shortage that threatened starvation for several million Rumanians in the rapidly approaching winter. The situation was exacerbated by the presence of more than a million sullen Russian soldiers who had fought as Rumanian allies and were now camped in Bessarabia and the rump of Rumania. Their presence helped keep away the Germans, but it imposed a problem of feeding the idle visitors, who were each consuming two pounds of bread daily, and whatever else could be begged, borrowed, or stolen. The Russians hadn't produced a pound of food for themselves in weeks, and now faced the prospect of starving together with their unfriendly hosts.

Boyle had found a couple of new companions, one of them

Lieutenant Count Beakendorf, the other Lieutenant R. A. Porters, a junior member of the British mission in Mogilev. They enjoyed a speedy run to Odessa where they parked Boyle's private car on a siding and boarded a small destroyer for a voyage up the Danube to Ismael and Lake Yalpool. They completed their journey to Jassy by train from the head of the lake. It was a useful journey, giving Boyle some idea of what was needed to maintain the water-borne transport in the area and how it could more efficiently be tied in with the railways. He returned to Stafka in a good mood.

There he was immediately brought up short. Waiting for him was a cable from Dawson telling him to return to London without delay. His first inclination was to go; he got so far as to reply, "If anything crucial hinges upon my being personally present can manage two weeks leave in London in December." But it was a momentary idea, for the same post brought a letter from Kennalley that General Turner had agreed to second Colonel Reid to Boyle if the Russians made a formal request. Now it looked as if Reid would soon be on his way and, with him to help, the work in Russia and Rumania could be advanced. Boyle had little hope of a reply from Dawson in order to apply for December leave. He was willing, but his heart was elsewhere, and his sudden return to Odessa en route to Jassy indicated his real feelings. He had stayed only a day at Stafka.

Before leaving he sent a cable to Reid urging him to pick nothing but first-class men for the Russian assignment. "It is a big job," he cabled, "and wants live men with both ability and experience. Our best are none too good to send to Russia at this juncture." He notified Kennalley he now would be asking for three additional loggers and four railwaymen, a total of twenty-one, with his original request included. With this he left Stafka.

Suddenly, within a day, he was back, to the astonishment of his Russian superiors and the British military mission members. A letter he sent to Sir George Barclay, British ambassador in Jassy, on 14 October, explains the strange behaviour. Reports of the War Office attitude towards Boyle, and of his quarrel with de Candolle, had reached Barclay, who notified the Rumanians that the British embassy "disassociated" itself from Boyle. The alarmed Rumanians dispatched a message, which had reached him at Odessa, that they could no longer use his services.

After long and thoughtful consideration Boyle wrote a measured, temperate letter to Barclay. He repressed any inclination to righteous anger, and showed that he could be a diplomat as well as a leader.

My position vis-a-vis your government, insofar as my work in Russia is concerned, is that I am a born British subject doing my best to help win this war and as such assumed that I was entitled to the assistance of its representatives and agents, all of whom are, presumably, at the present moment engaged in the same occupation.

In Russia I have received the most courteous and considerate treatment, and every possible assistance from the British minister at Petrograd, the British military mission here, and from General Poole's office in Petrograd.

I have not had any dealings with any other British agents except General de Candolle of whom I cannot speak so highly, but as I have no sort of connection with either himself or his mission I have naturally treated the matter as entirely personal and attached no importance to it.

It is, I think, unfortunate that your attitude in informing them that you had to "disassociate" yourself from my sphere of activities has frightened the Rumanian government into refusing to accept the help offered them, and which my position enabled me to render, and I only hope that the assistance they are accepting along the same lines may be effective and sufficient.

I cannot, of course, under the circumstances make any further overtures but should the assistance they have arranged for fail and an opportunity occur for me to assist them, and you can without embarrassing yourself convey to them my desire, I will upon request from them do anything in my power to help.

I am pleased to be able to inform you that all of the works advised by me in connection with the lines of transport leading to Rumania has [sic] been adopted and there is now no danger of any famine there on account of the lack of transport.

It was a reasonable reaction, and it enabled Boyle to regain the regard of the ambassador, who was able to have the Rumanians recall Boyle without loss of face when the tempest died down.

If for the moment the Rumanians didn't want Joe Boyle, it pleased him to find that the Russians had no such inhibitions. General Rattell and Engineer Lebedev added their support to his stepped-up efforts to get a Canadian contingent to Russia. Boyle used their recommendations to request Manikovski to put pressure on the Kerensky government to make the long-delayed formal request for the men.

Boyle now was dealing with yet another commander-in-chief, General Nikolai N. Dukhonin, who had assumed command after Kerensky had relinquished his foolish temporary occupation of the position. Boyle provided the new man with an account of his work and the situation as he saw it, in a report dated 14 October. It was a faithful and generally optimistic assessment of the new lines built, old lines reconstructed with increased capacity, and plans to step up water transportation on the Danube and Lake Yalpool by several hundred tons daily.

Perhaps to indicate the way things had been going, Boyle used a separate memorandum to speak of a 29 September conference with the Franco-Rumanian mission,* headed by the Marquis de Belvis, at which the Russian supply bureau chief, a

---

*Rumania had long been considered as part of the French sphere of influence.

201

civilian named Gorbel, had been forced to apologize for lack of instructions since he had consulted Petrograd and received no reply. Boyle stressed that no decisions had been reached about food supplies because a Rumanian ministerial mission, following his advice, had gone to Petrograd to negotiate Rumanian food purchases in Russia. They held, as an ace in the hole, an agreement made by the Russians with the Rumanians permitting these negotiations, dated April 1917.

These reports, translated by Rattell's staff, were forwarded to Dukhonin, who had them endorsed by Kerensky during a chance visit by the harassed provisional government leader on 10 October, when he was attempting to recover from a physical and emotional collapse which, Kerensky later wrote, "kept me in a critical condition for several days." This emotional explosion, Kerensky claimed, was brought about by the "flood of lies and slander" launched by the Bolsheviks. Dukhonin, he conceded, had brought him to his senses, but the ultimate fate of the Kerensky government becomes more understandable in the light of the mental condition of its prime figure.

Boyle sensed a hiatus; little seemed to be moving. Kennalley cabled that the Russian committee in London was still waiting for Petrograd to act. There was no report on Boyle's promotion. "Long and Morden would like to assist you," Kennalley reported, "but state this must be done officially as they cannot approach authorities. If Russian or British suggest, believe such action would be taken. . . ."

Promotion, Boyle realized, was unlikely. He had little hope that the British would recommend it after the de Candolle incident, and the Russians, who might have done so, had become incapable of any action, large or small.

The disheartening signs that the Provisional Government was about to drown in the ocean of its ineptitude did not discourage its friends. In mid-October the ACE members confirmed that they had located six Studebaker power sleds in Siberia and that they could purchase all of them for a token

£200. Purington cabled that the list of needed parts for railway repairs had been met and the material, which weighed twelve thousand pounds and had cost £105,000, was ready for shipment. But once again was the rider: "the committee here cannot move without authorization of Petrograd which has not been given."

October was a mournful month, an autumn of despair, and even the redoubtable Joe Boyle felt the weight of it all. Probably the best thing that happened to him was his meeting with Lieutenant George A. Hill, late of the 4th Manchesters and the Royal Flying Corps, who had been recruited for British army intelligence in Salonika, ostensibly as a staff officer, but in fact as a field-appointed agent of the British Secret Service. Hill, the son of a British businessman, had been born and raised in Russia and spoke the language fluently.

He met Boyle under dramatic circumstances. Like Boyle he was residing in the Bristol Hotel, where many foreign officers at Stafka were quartered. His secret duties included surveillance of suspected German agents at Mogilev, and Hill had aroused suspicions of his real role among those he was watching. One night, as he returned to the hotel during October's shortening twilight, he was savagely attacked. Although he appeared weaponless he was armed with a sword concealed in a walking stick. He quickly drew the thin blade, mortally wounded his assailant, and stumbled into the Bristol, bloody and shaken. There he almost fell into the arms of a large man wearing a British-type uniform who seemed more amused than dismayed. In the explanations that followed, I-K 8 (Hill's secret service code number) began a friendship with the Canadian that had important results for both of them.

It was a highlight in the life of George Hill, who would be a brigadier in the British Army in the Second World War, stationed in Russia once more, but who never forgot the comrade he had made that October night in 1917. Joe Boyle, he wrote twenty years later, was a born fighter, and blessed with exceptional common sense. He was independent to a revolutionary extent. Etiquette and procedure meant nothing to him, especially if a job had to be done.

He was in Russia to get on with the war, to harry the Germans and help the Allies, and in so doing he cared not over whom he rode roughshod. Such was Col. Boyle, a man whose equal I have encountered neither before nor since, and to have enjoyed his friendship, and to have worked under and with him, will always remain one of the proudest memories of my life.

Joe Boyle would have understood those words from his new friend, and he would have cherished them.

❧ NINETEEN ❧

The Moscow Knot

The record shows that in Russia's dramatic years of 1917-18 Joe Boyle was a long-standing prophet of catastrophe. However, when it descended he was no more successful in detecting the event, or its direction and impact, than the most optimistic officers at Stafka.

It was only after a trip to a transportation conference on 30 October that Boyle suddenly realized the climax was at hand. It was a fear that crystallized the evening after his return to Stafka from Kiev, when an agitated George Hill told him of a report that a mass meeting of military units had been called. They had been inspired, Hill insisted, by German agitators. The intent was to provoke demands for the expulsion of all Allied military missions. The meeting, Hill added, was due to start almost at once and he asked whether Boyle would attend the gathering and address the assembly, if possible. Hill agreed to act as his interpreter. He felt that the remarkable Canadian might have some influence since he was well-known at the Russian headquarters by this time.

Boyle's presence was greeted with suspicion by the meeting organizer, and the chairman was unwilling to let his unexpected guest take a bow. But this was no tame audience and when it began to react uneasily, someone suggested that a vote be taken. Boyle believed in democracy, but only up to a point in such a situation. Sensing that the meeting organizers would make sure he would be rejected, he strode brusquely past the men on the platform, seized centre stage, and began to speak in the clear, incisive voice that had impressed so many meetings in so many other places.

Hill, fearing the worst, courageously joined his friend in front of the unruly audience and began to translate. It was a faithful rendition, but as Boyle's emotional words poured out there were times when no translation seemed needed. Oratory delivered with passion and conviction eliminated the boundaries of race and tongue. The Russians, Hill commented, quietened and listened.

Boyle knew crowd psychology. He gripped the attention of his hearers. He began with stories about Canada. Then he switched into Russian history. The speech did not last more than 15 minutes and concluded with a stirring peroration in which he reminded his listeners that Russians never surrendered. They might retreat into Russia as they did during Napoleon's invasion, but it was only to attack with renewed vigor.

"You are men, not sheep," he concluded. "I order you to act as men." Thunders of applause followed. A soldier jumped up on the stage and shouted "Long Live the Allies" and "Down With the Germans." The ovation continued for some minutes. Finally Boyle and I were escorted by the mob to the hotel and an enthusiastic demonstration in favor of the Allied military missions was held, which was addressed by several of the Allied generals in turn.

Boyle's oratory had calmed the Stafka rank and file, but it may have lulled the Allied missions, for they did not become aware of the final disintegration in Petrograd until the night of 6 November, when General Dukhonin was warned by telegram that the Bolsheviks were carrying out systematic seizures of vital government buildings in the capital and making widespread arrests. News that the Cossacks had refused to leave their barracks to fight the uprising suggested that the government was irretrievably lost.

When Kerensky left Petrograd on 7 November to seek military assistance among units that might still be loyal, Joe Boyle, finally understanding what had happned, was on his way to Petrograd in his private railway car. He had only to look around and note the mob of undisciplined soldiery sitting on the roof, and hanging onto the sides of the car, to realize that Kerensky would find no help outside the capital. At Boyle's request, General Barter assigned Hill to accompany him, the first of a series of journeys they would take together across days and months of history-making in the world's greatest national upheaval.

At Orsha Junction, fifty miles from Mogilev, Boyle's car was detached and shunted onto a siding to await a Moscow-Petrograd train to which they could link up. The switch was made clumsily, at a high rate of speed that propelled Boyle's car into the buffers with a tremendous crash and damaged it so seriously that it was unusable. Boyle, convinced this was no accident, ran to the engine driver and knocked him stiff with a right-hand punch to the jaw. It was a sharp transition from riding in comfort and privacy to hauling their luggage aboard an overcrowded train, fighting their way into seats in which to conclude an uncomfortable journey to the scene of the ten days that shook the world.

A realist in most things, Boyle understood that Kerensky was finished and that it was time to take a look at his successors. Upon reaching Petrograd, he carefully donned full regimentals and buckled on his sword and marched down to the Smolny Institute to seek out the leaders of the October Revolution. As it had done so many times, boldness won the day. Boyle was quickly provided with a pass admitting him to both the Smolny and the Tauride Palace, the two nerve centres of the uprising. This important piece of paper gave him "right of free entrance" until 18 November.

Boyle and Hill were amazed by the apparent lack of security. They noted people wandering around unchecked, peering into ministerial offices, listening to conferences, and acting as if they were summer visitors touring a national edifice. For this brief period the Bolsheviks appeared to believe that they could conduct a government with a complete "open door" policy, a unique feature of the Revolution that soon vanished with experience.

After some patient questioning by Hill the two uniformed visitors were directed to the office of the Petrograd Revolutionary Committee President, Comrade A. Joffe. He received them with courteous interest and assured them that the new government was anxious to retain Boyle's services, of which they had received good reports, and hoped he would not only agree to maintain supplies to the southwestern front but would take time to deal with some problems closer to the capital. Joffe explained that a monumental rail traffic jam had closed all the lines around Moscow and created a chaotic situation at Moscow Junction. Would Boyle see what he could do about it? he asked, for it was threatening the supply of food to both Moscow and Petrograd.

Untying the Moscow Knot was a challenge Boyle was eager to accept. He moved quickly to prepare for the new assignment while completing a series of visits to other leaders of the new government. In the next several days he met and talked with Podvoisky, the new war minister; Antonov-Ovsenko, a future war and navy commissar and a fighting leader of the movement; Karahan, of foreign affairs; and finally, Lenin himself. All these meetings reinforced the assurances that his work would continue as in the past, that Russia still needed him, and provided proof that the new masters were men of action, in contrast to the procrastinating officials of the Kerensky government.

The Bolsheviks, practical men in an hysterical situation, were prepared to employ anyone who could help them. They felt sure Boyle could do so, and provided him with a fistful of passes and various authorizations that would permit him to go anywhere and take whatever action he felt necessary. One such "assurance" signed by Joffe and Djerjinsky read:

The War Revolutionary Committee of the Petrograd Soviet of Workers and Soldiers Deputies hereby assure that Colonel Boyle of the English service will continue to be at the Russian government's service until the final forming of the next war office.

The important Moscow assignment drew special documents. These sternly worded papers read, in part:

One puts no obstacles for free departure of Colonel Boyle of English service from Petrograd to Moscow. Immediately after his arrival the commander of the place must let the war staff at the Petrograd district know about it.

In his conversations at the time, and for a period afterwards, Boyle appeared to have been favourably disposed toward the new government. He had been told much about the rottenness of the Czarist regime and had too much knowledge of the ineptness of the Kerensky government to view the change in command as anything but a good one. It was not until he realized that the Bolsheviks intended to take Russia out of the war, and had seen for himself the brutality and horrors of the revolution, that this opinion was replaced by an unrelenting opposition to Bolshevism.

Heartened by his interviews, Boyle on 8 November sent a cable to General Turner asking the Canadians to send not 21, but 125 men to fill a new establishment, apparently drawn up after the 30 October Kiev conference. The group should include 22 interpreters, 10 of them officers. He may have stunned Turner but he had impressed the Bolsheviks, who immediately filed a formal request for the reinforcements.

Possibly at some risk to his own position, Boyle was able to do a good turn for a Russian friend. When the Bolsheviks complained that they could not quite see how they were going to be able to run things, Boyle boldly told them they could solve many of their problems by releasing General Manikovski from the prison cell into which they had tossed him. Surprised, delighted, and shaken by this turn in fortune's wheel, Manikovski found himself back in his old office, working for the new government, one of the first of thirty thousand former Imperial Army officers who would serve the Bolsheviks. They preferred to think of it as serving timeless Russia in a new aspect.

Two years later, Boyle explained his Moscow assignment to General Turner in these terms:

The Russian Northern and Western armies were very short of food and owing to the street fighting in Moscow ... during which no trains left Moscow at all, there was a freight blockade and Moscow itself was starving. The Bolsheviks were in a hopeless state of disorder and had no one to handle the situation.

Fighting was continuing when Boyle and Hill reached Moscow, and it would be some time before the Bolsheviks eliminated the small but determined anti-Bolshevik forces in the first manifestation of the coming general civil war. The sound of firing was a backdrop for Boyle's meeting in the offices of the Central Railway Board with N. Muralov, an enterprising individual who had been taking part in the fighting and was to become commander of the entire district. He estimated his forces at fifty thousand men, and the Cadet opposition at about ten thousand, mostly officers, students, and volunteers. Though badly outnumbered, the Junkers, as the Reds called them, fought desperately. It took ten days to capture the Kremlin and other White strongpoints.

Muralov had fifty thousand men, but not a Boyle among them, and he welcomed the big Canadian with enthusiasm and gave him full authority over all the rail lines in the region. The extent of his support was made evident within a few hours when some drivers and labourers refused to obey Boyle's orders. Muralov posted an order that all would be ready for work at seven the next morning; otherwise six would be selected by lot and executed on the spot.

Boyle not only gave orders, he showed how they should be carried out. Here, and elsewhere, he doffed his tunic and swung a pick with the strongest. Looking back over the years, Dmitri Tsevgintsov, who was to become his right-hand man, would tell of Boyle's great pleasure in getting down on the right-of-way and swinging tools in the middle of work gangs. Russian labourers were bewildered. It was unheard of for an officer to dirty his hands, but this strange foreigner actually seemed to enjoy proving he was a better man than any of them.

Boyle seemed to sense that the pace was slackening and would take steps to improve it. Upon occasion he would climb onto the roof of a railway car, placing interpreters at the four corners, and encourage the work gangs with praise, jokes, cheers, and song. From this elevation he would get them swinging picks and moving shovels in time to the beat of his hands and the measure of his songs. The vocalizing was purely North American and it is unlikely they understood a single word.

One of the Bear Creek gold camp favourites came roaring down the wintry wind, and listeners who heard him remembered that the words went something like this:

Yah, the boss was a fine man, all aroun'
But he married a great big, fat, far down.
She baked his bread, and she baked it—well
She baked it harder than the hubs of Hell
So drill, ye terriers, drill.

Muralov's grim threats and Boyle's inspirational exhortations permitted the untying of the Moscow Knot in a mere forty-eight hours of almost ceaseless labour. Boyle speeded the process with methods that might have called for a government inquiry in peaceful times. Where it was impossible to move the cars, they were levered over embankments to clear the right-of-way. Empty cars were deadheaded at high speed off the end of sidings into open fields. Railway officials were aghast. Railway owners were appalled, and some would have occasion to remember, in the safe haven of New York, how Klondike Boyle had ruined them financially on behalf of the Bolshies. Muralov and his associates were delighted as food trains moved into Moscow, forward to the armies, and north to the capital. Joe Boyle, thinking of the hundreds of thousands of Germans still engaged on the Russian front, felt doubly pleased that their opposition would not succumb to starvation.

Boyle and Hill left Moscow on 15 November, after watching a mass funeral of more than five hundred Bolsheviks killed in the fighting for the city. Thousands of Muscovites escorted these first "heroes" of the Revolution to their final resting place, a single grave near the Kremlin Wall.

Other foreign spectators on that day included John Reed and his wife Louise Bryant, the U.S. radicals who had made cause with the Bolsheviks. Reed wrote the monumental *Ten Days That Shook the World* and was fated to die in Russia of typhus a few years later. There is no record that capitalist Boyle and communist Reed ever met. It would have been quite a collision.

Three days later, back at Stafka, Boyle had to report the loss of his private car, wrecked at Orsha. The response was gratifying. He was invited to take possession of a very handsome replacement, Car No. 451. It was no ordinary coach, for it had been the private residence of the Dowager Empress Mother Marie Feodorovna, who had lived at Mogilev through the final months of her son Nicholas's playing at soldier as commander-in-chief. In this car she had said a terrible farewell to him as he left to make his decision to abdicate. Marie, stricken, had gone to live in semi-exile in the Crimea.

An official document recorded Boyle's temporary ownership: "This is to certify that railway car No. 451 was allotted on Nov. 4 (O.S.) to Canadian Military Transport Mission under the command of Col. Boyle of the Canadian service for a journey to Moscow." Boyle found more than a small satisfaction in the wording of the document. It was the first time that anyone in authority had acknowledged, on paper, that he was a Canadian officer. It was enough for him to be able to overlook the fact that he was not, unhappily, "in the Canadian service."

This luxurious vehicle, with its bullet-proof steel walls, contained a dining room observation lounge, a combined stateroom and bed sitting room, five double-berth sleeping compartments, a small kitchen, a heating plant, an electric generator, and a lavatory. Not the least of its advantages was the presence of a long-time former Romanov retainer, competent and fiercely proud Ivan, an attendant with few peers. Riding in baronial splendour, Boyle and Hill, now his permanent companion, rode safely and comfortably back to Petrograd, a small island of contentment in a sea of trouble.

There was good news for them in the capital. The Rumanians once more were requesting his assistance. Their delegation to the Soviets, waving the April agreement, had reached a satisfactory deal to purchase food and supplies in Russia on almost the identical terms suggested by Boyle's original recommendation. Clearly, this was a man to heed. On 25 November Count Di'Amandi, the Rumanian ambassador in Petrograd, signed papers commissioning Boyle—once more referred to as a member of the Canadian Army—"to procure supplies and equipment" for the Rumanian population.

At this moment in history the Bolsheviks were still prepared to accept obligations incurred by the provisional government. They would soon repudiate all such arrangements; but for the time vital to Rumania's survival in a critical winter they had recognized the moral as well as written requirement to provide food for a Rumania going hungry largely because of the presence of a large Russian army. After a full week of shopping for Rumania in various centres in central White Russia, Boyle turned Car 451 towards Mogilev, and arrived in time to become a spectator at a traumatic event.

When the Bolsheviks took over the government it seemed unlikely that General Dukhonin would be permitted to remain as army commander-in-chief, for he was a mild, soldierly leader who had remained aloof from politics as much as possible. His inevitable displacement was signalled on the night of 22 November when Lenin and Stalin conducted a telegraph conference with Dukhonin, ordering him to open peace negotiations with the Central Powers. Dukhonin refused, and the following day felt his position was reinforced when the heads of military missions at Stafka reminded him of Russia's agreement with the Allies never to make a separate peace. This was one earlier decision the Bolsheviks were not willing to recognize, but it might have been politically more acceptable for them, at a time when their power was far from consolidated, to have the army make the first overtures for peace.

War Minister Trotsky promptly accused the Allied missions of interfering in Russia's internal affairs in the hope of provoking a civil war. The council of commissars, Lenin's cabinet, announced that it would not be bound by any Czarist agreements. They dismissed General Dukhonin and appointed a former sailor, N. V. Krilenko, as commander-in-chief with instructions to open negotiations without delay.

As Boyle sped towards Mogilev, all these explosive elements were beginning to fuse. At Stafka the generals felt the ground shaking beneath them. Their concern manifested itself in a growing phobia about secret agents. Every chauffeur, every arriving messenger, was suspect, and some refused to talk on the telephone for fear of being overheard.

Sensing their peril, the Allied missions prepared to depart. They got away on 1 and 2 December, just a few hours before the arrival at Mogilev of Krilenko, who was accompanied by a large group of sailors, ferocious individuals who had led the uprisings in Petrograd.

Dukhonin, having ignored several warnings to escape, finally decided to depart by automobile on the morning of 3 December, but at the last minute he allowed himself to be persuaded to stay on for a few extra hours. It was a fatal decision. Early that afternoon Krilenko's wild men from the Baltic Fleet seized Dukhonin and dragged him to one of the many staff railway cars in which Krilenko was established.

At this juncture the train pulling Boyle's car rolled slowly into the compound. He and Hill saw the mob assembling outside Krilenko's car, a crowd that swelled by hundreds with each passing minute. There was an animal roar from the assembly, loud cries for Dukhonin's execution.

Krilenko came out onto the platform of the car and appeared to be vainly trying to argue against the mob, which screamed all the more as he seemed to be denying their request to kill Dukhonin. Just when it appeared that Krilenko might speak long enough to tire his listeners, a sailor loomed behind him, pushing Dukhonin out of the railway car. The general fell, or was pushed, into the mob that formed a gigantic circle and tossed their former commander into the air as if from a blanket.

Horrified and helpless to intervene, Boyle and Hill watched the nightmarish scene. Dukhonin's body went flashing up from the centre of the mob. Some at the rear fired shots at it as it soared above the station platform. Several with fixed bayonets rushed forward and caught the body on their points as it fell back. When it was evident that Dukhonin had become a lump of inert, ragged flesh, his corpse was kicked and dragged along the platform and thrown into a shed. The inflamed murderers then shouted that they would proceed into Mogilev, find Dukhonin's house, and murder his wife and family retainers. They missed her. Sick with fear at the likely fate of her husband, she had gone into a church to pray.

As the mob departed from the station Boyle forced his way into Krilenko's car, white-faced with anger and sick at heart. He realized that the Bolshevik cause was not one he could ever support again. With Hill as his interpreter he gave Krilenko a tongue-lashing, charging him with cowardice and calling him a man unfitted for command, who permitted his prisoners to be murdered. "I demand your solemn promise to release Dukhonin's body for honorable burial."

Krilenko, overwhelmed by this second devastating assault on his senses, meekly agreed. He later told associates that "thugs" had incited the crowd to violence and that one of the criminals, not one of his sailor guard, had killed Dukhonin by plunging a bayonet into his back as the general was about to address the mob.

There *were* thugs in the crowd, and thieves as well, but they wore military uniforms. Dukhonin's body, Boyle found, had been stripped of its greatcoat, uniform, boots, watch, and wallet. The twisted corpse was dropped into a rough pine coffin and taken by train to Kiev for burial. Interred with Dukhonin was three hundred years of Russian military history.

Many others recognized, as Boyle did, that there was no prospect of compromise and that Russia now faced the worst of all choices—civil war. Boyle's future hatred of Bolshevism was born that December afternoon. He would dissimulate with its leaders, even pretend to continue to work for them, but his inner soul was dedicated to their destruction. It was a decision that would cost the new rulers of Russia a great deal in the next three years.

Running the Gauntlet

Fatigue was painted on the broad face of the bulky, rumpled man sprawled in the drawing room of an imposing-looking private railway car, drawn up on the siding of the railway station in Jassy. It was 26 December 1917, but there was little sign of Christmas celebration inside the car or out. Its occupant, half undressed, had tossed aside a khaki military tunic, and one sleeve hung dangling, showing face up the insignia at shoulder level which spelled "Yukon," a word that puzzled the Rumanians who observed it. They knew of no British regiment of that name, or of any such country for that matter. Very few of them had ever heard of the tunic's owner, Lieutenant-Colonel Joseph Whiteside Boyle, although they would in the very near future.

Boyle had turned fifty years of age a mere fifty days earlier, and for the first time in his life he felt his years. He was alone for the moment, but there was work to be done in Car 451. Now the useful movable hotel was in a tiny corner of Rumania, and how it had arrived there was something that Boyle was about to explain to none other than the prime minister of Rumania.

He picked up a pencil stub and ruffled a sheaf of none-too-

217

clean official Russian telegram forms. There was no other writing paper available. Paper, like just about everything else except mud and misery, was in short supply in this benumbed capital of the small country engaged in a losing war with a host of enemies. This letter to the Rumanian political leader would be a rough draft. His aides, temporarily excused to enjoy themselves, could polish it in translation.

Your Excellency, as a result of a conference between M. Di'Amandi, Rumanian minister at Petrograd and General Manikovski, Russian assistant minister of war [and] at the request of M. Di'Amandi, General Manikovski charged me with the duty of procuring and forwarding to Rumania supplies due under the protocol of September 22, 1917. . . .

In connection with this work. . . .

He halted, drew a line through the five words and started once more.

While I was engaged in this work the Bolshevik uprising in Moscow so upset the transport conditions there that the Russian armies on the Northern and Western fronts were facing starvation, and I was sent to Moscow to endeavour to clear the blockade and get supplies through to the fronts and to Rumania, which work slightly delayed my work in the procuring of clothing for the Rumanian army but was of assistance in procuring of foodstuffs for the Rumanian front.

While in Moscow I was consulted by Mr. Guerin, Rumanian consul-general and representatives of the Rumanian foreign office and the National Bank, regarding the question of transporting to Jassy the archives of the foreign office, some paper notes and other valuables, and at their urgent request hurried through to Jassy with these articles.

"Hurried" hardly seemed the right word. After all, it took six days to travel eight hundred miles by railway, and more good fortune than any man had any right to expect. Talk about the luck of the Irish.

"Valuables," on the other hand, probably was the right word for part of the shipment. The prime minister must have known by then that the cargo included part of the Rumanian crown jewels as well as the four million sterling in Rumanian bank notes. He also knew that the Rumanian gold still remained in Moscow, so there was no need to emphasize that unhappy fact.

Before leaving Moscow I succeeded in locating and procuring orders for all articles of clothing due as of Nov. 1 ... and completed an organization for the loading and forwarding of these goods. ...

In connection with the procuring of clothing, great credit is due to General Bogateo, chief of the Russian intendancy at Petrograd, and to General Grudzinski, chief of the district intendancy at Moscow, both of whom exceeded their authority in taking steps to fulfill Russia's obligation to Rumania under the protocol; and to Lieutenant Sovine, a young intendancy officer who is in charge of the goods in storage in Moscow. All of these officials are entitled to recognition and I would respectfully recommend that they be awarded suitable decorations. ...

The notion delighted Boyle more than a little. What would his old pals in Dawson say when they heard that a sourdough was recommending Russian generals for medals?

In connection with the transport of the valuables brought from Moscow, one British and three Russian officers took part and in view of the dangerous nature of the undertaking, the fact that they were given their option as to whether they should take the journey, and the fact that on several occasions when trouble occurred with the Bolshevik soldiers their cool, determined and courageous behavior probably saved the mission, I recommend that they each be awarded a decoration.

He was having trouble with those Russian names, and the erasures were growing. Boyle decided to plunge ahead, and hope someone else would look after the spelling.

The officers in question are: Captain Galavin, 1st Smolensk Guards; Staff Captain Poritchinski; Staff Captain Count Tolstoy; Lieutenant George Hill, British Royal Flying Corps.

With regard to my personal connection with this work I wish to say that I have only done my duty, and in view of the fact that I am recommending officers serving with and under me, I would prefer that no award be made to me, as the fact of having been of assistance and the cordial thanks already extended to me by yourself and associates in the government have amply repaid me for any trouble.

Boyle read it over and shook his head. How hard it was to avoid sounding like a prig, or even an unmitigated liar, when talking about decorations. And had he forgotten anyone? Good Lord, yes, what about Borel?

Boyle read it once more, threw down the pencil and didn't bother to put a period to the final sentence. The letter would have to be improved, after he had had more opportunity to review once more all the details of that crazy train journey and the mad adventure surrounding it. For it had been a mad adventure, terribly exciting while it lasted but one that any man would think hard about before attempting it again.

Thanks to Manikovski's authorizations and the official papers provided by Di'Amandi, it had been relatively easy to get into the Russian warehouses. Removing those precious stores had required finesse and a deception of the hostile Bolshevik guards. In contrast there had been the friendly co-operation of the regular Russian troops, both senior and junior Russian officers, who acted with more than a slight risk to their lives.

Boyle's bold front and the reputation preceding him had helped, but some Bolsheviks had been hostile. One official had hijacked seven carloads of foodstuffs slated for the Rumanians and rerouted them to the Northern Front. Lieutenant Borel had demonstrated his courage there, risking his future in a brave but futile opposition to the actions of his superiors.

It was a minor setback, however. Thanks to the raid on the

warehouses, Boyle could report that the Rumanian soldiers would receive 600,000 woollen foot clothes, 1.4 million handkerchiefs, 700,000 towels, 150,000 water bottles, 700,000 sets of underwear shirts and drawers, 140,000 woollen vests, and 85,000 pairs of lined trousers. Soon to follow were 180,000 greatcoats, 150,000 tents, 150,000 cooking kettles, thousands of buckets, curry combs, and sundry other items—155 freight cars of supplies in all.

It was an unexpected relief that would enable thousands of Rumanian fighting men to survive the winter. It was a gift to warm the Rumanians physically, but the retrieval of the Rumanian treasury was a symbolic gift, lighting the fire of hope on a very dark Christmas Eve.

The treasures he had been asked to return to Rumania included the crown jewels, currency, the nation's archives, and the £25 million in gold reserves. They had been moved to Moscow for safekeeping when the crushing onset of the Central Powers had compelled a general retreat of Rumanian forces that saw Bucharest, their capital, fall into German-Austrian hands in December 1916, a few months after Rumania's belated entry into the war.

Two accounts of the daring exploits of the great train journey have been written by individuals who took part. Some fifteen years later, in his book *Go Spy the Land,* George Hill would dramatize the amazing days of the journey from Moscow to Jassy. The Boyle references, contained in documents prepared a few days after the actual event, lack the excitement of the Hill version but are more accurate. Between them they sketch one of the more dramatic moments in the lifetime of both men, caught up in the making of history beyond the inquiring eye and tongue of the war correspondents in other more publicized theatres of operations.

There was nothing illegal or subversive in the Rumanian decision to recall their treasures from Russian safekeeping. They had every reason to fear that the change in government might present obstacles to future recovery, and were wise to move as quickly as possible to claim their own. The problem was twofold: the possibility that the revolutionary, anti-monarchist Bolsheviks would refuse to co-operate, and the difficulty of moving several tons of special articles across a wasted land now menaced by civil war.

The Rumanians were fortunate that they had selected Joe Boyle as their special emissary, for he had personal friends among the Bolsheviks who were indebted to him for important services. Among Boyle's authorizations was a substantial letter from Muralov, now commander of the Moscow region, who had formed a high opinion of Boyle for his work in cutting the Moscow Knot. This, more than the authorization from Di'Amandi and Manikovski, made it possible for Boyle to remove the archives, currency, and at least part of the crown jewels from the awesome Kremlin treasury. Boyle did not write of any serious attempt to recover the Rumanian gold. In any event, it was not forthcoming, and as far as anyone knows, the Soviet Union still holds it to this day.

Hill was convinced that the Bolsheviks approved the removal of the treasures only because they were certain that no one could make off with it. Subsequent events indicate that when they realized they had been wrong, belated attempts were made to abort the great escape.

Rumanian officials, so bold at the outset, became frightened and delayed the removal, insisting on the receipt of a written authorization from Jassy, perhaps to evade responsibility if the plan failed. But Jassy agreed that it should proceed, providing two Rumanian treasury officials accompanied the shipment. All these concerns and hesitations are understandable. Even the leader of the attempt was aware that the route to Jassy led across southern Russia through the disaffected Ukraine, where a rapidly growing civil war had opened between the Ukrainian nationalists opposed to Bolshevism, and a Bolshevik army that was being steadily augmented. No one knew what side held what area, and where the next fighting would break out. Rostov, for example, changed hands twice in as many weeks.

Because railways were the one dependable communications route, much of this struggle, and the broader one that would follow it, was along the rail lines and for key junctions. And because both sides hoped to use the railways when they were victorious, there was amazingly little destruction of lines or rolling stock.

But it was along the rail lines that Boyle and his associates had to move, guarding a treasure worth millions. It is to the credit of all that, given the chance to go or stay, none begged off. Boyle makes it clear that the agonizing trip took six days. Hill, fifteen years later, thought it was a ten-day journey. There must have been moments when it seemed as if it would take forever.

Removal of the treasures from the Kremlin, once the word came, was speedily arranged, but the goods were not yet ready for rail shipment. Boyle stored the material in a Red Cross warehouse to facilitate handling and to permit disguising of the contents of the thirty-one small and five large packages that were made ready for shipment. Hill recalls that the jewels were placed in covered wicker hampers.

Stealth was the important ally in the movement of the cargo to the train. Boyle had hoped to make the transfer inconspicuously, but when the packages had been loaded onto sleds a detachment of sixteen Rumanian soldiers suddenly marched up and demanded to accompany the party. There was no time to argue. Boyle marched off the procession and, as he feared, it began drawing all the attention he had hoped to avoid. Bolshevik patrols asked questions. Boyle's interpreters fobbed them off with slick answers and the frequent waving of the sheaf of official authorizations.

At Car 451 an irate Ivan protested at the motley array suddenly threatening to take over his beloved vehicle. He finally helped load the shipment, which filled four of the compartments and squeezed George Hill out of his sleeping quarters.

A signed receipt, dated Moscow, 19 December 1917, shows how careful Boyle was in handling the cargo and the

Rumanians. It reads: "Under instructions from Colonel Boyle and in accordance with arrangements we have placed in his railway carriage thirty one (31) small and five (5) large Red Cross packages." The receipt was signed by V. G. Nedes and Ran Tourhers, on behalf of the Rumanian consulate and the Rumanian National Bank.

It had been easier to get the treasure out of the Kremlin and into the rail car than it was getting the car out of Moscow station. The stationmaster challenged Boyle's demand to hitch 451 on to the first west-bound train. As they argued, the train puffed impatiently. As usual, Boyle won the argument. When the train started to move Captain Count Tolstoi jumped aboard with word that the train was to be ambushed fifty miles along the line. The old Klondiker took the rumour seriously and mustered his scanty human resources. There were six able-bodied men, but he decided the treasury officials would have to be written off if it came to a fight. That left Boyle, Hill, Tolstoi, and Poritchinski, although the aging Ivan might be useful in a pinch. He certainly did not lack spirit.

All were placed on alert for the first few hours until the rumoured danger point was reached. The precautions were timely. The train stopped suddenly at a small station. Boyle and Hill slipped out and detected several shadowy figures bent over trying to uncouple 451 from the other cars. In the ensuing scuffle Boyle knocked out one of the strangers. The intruders took to their heels and escaped. The car was joined to the train with apologies from all, but there was no explanation for the unscheduled halt.

The encounter had made clear the Bolshevik intentions, so Boyle drafted a duty roster for a twenty-four-hour watch and warned his associates to be especially careful to look for an attempt to rush 451 from the forward carriages. Tolstoi and Poritchinski were cautioned to stay inside the car unless it was absolutely necessary to go outside. Boyle feared that their officers' uniforms might cause disorder among the Bolshevik partisans.

At Briansk the reality of the civil war became apparent, for a battle between the two combatants opened just as the train slowed in its approach to the station. The engineer, exercising good sense, increased the train's speed and roared through the terminal under a fusillade of small-arms fire from both sides of the track. Boyle thanked the former Imperial government for building royal trains with steel walls. The only damage was a couple of broken windows.

On the second night of the journey there was another unscheduled stop, resulting, it appeared, from a fire near the right-of-way which was discovered to be from a blazing vodka distillery. The temptation was irresistible. Passengers and crew swarmed to the fire zone to pilfer large quantities of stock, which they immediately began to sample. There was a good deal of snoring throughout the coaches when the train finally moved off.

Slow but steady progress followed until the next afternoon when a mounted Bolshevik detachment, commanded by a commissar, halted the train. Fortunately for Boyle they began searching the train from the front end, giving him time to prepare for their arrival. All the compartments were locked and the two Rumanian bankers were shut up in one of them while Boyle donned his full regalia and prepared to greet the commissar at the entrance to 451.

The Bolsheviks, he explained through his interpreters, could not come into his car because 451 was the carriage of a foreign embassy with extraterritorial rights that made it, in fact, a small piece of foreign territory. The commissar was intrigued. What country? he asked. Canada, replied Boyle proudly. His country, he explained, was a sort of American republic. He had no wish to explain how the King of England could also be the King of Canada.

The commissar seemed reasonably assured by the claims and explanations. Smiling broadly, Boyle then invited him to come in, explaining he would have to leave the rest of his party outside. Ivan produced food and drink. The commissar indulged and showed no disposition to inspect the Red Cross parcels being hurried to the starving Russian troops in Rumania.

This co-operation produced a promise from Boyle to recommend a decoration for the helpful commissar from the president of Canada. He promised to send a cable asking for it when he arrived in Kiev, a destination only a few hours away. Charmed by all this, the commissar reluctantly departed, bowing his thanks.

Believing that the run to Kiev was clear, the occupants of 451 settled back and relaxed—but not for long. The train slowed and finally stopped, evidently in the middle of a thick forest. Hill, sent out to reconnoitre, returned to report that the engine needed some minor repairs, but that, much worse, it was nearly out of fuel.

Determined to remedy the fuel shortage while the engine was being repaired, Boyle and Hill located a large stack of logs, nicely sawn into the right lengths and piled up along the right-of-way. They peremptorily assembled the occupants of the other coaches, explained the predicament, and persuaded them to form a human chain from the log pile to the engine, along which enough wood was passed to replenish the fuel tender. There was still a good deal of unconsumed vodka and teetotaller Joe Boyle was pleased, for once, to watch others indulge. Things were going swimmingly throughout the railway cars when the climate changed drastically as a burst of small-arms fire rattled out from a station.

The assailants turned out to be a detachment of Ukrainian nationalists under the impression that the train was full of Bolshevik troops. They seemed as relieved as the civilian passengers to discover this was not the case. They were suitably apologetic to find they had wounded a couple of the travellers, and distraught to find they had interfered with a train hauling the car of an important foreign mission.

Boyle had planned to take a breather at Kiev, a plan he immediately abandoned when the stationmaster informed him that he was aware of their journey and understood they were in charge of a large treasure being moved under armed guard. Arranging to be attached to the night train, the next to leave, Boyle and Hill begged transportation to the centre of the city and slipped into the Continental Hotel for a warm bath. There they met Captain Galavin, an old friend of Hill's, who asked to join them as he was anxious to get to Bessarabia. Boyle, glancing at Galavin's campaign ribbons, was quick to extend an invitation. He could use a veteran fighter at any time, none more so than now.

The two Rumanian bankers were permitted to report to their consul. Hill walked back to the train with Galavin while Boyle went to the regional headquarters of the Russian railways to talk with the officials he had met previously.

Departure time was 20:00 hours and Hill became more and more uneasy when Boyle failed to return. At the stroke of the hour he sought out the stationmaster and persuaded him to delay the departure. Thirty minutes passed; the official said there could be no further delay. Hill was about to order the uncoupling of 451 when Tolstoi whispered that they could stall departure by insisting on the application of the railway regulations. The safety cord, he pointed out to the stationmaster, did not extend the full length of the train and failed to cover the last two carriages as required by regulations. The stationmaster was a stickler for the niceties; he insisted on stringing a new cord to cover the whole train. While this was going on Boyle arrived, somewhat dishevelled and carrying a large parcel.

His failure to return on time, he explained, was the result of a bomb explosion. He had been making his way back when a bomb, apparently thrown by Bolshevik sympathizers, exploded, tossing Boyle through a store window from which the glass had been blown ahead of him. He had been knocked unconscious but recovered to find he was being treated by a group of Russians in the rear of what had once been a provisions store. As he lay there his eyes chanced on a large, brown decorated turkey, ready-cooked for the eating. As he made ready to depart he indicated his desire to purchase the festival bird, which he had wrapped in brown paper and carried along as a gift to appease his worried companions. Ivan was delighted with this acquisition and served it in proper style for a late-night supper.

It was easy going then for hours, slow but steady progress that seemed to hint that the worst was over. Fears dissipated and it was a very light-hearted group that moved towards the Bessarabian border that would give them entrance to the final stretch of the run to Jassy.

Suddenly, while the train rested in the station at Jamerinka, only forty miles from the border, all their fears came rushing back. For the first time on the long trip no one turned up to inspect the train, a departure from routine so marked that all Boyle's suspicions were aroused. The party was back on the *qui vive,* but despite this departure from the norm nothing happened. The train got under way once more, but Boyle's anxieties refused to vanish. They were justified. At the small station of Vapnyarka the train halted; without explanation, 451 was shunted on to a siding. A Bolshevik officer and a detachment soon arrived and told Boyle that his party was under arrest, and their car covered by a battery of field guns only a few hundred yards away. "We know you are stealing something from Russia to give to Rumania," he said sternly.

Hill advised against argument at the time. With true British phlegm he resorted to the time-honoured action of brewing a cup of tea while Boyle drafted a new duty roster and all of the prisoners talked of various fantastic ways in which to escape. In the end they were saved by Czarist bureaucracy, a most unlikely aide.

As they sat and schemed they became aware of a low, persistent noise, almost like a whistle. Hill, sent out into the night to scout, returned with the interesting news that it was steam escaping from an engine that was kept at all times ready to roll, as the result of an Imperial order made many years earlier that no one had bothered to cancel. The engine, staffed twenty-four hours a day with shifts of two men, had been puffing away uselessly for years. Now it had a chance to justify its existence.

Boyle and Hill walked casually over to the engine and talked with the crew, providing them with hot tea and food from 451's well-stocked larder. As they talked they had a look around. The Bolshevik hadn't been lying, for the field guns were as described and, worse than that, a detachment of Bolshevik infantrymen had now taken over the station.

From this nettle of danger the old White Pass troubador plucked the rose of escape. It was, he decided, a great night for a party, one to which all could come. Hill proceeded to the station and invited their captors to be their guests. Ivan was ordered to prepare the largest samovar of tea he could brew— and spike it with the vodka from the burned distillery.

Political philosophies were one thing, but a party was another; the Russian zest for the latter conquered. The soldiers drank, sang, and danced with and for their prisoners. They were particularly appreciative of Joe Boyle's rendition of the Klondike ballads, even though they didn't understand a word of any of them. When they left they stumbled back to the station with yet another large container of suitably strengthened tea. Soon the pre-eminent sound from that building was one of loud snoring.

Back at 451, the travellers were completing their preparations to escape. With the closest guards drugged with tea and vodka, the immediate problem was to move without alerting the more distant gunners with their fearsome artillery. Hill and Boyle awakened the two-man crew of the engine and explained that they wished them to attach it to the car and move off in the direction of Bessarabia with a minimum of noise and a maximum of despatch. The trainmen clearly were frightened of the occupants of 451, and obviously even more alarmed at what might happen to them if an escape attempt failed. Eventually, with the combined persuasion of future rewards and the immediate punishment that might be applied from the muzzles of the two revolvers facing them, the unhappy engineer and his fireman agreed to act.

Slowly they backed up the engine to the siding and coupled 451 to it. The train, increasing speed as quickly as it could, sped past the field artillery emplacement. All aboard—Hill and Boyle with the trainmen, and the nervous occupants of the car—waited for the crashing discharge they were sure would come as the train moved. Nothing happened. They had taken the soldiers by surprise. Several miles down the tracks, hoping that a warning of their escape had not yet been sent out, they halted the train. Galavin leaped out, threw ropes over the telegraph poles, fastened them to the rear of 451, and gave the signal to move ahead. The poles and the wires came down and dragged behind the train for several hundred yards before being released. Unanswered was the big question: had the sabotage occurred in time to silence those dangerous wires?

A few miles farther along, the reply was sharply in the negative. As the engine moved around a bend, the occupants of the cab spotted a series of red lights. Its headlights picked up a wooden barrier across the tracks with groups of armed men on both sides of it. Boyle, pushing his revolver into the engineer's ribs, shouted at him to increase speed. Petrified with fear the man refused, saying it would derail the train if he ran into the obstacle. There was no time for further argument, for already the train was beginning to lose speed. Boyle and Hill threw the two crewmen aside, seized the controls, and prayed that the close attention they had been paying to the train operation would qualify them to take over. They seemed to have picked up the hang of it, because the engine regained speed, rocking wildly as they crashed through the barrier, scattering the red lanterns like a rocket discharge. The terrified crewmen crouched on the floor of the cab and refused to return to the controls. Boyle took the driver's seat while Hill forced the crew to act as firemen, stoking the greedy furnace with wood.

The decision made, there was no stopping for anything, and

the tactics appeared to pay off, for there was no further attempt to halt them as they approached the Bessarabian border.

Suddenly, at the border crossing, a huge obstruction loomed, and it was clear that this one was large enough to stop them. Boyle applied the brakes but it was too late. The engine and its one-car cargo smashed into what turned out to be a huge pile of earth. The engine shuddered and coughed to a halt. As the passengers pinched themselves to be sure they had suffered no serious injuries, a volley of shots rang out and the engine began to ping with the thump of lead. Hill was sure they were out of Russia and began shouting to the unseen assailants. Finally the marksmen ceased firing. They were, they said, a Rumanian army outpost, placed to repel any Russians who sought to invade Bessarabia. The roadblock was to make sure that no trains of any sort got through. The new arrivals could attest to its effectiveness.

Dismantling the barrier took enough time to permit Boyle to notify Jassy about the success of his mission. The rest was a triumphal procession to the temporary capital of Rumania, where the Rumanian army and government officials had prepared to accept the gift that Joe Boyle and his stout companions had brought from Moscow. Their arrival was a Christmas present to lift the hearts of the Rumanians and so it was, on 25 December 1917, that two more officials provided Boyle with written proof of the accomplishment of his mission. The form release certifies that: "Under instructions from Colonel Boyle we have delivered to the representatives of the Rumanian National Bank the above-named thirty-one (31) small and five (5) large Red Cross packages." The names were those of N. Velloz and Lieutenant-Inspector Touchkin.

When the tired travellers returned to 451 several hours later, Ivan was waiting with a supper prepared from the last of Joe Boyle's Kiev turkey, following which Boyle graciously indulged an assault on 451's remaining stock of spirits. His companions had earned it.

His futile attempt to write a letter of recommendation for

honours and awards was more successful a few days later. As he requested, in a formal document that still exists, there was special recognition for George Hill, who was presented with the Order of the Star of Rumania. Boyle's request that he be pased over was ignored, as he must have expected it would be. He was immediately awarded the Grand Cross of the Crown of Rumania, the first drop in a shower of honours that would descend on him from the small, harassed country he had decided to succour.

If there were any honours for the Russians, they have not been recorded publicly. If they were recognized, it must have been done privately, for obvious reasons. No Bolshevik government would deal lightly with nationals accepting honours from a monarchy with which it was moving from undeclared into open war. The contributions of Generals Grudzinsky and Bogateo and their subordinates is preserved only in the written records that Joe Boyle left behind. Their fate in that time of turmoil is unknown.

✂ TWENTY-ONE ❧

Service Suspended

Among the Boyle papers preserved in Northern Ireland are several torn brown manila envelopes addressed to "Lieut.-Col. J. W. Boyle, General Manager, Canadian Klondyke Mining Co., Limited, c/o General Headquarters, Russian Army, Moghilev." The postmarks show that they had been mailed from Dawson City on 1 November 1917. None of them reached Boyle in Russia and one of them was never forwarded from Britain, for it is stamped "service suspended" and endorsed as having been "received in damaged condition at Vancouver, B.C."

Another, addressed to the Savoy Hotel in London, eventually was delivered at ACE headquarters. All these packages contained documents vital to Boyle's interests in the litigation begun in London regarding his Klondike holdings by Granville in June 1916, and continued in Dawson late in 1917.

Their failure to reach Boyle was critical because, as a result, he had no opportunity to defend his Klondike mines. Whether he would have deserted the mission he had personally undertaken to help the Allied-Russian cause, and in particular to work for impoverished Rumania, is doubtful, although he would at least have had the chance to fight for the estate he had built up over a score of years. But he was, by this time, so intensely devoted to the problems he encountered in Russia and Rumania that it is doubtful that he fully understood the business perils he faced, or really cared to worry about them when faced with all the immediate obstacles he was dealing with in Europe.

Yet he had evidenced some concern a few weeks after his arrival in Russia, as an 8 August 1917 letter to his old partner-rival Treadgold, written from Petrograd, demonstrates. He asked the Treader to forward without further delay documents relating to Pinder and Nadeau claims in the Klondike, assigned by mortgage from Treadgold to Boyle. Treadgold's past failure to act, Boyle wrote, "does everybody interested harm excepting the outsider interested against either Canadian Klondike or Granville Mining Company." It was, noticeably, a business letter, not a communication between old friends, and it seems to have elicited no response. To see Boyle's position firmly re-established would hardly have advanced Treadgold's long-held dream to consolidate all Yukon gold mining operations under one company, directed by Treadgold.

The breakdown in communications prevented Boyle from discovering, perhaps to his surprise, that Joe Junior was managing his Yukon dredges better than he might have thought possible, and demonstrating all his father's skill at persuading creditors to extend their assistance and the repayment deadlines. Although a $50,000 winter credit to CKMC from 1916-17 was unpaid, young Joe had persuaded the Northern Commercial Credit Company to grant the same line of credit for the winter of 1917-18. Some of his woes, he wrote to his father on 27 June 1917, were caused by socialist union organizers.

One of his operating difficulties was the necessity to submit for his father's approval any management decision of consequence. Young Joe, in desperation, made interim decisions that in the end became final.

From eight thousand miles away he could report to his father, who apparently did not receive the message, that despite

234

the bitter, ancient rivalry between CKMC and Yukon Gold he had been able to work out an arrangement with YGC that kept the two sides out of yet another expensive court battle. As a result of an arbitration YGC would be permitted to work some Boyle claims, paying everything recovered above thirty cents a yard to CKMC.

Still, there was a less antagonistic direction at Bear Crek which permitted E. E. McCarthy, resident manager of YGC, to replace a plank bridge across the Bear Creek pipeline over Boyle land that had been closed for months and seemed likely to end in yet another court case. Joe Junior wrote:

I trust the arrangement will be satisfactory, and it will certainly be a boon to us to again have the use of the bridge, as its closure has resulted in somewhat of a hardship to us, which I preferred to bear rather than enter into any transaction which might prejudice the position adopted by you and tenaciously lived up to for a number of years.

But this new, pliant attitude at Bear Creek could not ward off the impact of other long-standing feuds, now being pressed with vigour as it became known that Joe Boyle was stranded on the other side of the world.

A long-simmering dispute between the Dawson City Water and Power Company and the Boyle interests headed for a showdown. F. P. Burrall, head of the power company, served formal notice on Boyle to return all equipment, machinery, goods, and chattels loaned to him by the power company, including a transformer "rented or loaned on April 18, 1915." Burrall, a close associate of Granville officials and the heads of the Guggenheims, Boyle's most implacable rivals, wore several hats; the demand letter from his power company was signed by Burrall as "attorney in fact."

Junior Boyle, they discovered, was almost as nimble in a fight as his boxer father had been. His riposte was a counter-demand for return of all equipment, goods, and chattels to the

Boyle company. "I shall be pleased," he added, "to refer the matter to our president and general manager. As you are aware there will be considerable delay experienced in getting word to Mr. Boyle. . . ."

Fancy legal footwork was unavailing in London, however. The courts, acceding to Granville applications that went unchallenged because of Boyle's absence and lack of instructions, appointed Edward Dexter as receiver to investigate claims against CKMC and CKPC (Canadian Klondike Power Company). Dexter, just by chance, was one of the auditors whose name had appeared on the questionable financial statements of Granville several years before.

Eventually learning of the decision, Boyle appealed by letter from Russia to his old friend Lord Harris, asking him to intervene with the receiver to have proceedings suspended because his military duties made it impossible to take part in London hearings. Lord Harris, in seven short lines, declined to intercede. He said he had referred Boyle's letter to Dexter, who returned it with a note saying he could not act. Just how little Boyle could rely on his presumed friend was evident in a 21 September letter from Kennalley, who had asked to see Harris to inform him about Boyle's situation. The stiffly formal reply read:

Lord Harris presents his compliments and begs to thank Mr. Kennalley for the letter from Col. Boyle and for his kind offer of assistance. If there is anything to communicate Lord Harris will undoubtedly avail himself of the kind offer but he does not think it is likely that he need trouble Mr. Kennalley.

Having seen his master in action in Russia, it is likely that Kennalley realized Boyle could never be persuaded to return to defend himself. He urged Boyle to come back to London but added: "if you find you cannot leave there I will carry on to Canada as instructed just as soon as the various matters are settled, and I will do everything possible to strengthen your position."

Enclosed were statements from Dawson reporting accounts payable of $671,000, accounts receivable of about the same amount, and a fair prospect of extracting another $500,000 in gold before the end of 1917. At this point, despite the claims of Granville and other creditors, it is clear that the Boyle mining interests were still a going concern. On 18 October Junior Boyle sent a twenty-two-page letter reciting difficulties overcome and how past indebtedness had been paid off to the tune of $72,000. In the Klondike, the son added, he had a crew of ten Russians cutting two thousand cords of wood for winter use from the bush at Foster Gulch.

The future, he said, looked bright "if Congdon takes no action." But Congdon held the trumps and on 10 November, acting for Granville, he presented stock certificates on the Boyle companies for 649,993 shares. Yukon Explorations presented 150,000 shares, transferred to Granville, and the two applicants asked that the ownerships be registered.

The action followed a hearing in the Yukon court on 7 November in which Granville asked the Boyle companies, and Boyle and Treadgold personally, for execution and delivery of bonds, payment of complete CKMC indebtedness, registration of 765,000 Boyle company shares in Granville's name, payment of $156,000 under guarantees, and $200,485 under sinking fund, with a receiver to be named until the claims were met. Alternatively Granville asked for repayment of an unsecured loan of $1,350,000, retransfer of claims, properties, stocks and assets originally transferred, and accounting of all gold production and income.

Junior Boyle cabled for instructions on 11 November, reporting that he was confident he could stall off the application for a receiver at least until 10 December, but that he needed advice on how to meet allegations of mismanagement, needless costly lawsuits, and alleged unnecessary expenditures, such as the construction of a reservoir. Boyle knew nothing of this and it is unlikely that he ever had the full particulars of the case. Kennalley, valiantly playing for time in London, replied. The English court claim, he told Junior Boyle, had been an action by Granville for $1,350,000 under promissory notes, an action that repudiated an agreement allegedly made between Boyle and Granville in 1912. The Yukon suit, he said, was inconsistent with, and even antagonistic to, that launched in London.

Oppose the stock registration, Kennalley urged, and I will return to the Yukon as soon as possible to help. The promissory notes, which he said Boyle acknowledged, carried 6 percent interest, amounting to $400,000 for five years, "whereas mining and power companies have paid Granville approximately $800,000. . . ." Junior Boyle's evidence of management ability did nothing to halt the remorseless progress of the action against his father. In his absence Joe Boyle's enemies were intent on bringing him down. On 18 November Harold G. Blankman, clerk of the Yukon court, was named interim receiver until 12 December, when the motions would be heard. Junior Boyle retained E. C. Myers, a Victoria solicitor, but it was clear the defence would depend very heavily on Kennalley, who was having trouble getting a passage from London.

On 23 November, in some despair, Kennalley cabled that he could not hope to reach Dawson before the middle of January. He urged that a postponement be sought. "Communications with Boyle slow, conditions there very unsettled," he added. Kennalley then compressed all the bad news from Dawson into a cable fired in the general direction of his employer, somewhere in Russia. Boyle clearly could not have received it until he got back to Jassy with the Rumanian treasures on Christmas Day.

The proceedings in the Yukon moved on inexorably, without Boyle or Kennalley to provide a counter to the claims of his opponents. The outcome was inevitable. In mid-January 1918 a permanent receiver was appointed to take over the Boyle mining empire. Evidence that Boyle had agreed to certain conditions in London some five years before, when obtaining $1.5 million in cash from Granville to finance the construction of his third and fourth dredges, weighed heavily in the hearing. Boyle's refusal to conclude that agreement because he charged the terms of the deal had been altered might have made a difference, had he been there to explain it. The court preferred to accept evidence that Boyle had taken the money primarily in exchange for 29 percent of the CKMC capital stock, and an additional option to convert debentures into another 20 percent interest in the stock. There were other issues but the demand for the stock certificates was pre-eminent.

Although he wouldn't know it for some time, Boyle was no longer entitled to the $25,000 annual management salary he had been given, one he did not always draw. More important was the loss of the arrangement by which he received 25 percent of the net profits credited to his account in a Dawson bank. That had run as high as $250,000 in some years, money that he frequently did not entirely dispose of, despite his tendency to tell creditors to draw on him in Dawson. One year some $80,000 was left untouched.

So the battle for Boyle's extensive holdings, the work of his lifetime in the Yukon, was fought without his participation. To this extent—one involving millions of dollars—Joe Boyle was as much a victim of the Bolshevik Revolution as any financier or landowner in Russia.

Another cherished dream was expunged by the Bolshevik takeover. The downfall of Kerensky ended any hopes Boyle had for larger Canadian participation in the Russian transportation crisis. Boyle's imaginative project, finally approved by Canada after months of dilly-dallying, collapsed a few days later in the Bolshevik Revolution.

On 26 October 1917 a top-secret message, in Russian, was sent from General Manikovski reporting that an agreement had been completed with General Turner by which Canada would supply a fully equipped detachment of 123, all ranks, to be sent to Russia at once with equipment for three railway battalions on Canadian standards, this to follow in approximately eight weeks the dispatch of the personnel. The order, it was said, was being filled by the Canadian Pacific Railway, which had outfitted other railway battalions. This almost total acceptance of Boyle's persistently recommended plans paid tribute to his stubbornness and highlighted his wisdom, but it did nothing for him in the end. The deterioration in the Russian political situation was reflected in a telegram from Stafka to the transport directorate in Petrograd on 2 November, stating that the recruitment of Russian personnel to operate the railway equipment from Canada now was considered undesirable.

Boyle was the immediate loser, but thousands of Russians may have paid the ultimate price later. John Reed, reporting from that strife-torn country early in 1920, noted that millions had gone hungry and many had died of starvation because the transportation system was unable to get food to the large population centres from rural warehouses.

The painful final decision came in a letter from Kennalley in London which confessed that the Bolshevik seizure of power had killed the project. He noted there now were ten-day delays in communication, but the main problem was that

Lenin and his cohorts were in power; the Russian Committee here has repudiated the Lenin government; the British ambassador in Petrograd does not recognize the Lenin government and things were pretty topsy-turvey. . . . I guess we will just have to wait until things get normal again there.

The aid pledged to Boyle from American sources was made inaccessible when the United States placed an embargo on all shipments to Russia, a standard American response to events in Russia that continues to this day. The warehouses holding the goods for shipment to Russia were seized by government agents. Boyle's grand design to summon the resources of the New World to the relief of the Old had been blown away with the winds of change sweeping out of the vast, unhappy heartland of Russia.

There were others who shared his disappointment. In London, where he had been standing-by waiting to organize the troops to be sent to Joe Boyle was Lieutenant-Colonel Frank Reid. He swallowed his disappointment and returned to a base headquarters job in France until the end of the war.

Undoubtedly the pressures of immediate crises helped ease the sting of these setbacks for Joe Boyle. Fortunately for his peace of mind he was unaware of yet another assault on him, mounted this time by distant, obscure enemies intent on bringing him to heel for his disregard of military and diplomatic protocol. On 26 January 1918 a cipher telegram passed from Whitehall to the Duke of Devonshire, Governor-General of Canada, in Ottawa. The message, prepared by Colonial Secretary Walter Long, one of Boyle's London friends, gave a résumé of the tangled Boyle case. The British government, it made plain, wasn't employing Boyle. It failed to add that its representatives in Petrograd and Jassy were receiving his reports and benefiting from his services. The letter went on:

Boyle, since his arrival has negotiated directly with Russian authorities without reference to either British ambassador or British military attache. His activities extended to Rumania as well as Russia and he has been dealing not only with railway matters but also with political, financial, military and food questions. He has evinced utmost repugnance to co-operate with Inter-Allied representatives and refuses to recognize any party. His independent action has caused much trouble to Allied Railway Mission and his presence in Russia has been the source of constant embarrassment to British representative. . . .

In all this was the fine hand of de Candolle. In London, it appeared that the British authorities had disowned Boyle. The only solution, it was suggested, would be for His Excellency the governor-general to issue an official recall order to Boyle. "It is earnestly hoped that the Canadian government will send Col. Boyle instructions to leave Russia at once," the cable concluded.

Ottawa went into pained confusion. The message was circulated from the prime minister to the minister of national defence, then to the members of Cabinet, and discussed for five days. Then on 1 February 1918 the Duke of Devonshire issued an order unique in Canadian military history. He ordered the recall of this troublesome militia officer from Russia to Canada.

It was relatively easy to issue the order, but how to deliver it to a man who wandered around Eastern Europe in the middle of a civil war in his own private railway car, on private orders from two national governments? It would be difficult to locate him, and even more of a task to get this fiercely independent man, who had been relieved of any necessity to obey either the British or the Canadian government by their very actions in disowning him, to take any notice of such an instruction.

TWENTY-TWO

The Canadian Peacemaker

The convincing demonstration of Joe Boyle's ability to feed and clothe the Rumanians merely accentuated the demands on his services. In place of a furlough he might have used to defend his personal interests in an English court, he was given an immediate assignment involving Rumanian internal security, now menaced by the spread of the Bolshevik plague from Russia.

More than one million Russian soldiers remained idle in Rumania and along the Russo-Rumanian border. Many of them were on short rations, and all were subjected to incessant Bolshevik propaganda. Evidence that the infection was beginning to reach the Rumanians appeared in demands for the overthrow of the government and the removal of the king and queen. More immediate was the threat of a renewed Austro-German offensive to complete the occupation of Rumania.

These fears became magnified to the point that plans were considered to remove the royal family from Jassy to Mesopotamia. This wild scheme would have attempted to take the refugees from Rumania to the Tigris Valley by automobile, with the Red Cross providing a fleet of sixty trucks and passenger vehicles. A more foolhardy venture is difficult to imagine in an era when motor car reliability was low and roads for such a journey nonexistent.

At the joint request of General Tscherbatchef, commander of the Russian 4th Army in Rumania, and General Prezan, Rumanian chief-of-staff, Boyle agreed to inspect conditions in the Russian forces and to rectify them on the spot where possible. He was asked to take special note of one Russian corps in which agitators were urging the soldiery to kill or drive away their officers and loot the countryside to appease their hunger.

Boyle quickly diagnosed the problem as being primarily a lack of meat. He ordered the corps to slaughter 50 percent of its horses to provide meat not only for the soldiers but for the civilian population. This mass killing of the animals, whose meat could be preserved by freezing in the sub-zero temperatures, would ease the situation for many weeks, he was sure. In addition, because of the reduced demand on fodder, there would now be enough to feed the remaining horses for the rest of the winter, and many rail cars used for fodder transport could now be turned to other purposes.

Closely attended by his coterie of Russian interpreters, he concentrated on tracking down the known agitators, who were imprisoned by the army commander on his recommendation. Tscherbatchef was so pleased with this speedy resolution of the problem that he conferred the Order of Vladimir, Fourth Class, on the Canadian troubleshooter.

This success, and his earlier exploits, brought Boyle to the notice of General Henri Berthelot, doughty commander of a French military mission of some four hundred advisers to the Rumanian forces. Berthelot, like Boyle, was determined that resistance to the Austro-Germans would be continued. He had drafted a defence plan by which Rumania would oppose any attack, even one by the Bolsheviks. His hope was not to defeat the Central Powers, which he realized was no longer possible on the Russo-Rumanian front, but to delay as long as possible enemy occupation of the rich province of Bessarabia and the Don basin.

The Rumanians, for their part, were more worried about a war with Bolshevik Russia than any other invasion. In their despair they conceived the idea that Boyle, obviously on good terms with the new Russian regime, might be able to avert a war with the Bolsheviks. Prime Minister Bratiano, Foreign Minister Take Ionescu, Joe Boyle, and George Hill conferred at length on what might be done, and Boyle was provided with terms of reference on which to negotiate with the Bolsheviks.

Bratiano said that Rumania would facilitate withdrawal of the Russian forces to their own territory if that was the wish of the Petrograd government, requiring only that they leave their weapons behind for Rumania to use to defend itself against the Austro-Germans. He promised to withdraw Rumanian troops from Bessarabia, a land that both countries hoped to possess, as soon as Rumanian property and stores held in Russia had been returned to Rumania. To answer complaints being aired that Rumanians were arresting Russians, he asked Boyle to emphasize that such arrests had been made by the Russian military commanders, not the Rumanians.

The negotiating would require a visit to Petrograd, something that Boyle welcomed because he was carrying out another top-secret assignment he had assumed on an indefinite basis. In his 1919 report to General Turner he admitted that by this time he had become a double agent, ostensibly working on behalf of the Russians but, in addition, providing intelligence of ultimate benefit to the Allies. His meeting with Berthelot in Jassy had confirmed this role and a plan was devised whereby Boyle "was to use the Bolshevik authority ... to drift locomotives from the North to the South of Russia, and create as much disorder and confusion in the railway system in the North as possible." He was embarked on a daring and dangerous game. The Dukhonin murder on the Mogilev station platform was beginning to exact an unsuspected price.

Car 451 sped away to the northwest and quickly carried Boyle and Hill to Moscow where Boyle renewed his friendship with Muralov, now commander of eleven districts around the future capital of Russia. Muralov welcomed the negotiations to cement good relations with Rumania, and agreed to accompany Boyle to Petrograd to take up the matter of Boyle's future duties with War Commissar Podvoiski. Muralov proceeded to provide Boyle with new passes to permit priority movement of 451, giving him "full powers to unload artillery weights and buy and supply the army with aliments. . . ."

Muralov's offer to accompany his Canadian friend was a fortunate one, helping to ease Boyle's access to a government now deeply concerned with conditions in the capital that had almost become civil war. Sporadic exchanges of gunfire punctuated the night hours. Security now was a brutal fetish with the December mustering of the infamous Cheka, forerunner of the KGB, a fanatical secret police organization called the All-Russian Commission for Struggle with Counter-Revolution and Sabotage. The revolution was becoming a reign of terror.

Directing the terror machine were Felix Djerjinsky, a veteran Polish revolutionary, and Jacob Peters, a lifetime Latvian revolutionary, long exiled in Britain. Thanks to Muralov's presence, Boyle met both men. Peters, married to an English woman, asked Boyle to forward a letter to her in Britain by the British Embassy's diplomatic pouch, because he could not rely on ordinary mail services.

One of Boyle's first duties was to meet with Rumanian Ambassador Di'Amandi to inform him of what was going on. This proved impossible, for Di'Amandi and his staff had been imprisoned, apparently in reprisal for the arrest of the Russian agitators in Rumania. Allied mission leaders in Petrograd, Boyle discovered, believed the arrests were an attempt to provoke the very hostilities Boyle had been commissioned to prevent. It was a warning of sorts for all embassies. United in anger and concern, all the foreign ambassadors joined in a formal protest to Lenin and Deputy Foreign Minister Zalkind. As a formal representative of the Rumanians, Boyle added his voice to the complaints.

The ambassador's position remained precarious. Hill, scouting around, reported that his intelligence channels had learned of a plot to murder Di'Amandi and two former Kerensky colleagues, Cadet Party Leader F. F. Kokoskin and former Agricultural Minister Andrei Shingarev. Released and warned, Di'Amandi wisely fled to Finland. The former government members were less fortunate. Taken ill in prison, they had accepted the advice of friends and gone to the Marinsky Hospital for treatment. There assassins found and murdered them in their beds. Bolshevik newspapers blamed the assassinations on counter-revolutionary provocateurs.

Negotiations with the foreign office went poorly for Boyle because Trotsky, the foreign minister, was in Brest-Litovsk negotiating peace terms with the Central Powers. Zalkind, temporarily in charge, made it clear that he was opposed to the Rumanian proposals and openly expressed his doubts about the reliability of Boyle, who reported that Zalkind charged "it suited my purpose because the burzui were actually receiving benefits, and at first opportunity I got I would stab them [the Bolsheviks] in the back." Zalkind's instincts were sharp, but his associates did not share them. They knew Boyle and respected him as a man who could be depended on to get things done.

"After some interviews," Boyle reported, "Podvoiski and Muralov won out and I received further authority to go South to reorganize the repair shops, and try to increase the output of coal in the Don Basin and regulate its distribution and delivery." In addition, Boyle was continued in his appointment "as chairman of the All Russia Food Board which had been formed early in November for the purpose of dividing foodstuffs between civilian and military populations."

Podvoiski's support had been won partly on the basis of Boyle's long, honest reporting about the continuing crisis in transportation. Existing rough drafts of a memorandum, dated 28 January 1918, detail a frightening breakdown in rail services, place the blame for it, and outline remedies. Boyle charged that

Soldiers are travelling about the country in all directions, occupying approximately one-third of all railway wagons as living apartments, and one-third of all moving trains ... creating the utmost confusion at railway stations, holding up trains, and in many instances commandeering locomotives and deranging the whole system.

He identified the southwestern lines as the most critical point, being almost shut down because Bolshevik troops at Kharkov had prohibited all shipments of coal from the Don since 27 December. The ultimate result had been to starve all fronts, with a disastrous outcome for the army horses, now dying at the rate of one thousand per day for lack of fodder.

"The most satisfactory and probably only effective way [to avert famine and end the crisis] would be to effect an armistice between the warring factions in Russia, at least until spring." In addition to preventing a Russian war with Rumania, this bold emissary was not above a shot at ending the civil war. He urged a new, unified railway commission with a headquarters in Petrograd or Moscow to run the railways, and the use of troops to enforce the disregarded food laws.

In the end Boyle obtained everything he could have expected to get in Petrograd. He bade farewell to the Bolshevik leaders, charged with a dual mission to investigate the transportation difficulties for the Russians and to discuss Russian-Rumanian relations with Antonov-Ovsenko, a member of the Bolshevik government and currently commander of the southern front. A special pass provided for this dual assignment specifically included the names of Hill, Poritchinski, Tzegintzov and two British officers, Captains Nash and Crutchley, who were bound on a mission to the Caucasus. The attachment of the two British officers was made through the British embassy. Because his eventual destination was expected to be Jassy, the chargé d'affaires, Sir Francis Lindley, acting chief in the absence of the ambassador, persuaded Boyle to take along a pile of mail pouches that had been accumulating in Petrograd because there now was no service at all to Rumania, even for diplomatic mail. Boyle was playing mailman for His Majesty just about the time that the governor-general of Canada, at the behest of the British government, was ordering him recalled from Russia. The irony of the situation is more apparent now than it was at the time.

Car 451 carried Muralov back to Moscow, where Boyle stopped to conduct some routine business and check on the whereabouts of Antonov, who he was informed was at Kharkov, directing the Bolshevik campaign against the Ukrainian rebels. Boyle departed Moscow on a special train, with clearance for a speedy trip to Kharkov. The dilapidated condition of the railways was dramatically illustrated a few miles south of Orel when Boyle's special collided head-on with another train in the middle of the night. The engine was badly wrecked and Car 451 suffered major damage, its steel walls protecting the passengers from more than a severe shaking-up, however. Boyle commandeered the other engine and made it tow 451 back to the Orel workshops where the mechanics, spurred on by Boyle's exhortations and a promise of a substantial bonus, set some sort of shop record by completing the repairs in twenty-four hours of non-stop labor.

The delay was just long enough to foil Boyle's bid to meet Antonov in Kharkov. The Bolshevik commander had gone to Nikitia to set up a field headquarters for his campaign against the Cossacks. Anxious to discover whether Antonov would fight the Germans, Boyle caught up with the Russian commander at Nikitia and they held a long conference. Boyle was impressed:

Although Antonov had a very bad reputation I found him to be an excellent leader and very desirous of stopping bloodshed between the Russians and inclined to make peace with Rumania.

In addition he was decidedly anti-German . . . and I am quite sure one result of our interview was his very stiff position with the Germans whom he fought as long as he could hold his men together.

True to his pledge to the Petrograd officials, he examined the fuel and transportation system and duly reported to Podvoiski that the fuel-lubricant shortage arose from low production at the coal mines and oil wells. His remedies were twofold: close non-essential industries using these supplies; and recall former railway officials, dismissed when the Bolsheviks took over, to operate the lines. Two weeks after Podvoiski acted on this advice, Boyle could claim that oil and fuel supplies had increased by 47 percent. Had Zalkind's just suspicions prevailed in regard to Boyle, hundreds of thousands of Russians would have spent a much more uncomfortable winter.

Boyle's talks with Antonov about Rumania had been encouraging, but the Bolshevik leader stressed that he lacked the authority to conclude any kind of pact with Boyle. He directed the peace emissary to the Crimea. In Sebastopol he would find a senior government official, Dr. Christian Rakovsky, with the authority that was needed. Antonov supplied Boyle with yet another set of passes for him and his staff and Car 451. They would be needed in the Crimea, which had become an inflamed appendix of the nation on 9 and 10 January, when sailors of the Black Sea fleet had mutinied, seized their ships, and brutally tortured and eventually murdered some sixty officers.

Adding to their discontent had been rumours—fueled, it was said, by German agents—that Britain and Turkey had secretly made peace and a huge British fleet was en route through the Dardanelles to crush the revolutionaries and aid Rumania. A sailors' committee, after a wild meeting of the mutineers, ordered the arrest of all Allied subjects and threatened to kill ten prisoners for every casualty caused by the British fleet.

The cloak-and-dagger atmosphere was heightened when Boyle's train stopped briefly at Kherson and was met by the British consul. He informed Boyle that their mission was known to the German secret service, which would endeavour to sabotage it. To this end agents had been inserting notices in newspapers warning that the German army would soon be occupying the Crimea and there would be trouble for anyone aiding the Allies. Boyle moved relentlessly ahead despite the warning, but he was hardly prepared for the welcome awaiting his party in the Sebastopol station. The place was swarming with sailor mutineers who closed around the car and demanded to see its occupants.

Some parleying through his interpreters provided Boyle with the information that a clubfooted sailor named Speiro was leader of the would-be lynching committee. Boyle invited him to come into the car. Speiro charged that the arrivals were the advance guard of the British fleet. Boyle persuaded him this was not the case. His papers from Antonov helped dispel the charge, but it took some time and the mob, fearing its leader was in danger, appeared ready to assault 451. Boyle then invited the mob to send a delegation of eight to join Speiro and get the truth of the matter. In the calmer interior of 451 they, too, came under the spell of the Boyle story, an acceptance made easier with a dispensation of hospitality in the form of food and drink. Thus fortified, Speiro and his associates appeared on the platform where Boyle, ably assisted by Hill and the rest, harangued the mob whose anger changed to enthusiasm and turned into loud cheers. The machinations of the hated Germans was explained, which seemed to anger his listeners once more. To Boyle's astonishment they suddenly departed, running to the centre of the city where they wrecked the pro-German newspaper that had been publishing the propaganda.

It was a dramatic triumph, but Speiro said that Christian Rakovsky had departed for Odessa to preside over a session of the Rumcherod, the Supreme Council of the region. Speiro, however, wasn't about to let his visitors escape until he and his sailors had shown them true Crimean hospitality. Boyle and his party were given a tour of the Crimean War battlefields and asked to attend a meeting of all the revolutionary committees of the Black Sea fleet to meet the delegates from each ship. In this friendly atmosphere it was easy for Captains Nash and Crutchley to find a vessel sailing for Batum that very day.

Boyle has left his own account of the meeting he attended with the mutineers:

I explained through my British interpreter [Hill] the object of our visit which was, among other things, to let the people of Russia know we were still their friends, and that we did not assume to govern their politics and were anxious to see them stop killing each other and get ready to kill Germans, who were sure to advance into their country for the purpose of making greater slaves of them than they had ever been before.

This was received with wild acclaim and a British naval officer, Commander LePage, who attended the meeting wearing his uniform (which he had not had on for weeks) was also applauded.

That same day, 18 February, Boyle sent telegrams to General Poole in Petrograd and to Prime Minister Bratiano in Jassy. To Poole he despatched a brief summation of what had happened in Sebastopol, concluding:

there is every evidence that the feelings of uneasiness and suspicion created by the propaganda has entirely disappeared and the feeling of the whole fleet toward England is one of confidence and friendship. I am leaving for Odessa tonight. All well.

There was good news for Bratiano, too, for

providing satisfactory guarantees furnished that foodstuffs will not be commandeered for or used by Rumanian army I can procure arrangements with Russian revolutionary leaders to allow purchase in and transport from Russia to Rumania of foodstuffs for Rumanian starving civil population and distribution of such foodstuffs to be made by a commission to be formed by me consisting of British and Russian.

252

Having cleared matters with Petrograd, Boyle was able to conclude firm agreements of this kind with regional authorities. This stemmed from the early beliefs of Bolshevik authority that supported local autonomy, an arrangement the centralists ended in all the regions within a few years, the Caucasus being the last to be enveloped. For the moment, though, central government orders were conditional, not absolute, and depended on the approval of regional soviets to be effective.

The Allies, as confused as everyone, were at this time offering to support both the Bolsheviks and the Czarist Russians, their one objective being to keep Russia in the war and to prevent the removal of Austro-Germans from the Russian front to the endangered Allied lines in France. "Nothing surprising," wrote Tzegintzov, years later, to Boyle's daughter Flora, "that JWB felt like a duck in water in this atmosphere of chaos and general bewilderment." Among the confused he was a rare individual, who knew what he wanted, and knew how to get it.

The man he was now seeking to make peace for the Russians and Rumanians was Dr. Rakovsky. He had been born in Bulgaria, educated at the Sorbonne, and had become a Rumanian citizen. An individual of outstanding qualities, he eventually became Russian ambassador to Britain and co-author of the controversial British-Russian trade agreement of 1924. Boyle was about to engage an adversary worthy of his steel in what would become a classic confrontation.

Off to Odessa sped 451, the passengers looking forward to yet another triumph in a series that had started so badly in the Orel train wreck. They expected to take it easy, for there was no sign of the hostilities that had been plaguing the area. But at Elisavetgrad they had a rude awakening because there were neither passengers nor railway staff at the station. The train was halted while an explanation of this curious state of affairs was sought. A frightened Russian finally told them that everyone had fled at the approach of the special train, believing it to be one used by Maroussia Nikiforova, a notorious and cruel woman bandit whose exploits of pillage and robbery had become legend, almost on a par with stories of her many love affairs with prisoners to whom she took a fancy.

The most reliable source of what occurred in Odessa when Boyle and Rakovsky finally met is Dmitri Tzegintzov's diary. This shows that the Boyle party reached Odessa on 20 February 1918 and plunged immediately into a series of conferences with Rakovsky and the Rumcherod. Rakovsky, to Boyle's surprise, quickly confirmed the agreements about the shipment of food to Rumania that had been negotiated with Antonov in Sebastopol, but insisted on the additional proviso that Rumania must cease military operations against the Soviets. The negotiating continued for three days, during which Rakovsky agreed to further arrangements for ensuring that food supplies would be moved on Russian railways. The first draft of a preliminary agreement to restore peace between Russia and Rumania was drawn up.

Boyle's own account noted that:

Rakovsky was very bitter against Rumania . . . so I proceeded along the lines of getting every man set against him, and eventually got them [the Rumcherod] to submit terms of peace to Rumania under the authority of Mouravieff, commander-in-chief of Bolshevik forces fighting the Ukrainians at Kiev and the Bolsheviks fighting the Rumanians along the Dneister. . . .

Mouravieff probably had a total of 60,000 to 70,000 men and was in my opinion then verging on the point of insanity as there is no doubt he started out as a German agent. Whether it was the amount of killing he did, or the amount of power he got, he eventually completely lost his head and suggested leading a Russian army against the whole world, and then . . . was turned on by Lenin and Trotsky. He ordered all his forces to follow him to Petrograd to put them out of power, and when his forces did not follow him he committed suicide.

Insane or not, Mouravieff served Boyle's purpose on this

occasion. With his support and the rough draft of a treaty signed by all the Rumcherod members except Antonov, he was in a good position to beat down the final opposition.

Boyle had been carefully observing Rakovsky; he formed the opinion that his physical strength was less than his mental prowess. He laid a careful plan for negotiation by exhaustion, opening what he expected to be the final session at 10 P.M. To dress up the meeting he persuaded British, French, and U.S. consuls to attend in full dress, ostensibly to offer their services in adjudicating any unsettled points.

In its rough draft the treaty had three parts. In the first, Rumania undertook to formally declare a progressive withdrawal of its troops from Bessarabia, subject to the right to leave ten thousand men to guard the vital railway lines. Both parties to the treaty agreed to free all citizens of the other country currently under arrest.

Facing up to the possibility of military disaster, it was agreed that if Rumania made a separate peace with the Central Powers the Russian armies in Rumania would be permitted to withdraw. Meanwhile it was agreed to co-ordinate activities by the two signatories against the Central Powers.

The agreement accepted a point Boyle was anxious to have included. This provided that in case of dispute a commission consisting of Russian, British, Rumanian, French, and U.S. members would arbitrate the issue. One of its duties would be to settle any litigation arising in the event that Rumanian forces were compelled to retreat into Russia. This implied right of entry, and was fortified by a Russian pledge to shelter and feed the Rumanians in this event.

The rough, first draft is an unusual document, written in three hands, one of them Boyle's. The writing on the last page is a primitive scrawl in almost incomprehensible language, bearing out Boyle's belief that some of the Rumcherod were illiterate.

Signing for Russia were Udovsky, president of the public commissars of the Odessa district; A. Voronsky, of the Supreme

College; and Breschenan, commissar of international affairs. Rakovsky still refused to sign, despite the urgings of his weary associates and the artful pleadings of Boyle and the ambassadors. It seemed as if he would go on forever, and when the clock indicated it was 5 A.M. there was quiet despair. Suddenly, Rakovsky surrendered, called for a pen, and signed the formal document that had been prepared from the first draft.

He may have been a Bolshevik and a loser, but he was a gentleman Boyle would always remember. When he learned that the state of war existing along the frontier prevented Boyle from returning to Jassy with the treaty, he offered him his staff car. It would do, although piled with Boyle, Tzegintzov, and all that embassy mail. Boyle left Hill and the others in charge of 451. Even his departure was not as smooth as it might have been. As he waited to load the vehicle he was informed by the driver that it had been stolen by two soldiers. Mouravieff offered to find another, but the angry chauffeur vowed he would track down the thieves, and to Boyle's amazement he did so. The vehicle was located outside a private home in which a wedding party appeared to be underway. As the driver opened the door of the car someone in the house opened fire and wounded him. He returned the fire, killing two of the revellers. Unperturbed, and bleeding all over the front seat, he drove the car back to headquarters before surrendering the vehicle to another driver.

Well behind schedule, the peace treaty carriers moved off. Their delight at recent achievements began to wane when they realized the driver didn't know his way. Darkness overtook them and they sought shelter in a farmhouse. The next day was no better, for the engine began to sputter and finally failed completely as they drove through Tiraspol. Boyle's impressive manner coaxed a second car from the slim resources of a Russian army post. The commander warned them of possible danger as they approached the border, and thoughtfully provided them with a large white flag. It was a kind but not particularly helpful gesture. As the car reached the Benderi bridge over the Dneister, the dividing line of Bessarabia, a Rumanian outpost on the other side opened fire. The fusillade was sharp but, fortunately, the marksmanship was inadequate. Angry bellows from Boyle and hails from Tzegintzov halted the volleying and a Rumanian major came up, full of apologies that were not well-received. Barriers were removed and a few kilometres down the road a Rumanian general appeared and invited the travellers to join him for dinner.

Tzegintzov recorded that he and Boyle reached Jassy the next morning and were immediately ushered in to see War Minister Averescu by his Rumanian liaison officer, Lieutenant Stephen Lascar. "It took Boyle a long time to persuade the obstinate general to agree to enter into this pourparler with the Bolsheviks but he promised to put before the cabinet the draft offer of the Bolsheviks in Odessa," Tzegintzov wrote.

The Rumanian government, preoccupied with the problem of signing a peace treaty with the Central Powers, as it was being urged to do by pro-German elements, pushed the Russian treaty aside, despite Boyle's hopes for its speedy acceptance. "No one," the diarist complained, "cares about treating with the Bolshies or about what may happen to Rumanian notables in Odessa ... who are held as hostages." Some five dozen business and professional men, politicians, and national leaders were in prison in Odessa and Boyle had hoped that they would be set free in the prisoner exchange that was part of the treaty.

After seventy-two hours of procrastination the Rumanian cabinet signed the treaty and ordered Boyle to return with it to Odessa for final ratification by the Rumcherod. The delay was not entirely due to concern about the Germans. One section of the Rumanian cabinet was anxious to hold on to Bessarabia and was prepared to risk war with Russia to this end.

Convinced that time was vital, Boyle decided to make use of an airplane offered by Berthelot. It was a two-seater, which meant that only the French pilot and Boyle could travel. The Odessa scene had altered in the few days of his absence, he discovered. Alarming reports of a German advance on the region had been solid enough to make Hill move off with 451 when it appeared that Kiev had fallen to the invaders. He had decided not to wait any longer for Boyle. It was the end of Boyle's association with his own private car, which had served him so well for six exhilarating months of derring-do.

After all that, the intelligence reports proved premature. The Germans did not arrive for another week, giving Boyle plenty of time to complete the peace treaty arrangements, which were published in the newspapers and posted in handbills in the streets.

The German advance into Russia created panic in other places as well as Odessa. Allied military staffs in Jassy, fearing they would be cut off and become German prisoners, prepared to leave. Boyle, at Berthelot's request, agreed to fly to Odessa to act as advance officer for the evacuation of the Jassy missions and the volunteer organizations that had been serving in Rumania. There now was urgency, for it was learned that the Russian troops had permitted 130 lorries loaded with German troops to advance along the Danube and seize Galatz and Bolgrad. They were now believed to be heading for Benderi, where the missions would have to cross the border. Postponing his takeoff for Odessa, Boyle hurried to notify War Minister Averescu, who was equally indifferent to the fate of the missions or the hostages in Odessa.

Tzegintzov recorded that Boyle had been shocked to discover evidence of duplicity in observing the Russo-Rumanian treaty when he learned that the chief of army operations was planning a mopping-up drive along the Russo-Bessarabian Border. He warned that such an action might lead to the death of the Rumanian hostages in Odessa. Under pressure the war minister agreed that something would have to be done. Whether by design or accident the Germans, who had entrained at Bolgrad for Benderi, were unable to move because of an unfortunate collision between two shunting engines that damaged the rail line. This permitted the diplomatic train to get away. It would be a long journey, for its destination was Archangel. It departed well-fortified for the trip with food and alcoholic beverages sufficient to last for one hundred days. The train had cars carrying railway spare parts, a workshop, machine guns, and hand grenades. It did not lack other creature comforts because there were a number of stowaway Rumanian women on board.

Having done all he could to make the escape possible, Boyle flew off to Odessa, where he arrived 11 March 1918, two days ahead of its unopposed takeover by the Germans. Like others, he believed that the peace treaty he had negotiated was now a fact. It was certainly the first of the First World War, and even less permanent than some that followed it. Two months later the Rumanians abrogated the treaty and took formal possession of Bessarabia, an act that must have confirmed the Bolshevik decision to keep Rumania's gold.

TWENTY-THREE

The Pledge

At this critical juncture in the war, when his mind was totally fixed on his crusade to fight the Germans by keeping Rumania and Russia in the field against them, Joe Boyle fell in love for the last time. It may even have been for the first time, for there is some reason to doubt that his two marriages had been motivated by more than infatuation in the first case and convenience in the second. But his relationship with Queen Marie of Rumania, a truly regal personage by blood, upbringing and position, was something he had never imagined.

His impetuous marriage to Mildred Raynor, the petite young divorcée he had stolen from his brother Dave in 1887, had been the action of a lusty young man with little experience in the boudoir. In contrast, his 1908 second marriage to Elma Louise Humphries, the unassuming little woman from Detroit, was as much to escape the importunings of bolder women as anything else. In both cases the distaff side of the household took second place to his other interests. There were few of his activities that he could share with his wives. His was a male-dominated, masculine world. Boyle could campaign vigorously against tobacco and alcohol, but he was never heard supporting women's rights or votes for the "weaker sex." Nothing, in fact, had prepared him to meet such a woman as Queen Marie, a granddaughter of the great Victoria Regina and a relative of half the royal houses of Europe.

The queen, who kept a diary and was a busy correspondent, has recorded that she first met Boyle at lunch on 2 March 1918. It was a courtesy invitation to the unknown Canadian who was doing so much for Rumania.

Although full of anguish, I had a busy day and made the acquaintance of a very interesting Canadian, a certain Col. Boyle, who is working for us in Russia, trying to better our situation and especially our transport. A curiously fascinating man who is afraid of nothing and who, by his extraordinary force of will and fearlessness manages to get through everywhere; a real Jack London type.

Boyle was immediately attracted to the queen, as Tzegintzov noted in his diary. Boyle, he wrote, seemed jealous when Colonel Anderson of the American Red Cross appeared to be *persona grata* at the palace. The Klondiker then proceeded to make a *faux pas* that may have added to his pique. He was invited to meet King Ferdinand, a much lesser figure than the queen and one not greatly respected by those close to the court. Boyle, pacing the floor in rising anger over the delays in Rumanian acceptance of his hard-won agreement with the Bolsheviks, curtly responded that he was too busy to go to see the king but that if the king wanted to speak with him he could telephone.

Marie was not one to stand on etiquette where her feelings were involved. "I am," she once wrote, "and always was, moved by an irresistible instinct to give, without ever pausing to consider whether my overquick actions were wise or not, or if they would lay me open to unfavorable criticism or to being misunderstood." She realized that the Canadian was someone special, and she wasted no time in indicating her understanding of the fact, for Boyle visited the palace three times in the next week. These early meetings helped increase her interest in

Boyle but their relationship was cemented on the night of 9 March, one of the lowest points in the life of this unusual woman.

It was the night the Allied missions were moving out, but the queen was determined to stay up and say farewell to them, defying the warnings of the pro-German element now beginning to surface in the court and government. It was a miserable evening, rain pouring down in sombre background to the mood of despair permeating the palace. A decade later she would tell the Boyles in Canada how, as her final farewells were said, she was sitting alone in solitary anguish when Boyle, his garments dripping water, stalked into the palace and stood awkwardly in the reception hall until the queen advanced to greet him.

"Have you come to see me?" she asked.

"No ma'am," Boyle replied. "I have come to help you. And my God, woman, do you need help."

Joe Boyle, the Queen confided to her diary, sat up with her for hours.

I tried to let myself be steeled by the man's relentless energy, tried to absorb some of the quiet force which emanates from him. I poured out my heart to him in those hours. . . . I do not know all that I told him, the memory is a blur, but I made a clean breast of all my grief and when he left me and I said that everyone was forsaking me, he answered very quietly "but I don't" and the grip of his hand was strong as iron.

Later she said that an "irresistible sympathy" had sprung up between them at that time. "We understood each other from the first moment we clasped hands, as though we had never been strangers."

How could these two people, so suddenly thrown together, find a common thread that would never be severed except by death? Nothing in Boyle's life pointed to such a development though the queen was a woman of wide experience, reputed to have had a number of lovers to compensate for an inadequate marriage. This was hardly a romance in the style of Romeo and Juliet. Boyle was in his fifty-first year, handsomely middle-aged but beginning to show signs of wear. The queen, now in her forty-third year, remained a reigning beauty, lonely, but with the poise and self-possession of a truly royal personage. This mother of six children looked like a queen and played the part with a sense of theatre that some said might have made her one of the great ladies of the stage.

She was the eldest of four daughters of the Duke and Duchess of Edinburgh, her father one of the many children of Victoria and Albert, her mother the Grand Duchess Alexandrovna, daughter of Czar Alexander II, and a cousin to the Grand Duke Alexander of Russia, brother-in-law to Nicholas II by marriage to the czar's sister Xenia. All four of the Edinburghs' daughters were renowned for beauty and charm. Grand Duke Alexander wrote glowingly of the sisters. "Judges of pulchritude would have a hard time choosing between the four of them"—Missy, the future queen of Rumania; Ducky, who married the Russian Grand Duke Cyril; Sandra, the future princess of Hohenlohe-Langenburg; and Baby B, who was destined to become the Infanta Beatrice of Spain.

Rumania, to be sure, was less than what might have been chosen for the throne of a granddaughter of the Widow of Windsor, who ruled half the world. It was a lately sprung nation. Although its historical origins involved the ancient Romans, its modern form had emerged from pieces of real estate chipped from various nearby kingdoms. The architect of the Rumanian regal system was a commoner, Ion Bratiano, who had travelled much through Europe and, during a period of imprisonment in France for revolutionary activities, had come to the conclusion that Rumania needed a monarchy to survive. An obscure Prussian prince, Carol von Hohenzollern, a nephew of German Emperor Wilhelm I, was selected to be Rumania's first king. Bratiano, fearing republican interference, smuggled Carol into Rumania dressed as his valet, and kept him in hiding until Bratiano became prime minister.

Carol was married to Princess Elizabeth of Weir, a talented poet and writer known in literary circles as Carmen Sylva. It was an odd match and a disastrous one, for the union failed to produce the heir that the royalist supporters felt was imperative to survival of the kingdom. Eventually the royal couple separated. Bratiano the kingmaker was undaunted. He rummaged around in the German royal attic and came up with a successor in the person of an even less-inspiring Hohenzollern, a shy, backward young princeling named Ferdinand. It was now important to find a wife for Ferdinand, who would produce the heir to the kingdom that Carol had so signally failed to sire. While this search proceeded, Ferdinand, encouraged by Carmen Sylva, fell in love with one of her ladies-in-waiting, Helena Vascarescu. When the liaison was opposed by Carol, his heir presumptive ran off to Venice with the lady. Carol had them separated by force, exiled Miss Vacarescu from Rumania, and sent the poetess queen to a nunnery.

Finally, after much dabbling in the waters of royal protocol, it was arranged that Ferdinand would marry Marie, the eldest of the four daughters of the Edinburgh line, whose marriage would clear the way for the remaining three younger sisters to find husbands, in the custom of the day. Ferdinand was a very poor second choice for Missie. She could have married her cousin George, eventually through fate to become George V, but rejected him in a moment of youthful uncertainty that she later regretted. Marie might have been the queen of England, for the unexpected demise of an older brother projected sailor George on to the throne.

So this lovely, intelligent, shrewd, courageous, and enterprising English princess became the bride of gawky Ferdinand, still pining for his own lost love. It was a marriage of convenience, so accepted by both parties, and its main purpose was ensure the stability of the throne by the production of heirs to the kingdom.

It was evident from the start that the queen was much the stronger personality. But she had been trained in a family where the royal grandmother insisted that all the female members learn to keep house, cook, and carry out the duties of a proper wife. On the other side of things she had been taught *noblesse oblige* and accepted the duties implicit in royalty as it was conceived in Great Britain.

Marie immediately embarked on a campaign to learn to speak Rumanian, a hybrid language, and to popularize herself with its hybrid citizenry. She was buoyant, almost irrepressible at times, with great ability to charm anyone on whom she chose to focus her attention. Her actions were unconventional in many ways and her freedom in the selection of male escorts caused gossip, although Rumanian attitudes in these matters were closer to modern permissive society than to Victorian England. Her position in the nation was solid, despite the scandalous talk. It had been firmly established in the Balkan war of 1912-13 when the princess (she became queen in 1914) was frequently to be found in or near the front lines. She worked as a hospital nurse and frequently ignored her advisers to take great risks in nursing men dying of typhus and other infectious diseases.

More than any politician in Rumania she had been responsible for Rumania's 1916 entry into the Great War on the side of the Allies. Militarily and geographically it appeared to be a mistake to many of her countrymen. Ferdinand's inclination was to take the German side but the forceful Marie, sure that Britain and her Allies would triumph in the end, was more persuasive than her husband. British military men were sceptical. General Sir William Robertson, Chief of the Imperial General Staff, told a newspaper editor that he never thought the Rumanians would enter the conflict and didn't think they would be much good if they did.

After a brilliant beginning against the Austrians the Rumanians began to feel the steel of the German army, and like the Russians they could not withstand it. It was not entirely the fault of the Rumanians that they were defeated. The Allies had promised to send them three hundred tons of munitions daily and support them with a synchronized offensive that would sweep north from Salonika on the Aegean. The Russian breakdown had deprived Rumania of the munitions, and the Salonika offensive was a dismal failure. They were on their own and were soon forced back deep into Rumania.

The queen's problem—and it fell to her in the end—was to ensure the survival of the nation. At this desperate juncture the sudden appearance of a man of action who was demonstrating his ability to overcome insurmountable odds was like a miracle. His promises to summon food, arms, ammunition, clothing, and other necessities were kept. The impact of this confident success in a morass of failure was incalculable. Marie could truthfully say that in the darkest moment of her life Joe Boyle kept her from utter despair.

Now, as he prepared to return to Odessa to conclude the peace treaty her advisers had so reluctantly accepted, she reminded him that some seventy Rumanian notables—politicians, soldiers, sailors, civic leaders, and other faithful servants of the nation—were hostages in Odessa and should be among the first to be freed under the prisoner-release clause of the treaty. Boyle promised to look after them and any other Rumanians who might need help.

The limited capacity of Boyle's airplane once more left Tzegintzov in Jassy as his chief departed in high spirits on 10 March, promising to maintain communications. To the consternation of Tzegintzov and the Rumanians, there were no messages and concern arose when Hill sent word from Nikolaiev on 14 March that the Russians had been roundly defeated in a battle at Birsula as they attempted to repel invading Austro-German forces. As a result of the Birsula defeat, Hill added, he was taking Car 451 back to Kharkov, with Voronezh as his fallback base if Kharkov was threatened. The message continued:

There are rumors that Boyle has left Odessa on the same ship with the Rumanian hostages but as soon as Rakovsky heard that the

Germans were allowed to march through Rumania he gave orders to direct the ship to the Crimea. Commodore Pantazzi's wife [he was one of the hostages] informed Boyle of what was happening just in time for him to climb aboard the ship as she was sailing. Since then no news.

Tzegintzov frantically tried to confirm the rumour, but without success. All he and his associates knew was that Boyle had vanished. And if he was in the grip of the Bolsheviks, there was every reason to worry about his fate.

TWENTY-FOUR

Black Sea Odyssey

Hill's message that Boyle might be a prisoner of the Soviets was only too true. What the Russian revolutionaries didn't know was that they had a top spy in the British service in their clutches.

The extent of Boyle's participation in intelligence activities was known to very few—a handful in British embassies and close associates like Hill. It was in the dreary October of 1917, Boyle admitted in a private report six months later, that he had begun organizing an intelligence service to counter German propaganda and maintain scrutiny of German activities in Russia. Sabotage, where it could damage the Germans, was part of the program.

A handwritten memorandum from Boyle to General Ballard at the British embassy in Jassy outlined the growth of the network.

I started organizing small destruct units in Russia, my system being to select one good man, have him select for himself 10 men, preferably engineers—all of the men to be officers, all capable of caring for themselves financially—ready to take on any job required and to do exactly what they had been told to do, without asking questions as to who gave the orders or what relation their work had to do with any other work. Absolute secrecy and obedience were to be observed—no written orders or reports—no questions asked.

As soon as a man in any unit shows sufficient initiative and ability to handle men to warrant starting him out he is to be, in turn, deputed to raise and take command of a unit of 10 men.

Each unit commander works next to, and in contact with, the unit from which he sprang; receives orders from and reports to his original commander; uses his best judgment and initiative in finding work for himself and [his] men not filled by work instructions....

The work laid out for them by me is to get employment in repair shops of railways and coal mines—to carefully retard all work—"accidentally" break or do away with spare parts of machines difficult or impossible to replace particularly on imported locomotives and pumps; strip threads on fixed bolts and whenever possible do anything to a locomotive or pump that will cause a breakage.

On railways to blow up bridges and culverts on bad sidehill cuts; blow up any and all stores of supplies regardless of ownership or location; spread propaganda to the effect that the Allies, and particularly the British and Russia's friends in England, have stood and are still standing loyally by Russia, assisting and proposing to assist her in every possible way....

... Germany has destroyed Russia and is now entering her to the purpose of breaking her up, destroying her strength and securing, with military aid commissions, domination and authority.

Germany, in desperation and facing starvation herself, will rob Russia of her already insufficient stocks of good fats, wool and leather; starve her people, and when she has entire control make slaves of her people under a German Czar.

When Boyle drafted his memorandum in March 1918, he was in control of forty-four units with 484 members. Formed in the first instance to harry the Germans, it now operated against the Bolsheviks with the same enthusiasm as against the Austro-Germans. Accordingly, Boyle's return to Odessa to complete the treaty with the Rumcherod was only one of his objectives. He had his agents there and elsewhere and they were particularly useful in surveillance of the civil war and the German advance.

Such a network needed financial sinews, which were provided by Britain and France jointly, in immense amounts of money despatched to the southern front. Sums of £10 million and 100 million francs were made available for subversion and the financing of the information-gathering and sabotage. There were some French doubts about the value of Boyle's work around the time the military missions were fleeing Jassy, and for a while French support was withdrawn.

Reporting to Sir George Barclay, ambassador to Rumania, on 11 April 1918 Boyle referred to a 7 March meeting with Barclay and told of a subsequent meeting with Berthelot.

I told him just what I had reported to you. Namely that I had fairly wide authoritative powers from the Soviets and had been working in the Kharkov district, in the Crimea and in Odessa, and believed I had succeeded in getting the Bolshevik leaders in the South to refuse to abide by the Brest-Litovsk treaty and that they would oppose German entrance into the Ukraine; that I was sure protection would be given the Russians if we could get them to continue the war and retreat into Bessarabia and Kherson: that I had properly discussed the matter with you and declared my opinion that, if properly financed, I felt certain an organized effort could be made in the south of Russia.

He had also told Berthelot that a fairly strong guerrilla opposition could be mounted against the Germans and that the Black Sea fleet could be held solid, and that all supplies would be destroyed in a scorched-earth program as the Germans advanced. Boyle said he had asked Berthelot for two hundred of the French officers he had in Rumania to organize a fighting force and get it working with the Russian officer battalions mustering in the Don Basin. "[I] told him that you had authorized me to say ... that England would find one-half of any amount he would agree on with me. ..."

As Boyle made ready to fly to Odessa he received a cable from Rakovsky and Mouraviev asking him to notify the Russian units at Benderi of the end of hostilities with Rumania, because they had been unable to get in touch with them. Boyle flew to Benderi at considerable personal risk to himself and his French pilot and issued the instructions.

Boyle arrived in Odessa on Sunday, 10 March, with a number of things on his mind but charged by the queen and others to ensure the safety of the upwards of 70 Rumanian hostages held in the Turma Prison. They were to be exchanged, as arranged in the treaty, for some 400 Russians held in Rumania and the safe passage back to Russia of about 100,000 unarmed and disaffected Russian soldiers.

The hostages were to depart in a special train on 12 March. It all appeared straightforward, but soon it became an involved, deadly game into which a fellow Canadian, Ethel Greening Pantazzi of Hamilton, Ontario, wife of naval Commander Bruno Pantazzi, one of the hostages, was suddenly projected.

Mrs. Pantazzi had heard of Boyle in February from the U.S. consul in Odessa. Now the worried wife, appealing to Spanish Consul M. Mendicutti, who had been dealing with the hostages, sought out Boyle to discover what arrangements had been made to evacuate them. Mrs. Pantazzi was impressed at first sight, and later described the Klondiker as "a deep-chested man of splendid physique, about 50 years of age, his square jaw and bright blue eyes, under straight brows, giving the impression of reserve force." Boyle, she noted, was wearing a uniform with "Yukon" in block letters on the shoulder strap, and wearing on a blue ribbon about his neck the Rumanian Order of the Cross.

Boyle said that the hostages were being taken to Rumania by train the following day, and that she and her children could accompany them. He advised her to go home and pack. Meanwhile he sent word to the hostages of their coming release. At about 6:30 A.M. on Tuesday, 12 March, Mrs. Pantazzi was awakened by the persistent ringing of the telephone in her apartment. A voice whispered that the call was from the Turma and that the Rumanian Revolutionary Battalion, christened the Death Battalion, had taken over the prison two hours earlier. They had aroused the hostages and warned them to get ready for release prior to which they would have returned to them the money, jewellery, watches, and personal belongings that had been seized. Hearing a noise in the street, Mrs. Pantazzi saw several trucks loaded with people travelling in the direction of the waterfront. Some of them, she realized, were hostages. It was clear that they were not being taken to the railway station.

She ran outside, intent on finding Boyle. At the entrance to her home she met the Odessa prisons commissioner, one of the few Bolsheviks who had been kind and humane. He informed her that Rakovsky had no intention of keeping his promise to release the prisoners, who now were in mortal danger. Together they set out to find Boyle, who was quickly located. He found it hard to believe that Rakovsky had lied, but the exhortations of his visitors were so urgent that they commandeered a passing droshky and ordered the astonished driver to hurry to the waterfront. Seeing some of the hostages aboard two vessels tied up at the dock convinced Boyle that the situation was desperate.

Still doubting that Rakovsky was to blame, Boyle hastened to the Rumanian royal yacht *Stefan-cel-Mare,* tied up nearby, which had been seized as a unit headquarters by the Death Battalion. Mrs. Pantazzi interpreted for him as he was told that Rakovsky had indeed departed, taking the valuables owned by the hostages with him. The only officer now in charge, a man named Dichescu, argued strenuously with an irate Boyle, whose flaring temper finally forced Dichescu to agree to hold the ships in port until 2 P.M. to give Boyle time to make representations to the Rumcherod. After what he later described as "a good deal of running around" Boyle located one of the governing group, Breshenan, a signatory of the treaty, and obtained from him a document stating that the prisoners were now free and in Boyle's custody.

There was another mad dash to the docks, where it was evident that the ships were about to sail. On and around the *Imperator Trajan* soldiers in field packs blocked the way. A sailor on the deck claimed that the prisoners would never be freed. An infuriated Boyle once more tracked down Dichescu, who confessed that he had been unable to get the soldiers to give up the hostages. Boyle appealed to him as a man of honour to see the instructions were obeyed. To his surprise Dichescu agreed to make one more try, and both boarded the ship.

Dichescu's inability to direct the soldiers soon became evident on the deck of the *Trajan,* where a loud argument broke out. At Boyle's insistence it was agreed the hostages would be paraded on the dock. Down the gangplanks went the weary prisoners. Boyle remained on the *Trajan,* where he expected to sign a document saying that the prisoners had been turned over to him. Another argument broke out. As they shouted, a Rumanian-born stoker sidled up to Mrs. Pantazzi and urged her to get off the ship, or she would be kidnapped along with the hostages. She did so.

As the argument raged between Dichescu and the ship's officers, Boyle noticed that the guards were endeavouring to force the hostages back onto the *Trajan.* There was some resistance and an outbreak of firing led Boyle to cut short the debate and run down to the dock. The firing continued, apparently at some of the hostages who were attempting to escape. Confusion mounted as the guards began to force the prisoners back onto the ship. Boyle, held against some dock equipment by the press of the crowd, seemed pinioned. He spotted Mrs. Pantazzi a few yards away, still bravely trying to help. "I can't stand this, I'm going with them," he shouted to her.

"Go," she shouted back, "or they are all dead men."

Bulling his way up the gangplank, Boyle strode on to the deck where the terrified hostages cowered. He saw two armed guards brutally beating one of them, an old man who was unable to resist. Boyle seized the tormentors, one in each strong hand, banged their heads together and threw them on the deck. Realizing that the guards were in earnest, Boyle shouted to the rest of the hostages on the dock to come aboard before they were shot.

There was no further brutality. The guards gazed in astonishment as Boyle assembled the prisoners and counted them. A number had been injured, and nine of the original party were missing. It was not until much later that it was learned that only two had been killed in the riot on the deck; seven others managed to get away in the confusion.

Meanwhile a car bearing four German officers drew up at the city hall, the advance party to arrange the takeover of Odessa. The German army marched in the next day. Boyle and his charges would escape the Germans, but could they get away from the Death Battalion?

It was an unanswered question that troubled the hostages as the *Imperator Trajan* moved away from the pier. They could expect little from the armed guards who roughly forced them into one large room. It was a miserable voyage, for the only sustenance was a few tins of cabbage thrown into their floating prison cell by guards. There were occasional servings of tea with a sugar so adulterated that few risked using it. Boyle observed that the ship was sailing east. Clearly, it was not on a course for Rumania. Several times it slowed down and appeared likely to move into small ports on the coast. After three days of bouncing around in rough seas, the *Trajan* docked at Theodosia, a small community on the north Black Sea coast near the Crimea.

Getting ashore was a relief, but it was soon evident that Theodosia was no rest centre. As the prisoners were marched from the waterfront they came under fire from two sides, for they had walked into the middle of a skirmish between

Bolshevik and White factions. Boyle hurried his charges behind a stone wall until the battle died away. Their march ended at what they discovered was a sanatarium, used more recently as a cholera hospital. It was virtually unfurnished but the prisoners were given straw for bedding. They had one thing in common with their armed jailers—no one had any food. When roubles, hidden in their clothing, were produced, the captors agreed to find something they all could eat.

Boyle, who had boarded the *Trajan* with only the clothes in which he stood, was pragmatic as usual. He removed his undergarments and socks, washed them, and walked around barefooted as they dried. One hostage found a pack of playing cards in his belongings and they were at once recruited for twenty-four-hour duty to amuse the group.

Now that they were far from Odessa the jailers hardly seemed to know what to do with their prisoners. Boyle, with Commander Pantazzi assisting the interpretation, was given permission to communicate with the British vice-consul in Theodosia, a Swiss named Von Stuler. Immediate execution now seemed less likely but Boyle was taking no chances. With the help of Von Stuler a detachment of twenty Chinese soldiers from the Bolshevik International Battalion was obtained, ostensibly to help guard the hostages but, in fact, to keep an eye on the wild men of the Death Battalion.

The discomforts of the prisoners were eased, food supplies were assured, and Boyle was granted the privilege of sending telegrams. His first went to Odessa, where he urged Breshenan to act. That honest Bolshevik responded by hastening to Theodosia and ordering the Death Battalion to give up the prisoners. They ignored the command and put him in with the hostages for safekeeping.

Imprisonment in Theodosia was uncomfortable, but much easier than confinement in the Turma. The relaxed atmosphere even permitted Boyle to hire a photographer to take a group picture. It is an amazing record. Inhabitants of the town look over a stone wall down into a courtyard, where Boyle and the hostages sit calmly for the Theodosia cameraman. Armed guards loll around on the fringe. Boyle, conspicuous in the centre of the group, is properly dressed and looks very regimental and very much the boss of the party.

Breshenan's presence was useful, for he was able to work with Boyle in obtaining the help of the Theodosia Soviet in planning a getaway. Convinced that their ultimate fate was death, Boyle was determined to break out. Through Breshenan, Von Stuler, and the local officials it was now possible to plan.

When two secret sympathizers among the ship's personnel warned Von Stuler that the intention was to march the prisoners to a munitions shed that would "accidentally" be blown up, the escape conspiracy, funded by money provided by Von Stuler, advanced quickly. In negotiations oiled with the payment of 150,000 roubles Boyle arranged with the captain of the *Chernomore,* a small freighter tied up at the docks, to take the hostages to Rumania.

Shortly before sailing time the prisoners boarded the *Chernomore,* their passage guarded by the Chinese soldiers sent to watch the Death Battalion watchmen. The revolutionaries were caught off-guard, resting on the *Imperator Trajan,* but as the *Chernomore* made ready to cast off someone sounded the alarm and two of the Death Battalion ran over to see what was happening. Boyle asked them to come aboard so that he could explain things. They did so, and as soon as they stepped on the deck the gangplank was raised and the *Chernomore* departed. It was an unopposed departure, except for a few belated artillery shells that were wide and short of the target.

The *Chernomore* was safely away, but far from safely home. There might be pursuit, and the Austro-Germans now controlled all the Rumanian seaports. Boyle's decision to go to Sebastopol was wise, for there he could renew old friendships with the local Soviet leaders and the men of the Black Sea fleet.

Speiro was delighted to see the big Canadian and readily agreed to support a request that the Sebastopol Soviet make a declaration establishing the freedom of the hostages. Boyle was

A Boyle dredge works the Klondike River beside the rival Guggenheim offices (left).

The Boyle dredge after the mysterious 1916 explosion.

Above: Joe (standing) and Charles Boyle (seated with stepson Ralph Morgan) with Dawson school teachers at Bear Creek.

Right: Boyle ferrying a young picnicker.

Below: Guests at the picnic included: Elma (far left), Joe (holding child), Martha Black (centre foreground) and MP George Black (far right).

PROHIBITION MEETING

A Monster Prohibition
MASS MEETING
Will Be Held
TONIGHT
A. B. HALL
At 9 o'Clock

Chairman, J. W. BOYLE
Speakers, REV. FATHER LEWIS, THOMAS
PARKINSON, J. T. PATTON,
REV. ARTHUR ROSS
The Licensed Victuallers Are Invited to Address the
Meeting. EVERYBODY WELCOME.

Come and Hear This Important Question Discussed
THE PEOPLE'S PROHIBITION MOVEMENT

Above: (Left to right) Nan Boyle, Elma and Elsie Lanning at North Forks site.

Left: The Boyle-led "dry" forces lost by 3 votes in 1916.

Below: Dec. 24, 1913. Joe and Elma sit in front of tree. Standing at rear (left) is Joe Jr.

Flora (left) and Ida May Burkholder in
the garden at Singapore's Raffles Hotel.

The Boyle Yukon contingent in Dawson, Oct. 5, 1914.

(Left to right) Crown Prince Carol, Princess Helene, Marshall Pilsudski, Queen Marie, King Ferdinand, Princess Irene of Greece, Prince Nicolas, Minister of Poland to Rumania (BBC).

Zizi Lambrinos.

Marie and Ileanna on a 1925 visit to Wales (BBC).

Above: Boyle (seated centre) and Rumanian hostages under Bolshevik guard at Theodosia.

Right: Boyle reputedly at Ekaterinburg where the Romanovs were imprisoned.

Above: With U.S. Navy officers in 1922 are (left to right): Tzegintzov, Claude Solly, Nurse Dorothy Wilkie and Boyle. Photo taken by George Hill.

Left: Boyle recovering in Bessarabia, 1918.

Below left: Joe Boyle Jr. (Shell). *Centre*: At 96, Rev. John A. Davies presides at Boyle's re-interment in Woodstock. *Right*: Flora places orange flowers in Rumanian urn. *Background*: The Royal Canadian Regiment fires a salute.

given complete access to the cable office and began firing-off messages all over the world, including one sent to Canada to assure his family that all was well.

The plight of the hostages was widely known because the stout-hearted Mrs. Pantazzi, only a few hours after the abduction from Odessa, had made formal requests for help to several governments. She notified the Rumanians and even appealed to the good offices of the German naval commander a few hours after he took up his station in Odessa. She urged him to bring the matter to the attention of General von Mackensen, commander-in-chief of the Central Power forces on the southern front.

Boyle became aware of all this in Sebastopol and added his voice to the clamour, asking that von Mackensen permit the *Chernomore* to discharge its passengers at the port of Sulina in one of the mouths of the Danube Delta. There, it was suggested, the Russian prisoners in Rumania could be exchanged and taken back to the Crimea by the *Chernomore.* The exchange of the 100,000 disaffected Russians would proceed when Boyle returned to Jassy.

The proposals must have confused von Mackensen who would be, indirectly, party to an exchange of prisoners between two other countries partly occupied by German troops. The agreement would have to include safe-conduct for an enemy alien wearing the uniform of the Canadian militia. He thought about it and finally agreed to let the program proceed. Repeated pleas from Jassy appear to have been the compelling factor. The plan looked foolproof, but it was a German arrangement and no one thought to inform the Austrians about it, although they were in charge of Sulina.

Once approval was received, Boyle was off, hurrying the *Chernomore*'s captain directly to the Rumanian coast. His impatience surfaced when he told the captain to ignore an uncharted minefield and not bother to wait for a pilot who would ensure a safer approach to Sulina.

Excitement ran high that Monday morning, 1 April 1918,

when the *Chernomore* reached Sulina. The joy was premature. The Austrians refused permission to dock, saying they had no knowledge of the vessel, its cargo, or any arrangements. They ordered the ship to anchor in mid-stream, under the close scrutiny of four Austrian monitors and periodic aerial patrols. There was one small straw at which to clutch. The Rumanian cruiser *Elizabetta,* commanded by Lieutenant-Commander S. Lazu, was anchored nearby. Lazu quickly volunteered to try to reason with the Austrian senior officer, a Commander Wolff.

Wolff was obdurate. He said he was not interested in claims that von Mackensen had approved the transfer. He would act, he said, only when instructed by his Austrian superiors. Furthermore, he added, force would be used to prevent any movement by the *Chernomore.* Boyle immediately responded that the *Chernomore* would sail and complete its mission, regardless.

Into this charged situation came a small vessel carrying some three hundred Russian prisoners, who arrived at Sulina in the charge of Tzegintzov and one of Boyle's Rumanian aides, Stefan Lascar. They had spent the previous night huddled on the banks of a canal at Remi waiting for their transportation to Sulina. Tzegintzov and his associates sailed into Sulina at 8:30 A.M. and were astonished to see the *Chernomore* in the middle of the river, ringed by warships with two Austrian planes flying overhead.

Boyle could be seen on deck surrounded by civilians. Tzegintzov set out to find the Austrian commander, but when he asked Wolff what was going on the Austrian said that because Austria was at war with the Bolsheviks, and there was a British officer on the *Chernomore,* it would not be permitted to move. The Russian produced a copy of von Mackensen's free-conduct for Boyle and his party, but Wolff said he could not accept those instructions.

Boyle, his mind made up, announced that the *Chernomore* would sail on Thursday, 4 April. It was a bold challenge that the Austrian commander appeared willing to accept. Boyle told what happened on that anxious Thursday morning.

I refused to change my sailing, and on Thursday morning he [Wolff] had steam up and all four monitors had their guns cleared for action. He dropped one monitor down stream and tied her up behind us, and placed one on the opposite side of the canal from us, and the two others in front of us, and he then, with men seated in each of his seaplanes at machine guns, trained them up the river.

Boyle thought the Austrian meant business and that it would be good Allied propaganda if Wolff could be forced to sink the ship. He put the Rumanians ashore, and continued with preparations for sailing. The *Chernomore* had begun to get up steam about 8 A.M. Boyle ostentatiously sent out a crew to work on the two-pounder, an ancient gun fitted more in hope than expectation that it could sink any submarine that might attack the vessel on the high seas. As this went on, he sent a letter to Lazu protesting Wolff's conduct and asking the Rumanian cruiser's captain to officially inform Wolff that he was going to move the *Chernomore*.

For ninety minutes the adversaries stared eyeball-to-eyeball. At 9:30 A.M. Wolff blinked.

He signalled the *Chernomore* requesting that Boyle visit him. Inviting Lazu, Tzegintzov, and Lascar to attend, Boyle did so. Wolff said that he had just received word that the exchange was to be permitted. He provided Lazu with a document in French confirming his statement. French in those days still was the working language of diplomacy.

Boyle, in retrospect, was happy to admit he had been bluffing, "as the little boat I had was a very poor type of freight boat and with a two-inch gun on the stern."

Victorious in the debating field, Boyle moved quickly to effect the prisoner exchange. There was a moment of sadness as one of the Rumanians, in his excitement, fell into the

Danube and was drowned before the eyes of his wife, waiting on the dock. The Russians marched immediately aboard the *Chernomore,* which made ready to sail as soon as they were embarked. A number of them shouted their thanks to Boyle, and all of them joined in singing the "Internationale." Some of the Chinese soldiers who had safeguarded the hostages waved their caps frantically as the vessel moved off.

On the pier the thankful Rumanians, tears streaming down their faces, sang the national anthem. They weren't quite home though. No transportation was ready and Boyle had to find an old iron barge on which the former hostages and their wives and families could be taken to the railhead at Galatz. A few found passage on the small tug that towed them away. They arrived in Galatz on 5 April, and once more incompetence was in command. The station master, it was discovered, had neglected to reserve seats for the party, although he had carefully saved one for Boyle.

What Tzegintzov recorded as "a terrible row" followed. Boyle refused to go without those with whom he had shared dangers and almost unbelievable experiences. The station master dispatched the train despite the protests. Boyle sent a torrid telegram to Jassy. Two hours later the train returned. Miraculously there was room for everyone. What happened to the station master is not recorded. So, six hours late, the former prisoners and their rescuer began the last leg of their long journey from Odessa, a nonstop trip at such a pace that there were fears the cranky little engine would jump the tracks. The engineer, it turned out, had been ordered to convey Boyle to the palace in Jassy in time for lunch, and railway officials, worried about the royal wrath that might descend on them, ordered the engineer to proceed at top speed.

Boyle, dog-tired and as dirty as a miner fresh from the creeks, was rushed to the palace and ushered into the royal presence, where King Ferdinand immediately decorated him with the Star of Rumania and sash. "Some of our friends," Tzegintzov told his diary, "considered he should have been awarded Michael the Brave Order"—the highest Rumanian award for gallantry in the field.

Exchange of the Russian soldiers took three days, and began as soon as Boyle had had his first proper night's sleep in many days. He was unhappy, just the same, for he had learned that Rumania planned to abrogate the treaty by seizing Bessarabia, an event that occurred the next month.

The epic adventure was over, but the nation would not forget it. In the hour of defeat it had found a national hero, and for weeks to come Joe Boyle was almost overwhelmed by the thanks of great and small. His daily walks became triumphal processions, many stopping him to shake his hand or just look at him. The newspapers extolled his deeds. He was hailed as "The Saviour of Rumania." One reporter even did something no one else seemed to think necessary: he collected and had published the names of all the rescued hostages.

Those Boyle had saved were full of gratitude. Joined by leading political, civic, and military figures, they publicly expressed their thanks in a luncheon at the Rumanian Jockey Club on 11 April. J. Lucasiewicz, one of the hostages, spoke for all as he told Boyle that they considered his service "an act of deep sympathy for the whole nation." All Rumanians, he continued,

have been able to realize your qualities of great energy, courage, strength [and] will keep it in mind and ... transform it into the symbol of the creed that nations have the duty, and the power, to struggle until the last breath. So, thank you colonel, for everything you did for the Rumanians. Thank you especially for the lesson of energy you gave us by your example.

Unbending for one of the few times of his life for the press, Boyle gave an extensive interview to reporters. One of them underlined the answer Boyle told them he had given to Zalkind when the Russian assistant foreign minister told him that Rumania was suffering from an illness that only a revolution could cure. "I told him that Rumania is not sick—she is starving and I know that a revolution of the kind you mention will produce a greater starvation and the destruction of the people you want to save by revolution."

The people, this story went on, were calling their hero Sherlock Boyle, for his feats were as amazing as those of the internationally known great detective. "You call me Boyle," said the Canadian, "but the Bolsheviks call me Colonel Boylsheviki."

Queen Marie confided several hundred words of admiration for Boyle to her diary. She was aware of more than his deeds. "Though their grip was of steel, his hands were unexpectedly refined. Dogged strength emanated from the man, a stubborn tenacity. Here indeed, was eine Manne, ein Wert."

And there was, on 22 April, a secret message from Downing Street to the Duke of Devonshire in Ottawa.

With reference to your Excellency's telegram of February 1st regarding the recall of Lieutenant-Colonel Boyle from Russia, the terms of which I communicated to His Majesty's representative at Petrograd, I have the honor to inform you that Mr. Lindley subsequently reported that Colonel Boyle was doing useful work in Russia in connection with food transport, and that [as] he was on very good terms with Monsieur Muralov, the Bolshevik commander at Moscow, he thought he had better stay in Russia.

Later His Majesty's Minister at Jassy reported that Colonel Boyle had arrived there and that his retention was desired by General Berthelot and, he believed, by the Rumanian prime minister to act as intermediary between the government and the Bolsheviks. The minister was accordingly authorized to retain Colonel Boyle so long as his services were considered useful.

The Duke was further informed that the British Embassy in Russia had stated that "Monsieur Trotsky has frequently asked about Colonel Boyle and would be glad to make use of his services."

On this note ended the unprecedented recall of Honorary Lieutenant-Colonel of the Canadian Militia J. W. Boyle. Fortunately, he was far too busy doing important things for the causes he cherished to be aware of what they had been trying to do to him in less hazardous regions.

With a rare sense of the fitting, someone in Ottawa sent the notification of the change in attitude about Boyle to two branches—the militia office and the department of trade and commerce.

A week after his return Boyle sat down once more to grapple with the authorities about recognition for his faithful companions in his adventuring. The first appeal was ignored. Now he tried again through a now-proven friend, Sir George Barclay, the ambassador in Jassy, who replied that he was forwarding the recommendations to Whitehall "in accordance with your request." The knowledge that Sir George had done so made Boyle feel reasonably confident there would be a response.

He asked that Hill and Tzegintzov be awarded the Distinguished Service Order; and that the Military Cross should go to Lieutenant-Commander Lazu, Lieutenants Lascar and Bucer of the Rumanian Army, and Captain Cheval and Sergeant Vincent of the French Army. He also drew attention to the valuable services, rendered at risk, by the British vice-consul in Theodosia. At greatest risk of all, he added, had been Captain Cheval, who had been left behind by Berthelot to assist Boyle and Hill with their intelligence work in the Odessa area. Vincent and Bucar had skilfully flown Boyle on many missions, taking great risks in night flights at a time when they were almost unknown.

It remains strange that no one in London or Ottawa noted that Boyle himself, decorated for exploits in the field by two Allied nations, received no recognition from his own people.

❧ TWENTY-FIVE ❧

A Heart Bowed Down

That safe-conduct that von Mackensen granted Joe Boyle quickly turned out to be a one-way pass to Jassy, with no legal opportunity to travel elsewhere. The Central Powers now controlled a vast area of the west and south. They were on the Russo-Bessarabian border, in control of Odessa and advancing on Kiev and the Crimea.

Accompanying the swift Austro-German advance had been the equally speedy disappearance of the pro-Allied Bratiano regime in Rumania. It was replaced by a government headed by the pro-German M. Marghiloman, a switch accomplished almost by sleight-of-hand in a farcical election staged on a few days' notice. So it was with Marghiloman that Boyle had to deal when he returned with the hostages. The strictures of his safe-conduct angered him immediately and he asked the government to intercede with von Mackensen on his behalf to permit him to return to Russia. He found the prime minister unresponsive, even obstructive. Boyle arranged to meet him on 10 April, but Marghiloman just happened to be away from Jassy and unavailable. Boyle's daily pleas for a meeting were courteously acknowledged and totally ignored.

This temporary incarceration brought him the daily pleasure

of meeting with Queen Marie. They frequently rode together on horses from the royal stable as the queen showed Boyle the beauties of the countryside she had come to love, and found him sharing her enthusiasm for it and for its kind, simple people.

Boyle, not one to be confined by a mere safe-conduct, found means of travelling that permitted him to go about his intelligence business and meet with those who shared his intense determination to continue to oppose both the Germans and the Bolsheviks.

On 25 April he escaped by car to Roman, an ancient community also beloved by Marie, and there he had a long meeting with former War Minister Averescu and General Tscherbatchef, still commander of Russian troops in Rumania.

His activities advanced another step on 1 May when he met with the queen, Averescu, former Rumanian ambassador to Britain Nicolae Misu, General Ballard, and some others. The conference covered a wide spectrum, concentrating finally on how to fashion a national program to preserve the dynasty and the nation against the Bolsheviks, now recognized as by far the greatest menace to Rumania. These activities were bound to attract attention, and did. Two days later Ballard passed along word that some Rumanian ministers had asked him to see that Boyle was kept away from Averescu.

There was some social activity, as well, in which Boyle joined with pleasure. At Easter, after attending a midnight service in the royal chapel, Boyle and Tzegintzov joined the king and queen and with them drove to Khontseshty, where they were guests of Mme. Navruz Khan. The return to Jassy after this pleasant interlude was complicated by two breakdowns in the car motor, necessitating overnight stops. Boyle fretted at the forty-eight hour delay before he and Tzegintzov were returned to their billets at 4 Strada Pozoiou, the residence of Princess Marie Morousi, divorced wife of the politician Ion Bratiano.

All these journeyings, and suspicions that there were more of which he knew nothing, worried Marghiloman. The prime minister got the impression that Boyle was still active and taking orders from his opponents. That suspicion was re-inforced in mid-May when Boyle drove to Kishinev, capital of Bessarabia, for consultations with General Ystrati, commander of Rumanian occupation troops in the province. Tzegintzov noted that Ystrati was reputed to be the only official there who refused to accept bribes—a compliment tempered by suspicions that Madame Ystrati did the collecting on her husband's behalf.

Bessarabia was a comfortable billet for the six occupying Rumanian divisions. It was a province abounding in food and other necessities, but Rumanian arrogance made things miser-able for many in some areas. Boyle's anger was aroused when he learned of one Rumanian commandant who ordered every-one in the town he was occupying to salute his cap, which he had carried around the streets on a tall pole.

The excursion to Kishinev had one important benefit for Boyle. Undoubtedly under royal orders, the Rumanian air squadron at Kishinev placed two airplanes at the direct orders of Boyle and Tzegintzov. They once more were mobile, far beyond the radius of those cranky automobiles.

The remainder of May saw Boyle constantly on the move, Marghiloman unable to interfere, and the Germans too busy elsewhere to do anything about it. Unquestionably his time was taken up with the direction of his now-invaluable intelligence circuit, but there were odd moments of relaxation. One was a happy two-day pleasure jaunt to Cotafanesti where Marie entertained Boyle and Tzegintzov at a royal hunting lodge, from which she escorted them on a tour of the Rumanian positions along the River Bystritza. On the second day Marie and Ferdinand entertained their guests, and officers of the 15th Division, at lunch, following which they drove to Bikaz for dinner at a royal summer palace, beautifully situated in the valley of the river.

Boyle, it seemed, was seldom in one place for more than a few hours. He met with the Marquis de St. Clair, French ambassador in Jassy, and then in company with Tzegintzov flew to Kishinev. Unrecorded business concluded, they flew back to Jassy, climbed into an automobile and drove to Roman, touched at Cotafanesti, and returned to Jassy for another series of meetings, after which they flew off once more to Kishinev. All this activity took place in the first ten days of June.

These were far from the aimless wanderings of a bored man of action. Boyle, to his great delight, was engaged in a new kind of war with the Germans. The two sides were battling fiercely in a contest to buy up all the foodstuffs and supplies available in Bessarabia. This commercial conflict was financed by the Allies and carefully planned and carried out in co-operation with many Rumanians still devoted to the Allied cause. Recent events in France, where it began to appear that the Germans had made one throw too many, helped bring out supporters in even greater numbers.

One thing is certain. In those few weeks of Rumanian spring the relationship between Boyle and Marie deepened. That they became lovers seems certain. Both were full-blooded, passionate individuals who made their own rules. They were mature enough to understand the rewards and the penalties of such a relationship and wise enough to risk them. Boyle was everything that the king and the other men Marie had met never were. She was the kind of woman who could match him in courage and devotion, far beyond any woman Boyle had ever met. Marie's affection was not lightly bestowed but, as she herself hinted, when it was, the gift was complete. They were living at a pace only those who have survived a war can understand. When you may be dead tomorrow there is every reason to live today.

On 8 June these two admirable people joined in an act of defiance that enraged the Germans and cheered the Rumanians. As a gesture to rally the nation, and in part as one of evident defiance and protest, a national day of mourning had been promised in honour of the fallen. It had been postponed several times under pressure from von Mackensen, but was finally and definitely set for Saturday, 8 June. This brought relief to the queen, who found the postponements intolerable and asked in her diary: "How shall we be able to live through it without a revolt?"

The queen announced that she would attend a requiem mass in Jassy cathedral and invited a number of people to attend with her, among them Boyle. The Germans announced that no Allied officers would be permitted to attend. The queen, as good as her word, marched to the cathedral with her retinue, prominent among them Colonel Boyle in full regimentals, proudly wearing the decorations he had earned and received from the Russians. "I had invited him and that was quite enough for him," the queen wrote. "What others thought about him being there was a matter of glorious indifference to him."

Several days later, personally confronted by von Mackensen, Boyle was ordered to remove his uniform. He coolly refused, saying it could be taken from him only by force, and that he would shoot the first man that attempted it. The general did not pursue the issue. He knew that Boyle meant what he said.

Boyle's many private hours with Marie had given him a chance to advance ideas for the reform and improvement of Rumanian political and social life. He urged the queen to improve the lot of the peasants, who constituted 80 percent of the population. He did not stand on ceremony, for "he was always in earnest but his heart was in the right place."

In the relaxed evening hours, then and later, Boyle brought new pleasure to the royal family, and especially to the royal children, with his mind-boggling stories of the great gold rush, frequently punctuated with the recitation of poems by the Yukon's Robert W. Service. Marie found that

In time of depression he was an extraordinary, refreshing and invigorating companion. And an unexpected touch of early Victorian puritanism added much to his quaintness. He neither drank nor smoked. My Ileanna adored him and he filled her young soul with strong and healthy maxims which she later carried with her out into life.

Boyle's closest relationship with Rumanian women was in the privileged homes of royalty, but he found himself distressed by the condition of those less favoured. He saw the peasant women condemned to lives of hard work and childbearing, and found it offensive that young Rumanian boys were permitted to be idle while their sisters and mothers worked. He urged that Rumanian boys be obliged to work from their early years to ease the burden on the females of the family. He hoped to help the queen design a new, better nation.

He had been without a real holiday for more than a year, calling unceasingly on his great physical strength. But there was a war to finish winning, and he drove himself with all the intensity of that much younger Boyle who had fought his way into the Klondike in 1897. In the end, it all caught up with him. On 18 June, a good day for action—for it was the anniversary of Waterloo, a battle that had ended another long war—Boyle and Tzegintzov flew off to Kishinev for yet another round of intelligence visitations. The next day Tzegintzov found time to pen two sentences in his diary: "Boyle has a stroke. Got him to Kishinev Red Cross hospital under Dr. Klisich." Days later a romantic tale reached North America. Klondike Joe Boyle, it was said, had been stricken with a heart seizure while flying an airplane nine thousand feet over Russia. The truth is somewhat less dramatic. Tzegintzov later told Flora Boyle that her father had been stricken in his hotel room soon after their arrival in Kishinev.

Boyle's life depended on the skill of Dr. Klisich, a Serbian heading the Red Cross hospital, and on the care of a medical team assembled to look after him as quickly as possible. Tzegintzov sent a telegram to Marie, who hurried her own physician to Kishinev. She told her diary of her anguish.

It seemed incredibly unfair that fate should thus lay low this only friend who had remained with us ... and what made it doubly hard was that it was absolutely impossible for me to go to Bessarabia ... so that I, who had looked after so many hundreds of anonymous sufferers, was not able to hurry to the sick bed of my friend.

Klondike Joe Boyle, the stout Canadian who had lifted 150 pounds of Yukon gold with one arm, who had seldom known a minute of ill health since childhood, lay paralyzed on his right side, a cripple who might never again be wholly fit.

Comedy and Tragedy

Joe Boyle's life hung in the balance for two weeks before he could even begin to hope that there would be any future to worry about. The prospect, at best, was forbidding. He was partially paralyzed, his features were misshapen, his circulatory system was damaged, and his heart weakened.

Faithful Tzegintzov stayed with Boyle until 1 July, despite the duties that had fallen on his shoulders in directing Boyle's affairs, public and private. On that date he flew to Jassy to meet Sir George Barclay and General Ballard, obviously to talk about the intelligence network and how it would be maintained in Boyle's absence.

Marie, full of concern, told Tzegintzov that she was arranging to have Boyle convalesce in the Rumanian hill country near Bikaz, and planned to install him in the summer palace there. Boyle, fighting stubbornly to overcome his affliction, balked at the arrangements but gratefully accepted Marie's offer to house him in a comfortable peasant cottage not far from the royal residence.

Toward the end of July Boyle could be moved. In the capable hands of Tzegintzov he set off by car, travelling slowly through Jassy to Piatra and eventually to Bikaz, where he arrived on 1

August. The queen had personally supervised the preparation of the cottage and was there to meet Boyle, who had been joined by General Ballard and Rumanian ambassador Misu. Boyle was too tired to attend dinner, but was well enough the next day to visit Marie, who found his speech, intelligence, and wit as good as ever, although she detected a sadness in her great friend and admirer, as if he realized something permanently had been drained from his great physical powers.

Quiet at first, Boyle began to expand in this environment. Laughter returned. He began to tell his stories again, and established a great friendship with Princess Ileanna, the youngest daughter of the royal family. (Years later, after a failed marriage with an Austrian prince, Ileanna moved with her children to America, and eventually became abbess of a monastery in Pennsylvania.)

Life at Bikaz fell into a pattern. Each day Marie had breakfast with him and, unless the weather was inclement, she and her children joined him for a drive. Frequently they carried a picnic lunch brought from the palace. It was exactly what Boyle required: quiet, the care and loving attention of good friends, good food, and an opportunity to rest, which had escaped him all his previous years.

As his health improved, Boyle's excursions ranged to more distant points, among them a large and lovely river valley that appealed to Boyle as the spot at which to construct a hydro dam to provide power for the whole of Moldavia. The idea intrigued him and he spent a good deal of time accumulating French and Russian electrical systems data that might be adapted. His vision was justified, years after his death, by the building of just such a system.

Little more than two months after being stricken Boyle was involved, Tzegintzov noted, "in trying to help our Red Cross representative to get hold of the Red Cross stores seized by the Rumanians," a project in which the Russian aide became deeply involved. His diary provides a background to the project that neither Marie nor Boyle would record in their public records:

"He has interested the Queen in the subject and persuaded [Colonel] Iiline to sell part of the R.C. property to the 'Regina Maria' and the Queen will then help to get the remaining part out of the country."

The queen, who had been concerned by Boyle's passivity—"I feel that he knows he will never be quite the same again, and this is terrible to him," she wrote—was delighted by his interest in the Red Cross matter. Boyle had a twofold interest in acquiring the stores. He wanted some of them to be the foundation of Queen Marie's private medical organization, the Order of Maria Regina (about which he had advised her), and he and the queen secretly planned to divert a substantial part of the stores to the White Armies in Russia, which were in desperate need of medical supplies. The Volunteer Army, as it was called, had been assembling under General M. V. Alekseev, whom Boyle knew from Stafka days. Alekseev died within a few weeks, killed in a small battle.

Ileanna and "Uncle Joe" joined forces in their own private aid program, collecting supplies which they distributed to the villagers. "Our excellent colonel was very generous with his money," the queen noted. Her spirits were rising, like those of the man who loved her, for it was clear now that the Germans could not hope to win the war, and its termination would redound to Rumania's benefit.

Some of her delight was clouded by a family problem of national concern. Prince Carol, the heir apparent, had long been at odds with his mother, displaying what she and Ferdinand considered a refusal to accept the obligations of his position. Carol was the oldest of five living children. There were three girls, in descending order of age, Elizabeth, Mignon, and Ileanna, and a younger brother, Nicholas. There had been another, Mircea, the last of the royal brood and like so many youngest children the most beloved by the mother. But Mircea had died of diphtheria in 1916, a loss that distressed Marie intensely but did nothing to bring her and her son and heir closer.

The laws of primogeniture ensured that Carol would be the next king, but his inability to find a royal princess was becoming a source of family discord and national unease. Like his father, Carol preferred a commoner, in his case Mlle. Zizi Lambrinos. When the marriage was forbidden he left his regiment and ran off to Odessa with her, where they were married in the cathedral with the blessing of the German commander, who undoubtedly welcomed the opportunity to embarrass the Rumanian royal family.

It was a scandal of major dimensions and an additional problem for the reviving Boyle. He became deeply involved in the family crisis and worked hard to persuade the young prince to give up his morganatic bride. Boyle had several long meetings with him, and during one in Odessa, the Prince, having something of his mother's flare for the dramatic, threatened to commit suicide if he was forced to return home. Boyle smiled and offered to loan him his pistol to facilitate the attempt. Carol withdrew the offer, came home, and eventually his marriage was annulled.*

Meanwhile the strange case of the Red Cross supplies lying unused in warehouses in Botosani, Jassy, Roman, and Kishinev was developing under Boyle's probing examination, with much of the legwork done by Tzegintzov. The stores, technically the property of the Russian Red Cross that functioned during czarist days, were closely guarded by the Rumanian army. The cast of this comedy-mystery, as it developed, included:

Queen Marie—interested in obtaining supplies to stock her

---

*Carol later made a royal marriage on 10 March 1921, when he wed Princess Helen of Greece, an arrangement in which Boyle played a role of royal matchmaker. It was a short-lived, unhappy union that produced the last king of Rumania, Prince Michael. Carol, still with an eye for commoners, made a life with Magda Lupescu, finally marrying his mistress after a long sojourn in England.

Order of Maria Regina and to assist the White armies in southern Russia.

Joe Boyle—a national hero sharing the same interests as the queen, a trusted royal adviser behind whom the court, and some less savoury characters, could operate.

Dr. Mamoulia—the queen's physician, who had helped nurse Boyle but whose interests were not necessarily the same as those of his royal sovereign.

Iiline—a pompous but honest Russian Red Cross official in charge of the stores and a White sympathizer hoping to send all of them to the Don armies.

Nicolesco—a merchant who preferred to make a dollar honestly, and who would act as the queen's agent in the purchase of the supplies.

Salini—a Rumanian wheeler-dealer with valuable connections to the pro-German Marghiloman government, whose interest was to divert as much of the sale price into his own pocket as possible.

Stan—a Rumanian lawyer providing whatever legal fiction might be needed to cover dubious deeds.

Plus a cast of sundry lesser characters, including General Bailiff and members of the court.

The play began when Salini induced Mamoulia to put the idea of purchasing the stores into Boyle's mind, certain that Boyle would mention it to Marie. Boyle spoke with Iiline and the queen, and after some days of negotiation made a contract that permitted the queen to stay in the background by subletting the deal to an agent, Nicolesco.

Iiline's reluctance to sell in Rumania was overcome when Salini whispered that the stores were going to be seized by the Germans. Iiline, totally opposed to such a disposition, agreed to sell them to the Rumanians rather than lose them. The arrangement called for a good-faith payment of one million lei, about $250,000 at that time, on an agreed-upon scale of prices based on 1915 values plus inflation, and graduated according to the condition of the stores.

Salini, hoping to increase the size of his cut, asked Nicolesco whether he would pay him (Salini) more if he could get the price of the stores reduced. Nicolesco agreed. Salini then gave the signal and Mamoulia and Stan made complaints that Iiline was swindling Rumania, and threatened to have the contract cancelled. Secretly pleased at a possible cancellation, for he had discovered that the threat of German seizure was a lie, Iiline said he would cancel the arrangement. This angered Salini and Stan, who threatened to make it impossible for Iiline to remove the supplies at all.

The delay in the completion of the contract made Boyle suspicious. He had dealt with the wolves of Wall Street and the freebooters of the Klondike, but this was a new experience. He assigned Tzegintzov to investigate the whole matter. When it became known that Tzegintzov was asking questions, Iiline came to him and wanted to know whether Salini could block the transfer of supplies to the White armies. Tzegintzov assured him that, things being as they were in the government, they assuredly could. Nicolesco, who said he was prepared to deal on the original terms, met Iiline and completed the deal. Unquestionably at Boyle's suggestion, Nicolesco made amends by permitting Iiline to retain certain special items needed for the White armies, and arranged the gift of free supplies to the Order of Maria Regina. It was Boyle who found the one million lei that was the final price for the supplies.

Far from losing favour with anyone, Salini, Stan, and Mamoulia managed to obtain a slice of the purchase price. Boyle was not amused and found it difficult to accept Tzegintzov's rationalization that "it is the way of things in Rumania." But in the end, despite the roguery, the queen's Order got its supplies, and the White armies benefited by a shipload of vital items including 104 kinds of medical stores, medicines, operating room equipment, and—doubtless to their surprise—forty Russian Imperial and fifty Red Cross flags.

A small final bit of skullduggery was required to move the stores out of Rumania. When they were loaded at Ismael the manifest gave Rostov-on-Don as the destination, a port to which the Germans approved shipments. But the vessel sailed directly to Novorossisk, a forbidden destination.

Completion of this assignment brought Tzegintzov to a sharp turn in the road. He had long desired to join the Volunteer Army despite Boyle's suggestion that he could do more for the cause working with him. But the able Russian aide, a career soldier, decided he had to go, said his thanks and farewell to the queen, Boyle, and his other associates, and departed for the Kuban. He promised to keep Boyle informed of all that he saw and did, and quickly demonstrated his value in that regard. His report from Odessa contained information arising from a visit he had with Grand Duchess Marie Pavlovna, who was living there with her family in difficult circumstances. She feared for their lives, for the city was now menaced by yet another uprising among the Ukrainians. Tzegintzov urged Boyle to do what he could to help the grand duchess escape to Rumania, an appeal reinforced soon afterwards in a letter from N. Golejewski, a member of the Pavlovna household, who said that he had been advised to write Boyle by Tzegintzov. "We are a small party consisting of the Grand Duchess Marie Pavlovna [sister of the Grand Duke Dmitri, now at British headquarters in Persia], her husband Prince Putiatine, Mr. Peter Tolstoy [an ex-ADC of the Grand Duke Dmitri], his wife and family, and my wife, my child and myself."

Failing to hear from Boyle or anyone else for nearly a month the household had abandoned hope of relief from Rumania when, one morning in November, while the grand duchess was still in bed, a Russian officer came to her apartment and reported that Colonel Boyle of Canadian intelligence in Rumania was ready to arrange the escape and she would be further informed. "Somehow," she wrote later, "I did not put much trust in the desire of a Canadian colonel to save us, but I was utterly mistaken." A week later the same Russian returned with a letter from the queen of Rumania, inviting the grand duchess and her family to come to live in Rumania. The message found the grand duchess in bed, suffering from influenza (it was the year of the great 'flu epidemic), but despite her illness she was determined to go. The refugees were taken to the railway station, where they were invited to occupy a special carriage guarded by White Russians assigned to protect them en route to the hospitality of the Rumanian royal family.

The long delay in responding to the appeal for help was not typical of Boyle and was hardly his fault. There is a gap in his story the first two weeks in October 1918, which has never been explained but which may involve the most secret of all his assignments. In 1920, during a visit to New York, Prince Carol spoke of the mission with Flora Boyle, and several years later Queen Marie in a private audience in New York told her the fuller story.

When the Bolsheviks announced that the czar had been executed, there was no reference to the fate of the other members of the entourage held in close confinement in Ekaterinburg. The admission that the new rulers of Russia had authorized this regicide sent shock waves around the world. Many other Romanovs and Russian nobility simply refused to believe that Nicholas had been killed. Among the most doubtful was Dowager Empress Marie Feodorovna, who was in regular communication with Marie in Rumania. Boyle was asked whether he would go to Ekaterinburg to investigate the matter and, although far from completely well, he accepted the mission.

Flora was told that he inspected the Ipatieff house in which the royal prisoners had been assassinated. He talked with the

White occupiers, with Tchemadurov, a Romanov servant who survived, and with residents of the town, but was unable to get to the place where the bodies were alleged to have been burned with the ashes tossed into a mine shaft.

Marie gave Flora a photograph of Boyle, said to have been taken in front of the fireplace in the Ipatieff house. It clearly is Boyle after his summer illness. He is wearing his ribbons on his uniform but seems far from well, his face creased and drawn and his hair greying at the centre part. But Boyle left no documentary evidence of this mission. His notes, Marie told Flora, were written on scraps of paper from which he compiled his final report, pieces that could easily be disposed of if he had fallen into Bolshevik hands on his return.

It is difficult to know what to make of this story. Boyle could not have made the one-thousand-mile journey by train or car. There were few roads and, as he had discovered, train journeys seldom provided better travelling than ten to fifteen miles per hour on average. In any case, it is unlikely that he could have made such a rail journey without being intercepted by the Russians. So if Boyle made this long trip, he must have gone by air in one of the planes that had been made available to him.

If Boyle made a report directly to King George about the fate of his Russian cousin and the Romanovs, it may well be resting in the royal archives in Windsor castle. A few years ago former British MP Peter Bessell claimed that years of research had convinced him that the Romanovs were not killed, and that the Allied and Soviet governments had proof of the fact. This has led to speculation that he had obtained some information from the British royal archives.

What is known for certain is that Boyle had his intelligence network searching for answers to the mystery of the Romanovs' fate. In December 1918 he received a lengthy report from A. Kasman, one of his agents in Kishinev. This included an extract from a letter written by a former member of the Cadet Party named Stepanov, who had lately taken up residence in Odessa.

Stepanov told of a meeting with General Grishin-Almarov, who had been with the Siberian White armies and had been one of the officials investigating the assassinations a few days after the fateful 16 July. He had provided Stephanov with the copy of a report he had made on the events in Ekaterinburg, which was being forwarded to the Rumanian ambassador in Bucharest. According to that report:

During the night following the 16th of July the whole family, consisting of the Emperor, the Empress, the heir-apparent, the Grand Duchesses Olga, Tatiana, Marie and Anastasia, have been shot. ... [T]he Emperor and family and all persons accompanying them were removed to a cellar situated under the house, were placed against a wall and shot. The Emperor died holding his son in his arms; the poor boy was ill at the time. Grand Duchess Tatiana didn't die on the spot, though wounded by several bullets; they finished her off with rifle butts. The corpses were put on a motor camion and taken to a place forty versts from the town and there they were burned.

This account of the murder of the Imperial family has been seriously challenged on many counts, with more recent commentators claiming that only the czar and his son were shot and that the rest of the family was spirited away in a sealed train and kept in poverty in other cities of the area, where they eventually expired from hunger and grief. The fact is that no one can be sure. One of the great propaganda triumphs of the Lenin regime, which was skilled in deception, was the way in which it covered up the truth of what did happen to the imprisoned ex-czar and his family.

At the time, Boyle appeared convinced that the family had indeed been murdered, and drafted a report to the dowager empress and other royal personages, including Marie and Prince George. His opinion may have altered; he was said later to have disputed the claim. Whatever his opinion on the matter, the murder of the Romanovs cemented even more firmly his determination to work against the new regime in Russia, even as he toiled to advance the eventual triumph of the Allied cause. It was an event now close at hand, that October in 1918 when he vanished from view for two weeks.

To his intense personal satisfaction he was able to celebrate Armistice Day, 11 November, in Jassy, guest at a dinner party hosted by General Ballard at the British embassy. Among the guests were Queen Marie, her two older daughters, and her aide General Bailiff. It must have been an evening of great significance to all of them. For Marie it proved her position to have been the correct one in putting Rumania into the war on a side that had looked, at that moment, in danger of losing. Boyle's place in the scheme of things was obvious. And for him it was an opportunity to celebrate at the side of the woman he now realized he loved deeply.

Those few, happy hours were a temporary respite, for even as they commenced Klondike Joe was deep in preparation for a bold move to snatch the exiled Dowager Queen Marie Feodorovna from her exposed summer palace near Yalta. Boyle had conceived the plan some two weeks earlier, charting the operation with the help of Commander Pantazzi, the resolute young Rumanian seaman he had met first as one of the Odessa hostages. Boyle broached the proposal to the queen on 2 November, explaining that his concern for Marie Feodorovna had been aroused by intelligence reports that the Bolsheviks were massing forces to take over the Ukraine and the Crimea as the defeated Germans withdrew. There was, he said, "a deliberate plot to kill the members of the royal family residing in the Crimea."

The king gave him command of a ship going to the Crimea, and with his usual thoroughness Boyle hand-picked his crew and a detachment of two hundred soldiers. He insisted that they be well supplied with machine guns, for his faith in that weapon had been more than justified from 1914 to 1918. It was a luxurious outing in many ways. The ship's larder was crammed with the finest foods and wines that could be obtained. Finally, just before sailing, a large automobile owned by the Rumanian prime minister was deposited on the deck.

By this time Boyle's agents had informed him not only that the empress was at Yalta but that the Grand Duke Nicholas, the Duchess Xenia (oldest sister of the late czar) and her husband Grand Duke Alexander, as well as the Grand Duchess Olga, all lived in royal summer residences in the area, close to Yalta and about sixty miles from Sebastopol.

The expedition was full of hazards, not the least being the presence of uncharted minefields, free-floating mines, the possibility of opposition from forces on the shore, and the strong prospect of diplomatic explosions if Rumanian troops landed on Russian soil. However, it was smooth sailing across the Black Sea. Their Sunday morning arrival 17 November created a local sensation, for it was the first ship to dock in several months and the townspeople flocked to observe it.

Boyle discovered that occupying German forces were not interested in him or his party. They were preparing to return to the Fatherland within forty-eight hours. Bolshevik forces, he was informed, were waiting for the Germans to leave, intent on seizing power as soon as the occupiers left.

He was bemused to discover that the Bolshevik show of energy was sparked by a fiery woman leader who had shown admitted talent in organizing the projected takeover. "Fortunately," Boyle wrote, "the leader of the Bolsheviks took sick and died that day." People, as they usually do, suggested she had been poisoned. This timely fatality put an end to reports that the Bolsheviks planned to seize the ship. Boyle discouraged that sort of talk by mounting his machine guns and telling any who would listen how good his troops were, and how well-prepared to resist any hostile actions.

Dropping the stick for a moment, Boyle dangled the carrot, in this case an invitation to the Bolshevik leaders to attend a party on the ship. This social event became an endurance contest in which the guests seemed willing to stay as long as the food and drink held out and their heads could resist the onslaught of Demon Rum. Boyle just *had* to win that contest.

Boyle left Pantazzi in charge of the guests and drove off in the prime minister's automobile to find the dowager empress. She was soon located, living uncomfortably but confidently in a small villa, her needs cared for by an English companion, Miss Dane, and a small retinue of servants. The exiles were overjoyed at the arrival of the party and engaged their visitors in long, lively conversation during which Boyle realized that the empress simply did not believe that her son Nicholas had been murdered.

Boyle presented letters from Ferdinand and Marie and strongly urged Marie Feodorovna to accept the proferred hospitality, particularly in view of the Bolshevik menace. The empress declined to move, saying she had been informed that a British naval squadron was en route to the Crimea and she felt she would be safe until they arrived. She assured Boyle that while the Bolsheviks had been very cold and formal in dealing with her, they also had been correct. Her only problem, she added, was when she insisted on signing her ration card with a regal "Marie." Told that she would be penalized if she refused to put down her second name, she had a ready answer. "I have been signing Marie for fifty years," she told them. "If that is not sufficient I can do without sugar."

Boyle tried every trick he knew, but the empress was adamant. He departed with a farewell message that he would return in twenty-four hours, after she had had more time to think about it. Aboard the ship in Yalta harbour the party was still underway, and was at a stage where his disappearance had hardly been noted. Pantazzi warned that the real danger was that they might run out of drinks before the mission was concluded.

The following day Boyle once more slipped away to see the empress. She was unbowed, prepared to wait for the Royal Navy, she told him. In the interim she had written long letters to the Rumanian king and queen, to her sister Dowager Queen

Alexandra in London and others, and commissioned Boyle to personally deliver them. As they said their farewells the tiny, lion-hearted empress extended her hand. Boyle's Russian and Rumanian aides kissed it in courtly fashion. Klondike Joe looked her squarely in the eye, his face shining with admiration, and wrung her hand warmly, in the fashion of the faraway Yukon.

Boyle's fears that the Bolsheviks would take over Yalta were removed when a detachment of the Volunteer Army arrived and took possession of the area without having to fire a shot. Arrival of the White Russian forces made it safe for Boyle to depart. He set a course for Sebastopol to investigate a report, on 27 November, that a British cruiser and two destroyers had arrived there. He left behind his precious machine guns as a gift for the volunteers.

The report was true. The end of the war had opened the Dardanelles to the long-frustrated Allied navies. In Sebastopol the Boyle party met Vice-Admiral Sir Somerset Gough-Calthorpe, commander-in-chief of the British squadron. After his talk with Boyle the admiral sent two destroyers to Yalta to protect the members of the royal family. Boyle made ready to return to Rumania, satisfied that the reluctant Romanovs in the Crimea were reasonably safe for the moment. Before departing he persuaded the captain of a Rumanian ship that had been idled in Sebastopol after seizure by the Bolsheviks to return to Rumania with him. It was a valuable consolation prize.

During Boyle's absence in the Crimea the Rumanian government had returned in triumph to Bucharest. A new prime minister, General Coanda, was at the helm, having replaced the hated Marghiloman, who had resigned a few days before the final German collapse on the western front. So it was that, at the Cotroceni Palace in the national capital, Boyle reported on the events of his mission to the Crimea.

November had been a good month for Joe Boyle, and his services were recognized as never before. There was the presentation of the Croix de Guerre by General Berthelot, to add to the Order of Maria Regina that Marie had bestowed on him for his services in the Red Cross supply problem. And at the British embassy Sir George Barclay was penning an official document paying tribute to Boyle that brought the Canadian a DSO (Distinguished Service Order) in the 1919 royal birthday honours list.

TWENTY-SEVEN

The Duke from Dawson

The sudden silence of 11 November, which descended on all the world except strife-torn Russia, turned the attention of people wearied of making war to the problems of finding peace. It was 180-degree change of course, requiring an emotional and mental adjustment of all those who would soon assemble at the former royal palace of Versailles to negotiate a peace treaty. There, among the politicians, the generals, the opportunists, the genuine, and the false, was the Honorary Lieutenant-Colonel of the Canadian Militia, Joseph Whiteside Boyle, newly minted Duke of Jassy in the Kingdom of Rumania.

Only a few weeks earlier Boyle had been granted a dukedom by the king and queen, a crowning gesture of the nation's gratitude, some believed. Others whispered that it was a personal gift from Marie to Joe. The elevation, they said, permitted her to seat Boyle close to her at formal functions. As a commoner he had been obliged to sit below the salt, too far away in her estimation, and yielding no escape from the many boring people who sat closer.

Boyle's dukedom has been a matter of argument, but it does appear to have been a fact, although he may well have wished to forget it later. There are, in the Boyle papers, formal documents relating to a sizable ducal estate, a former Russian appanage, in Bessarabia, apparently the lands conferred on Boyle with the title.

Reports reaching Canada that Boyle was a duke infuriated his Woodstock relatives. Brother Dave angrily charged that it was a newspaper hoax. A Toronto newspaper published a picture of Boyle's neglected second wife and asked, "Is She the Duchess of Dawson?"

Boyle's presence at Versailles followed his return to England in December 1918, after eighteen unbroken months of field service in Eastern Europe. This long-overdue furlough, which ought to have provided plenty time for rest and relaxation, became merely an extension of assignments in a different location, with no time for vacationing. Before saying farewell to Marie and the royal family in Bucharest, Boyle had been commissioned to carry out a series of missions, the most immediate of which was to convey Prince Nicholas to England and install him as a student at Eton College. He was further charged with negotiating for food, clothing, and industrial and agricultural aid for Rumania. And on his person he carried messages from Dowager Queen Marie Feodorovna to her sister Queen Alexandra and other members of the royal family.

His own long-neglected business was crying for his attention, but he would be too late to prevent the disaster that had befallen his Klondike operations. Not the least of the items bothering him was the matter of his status as a Canadian soldier.

Perhaps the most important task of all was one he had assigned himself: to persuade Allied leaders to support massive intervention in the Russiain civil war and ensure that Bolshevism was defeated.

Prince Nicholas, departing Bucharest in the care of Misu of the Rumanian foreign office, had preceded Boyle to Constantinople. An undated cable from Boyle to King Ferdinand reports that he had met Nicholas and Misu, and that they would sail to

Taranto on HMS *Heroic* that evening. From Taranto the trio travelled by train to Paris, where Misu, who was to be a delegate to the peace conference, left them.

Boyle and his royal charge arrived in London 24 December and registered at the Ritz Hotel. London was *en fête*, gaily decorated with flags and bunting to celebrate the victory and honour the constantly arriving and departing foreign diplomats. There is no record of what Boyle did on Christmas Day but he has recorded that on 26 December, the traditional Boxing Day holiday, a note was received from Hugo Erskine Wemyss, private secretary to Princess Christian of Denmark, a sister to Queen Alexandra, inviting Boyle and Nicholas for lunch at Schomberg House on Pall Mall. "I do hope it will not rain and spoil the decorations," Wemyss added.

Boyle was able to pass along the message from Marie Feodorovna to her sisters and inform them personally of the events in which he had been able to serve the Romanovs.

The long journey, far from tiring Boyle, had left him feeling better than he had for many weeks. His priorities quickly came into focus, for one of his first actions was to write to Lord Reading, the war secretary, for an appointment in which to advance his plan for vast, direct intervention by the Allies on the White side of the Russian civil war. Reading was understandably busy but agreed to meet Boyle on Monday, 30 December.

While he waited, Boyle renewed his Canadian links through an interview with Sir Robert Borden, the Canadian prime minister, on Sunday, 29 December. Borden's memoirs record that Boyle gave a

most vivid and interesting account of his work in Russia during the last year and a half and of conditions in that country. He says that triumph of Bolshevism in Russia means that it will overrun Germany and that Germany and Russia will overrun the world or reduce organized society to anarchy. He insists that it must be put down . . . and declares that an army of a million men can do it. He says it will be a fraud and a sham if Peace Conference concludes its labours without terminating the war and that cannot be done until anarchy is ended in Russia.

Also discussed was regularization of Boyle's military status, which he pursued again on 3 January in an interview with General Turner at Canadian military headquarters in London. This meeting resulted in Boyle drafting a long report of his activities in Eastern Europe, at the request of Turner, a document he erroneously dated 4 January 1918. There was no immediate reaction to these pleas for full recognition as a Canadian officer on overseas service, rather than a free-lancer all too frequently pricking the boils of military displeasure.

In search for aid to Rumania the Klondiker turned to his old friend and associate, Herbert Hoover, who directed Red Cross programs. He then approached the British Royal Commission on Wheat Supplies. The responses must have been reasonably encouraging, for he began dickering with shipping companies for vessels in which to move the anticipated aid. As usual, Boyle was thorough. His approach to the wheat commission was so well documented with statistical and other data that the commission accepted Boyle's submissions and cancelled a plan to send an investigating team to Rumania to survey the nation's needs. Boyle tried every legitimate device, including psychological warfare, in his appeal for British help. He pointed out that the French and U.S. response was so generous that Britain could hardly afford to stand aloof, and he asked the Foreign Office to accept the principal that it was in Britain's wider international interest to participate.

Boyle's grasp of things was amazing. Administratively, he urged, there should be an interdepartmental committee, including London delegates of the Rumanian Red Cross, which would be assisted by another in Rumania to include representatives of the food and shipping ministries, the war office, and a number of prominent Rumanians "of known British sentiments."

During the war Rumania had been considered to be in the French sphere of influence. Boyle, almost certainly at the behest of Marie, was actively engaged in making it a new sphere of British influence. From a temporary office set up in the Ritz the Canadian dynamo hummed for hours on end, engaged in a variety of projects. His links extended to Paris, where he worked in concert with Misu and Director of Marine Affairs Ghica in the hunt for ships in which to send the supplies he felt certain would be granted. Rumania had only a few merchant vessels that had survived the war, chief among them the familiar *Imperator Trajan*.

The *Trajan* had sailed for Marseilles where Hoover had promised to supply Boyle with a cargo of Red Cross supplies, but the cranky, weatherbeaten vessel was overdue and there was no word of her whereabouts. There were other difficulties. Boyle sent a message to Hoover at the U.S. embassy in Paris on 7 January, asking for information about the delivery of the promised cargo. Three days later the outlook brightened when Rumania was offered nine cargo vessels of from 3,500 to 7,000 tons, seven of them immediately available. Now Boyle could stop worrying about the *Imperator Trajan*.

On 13 January he made formal application to the French mission in London for full equipment and supplies for 240,000 soldiers, as well as unspecified quantities of food, clothing, and medical supplies for the Rumanian civilian population. Then he requested that Britain provide 7,500 tons of biscuit, 5,000 tons of pork and beans, 5,000 tons of preserved meats, and 2 million tons of condensed milk for immediate shipment to Rumania.

Even as he won aid for Rumania, Boyle was trying to persuade the Canadians of postwar trade opportunities there. His contacts extended not only to the prime minister of Canada but to the Canadian Trade Mission, chaired by another former Woodstock College graduate, Lloyd Harris. And he apparently made some progress. The *Times* reported that Boyle had received a proposal from Sir Robert Bordon to advance £5 million in Canadian credits. The report was premature and put Boyle in a bad light, the suspicion being that he had leaked the information. Given Boyle's aversion to the press, it is more likely that the leak came from other sources.

Through this entire period Boyle reported regularly to the queen in Bucharest. Boyle had proceeded to London with the full authority of the Rumanian government as a commissioner for Rumania, but he found the Rumanian embassy in London uncooperative. His never-ending exertions finally took their toll, for he appeared to have come down with influenza early in the New Year, an illness he had great difficulty in shaking and from which he was still suffering when he departed for Paris and the peace conference on 25 January 1919. The grand assembly of the world's leading figures had come together a week earlier, but Boyle was not destined to watch them in action for a few days more, as he was immediately confined to bed.

Paris was to be a disappointment in many ways. On his arrival Boyle found that the leader of the Rumanian peace delegation was to be Ion C. Bratiano, who had supplanted Coanda as prime minister after Boyle's departure from Rumania. Bratiano's refusal to honour the credentials given Boyle by his predecessor became public knowledge, and embarrassed him in his dealings with Hoover and others to obtain relief supplies for Rumania.

Periodically there were echoes of his earlier, more exciting days in Russia to warm him. Early in January he had a letter from Captain R. A. Porters, a British staff officer at Mogilev, who had accompanied Boyle on one of his many excursions in Russia. Porters wrote to express his delight that Boyle was safe and had been able to get back to Britain, "out of the chaos that once was White and Holy Russia." Their trip from Stafka to Rumania, he added, was pigeon-holed in his memory. Now stationed at the British embassy in Paris, Porters was a highly critical observer of the passing scene. "I hope, in fact I know," he wrote, "that you humbled the British F.O. right up to the last. I still have a delightful souvenir of one interview in Jassy. But that 'ivory dome' mentality apparently exists everywhere. It is just as bad here, especially as regards propaganda."

Boyle, recovering slowly at the Hotel Westminster in Paris, was heartened to learn that the *Trajan* finally had arrived in Marseilles, that Ghica was going to supervise its turn-around, and that F. Rattigan and his wife would be sailing on 1 February for Rumania, to relieve Sir George Barclay, who was leaving on furlough. Despite Bratiano's stance, which was hindering his work, Boyle had arranged with Hoover for three more cargoes of flour, and two shiploads of fats and milk, to follow the *Trajan* within a matter of days. The British government had agreed to advance funds, leaving it to Rumania to make repayment arrangements later.

In informing Bucharest of his success, Boyle was particularly pleased to add:

Have a written offer from Canada to loan to Rumania twenty-five million dollars to be spent in Canada, five million of which will be granted at once pending completion of loan which will be at 5½ per cent which is the rate of interest Canada pays on her public loans. All purchases made under this arrangement will be made through either the Inter-Allied Food Commission or the Canadian Government Trade Commission. Mr. Misu should immediately be empowered to sign the necessary documents.

Bratiano, who was about to set out for Paris, immediately cabled his acceptance of the offer. His opinion of Boyle rose steadily thereafter.

Hit hard by his illness—his shakily drafted letters from Paris show how weakened he had become—Boyle felt well enough by 2 February to ask for a second interview with Prime Minister Borden. Borden agreed to meet him on 4 February and invited Arthur L. Sifton, minister of customs and a member of the Canadian war cabinet, to be present.

Boyle expressed his gratitude for Canada's aid to Rumania,

and once more fervently pressed the need for the western world to support the anti-Bolshevik cause. There was no talk of a million men this time. He concentrated on a proposal that Canada send a highly experienced corps of some 250 machine-gun experts to instruct the White Armies. Borden was polite but did not respond. "I told him there was no probability we would entertain any such proposal," he wrote to Sir Edward Kemp the next day. Meeting Joe Boyle was too much for Sifton who, Borden recorded, was not highly impressed "except by the fine quality of Boyle's imagination." Which says more about Sifton than it does about Boyle's performance.

The prime minister was more helpful on the issue of Boyle's military status and promised to see what he could do to regularize it and authorize the wearing of the foreign decorations that Boyle was proud to spread across his broad chest. Borden asked for a letter outlining the case. Boyle, never slow to strike, responded by writing that afternoon.

It was well that he was prompt, for his enemies in the military establishment were once more pursuing their vendetta against this upstart, amateur soldier who rode around the streets of London in a Rolls Royce driven by a Rumanian prince, and claimed to be a Rumanian duke. There had been an exchange of letters about Boyle's rank and position in January between Lieutenant-Colonel O. M. Biggar, of the Canadian section of the British legation in Paris, and Major Everett Bristol at Canadian headquarters in London. Writing to "Dear Everett" on 22 January, Biggar concluded that "in the circumstances . . . Boyle really has no right to be wearing a Canadian uniform."

The matter could hardly stop there. It was drawn to the attention of Lieutenant-Colonel E. W. Pope, adjutant-general at the Canadian Overseas Military HQ, who was asked to investigate the fact "that an individual called Boyle, wearing the uniform of a Lieutenant-Colonel of the Canadian Forces, was in the city. On General Turner's instructions I sent Boyle written orders to the effect that he was not entitled to wear uniform and requesting him not to appear again in the uniform of a Canadian officer."

In a report dated 7 February 1927, Pope wrote:

Some two or three days later, I saw Boyle for the first time. He...told me that he would like to tell me exactly what he had been doing in Russia in order that he might right himself in the eyes of the Canadian Military Authorities. He said that he had duly received my letter regarding his wearing uniform and that in consequence he had put on civilian clothes the next morning. He was stopping at Buckingham Palace and His Majesty, on meeting him that morning remarked on the fact that he was not in uniform. Boyle told the King he had been forbidden by Canadian authorities to appear in other than civilian attire. His Majesty, according to Boyle, then told him that as his Sovereign he ordered him to get back into uniform. He (the King) considered that he had justly earned this privilege for his work on behalf of the Allies in Russia and Roumania.

It was obviously impossible for me to verify the truth of this statement, but I did definitely ascertain that Boyle had arrived from Roumania . . . in charge of the Crown Prince who was to attend either Eton or Oxford. I ascertained that he was staying at Buckingham Palace and as far as I could I verified and had confirmed other statements which he made. Boyle from then on was permitted to wear uniform.

Borden directed Sir Edward Kemp to investigate the matter. Kemp began a protracted paper chase with letters to General Turner. He was told by the general that the British did not now oppose taking Boyle on Canadian strength "with a view to regularizing his work in Russia," if that was the Canadian wish. Boyle, he added, had proceeded to Russia on his own and should not, in any circumstances, be given pay and allowances back-dated to 11 June 1917. That gratuitious sniping overlooked the fact that Boyle, from the start, had waived any claim to pay or allowances from the Canadian treasury, and Turner was aware of the fact.

Sir Edward was still uncertain. He wrote to Borden that it would "facilitate matters if some government were to ask for his services," for the War Office did not appear anxious to take the initiative in straightening out Boyle's status. On 3 March Colonel Pope prepared a résumé for General Turner in which he reported contradictory views at the War Office and Foreign Office.

The Foreign Office commended Boyle's work and stated that although they were aware that certain friction had existed between this officer and Gen. Candolle, the latter never mentioned the fact in any official report. On the other hand the department of military intelligence at the War Office makes certain strong allegations against Col. Boyle... that the man is a bluffing adventurer who knows how to make the most of his chances and should not receive official encouragement. . . . What he did in Russia is unknown, but in due course he found his way to Roumania where he ingratiated himself with the Royal Family and finally was sent to England in the company of Prince Nicholas with an introduction that took him to Buckingham Palace. The Roumanian legation, from which he borrowed £100, disliked him strongly and their feelings were not softened when he produced a parchment, apparently faked in Canada, conferring a Roumanian "Dukedom" upon himself. There are certain outstanding law suits against Col. Boyle and it would appear inadvisable that he should be granted military status. . . .

The comment from the War Office represents a display of falsehoods and ingratitude that is almost stunning. For more than a year it had profited directly from the reports of Boyle's intelligence network. Back in London was Captain George Hill, one of Boyle's closest associates, who could vouch for the truth of all his actions. Hill made a long verbal report on his activities to the director of military intelligence in mid-November 1918. That he could have avoided mentioning Boyle in that recital defies belief. There was other evidence, including Sir George Barclay's commendatory report of 16 November 1918, in which

315

he said "there has never been a moment when the services of Col. Boyle here have not been useful both to His Majesty's Government and the Roumanian Government."

Borden, one of Canada's wisest and most underrated prime ministers, was not to be deceived. On 18 March he suggested to Kemp that Boyle be made head of a small Canadian mission to Rumania to direct distribution of Canadian aid and act as a trade commissioner. He was cautious, though, urging that someone be sent with Boyle to restrain "his impulsiveness and occasional lack of good judgement. There is no doubt about Col. Boyle's possession of remarkable initiative and resourcefulness, his great courage and iron nerve." This instruction by the prime minister did not end the long struggle, but it ensured that Boyle could not lose it.

General Turner, mumbling to himself, retired grudgingly. On 8 April he wrote:

As far as we are concerned he is a private Canadian citizen. As regards the verbal statement that he made that the King desires to see him in uniform; I think a letter should be sent to the secretary of the War Council, on the above lines, so as to clear the ministry and these headquarters.

Before concluding his first visit to the peace conference Boyle was seized of a very bright idea. Why not have Ferdinand and Marie attend the conference and plead Rumania's case? A word from Boyle was all they needed in Bucharest, and the government was wise enough to send Marie without her husband. She was a good negotiator and a beautiful royal personage. She would get Rumania more attention in the world press than any other single person. And she did, charming world statesmen in both London and Paris and providing extra impetus to her Canadian adviser's pursuit of assistance.

Before returning to London where other business was waiting, Boyle conferred at length with Prime Minister Bratiano. The reason for the earlier Bratiano antagonism is not clear, though one possibility is that some dispute had arisen when Boyle had lived in the home of the prime minister's divorced wife for a time. Boyle told Bratiano that he expected, eventually, to return to Russia. "In the meantime," he added, "if there is anything I can do for Rumania I trust you will let me know as I am only frank when I say I would sooner be helping her." By this time the prime minister knew Boyle well enough to understand that he meant every word of it.

The acclaim and attention that would be accorded Marie in Paris was not without some self-serving on the part of her most powerful flatterers. The Allies hoped to use Rumania as a bulwark against the bolshevism they were not prepared to fight themselves. This doctrine had been first sketched in a meeting in Jassy at the moment that Boyle was crossing the Black Sea to attempt to rescue Marie Feodorovna.

"Wilson," wrote one observer, Arno J. Mayer, "worried about weakening governments, including the Polish and Rumanian governments, that carried the brunt of the containment and intervention in Russia." It had been contended that "Rumania had been chosen to strangle the Soviet Republic since none of the great powers wanted to serve as hangmen themselves."

Boyle's grand design for a one-million-man Allied army never had a chance of acceptance, but the Allies did send small groups of men and masses of war materiel. More than two thousand British observers aided the White armies, and volunteer aviators formed the backbone of its small air force. The net effect was to prolong the bloody, losing struggle that killed more Russians than all the battles of the First World War.

In 1939, on the edge of a renewal of the great global conflict, Lord Beaverbrook told Flora Boyle in London that even Churchill was ready to admit that there might have been something in the massive intervention theory. "If we had taken Boyle seriously," he had told Beaverbook, "we wouldn't be in the difficult position we are today."

TWENTY-EIGHT

Reunion in London

The grim shadow of postwar disenchantment had yet to descend on the London to which Boyle was returning. The celebration of the victory after so many years of struggle, and at such a price in men and treasure, continued. London was the focal point of attention for all of the Empire, and people kept bobbing up there from all over the world. Among them was Mrs. George Black, living with her soldier husband in the Empire's capital and enjoying every minute of the peace.

She told of preparing a dinner for a group of Yukon soldiers, some of them Boyle's originals. As she awaited for their arrival there was a knock on the door. When she opened it she was hugged by Klondike Joe Boyle, who apologized for not coming to visit the Blacks earlier, as he had been busy at Buckingham Palace. The apartment was soon awash with excited talk, much laughter, many stories of the good old days, and the more recent bad ones. The meeting dragged on into the small hours, and when it ended Boyle promised to keep in touch.

Some two weeks into March 1919, Queen Marie arrived in London by train from Paris. Among the notables waiting to greet her, she saw, was faithful Joe Boyle. Her return projected him once more into the centre of things. He was at her breakfast meetings as she planned her day, and worked tirelessly with and for her for even more aid to Rumania—agricultural supplies, seeds, locomotives for her war-torn railways, anything and everything that would be useful.

Boyle's widening acquaintance with the people who counted now included the likes of Winston Churchill; Lord Astor; Lord Curzon, the foreign minister; General Greenly, head of the British military mission in Bucharest, who had carried letters to Boyle from the queen; and many more.

Late in March the Canadians in London played host to the queen at a tea party at the Ritz, clearly organized by Boyle, who frequently stayed there. Hundreds attended, including High Commissioner Sir George and Lady Perley. Boyle had insisted that the Blacks be among the guests and he led his old Dawson friends over to meet Queen Marie. Mrs. Black noticed that the queen lightly scolded Boyle, saying that she hadn't seen him for three days.

The queen, wrote Mrs. Black, wore an ermine-lined sable cape, which she handed to an equerry, revealing "a handsome panne velvet gown, coloured and patterned like an Indian shawl." Covering her golden-brown hair was a silver turban with gold and bronze flowers, from which a delicate brown veil was suspended. She wore a long string of pearls and pearl earrings mounted with solitaire diamonds, and carried a sable muff trimmed with ermine.

The queen greeted the Blacks with warmth. Boyle, she told them, "is a miracle man. He is Roumania's Saviour. When everyone else ran away, deserted us, Col. Boyle knew no fear. He remained. He saved our people." It was a message that she would later carry across the Atlantic in almost identical words.

Other receptions and parties followed, to which Boyle was able to invite some of his Canadian associates. A small select group, invited to attend a party at the Rumanian embassy, spoke at length with the queen about her favorite subject, Joe Boyle. They noticed that she wore a necklace of gold nuggets, a gift from the former King of the Klondike. Once more Marie told of

Rumania's eternal gratitude to Boyle who, she told them, had been created Duke of Jassy.

One assignment that took much longer than Boyle had anticipated was the acquisition of sufficient seed grain to guarantee a 1919 harvest adequate to supply the needs of a nation greatly enlarged as a result of the war. The addition of Bessarabia, Bucovina, Transylvania, and other border regions, many of them desolated by the war, had increased Rumania's population from a 1914 total of 7.5 million to more than 17 million, of which 14.5 million lived in rural areas and depended almost completely on agriculture for their livelihood.

Marie was no pasteboard queen. She realized that revolutions spring from empty bellies and took the problem under her direct control, forwarding a list of necessities for Boyle to supply in a letter written in her own hand. The queen asked for 2,375 carloads of wheat seed which, she specified, "must be Manitoba wheat." Boyle was ordered to find 70 farm tractors, 1,500 seeders, 3,000 reaping machines, 1,500 mowers, 1,000 raking machines, 200 threshing machines, 650 hand threshers, and a multitude of smaller items including 600,000 pickaxes, 133,000 spades and shovels, and 190,000 garden forks. "The quicker we are aided the better for our general peace and the better for the throne," she reminded him. She added her familiar "Marie" and a sentence, "The Queen You Are So Faithfully Serving."

As he persisted in these vital matters Boyle also found time to pursue his demands for British decorations for his Rumanian aides, in particular his recommendation for some honour to Commander Lazu, who had helped him defy the Austrian Commander Wolff with his monitors and airplanes. When Boyle learned that the Admiralty had not acted on the communication forwarded by Sir George Barclay, he renewed his appeal. When asked to provide full details of the incident, he patiently reconstructed the crisis, enclosing copies of all the correspondence with Wolff. Two months later he was gratified to hear that the Admiralty had decided to accept his recommendation to honour Lazu.

He would dearly have loved another visit to Ireland, but was kept so busy that he apologized for his failure to visit Buckna in a letter to Cousin Charlotte on 23 February. His Irish relatives were not alone in wondering what had happened to him. There had been little or no direct news of him at Bear Creek after he arrived in Russia. A letter sent in November 1917 did not reach Dawson for four months. On 4 December 1918, L. E. Lowman, secretary of the Soldiers Aid Commission in Woodstock, wrote to Ottawa on behalf of the Boyles at The Firs, asking for some news of the missing colonel of whom they had heard nothing for six months "and fear he is a prisoner in Rumania." Ottawa knew little more than his kin in Woodstock but made some inquiries and was able to report that the Foreign Office said Boyle was in Jassy on 30 November and would soon be leaving for England.

At Bear Creek, on 28 February 1919, Kenton Shane, a relative of Elma Boyle, dropped him a note on CKMC letterhead. "Would appreciate a few lines from you. Very anxious to get some news of your work. Am sure it would be interesting to read. Everyone here well. Can I do anything for you? Command me. Elma and Sadie anxious to hear from you. Trust you are enjoying the best of health." It had been a long, long time since plain Joe Boyle had told Elma to wait for him in the Butler Hotel in Seattle where he would meet her after his quick 1916 trip to England. Now she had an emissary pleading for news.

Whether Boyle responded is unknown. His feelings for the queen were such that he could hardly view returning to Elma with equanimity. With his mines in receivership and beyond his redemption, he seems to have decided to drop the curtain on that part of his life. He had done the same thing in 1896, when his first marriage foundered. He was not a man to live with failures when they could not be retrieved. Some will account it a major flaw in an unusual man, but it was the way he was.

In London he was still pursuing his dream of massive Allied intervention to crush the Bolsheviks, turning now to another advocate of such a policy, Winston Churchill, former Lord of the Admiralty. Churchill replied through his secretary, Edward

Marsh, that he was too busy to see him but advised him to "have a talk with General Greenly.... Mr. Churchill knows that General Greenly shares your view on the subject."

It was a poor time for the advocates of intervention. The Grand Duke Alexander of Russia, urging the same policy as Boyle, was rebuffed by leading generals and statesmen. He marvelled at their ignorance and particularly at that of a French general who insisted that two divisions landed at Odessa could take the new Russian capital of Moscow in a matter of weeks. There was no need for troops, Clemenceau assured the baffled duke, for the *cordon sanitaire* would topple the Bolsheviks in a matter of months.

Churchill was the only statesman of any stature supporting intervention, but following his thundering speech at the peace conference on 4 February he had been effectively muzzled by Lloyd George and Arthur Balfour. Balfour's ignorance appalled Boyle. He also recorded that Lloyd George once spoke learnedly of the civil war victories of General Kharkov, mistaking the city for Cossack General Krassnoff.

Boyle's search for aid to Rumania was global, and his successes in this helped offset the frustration of his fruitless days advocating intervention. On 3 March a message from T. M. Stevens of Vancouver reported that he could supply 1,500 tons of milk, 1,000 tons of rice, 1,500 tons of salmon, and 2,000 tons of flour every month if Rumania provided the bottoms to move the cargo.

Stubbornly pursuing the dream of intervention, Boyle penned on 28 March a joint letter to Churchill and Sir Henry Wilson, Chief of the Imperial General Staff, outlining his approaches to Borden and Kemp and a subsequent private talk with Lieutenant-Colonel H. F. Meurling of the 2nd Canadian Motor Machine Gun Brigade. Meurling, he said, had indicated that Boyle could easily obtain as many as one hundred machine gun officer experts from the Canadian army to serve in Russia.

My idea is to take a picked lot of men—use them as instructors and

322

teach the Rumanians and Russians modern machine gunnery. By so doing, and by organizing men into machine gun brigades we would, if provided with plenty of guns and ammunition, increase the gun power of such men tremendously, and for the class of guerrilla warfare to be waged would be of incalculable value.

I am satisfied that the Imperial Government will finance them, that the Canadian Government would agree to send the men here and they could be made of immediate use. . . .

There was need for haste. The Canadian Motor Machine Gun Brigades were under orders to return to Canada on 12 April, and Boyle had another trip to Paris on his agenda.

Without waiting for a reply from Churchill or Wilson, Boyle began his own search for recruits for the Volunteer Army by enlisting the services of Captain F. F. Worthington of the first brigade in compiling a list of those likely to be willing to serve in Russia. Worthington, who would be a founder of the Canadian Armoured Corps and a major-general of tanks in the Second World War, had been involved in Central American revolutions and other exciting events. The idea of a sojourn in southern Russia was definitely appealing to this man of action.

After a quick look at his own brigade Worthington reported that he had the names of seventeen officers and forty-five NCOs prepared to fight for the Whites. Because Colonel Meurling was absent he did not approach the second brigade, but Boyle noted that the top man on the list was the commander of the first brigade, Lieutenant-Colonel W. K. Walker DSO, MC. Two days later Meurling wrote angrily to Boyle protesting against this "improper" recruiting, without authority. He urged Boyle to ask General Brutinel, commander of the brigades, to organize the detachment. Meurling added that while he was in sympathy with the program he could not become involved because of the irregular way in which it was being pushed. He concluded this somewhat hysterical, and undoubtedly jealous, outburst rather oddly, wishing Boyle "all success and assure you if there is anything I can do to further this expedition, I will gladly do so."

It was too late to bring the project to completion. The brigades sailed for Canada, as scheduled, on 12 April. Colonel Walker wrote Boyle a short note from the SS *Adriatic*. He had not forgotten the proposal. "Keep in touch," he wrote, "and let me know if you need officers or NCOs. They will be on hand if required."

In other respects Boyle's relationships with the military were improving. On 7 February 1919, a copy of Berthelot's order-of-the-day, issued in Rumania the previous autumn, was received at defence headquarters. It seems unlikely it was mere coincidence that an order authorizing Boyle's wearing of his Rumanian decorations was published twelve days later. This was partial satisfaction but there had been no mention of his right to wear his Russian decorations, and Boyle wanted to know why. He called on General Barter, who knew and appreciated Boyle's services in Russia.

On 14 April Barter wrote from Bournemouth that he had communicated with the War Office on the subject.

I said I could testify to your receiving them from the C in C at the time as I was present at General Headquarters when they were bestowed on you. I also added that I considered them richly earned and I myself had recently put forward your name for a British decoration. . . . I hope to see you on my return and that by then you will have heard something about a DSO or CMG.

By the spring of 1919 the peace conference was becoming a sad disappointment and a bore for the likes of Boyle and another man of action, (T. E.) Lawrence of Arabia. The posturing, manipulation, and careless breaking of promises contributed to their disillusionment. Intervention in Russia was a dead issue, as Boyle finally realized. He surely would have agreed with the historian who observed: "What condemned the intervention and made it condemnable was its inadequacy. The crime was that of failing to measure up to the opportunity."

324

In London Boyle continued to pursue private assignments while anxiously hoping for a return to action. One of these private assignments was at the request of the Dowager Empress Marie Feodorovna, who asked him to investigate a report that her son, the late czar, had left a large amount of money in the the Bank of England. Armed with a power-of-attorney from the empress he opened negotiations in conjunction with Arthur Davison, private secretary to Dowager Queen Alexandra. They were seeking the truth of a rumour that £10 million had been secreted in England by Nicholas, a rumour that had a number of Romanovs looking for a share of the treasure. The legend of the Russian treasure has persisted to this day, although Boyle long ago found it to be false. The matter was cleared up in a report from Davison to Boyle dated 7 April 1919:

the Bank of England holds nothing, either in the way of cash or securities on account of the Russian appanages, so I am afraid your informant must be drawing on his imagination when he told you there was ten millions deposited on that account in the Bank.

Although he had entertained thoughts of returning to Russia, it was time to return to the country he had adopted; Marie, who had returned to Rumania in April, was urging him to come back and help her handle growing political and economic problems, as well as a few family matters giving her concern.

He was pleased, then, to read orders dated 22 May 1919, of the Overseas Military Headquarters of the Canadian Forces granting him indefinite leave to proceed to Rumania on a special assignment for the Canadian mission in London. It was odd that the army that had continued to say he was not part of it was now granting him leave as if he were. Borden's proposal, it is clear, had been accepted, with one amendment. No one dared send along a companion to keep a watchful eye on Boyle.

Final proof of his acceptance followed on 3 June, when the *Gazette* carried a notice of the award of the Distinguished

Service Order for services rendered in connection with military operations in Russia. Boyle was pleased, but may have been a little upset that the notice carried the name of "James Whiteside Boyle."

TWENTY-NINE

A Man of Many Parts

As Joe Boyle prepared to leave England, news came from Woodstock that his aged father had died. Charles Boyle and his world-roaming son had always been close, but there was little time to mourn. Rumania and its queen were waiting.

Had Canada been a little more gracious, the erstwhile King of the Klondike might have returned to Bucharest as a regular soldier with a much higher rank. The War Office at one time had asked the Canadians to give Boyle the rank of major-general. The politicians spurned the suggestion, according to General Turner in a report written in 1927, and replied that the War Office could do so if it was the desire of the queen of Rumania. Boyle's close association with the queen had become known, and probably was the subject of critical talk in some circles. To promote him at the queen's request would be to acknowledge the relationship, and Canadian politicians were not about to do anything like that. Now, still an honorary lieutenant-colonel but unchallenged in the right to wear his uniform, Boyle was back in Rumania with another load of major assignments.

First he was to supervise distribution of the $25 million in aid from Canada, which had been made official in Paris when Primer Minister Bratiano signed an agreement with Trade and

Commerce Minister Sir George Foster. Marie was delighted with the long-term repayment clauses. So were those who came after her, for the loan never was repaid.

But the Canadian program was only part of Boyle's work. He was, as well, the representative of the Red Cross aid committee run by dour Herbert Hoover, one of the few who does not seem to have been charmed by Marie.

Boyle's intelligence network, now working for the Whites, was also still in action. He was advising the Volunteer Army on a multitude of subjects, acting almost as a staff officer while rejecting periodic requests to become one in fact.

The trip to England and his own efforts also had placed Boyle in a new position. In his advocacy of help for Rumania he could hold out the rewards of her petroleum reserves, for it was clear that oil would play a much more important role in the postwar world than it had prior to 1914. This brought Boyle into contact with the officials of the British Petroleum Executive, an event that had great significance for an entrepreneur whose main interest had been gold, and who still held secret hopes of developing the gold gravels of Siberia. His contacts with the Petroleum Executive had given him a role in ensuring that Britain received some needed oil from the great Ploesti fields in Rumania, which had been devastated by British special service men in 1916. Finally and not least importantly for him, he was at this time still a confidant of the queen on the not yet resolved difficulties with Prince Carol.

With all these assignments to complete, it was fortunate that after two years of fruitless pleading for his services Boyle was able to take Lieutenant-Colonel Frank A. Reid with him as one of his staff. For Reid, who had waited so long for a military assignment and might have had it but for reaction to the Bolshevik Revolution, there was a certain irony, for he now was on a civilian footing. Boyle had two other assistants, "Sandy" Arkwright and Charles Sutherland, whose names have been preserved because of a long letter Sutherland wrote to relatives later in 1919.

It was a fascinating life for Reid, who stayed with Boyle for three years, in contrast to the brief stay of the other two assistants. Reid shared enough experiences to give him the idea of writing a book about his fantastic boss, a design long postponed and finally frustrated by his death some twenty years later, but not before he was able to tell Flora Boyle about some of his experiences in Rumania.

The Canadian mission, Reid recalled, was installed in what he described as "a very large castle with unlimited servants."

I was dumbfounded at the power Boyle wielded. It was unrestricted, his influence unlimited. He had complete control of all the secret police and he was a dictator, not only politically but throughout the entire country, and as the country was full of intrigue he had an extremely busy time. We had secret agents working throughout the Russian oil fields and also agents throughout Rumania. Boyle's position as Red Cross commissioner was a clever cover-up.

The royal rulers, with a strong man on whom to lean, relied on his judgment in many areas. Reid said that no statute was enacted in the Rumanian parliament before it had been discussed with Boyle, a fact that created resentment among the politicians, many of whom were angered at his dukedom and the wide-ranging powers given him by the king and queen. They particularly resented his liberal inclinations and his support of populist measures, such as lowering the property qualifications for holding office and the extension of the franchise to several million previously voiceless Rumanians.

"Boyle," Reid said, "was responsible for the law that enabled the peasant to buy land from the proprietor-landlord." He openly sought an even more infuriating change for the wealthy in advocating the expropriation of large landed estates and the distribution of property among all deserving citizens, an act that appeared likely to enfranchise every adult. Like so many reformers in history, he was ahead of his time, but he presented these radical ideas with all the conviction he could muster, for he was intent on preserving the monarchy by widening its support base and safeguarding it against the pressures of the Bolshevik experiment on the national borders.

A sparkling view of what it was like to be with Joe Boyle in those halcyon days is offered in Sutherland's letter to his mother, Mrs. H. T. Sutherland of New Glasgow, Nova Scotia. Sutherland was a young engineer with some experience in transportation problems. He had joined Boyle on a short-term arrangement, ostensibly to deal with renovation of the Rumanian rail system, but soon found his duties led him far outside that specific area. At one time, he wrote, he was called in

to inspect a proposition for heating the two royal palaces. . . .

I found the Germans had damaged the furnaces so they had to be replaced and that a Swiss firm was bidding 800,000 lei to replace them, and it was recommended to accept it. . . .

After visiting the palaces . . . it did not take long to decide there was a big margin of profit and about 60 or 70 per cent was being paid as graft. . . . So I condemned the whole affair and offered to get the furnaces from Canada for a fraction of this.

With Boyle as his mentor the young engineer met many of the most important people in Rumania. He dined with the Odessa hostages and found their gratitude to Boyle burning as bright as ever, and the Grand Duchess Marie and her family had the same high praise for him. One of Sutherland's most memorable experiences was attending a special service to mark the signing of the Treaty of Versailles, in company with the king and queen, the leaders of the nation, and members of the diplomatic colony. "The music was a treat," Sutherland wrote, ". . . better than the Mason's work in the First Presbyterian Church." Following the service everyone went to the race course where the King's Cup was being run, and the day ended with impressive fireworks and illuminations.

Like most men, Sutherland was entranced by Marie, who won

his heart at a special luncheon for the Canadian mission in the Cotroceni Palace on Dominion Day, 1 July.

My place was on the Queen's right and I was so nervous after being told that I needed several aperitifs to put me right. However, when I took my place I found her so charming that I was quickly put at ease. The King sat directly opposite the Queen and only three feet away and Colonel Boyle opposite me. . . . It was very gay as they told stories and joked and laughed until they got us all doing it. Afterwards we went back to the waiting room and I had a long, serious talk with the Queen . . . for almost an hour and a half and I learned more about the country than I had from all the others I met in Rumania. The King was chatting with the others . . . and I only had a word with him . . . but I much preferred to talk with the Queen as she has the brains of the combination and I should say she is the boss as well.

Boyle's wide interest in so many phases of Rumanian life were forward-looking and constructive. At the war's end he had ready for the consideration of the government a national plan of reconstruction to parallel long-prepared programs for the rehabilitation of the devastated areas of northern France and Belgium.

Unknown to most, he continued to conduct his intelligence circuit, which was for a time almost the only reliable network in southern Russia. It was uniquely a Joe Boyle operation, the creation of a private individual, financed by two world powers. To him flowed information of many kinds—military, political, and economic. Some reports were a few sentences, scrawled on scraps of paper; others were long and detailed. In Rumania his agents kept an eye on Bolshevik agitators and spies who then, as now, seemed to have little difficulty in finding their way across protected borders, particularly when there was a flood of refugees to deal with. Rumania kept a close watch on annexed Bessarabia.

Boyle's surviving records indicate the extent of the agents' activities. Ingenue Coopisdorf of Kishinev, like many of the Boyle men, sheltered behind a business address. Over a brief period he collected 100,000 lei and 4,135 roubles, some of it distributed to other agents. Boyle's meticulously kept record of disbursements and of payments made ranged from pittances to small fortunes during his first stay in Rumania. In June and July 1918, when he was in hospital in Kishinev, Boyle directed aides in the operation of the circuits. Tzegintzov in that time paid out 27,000 lei to one Kenno; 300,000 lei to the French officer Cheval, who bravely volunteered to remain in Odessa and run things in that region; one million lei to an agent named Aynadino; 150,000 lei to Peter Troubetskoy; and more suspiciously, 500,000 lei to Vaitoineau, one-time Rumanian interior minister.

Modern values of the currencies are difficult to determine but the pre-revolutionary rouble was worth about fifty cents U.S. and considered equal to two lei. Tzegintzov himself signed for 150,000 roubles while attending Boyle in Kishinev. Geroge Hill, separated from Boyle in March 1918, received 10,000 lei from him in June through an N. H. Konopke.

Some of the Boyle agents were put to work investigating complaints of Russian commanders that their men were being subjected to "open, shameful plunder" in Bessarabia. One of Boyle's networks provided detailed information dealing with the fate of the Russian Black Sea fleet, which had fled from Sebastopol to Novorossisk, at the eastern end of the Black Sea, when the Germans marched into Sebastopol. Throughout 1918 and into the next year Boyle's network provided an accurate picture of conditions. They sketched the landscape of a countryside held down by German occupation troops vainly trying to win favour by food distribution and arousing opposition of the seizure of vital war supplies such as copper and oil.

The same reports indicated that things were becoming difficult for Bolshevism as early enthusiasm for the freedoms they had promised, such as distribution of land, vanished in the evolving reality of the severe and brutal tyranny. One agent sent news of an anti-Bolshevist uprising in the remainder of the Black Sea fleet during which two hundred commissars and Bolshevik adherents were killed. In Moscow, he added, Trotsky had surveyed the scene with deepening alarm and declared: "It is possible that we will have to go away from power but in so doing will bang the door so hard that all Russia will shudder."

Boyle's summaries revealed the difficult conditions in occupied Russia in 1918. In the larger cities such as Kharkov and Odessa there were daily murders of German soldiers. Closure of industries had created civil discontent, reflected in continuing trouble among railway and transport workers, for which Boyle could claim some responsibility. Peasants were hoarding their grain and refusing to sell their produce. And Boyle's destruction squads continued to blow up anything that could be of use to the Austro-Germans or the Reds. "Destruction of Yscherkassy was complete," he noted. "No cost to the destruction unit."

As conditions worsened, so did German treatment of the populace. Executions as warnings only stimulated more bloodshed. The Germans of 1918 were no more able to win over the Russians than their Nazi successors a quarter of a century later. Some of the reports reaching Boyle were horror tales. "Specific case," he wrote, "Proskuroff—Peasants attacked Germany company, killed 12, wounded many. Number of peasants captured. Some system (not known) selection adopted and 100 shot. Country in this vicinity is wild. Nothing to be done. Six German sentries killed in Kiev railway junction on Good Friday."

Bessarabia continued to be a thorn in the flesh of its new Rumanian overlords. Reports of disorders, arrests, expulsions, and other reactions are part of the Boyle record. There was, as well, the surfacing of the anti-Jewish feeling that has always existed in that part of the world and was an ugly fact of life in both Russia and Rumania. A Kishinev paper that Boyle collected reported the arrest of "a Jew boy on a charge that he some time ago was selling a revolutionary newspaper and is a Bolshevik. Boy carried away from Kishinev and vanished."

Russian newspapers made great capital of the Bessarabian disorders. The Odessa *Leaf* charged that when the Rumanians occupied Benderi they killed two hundred railwaymen supposed to be Bolsheviks, looted and destroyed shops, and exported their stocks to Rumania.

From the Kuban, on 20 October 1918, Tzegintzov wrote Boyle a sobering report of conditions there. It took two months to reach Bucharest and was opened by Troubetskoy in Boyle's absence. Tzegintzov, it turned out, had been employed on a raid beyond Petrovsk that had been abandoned because a planned airlift had been endangered by the Bolshevik seizure of territory between the Caspian Sea and Petrovsk. The Volunteer Army, Tzegintzov had found, was in great need of money, ammunition and weapons, medical supplies, and other things. Their absence meant that there was little or no growth in the rank-and-file numbers of the army, which was heavily manned by officers who, fighting as infantrymen, were suffering losses that imperilled the whole situation. It was a "no quarter" war, he had been horrified to find.

Two weeks ago one of the regiments was partly surrounded and during the retreat they lost nearly 30 officers of the Guards regiment. Those who were wounded and could not be carried away were found afterwards horribly mutilated. Even their parents wouldn't recognize their bodies. You cannot imagine the horror of this kind of fighting— when the wounded cannot be taken away they have to be killed for if they fall into the hands of the Bolsheviks they are sure to be tortured. We live here in hope of the arrival of the Allied Fleet and the Volunteer Army will have an ample supply of ammunition and guns.

This former Imperial Army colonel was scornful of some of the White regiments that opted to follow the Bolshevik military system, or lack of it, in army discipline. He was full of praise, however, for the Siberian units "based on principles of before-revolution times, full of authority of officers, no politics, no committees."

Tzegintzov appealed to Boyle to try to find his wife and their children, whom he had lost track of since they fled from Simbirsk. "Please give my best thought to my little friend Princess Ileanna," he concluded. Five days .after that letter reached Bucharest he wrote again. This time his report was only received on 28 January, 1919, when Boyle was in Paris. It was a more hopeful message, recording volunteer successes and commenting on the more friendly attitude of the eternal turncoats who afflict every conflict of this sort. He conceded that Boyle had been right in advising him not to go to the Kuban. His only job, he said, would be leading a group of other officers, without men or horses and with little prospect of fighting. The long-awaited Allied help, thanks to Marie, Boyle, and others, had received Novorossisk on 23 November.

Even Tzegintzov's career looked up, for he found employment as a liaison officer and interpreter on the army staff. He had made enough of an impression on visitors that his name pops up periodically in books written by the Allied officers who had the advantages of his capable services in the campaign in the Kuban.

Although he refused to work as a staff member with the White headquarters, after his return to Rumania Boyle provided useful services for them as an adviser. It was reported on 1 October 1920 that he had accepted the position of chief-of-staff to General Wrangel whose defeated armies at that time were falling back into the Crimea. Boyle did go to the Crimea briefly, and probably helped in the evacuation of the armies and thousands of civilians, a military feat of some consequence. But Boyle had refused a staff job under General Denikin when the White cause was in the ascendant. That he would join a cause that was doubtful of success was unlikely, given the other assignments with which he was charged.

Like other observers he was astute enough to understand that the White collapse arose from its failure to appeal to the ordinary Russian. The Bolsheviks had one goal; their opponents were hopelessly divided. A few wanted a return to czardom;

others the reinstatement of a Kerensky-type regime. Failure to co-ordinate both strategy and goals doomed the Whites despite the early loss of favour by the Bolsheviks. Denikin, as he advanced, had re-established the large landowners, many of whom had learned nothing and began settling accounts with those who had been virtually their serfs. The Whites, lacking supplies, lived off the land despite vain efforts to quell their looting and violence.

Boyle was one of the few who realized the folly of trying to campaign on these terms. He helped draft a proposal to put the Volunteer Army on a basis of guaranteed rates of pay and allowances, death benefits, pensions, and other conditions to be found in true professional national forces. These "Laws for Serving in the South Army" included a code of honour and military conduct. It would have limited volunteers to eighteen years of age or older, and rejected the services of women in fighting units. It was a noble idea, and like so many such ideas, inoperable. It was the Reds, under Trotsky's genius, who found the discipline that escaped their opponents and that, in the end, ensured the Reds victory.

Word that had reached the Rumanians in Paris, of Bela Kun's Bolshevik seizure of power in Hungary, presented another threat to Rumania's western flank, placing Rumania between two Bolshevik powers. It was a menace that Rumania was not prepared to tolerate, and in the summer of 1919 the reinvigorated Rumanian army marched into Hungary and took effective control of the country. Boyle could not avoid inspecting the situation, about which it is likely the queen wanted information from a trusted, impartial observer.

As they had in Bessarabia, the occupying Rumanians began to act arrogantly and outrageously, creating a storm of charges that they were stealing Hungary's food and art treasures and oppressing the people they had, ostensibly, come to liberate from the Red plague. The Allied leaders in Paris, perhaps because they felt the Rumanians had turned their forces against the wrong set of Bolsheviks, sent Sir George Clerk to Budapest to investigate matters and present the Rumanians with an ultimatum to withdraw. The mission, far from accomplishing its purpose, merely disclosed wide differences between the French, British, and Americans.

It was into this nest of conflicting interests and backstabbing that Joe Boyle and Frank Reid moved, hardly aware of the facts of the case. Reid related the story of their journey, having gained the impression that his employer created an assignment for himself out of an urgent sense of curiosity and a desire to be where the action was.

They started out in two large touring cars—Boyle, Reid, three interpreters, and two secretaries. Reid later reported that:

Apparently the car drivers were Communist sympathizers, because we encountered constant trouble from the moment we left Bucharest. Our tires were mysteriously slashed, one car caught fire, and on another occasion we had serious engine trouble and a car refused to operate.

Boyle and I decided to take a walk. We didn't have our military passes as they were with the interpreters who remained to direct the work on the car. After a mile or so we suddenly were challenged by a sentry who was armed and had a sword bayonet on his rifle.

As neither Boyle nor I could speak any Rumanian we were unable to explain why we were on this road, a forbidden area, and the sentry called out a guard of about 16 men, a raw-looking lot of peasants, all armed with sword bayonets, who completely surrounded us. I was in civilian clothes but Boyle was in uniform with all his decorations and they mistook him for a Communist. We found ourselves in quite a serious position.

They conversed, but their English did nothing to reassure the guards. Reid reported that the conversation went like this:

Boyle: Tell them who we are.
Reid: How the hell can I, I don't speak their language.
Boyle: Well, tell them something.
Reid: I'll try.

He did, utilizing some of the pidgin French he had learned on the continent in some two years in France. It seemed to make their captors even more suspicious. Boyle became impatient.

Boyle: Let's get back-to-back and swing on them. If you hit them they'll run like hell.
Reid: No, I have no intention of being poked by one of those bayonets.
Boyle: Are you afraid?
Reid: Certainly I'm afraid. They'll go for us and if they do they'll only be doing their duty. I think I'll try my French again.
Boyle: Well, do something.

Reid, in desperation, poured out his French patois with frantic speed. The Rumanians, fascinated by the outpouring and the strange defensive posture of their prisoners, began to argue among themselves. Suddenly they came to an agreement, a decision to take Reid to the guard post in which their commanding officer was beginning to arise, the hour being near noon. Boyle was left surrounded by bayonets.

The officer's room smelled like a French brothel, Reid recalled, but the man could speak French. "I explained that his men were holding Boyle down the road and that Boyle was head of the Rumanian secret police and was very annoyed; that our cars were farther along the road and our interpreters were there and they had documents to prove our identity."

It was patois but it was understood. The stricken officer threw on his tunic, mounted a horse and rode off at a gallop, passing the red-faced Boyle without stopping. He returned quickly, bowing and scraping and apologizing, to no avail. "Boyle," Reid added, "never got over the desire to have this officer's blood." As soon as they reached Budapest, Boyle had the two drivers placed under arrest.

As always, Boyle went first class. "We stayed at the Hotel Hungaria," Reid recalled, "the best hotel in Budapest. It was commandered by the Rumanians. . . . It was impossible to conceive how intensely the Hungarians dislike Rumanians, and

338

when they were in occupation of Budapest they gave them a very bad time." The dislike of Rumanians, in fact, was about the only thing that the Bolshevik Hungarians and their local opponents held in common.

Boyle looked over the scene for four or five days, formed a few opinions to report to Marie, and returned to Bucharest more expeditiously than he had departed it. The Rumanian army, having saved Hungary for the landowners and business elite, followed Boyle home soon afterwards.

THIRTY

To Win or Lose It All

One of the mysteries to those who knew Joe Boyle's combative nature and his tenacity under fire must have been his failure to make any fight to regain his Klondike holdings once he returned to England at the end of the war. His properties had not long been in receivership and, although his temporary manager, Joe Junior, departed soon after the receiver took over, his son had demonstrated that they were still viable and could be worked at a good profit for an indefinite period.

Boyle, who liked money only for what could be done with it, had spent it freely, and his resources were badly strained by the time he left Rumania in December 1918. Yet he made no apparent move to recover his hard-won position.

The answer to the mystery seems to be that he had found a greater dream, a brighter goal for his ambitions. He was only too well aware that his health was not what it had been, but he had recovered to the point where he could at least contemplate one more great adventure. He found it in the black gold of the petroleum industry, in the oil wells he had seen in Rumania, and in those he knew existed in the Russian Caucasus. He was sure he was capable of one last, great thrust.

One of his 1919 assignments in Rumania had been to obtain

oil supplies from the Rumanian wells for postwar Britain, where the shrewd men of the Petroleum Executive knew that oil would be a vital energy source in the postwar world. His connection to the Petroleum Executive unquestionably came from his friendship with Walter Long, the Secretary of State for Colonies and a long-time associate in London.

So Boyle returned to Rumania with an oil contract to win, having made the acquaintance of another thruster, one of the most powerful oil magnates in the world—Sir Henry Deterding of the Royal Dutch–Shell. Deterding was able and ruthless, what might be called in these days "a fitness nut," in which area he held the same convictions as Boyle about exercise and abstention from deleterious substances such as tobacco.

Technically, Boyle was negotiating with Rumania to obtain 70,000 tons of petroleum for a Shell subsidiary, Anglo-Saxon Petroleum. Agreement for him to handle the oil work had been given by the Canadians, although it is doubtful that they fully understood the extent of his assignments. Boyle was paid £6,000 as a token of Anglo-Saxon's serious intent, and it was obvious to the former gold miner that he might find a fortune in this new field of resource extraction.

Early in August 1919, and somewhat to Boyle's astonishment, the Canadian mission to Rumania was terminated and he was ordered to return to London in peremptory terms. Rumours of the extent of Boyle's other interests may have been the reason for his recall. While he regretted the cessation of his Canadian assignment Boyle had no intention of returning to England, and those who relied on him, such as the Petroleum Executive and the royal family, had no wish for him to depart.

For Boyle there was another important reason. The arrogant Rumanian regime in Bessarabia had thrown many Russians into prison, including a number who had worked with Boyle's espionage and sabotage units. He was determined that they should be looked after and that nothing would be made public about the intelligence network.

The wrecked Ploesti fields had been restored to operational

status in a matter of months and were functioning more efficiently than ever. This good-quality oil was a most desirable prize, and Boyle was able to get contracts for it for Britain. By this time Deterding's sights had been raised several notches in consideration of what might happen to the abandoned oil lands in the Caucasus. He was hardly a Communist sympathizer, but he was a good businessman and was convinced that a deal could be made with the foes of capitalism in Moscow to regain the oil properties.

Boyle, a man who knew some of the leading Bolsheviks personally, and who had demonstrated his ability to work successfully in the chaos of that nation, was the logical man to head up this much greater mission. But there was another consideration. Boyle, a most versatile fellow, was a White sympathizer, and in mid-1919 it seemed possible that the Bolsheviks might be beaten, in which case he would have the inside track with the winners. Certainly when Boyle visited Tiflis and Baku in the fall of 1919 he was able to assess the possibilities as being very good. The White armies were at flood tide. On 18 October Denikin's army took Orel, eighty miles from Moscow, and boasted that the capital was the next objective.

Royal Dutch–Shell began buying up properties from smaller companies that had become discouraged about regaining their lands in Russia. Regardless of who won or lost, it looked like a good gamble for Shell.

The greater vision of Deterding created new grand prospects for Joe Boyle. Aside from defraying his expenses, he had received no salary for his work in Rumania. Now he was offered an almost-unlimited expense account and the right to 5 percent of all new oil production revenues that might arise from his work for Shell in Russia.

In the domestic circles of the king and queen he continued as adviser on the future of Prince Carol, sent in 1919 to join his regiment on the Hungarian frontier, and so neatly separated from Zizi, the woman he had married under the German shield in Odessa. Frequent meetings between Boyle, the Prince and the royal family continued throughout 1919; it was not until January 1920 that Carol agreed to give up Zizi. To provide the prince with a cooling-off period it was arranged, at Boyle's suggestion, that Carol should visit the United States (where in New York he met and talked with Flora Boyle). Annulment of the marriage made it possible for Carol to marry Princess Helen of Greece, a match in which Boyle also had some part. He would not live long enough to see that it, too, was a disaster.

This service to Marie and the king had unfortunate consequences for Boyle when it became known publicly. Politicians who hated his influence at court and his liberal notions of operating the country joined with the nobility, who scorned his position and hated him for his proposals to give their land to the peasants. Anti-royalists who looked for any stick to beat the monarchy made cause with Carol; their newspapers ran scurrilous and highly critical, sneering stories about the erstwhile saviour of Rumania. Scandal-mongers told tales of Boyle's alleged flagrant conduct with the queen. One recounted how he had been seen leaving her quarters half-undressed and totally embarrassed when an unexpected caller arrived.

Such stories were damaging to Boyle and to his royal patrons. His own relationship with the queen suffered a setback in 1920 when someone mailed her a clipping of the Toronto newspaper article that asked, "Is Elma Boyle the Duchess of Dawson?" Boyle apparently had told her about Milly, his first wife, but had neglected to mention Elma. Marie knew he was divorced but not that he had remarried. The queen carried the clipping to North America with her in 1926 and presented it to Flora Boyle, telling of its unexpected arrival and her unhappiness that Joe had not been completely frank with her.

Despite the growing pressures on him, however, life in Rumania continued to hold a certain magnificence for Joe Boyle and his staff. He was most generous in his gifts to Marie, presenting her with furs on one occasion and with riding horses on another. Reid related how he was despatched to England to inspect

and take delivery of two magnificent horses that had won prizes in shows, from the stables of Sir Henry Deterding.

Not being satisfied with this, Boyle detailed me to buy a third horse, also a show winner, for Princess Ileanna. The horses were equipped with blankets with the royal crest on them, new saddlery and all the other trimmings and with this circus (I was supposed to be in the international oil business) I proceeded to Paris where the animals were inspected by the Queen.

Boyle's delight in the gifts led him to arrange a large military parade in Bucharest that ended in a field day at which the horses were presented to the royal family. Thousands lined the streets to watch the procession. The queen's horse, a fine white stallion, was one of her favourites; she rode it annually when she inspected the 4th Cavalry Regiment of which she was honorary colonel.

With Boyle's popularity in decline, at least among the court's enemies, some of his older enemies emerged, pursuing him even beyond the borders of the kingdom. In London a new Canadian chief-of-staff, Major-General J. H. MacBrien, received a letter on the stationery of the military attaché of the Rumanian embassy, asking that old question about Boyle's status in the Canadian army, whether he had an official mission in Eastern Europe, and whether he was "a demobilized Canadian officer authorized by your regulations to continue to wear uniform?" MacBrien, noting that the signature was an illegible scrawl, forwarded the letter to the Militia Council in Ottawa, suggesting they might like to answer it. He was wrong.

The efforts to get Joe Boyle out of his uniform continued in London, however. It became a long-playing comedy. The War Office ordered Boyle to take off his uniform; the War Council did likewise. Boyle replied, battling them with all the lawyer's guile he might once have exercised at the bar. The Rumanian king and queen wrote on his behalf. Sir George Barclay was involved. Aide d'Affaires W. F. A. Rattigan, whom Boyle had been able to help reach Bucharest, was caught in the middle. Finally Boyle was told he must stop wearing his uniform as of 1 September 1920.

That alarmed the Petroleum Executive and Royal Dutch–Shell. A representative in uniform was much more useful dickering on their behalf with Russians and Rumanians than a man in civilian clothes. Walter Long and his associates had the date for doffing the uniform put off until 1 January 1921.

Boyle, so magnificent in times of real stress, and sometimes petty when the issue was inconsequential, was in a fight he couldn't win, particularly since criticism of his role at court was mounting in Rumania.

The pressures on the royal family, and most of all on Marie, were beyond their control. She was told Boyle must leave, and had to inform him of the decision. Later she would write:

After having made a hero out of him, almost a demi-god, they set upon him later, trying to blemish his honor, to pull him down, only because I knew he was big and trusted in him beyond what others considered it was wise to trust a man and especially a stranger. So they had to take him from me. I fought hard but finally had to surrender.

Boyle had been criticized in Rumania and elsewhere for the oil deal he had negotiated for Anglo-Saxon. It had been dishonest, it was said, arranged by his royal patrons. Unquestionably because of political interference, Rumania had not lived up to the contract, shipments being far under those required. Boyle applied what pressure he could, but his grip had been loosened and his power was vanishing. As much as he disliked the idea, and as much as he fought it for a time, he realized it was the moment to depart the country whose cause he had made his own, and for which he had so successfully toiled.

He would not be unemployed. Royal Dutch–Shell beckoned

and there was much to be done in the Caucasus and elsewhere. As one who savoured success more than money, he was aware he was joining a company that was an outstanding example of achievement. Shell was founded by Marcus Samuels in 1897 and backed by the House of Rothschild. It quickly became involved in a wide-ranging struggle with Royal Dutch of the Netherlands and Standard Oil of the United States. In 1901 after successful negotiations by Frederick Lane, Deterding, and Samuels, their interests were merged in the firm of Royal Dutch–Shell, a giant combine ready to take on the flexing muscles of Standard Oil. The timing could hardly have been better, for the British Navy was on the verge of switching from coal-fired boilers to oil burners. The navy required assurance of global supplies in fueling depots that would replace the old coaling stations, and an arrangement guaranteeing control of this vital resource and security of supply.

Deterding was an organizational and administrative genius, a man of infinite patience and long-range perceptions. The result of his enlarged association with Boyle was an agreement made with him in, or about, May 1921,

whereby Col. Boyle should be employed by Shell and associated companies to attempt to recover certain properties and assets of Shell and associated companies in Russia which had been seized by the Soviets and/or others, and in acquiring or attempting to acquire new properties or assets in Russia, Col. Boyle was given powers of attorney by all the Shell Companies.

This wide authority was confirmed in the summer of 1921 when North Caucasian Oil Fields Limited of London, one of the Shell group, notified its Grozny office of Boyle's appointment as general representative of their interests in Russia, with full power to act.

About the same time, Deterding wrote to Boyle confirming the terms of their agreement. The letter noted that all expenses were to be paid by Shell, and the royalty on the basis of the five per cent on the marketable production of any new oil territory he [Boyle] brought in; further, that the royalty paid to owners would be 7½ per cent exactly, after which it would be on a sliding scale up to 17½ per cent or more paid to the owners; no royalty would be paid to Boyle.

Joe's 5 percent would be found in new oil in an area he had already determined was capable of vast expansion. There were other clauses guaranteeing Boyle a minimum £50,000 for recovery of existing properties and an agreement that Shell would meet all expenses with no limit set on what was bound to be an expensive operation.

Although the oil consortium had been hoping that the Whites would win, the timing was not unfavourable for what had to be an approach to the capitalist-hating Bolsheviks. Russia was exhausted by years of struggle, and many of its regions were not under the complete control of the central government. The Caucusus, the last to succumb, bowed only late in 1921. Lenin and his comrades were very conscious of the need for economic stimulus. One economist estimated that the living standards of the Russians had declined 300 percent below that of 1914. In three years of war among the Russians themselves, production fell to 13 percent of prewar output, and agriculture was at one-half of its 1914 level. Recognizing the urgency and the very real prospect of widespread famine, Lenin proposed to admit foreign capital and entrepreneurs to develop the natural and industrial resources of the country on a concession basis. Royal Dutch–Shell was early in the field as the scramble began. The opportunities that Joe Boyle had foreseen and hoped to have Canada compete for were emerging. But Canada was nowhere to be seen in the hunt.

A telegram from Maxim Litvinoff to Lenin from Reval, Estonia, 16 January 1919, spoke of a request he had received from Royal Dutch–Shell for a monopoly concession in petroleum and kerosene and the right to explore for oil in the vast underdeveloped regions of Russia. "I favour experimental negotiations, supremely cautious," Lenin replied. He considered the matter important enough to order the drafting of a set of specific instructions dealing with such situations.

On 24 January 1921 the Russian Supreme Council of National Economy approved a proposal for formal negotiations, and on 1 February the Sovnarkom went a step further and sanctioned negotiations for Caucusus concessions. The Sovnarkom decision was on a split vote, for many of the old-line Bolsheviks were horrified by Lenin's pragmatism, but as Louis Fischer pointed out in his book, *The Life of Lenin*, the leader usually had the last word. In this case he told the Sovnarkom that concessions in Grozny and Baku would provide "an opportunity to overtake the advanced techniques of advanced capitalism" and he promised that no more than 25 percent of the resources of the field would go to foreigners.

Lenin cabled the decision to Leonid Krassin in London on 19 March 1921 as guidance in his task as head of a Soviet mission negotiating a commercial agreement with the British government: "The party congress has approved the policy on concessions in Grozny and Baku which I defended. Accelerate negotiations for them as well as for other concessions. Inform me more frequently."

Boyle and Deterding were delighted and reached the agreement for his services previously mentioned, proof of which has been provided by Shell House in London. They might have been more wary had they understood that Lenin was ready for the capitalists to become engaged in a bidding war, and that he was hopeful that U.S. firms would become interested in participation.

One U.S. oil man scouting the Russian possibilities in Moscow and elsewhere was Washington B. Vanderlip of Standard Oil, who made it quite clear that his company would like to take over any concessions the Soviets had to offer. During April of that year Lenin reminded Foreign Affairs Commissioner G. V. Chicherin of this prospect. "Has it been explained to Vanderlip," he wrote, "that we could grant the Americans a concession to tremendous oilfields [Baku, Grozny, Euba, Ukta] and that America would thereby beat England? Telephone us as soon as you have read this."

Regardless of which side might emerge as concessionaire, Lenin regarded this foreign intrusion primarily as a training school for Russian scientists and technicians. He spoke of thirty-year concessions but privately hoped that "within 15 years the Russians would be able to buy out the concessionaires and run the field themselves." He told Bolshevik, old-line opponents that it would be "leftist infantilism or foolish doctrinaireism" for Russia to attempt to operate the fields itself at that time. His plan, simply put, was "to overtake [capitalism] with the aid of foreign capitalists," as Fischer put it. He was prepared to bury the foreign exploiters with the shovels they would so willingly provide.

Royal Dutch–Shell, seeking to recover its Caucasus properties, purchased years before from the Rothschilds, felt that Lenin had no option but to renew dealings with the men who knew how to operate the oil wells, even if they had been secretly engaged in trying to drive him from power only a few months earlier. Lenin was a realist, like Joe Boyle who, now that the White cause had been wrecked, saw the establishment of commercial relations with the winners as a more reasonable course than sulking behind a French *cordon sanitaire.*

Boyle's visit to the Caucasus introduced him to an area as large as Texas between the Black and Caspian seas. It had been producing oil since 1863; and in 1914 some 83 percent of the Caucasus production was supplied from the Baku region, the remainder coming from the Grozny and Maikop fields.

Boyle started his assignment with many advantages: his experiences in Russia, his knowledge of the men who ran the new Soviet state, and his ability to call on trained and valuable personnel from his own intelligence networks. His unlimited expense account made it possible for him to reassemble some of his most valuable people, like Dmitri Tzegintzov, George Hill, and others anxious to take well-paid employment with prospects of travel and excitement, while thousands of their wartime associates walked the streets jobless. Boyle's first effort to enlist Hill failed, for the former intelligence agent was engaged in a personal business venture. This effort to make his own mark failed within a few months and Hill was delighted to find that Boyle still wanted him, albeit at a somewhat reduced salary. Frank Reid also was delighted to remain with him as personal secretary and jack-of-all-trades. Tzegintzov was posted to Constantinople, a listening post of high importance through which all who might travel to the Caucasus would be likely to pass. Tzegintzov's White Army past would make it impossible for him to work in Russia, but his many contacts and his linguistic abilities would be invaluable. A Shell employee with long experience in the region, Claude A. Solly, was also enrolled in Boyle's group.

Boyle was engaged in protracted negotiations with Krassin in London, and his hand was strengthened on 19 October 1921, when Foreign Minister Marquis Curzon had his secretary Esmond Ovey dispatch a note to Krassin:

The Marquis of Kedleston is informed by Colonel J. W. Boyle that Royal Dutch–Shell group are anxious to obtain a concession from the Soviet Government for the production of oil from their properties in South Russia and the Caucasus. I am directed to inform you that it is with the full approval and support of His Majesty's Government that Colonel Boyle has addressed himself to you on this subject. His Majesty's Government trust that these negotiations may result in early and satisfactory settlement.

Krassin, who had worked for international business firms before the war and had been a representative in the Caucasus for a German electrical firm, must have studied the brief communication with great interest. It certainly was ambiguous enough, for in one reading it appeared to talk of Royal Dutch–Shell as proprietor of the oil lands asking for permission to operate. The oil companies had been hoping, rather foolishly, to be restored to ownership. The question of restoration had been up in the air, to be settled later. Curzon's letter ignored that issue in the hope that the parties would get on with the more important job of production.

Krassin's position was strong, arising from his conclusion of an accord with the British Board of Trade in May 1919 that covered financial claims, trade, and other concerns in a way that gave *de facto* recognition to the Soviets, which would in its own way imply recognition of ownership of the oil lands. In any event, Krassin was not to be decoyed. He replied that he was willing to negotiate about "the oil wells formerly owned by them in South Russia and the Caucasus."

There was good reason for the Soviet caution, for Deterding had been busy buying up property rights from any who would sell—émigré Russians, small oil firms, and proprietors. From the first-named he had acquired a factory in the Nikopol-Mariupol region that specialized in making piping for oil companies. Little escaped his gaze in advancing the new venture.

There were others in the same kind of business. In 1920 Standard Oil had purchased a half-interest in the Swedish Nobel firm's Russian concessions, one of the oldest in the Caucasus which had, in 1914, produced 50 percent of all the Baku-region oil.

Boyle's plan of operation relied heavily on the fact that technically the Caucasus was an independent republic, capable of making its own treaties. It was a strange condition, stemming from a "Declaration of the Right of the Peoples of Russia," issued early in the regime's takeover by Stalin and Lenin. Clause two of the declaration spoke of "the right of the peoples of Russia to free self-determination, even to the point of separation and the formation of an independent state."

At Kiev the Central Rada immediately declared a free, independent Ukrainian Republic. Finland, Siberia, and the Caucasus followed suit. Even the Polish troops in the Russian forces sent away their commissars and formed their own military committee. It was a situation that could not continue, but it took several years to bring the dissidents back into the national fold by force of arms. Bolshevik theory was one thing; its practice was another. An agreement with Moscow would be very helpful, perhaps in the end a necessity, but one signed and sealed by the autonomous Georgian-Caucasus government could hardly be ignored.

To facilitate negotiations, all the Russian holdings of Royal Dutch–Shell were transferred to the British side of the consortium. In addition to having the financial resources with which to repair damage and neglect on the properties, Shell now possessed some shadow of legal claim to them as well. Boyle was sure the Russians lacked the monetary sinews to undertake the work themselves, whether it was directed from Moscow or Batum.

Even as he worked to advance the interests of his oil industry associates Boyle continued to think of, and work for, Rumania and its queen. He wrote frequently to Marie, offering counsel on many subjects, reporting to her on Prince Nicholas's progress at school in England, words of wisdom about agriculture, and cautions about the way in which she handled Carol.

His new position gave him opportunity to travel, and in June 1921 Boyle set out for Constantinople, pausing for two weeks to visit Marie and enjoy her company. It was a poignant meeting in many ways. They took trips to the countryside spots where they had first learned to understand what was in their hearts. The queen spoke, too, of her affection for this strange land and how she intended to have her heart kept in a special vault there when she died. Death may have cast a shadow on their meetings. This was not the Boyle she had first known, but he was attempting to drive himself at the same old pace in another great design. When he departed she could not have known that she would never see him again but, as a believer in psychic phenomena, she may have sensed it.

Negotiations were necessary, and Boyle could be patient when necessary. But he had no reason to wait around for the diplomats to cross the T's and dot the I's. He joined Hill, Tzegintzov, and Solly in Constantinople and approved a plan to purchase two speedy vessels that could be used in their activities on the Caspian Sea. Solly, the transportation expert, and Hill, the linguist and intelligence man, planned to travel to the Caucasus, visiting Batum on the extreme eastern limit of the Black Sea, and Baku on the Caspian. It had to be self-sustaining because of the shortage of food in Russia and the uncertainty of transport and communications. The vessels, two high-speed anti-submarine patrol ships offered for sale as war surplus by the British Admiralty, were found to be seaworthy, with good performance records and a list of submarine "kills" to their credit. They were renovated and their facilities increased to permit six travellers to move in comfort with the ship's crew of five. These were to be sailed to Batum, then moved over the mountains to a permanent base at Baku, from which they could service the entire Caspian oil area.

Boyle returned to London where he attempted to speed approval of the purchase, which did not arrive, however, until 15 December. With his preparations well advanced, Boyle formally approached the Foreign Office with news of the project he was launching and asked for formal support, which emerged a few weeks later in the form of Curzon's letter. Royal Dutch–Shell, he informed the Foreign Office, had twenty holdings in Russia that it hoped to exploit.

The confirmation of the sale of the vessels permitted Hill and Solly to depart for the Caucasus, where for two months they worked unceasingly, stitching together an oil deal on the terms Boyle had outlined. They had been armed with a power-of-attorney to act for Boyle, so they were in a position not only to make proposals but to close deals. It went swimmingly for them, and after two months of non-stop talking to Bolshevik leaders of the region, national committees, and the Georgian foreign office in Tiflis, they were ready to present agreements for the signatures of the various notables.

As they were unwinding in a Batum hotel they were informed that a Colonel Boyle was on a ship in the harbour and wanted to see them. For some two months they had lived in virtual isolation, unaware of what had been going on elsewhere; therefore they could not even guess the reason for this unexpected visit. They found Boyle on the ship with a new assistant, Frank Douglas,* an old Klondiker, and noticed that he looked drawn and unwell, although he appeared in good spirits. Hill, who recounted the events in his book, *Dreaded Hour*, noted that Douglas took lengthy notes of the conversations.

Although he was quick to applaud the success they were reporting, their employer insisted on being personally conducted over the ground they had travelled and to meet the people with whom they had been dealing. They could only agree, and they set off by railway over the mountains to Baku, thence to Tiflis, stopping en route at all the places they had visited. Boyle's conduct baffled them. Usually charming when necessary, he appeared deliberately rude and out-of-sorts, short-tempered, and anything but diplomatic. After a week it was clear that the regional pacts they were on the point of concluding would never be accepted, and that this result appeared to be what Boyle was after.

When they reached Tiflis he told them that he had to return to Europe to attend a world economic conference in Genoa, at which an agreement about oil resources would be reached at an international level. Their disappointment was tempered by the

---

*Douglas, a former Canadian Army sergeant, had been named along with Boyle as illegally wearing Canadian uniform in a 27 March 1920 letter received by Canadian Army Headquarters in Ottawa. The writer was an Algernon Sladen, who charged that these actions, and others, were bringing discredit on the Canadian nation.

realization that their Canadian chief had overtaxed his strength in making the trip, and they were genuinely alarmed for him as they assisted him into the train for the wearying, six-hundred-mile trans-mountain journey from Tiflis to Batum. The train was heavily loaded with passengers. As it made ready to depart they saw a private car attached to it, and were told it was for a group of Bolshevik dignitaries.

The Caucasus mountains were a challenge for the trains, with steep gradients and breath-taking hairpin curves, a difficult enough route at any time but positively dangerous when traversed by the war-worn equipment on which they had to move. The hours passed slowly for Joe Boyle in his distress, and his companions shared his discomfort. It was bad enough going painfully upgrade, but worse when they had passed the height of land and went rushing down with cars swaying and jolting as brakes were applied. The speed of the train seemed to increase as they plunged into a particularly steep gorge. There was no indication that the brakes were being applied.

Hill reported that trouble began as they went through the Suram tunnel approaching a small station. The train added to the clamour for it struck a series of gongs, set up at thirty-yard intervals, which signalled instructions according to the position in the tunnel. The train gave a terrific lurch and threw Hill from his bunk. Boyle, aware that something was wrong, staggered in from the adjoining compartment. He ordered Hill to see whether he could apply the handbrake at the rear of the car, while he attempted to brake it from the front. They soon realized that the brakes had been sabotaged and the train could not be halted. The berserk engine and its cars tore through the station, went partway up the grade on the other side, and jolted to a stop over the bank of a steep ravine. According to Hill, the train crew and almost everyone in the first two carriages were killed. An inquiry established that the train had been sabotaged by dissidents trying to kill the Bolshevik officials. Almost miraculously, none of the Boyle party was seriously hurt. Another train took them to Batum the next day.

Colonel Joe, apparently reinvigorated by the incident, became talkative and amiable, a welcome relief from his dark moodiness. He gave his companions a full report of what was happening, and told them why he had sabotaged their mission, in order to delay any local agreement. He followed that with what Hill remembered as an amazing and wide-ranging exposition of global political and economic conditions. After learning of the international conference at Genoa, "he was positive," Hill wrote, "that any local settlements made now would not hold for long—unless supported by and based on an international agreement."

Boyle's mental condition, unfortunately, was not matched by his physical well-being. As the hours passed his legs, they noticed, began to swell and his breathing became laboured. Boyle gasped that Solly should remain in Batum while Hill accompanied him to Constantinople.

The sea voyage was a nightmare. Boyle, conscious and in great pain, become so swollen about the legs that his companions had to slit the legs of his pajamas to ease him. He was nursed throughout the night, but at dawn fell into an exhausted sleep suddenly ended by the pitching and rolling of the ship in a sudden Black Sea squall.

Boyle was carried on a stretcher to the Pera Palace Hotel in Constantinople. It was imperative that he be treated, but doctors were difficult to find. Hill came back with a small Greek who spoke English. He examined the exhausted patient and warned him bluntly that he would be risking his life if he attempted to proceed to Genoa. There were only two doctors, to his knowledge, who could treat the Canadian. One was a Swiss, the other Sir James Mackenzie, a London heart specialist who had attended King George V.

Boyle insisted that he had to move on and asked the doctor to do anything he could to help him. He lay patiently curious as he was treated by cupping. His companions watched in fascination as the doctor cut cross-like incisions in orderly fashion across Boyle's back. He heated several small glass cups by filling them with methylated spirits. After putting out the flame, he inverted each cup over an incision. The cups clung to the skin, and each, by the vacuum created in the process, drew off a portion of blood.

The incisions were treated with an antiseptic and dressed. This witchcraft astounded the onlookers, for within minutes Boyle had fallen into a deep, restful sleep. By the next day his legs were down to their normal size. Three days later he boarded the westbound Orient Express, clutching a ticket for Genoa.

THIRTY-ONE

The End of the Trail

The pilgrimage to Genoa, where Boyle hoped to conclude his pact with the Soviets, began on a low note. As soon as Boyle had shaken hands with Frank Reid and representatives of Royal Dutch–Shell, Hill insisted that his chief go to bed. They had taken up quarters in the Hotel London, but he was not to be permitted much time to recuperate after his 13 April arrival, for the conference had begun on 10 April.

Hill left Boyle briefly. While out of the hotel he met two journalists, Steven Smith of the Associated Press and G. Ward Price, a flamboyant London writer. Hill had been searching for a doctor, but his report that he had found one was of much less interest to Boyle than the story of his encounter with the newsmen. "Podge, keep your mouth shut," he ordered. He was only too aware that a few careless words might imperil the outcome of his work, for the world press, along with a glittering array of world political leaders and oil company representatives, had congregated in Genoa. It was an era of loudly heralded conferences to find solutions to the problems of the world, and this one, like most of the others, never lived up to advance billing.

It was imperative that Boyle meet with the Russian representatives, but they were quartered in Santa Margharita, a small village about an hour's drive from Genoa, so Boyle made what was now for him a difficult journey. Almost the the first member of the Soviet delegation he met was Christian Rakovsky, who greeted him with "Well, Colonel Boyle, I've still got your treaty in my pocket and despite Rumania's protestations in it they still have Bessarabia in their pocket. I hold you responsible. Please remember I shall always be willing to exchange the treaty for the province." It was sharp but good-natured raillery, a fair omen for the negotiations Boyle hoped to have with Krassin, Rakovsky, and the other members of the delegation.

The same talks would tell the Russians how Boyle assessed the Caucasian fields, and they were anxious and willing to accept his judgment of future development. Despite the good will between them, however, they reached an impasse, for the Russians hinted they were prepared to negotiate an immediate pact with Boyle's employing companies, while he was under instructions that such an agreement could only follow the conference. The Russians were politicians prepared to act immediately on economic measures, but Boyle was a business-man inhibited from decision-making because of instructions from his politicians. But all would be well—if only the conference gave its blessing to arrangements of the sort he was pursuing.

That there ever was a prospect for a quick and easy approval seems unlikely. A. C. Bedford of Standard Oil had set the tone of the whole meeting when he publicly demanded on the third day of the sessions that there should be "no attempt at Genoa, or through private agreement through various nations, to exploit the resources of Russia; but that it should be understood that a fair and equal economic opportunity should be preserved for all concerned." On those terms the conference could not succeed, for the British were there for entirely opposite reasons, anxious to see Royal Dutch–Shell in the driver's seat not so much for the future of the company as for the advantage of the British homeland and its interests overseas.

It was in many ways a strange sort of gathering, for the United States, having rejected Wilson and the League of Nations and internationalism, refused to send an official delegate, but made sure an observer was present with power to interfere. Strangest of all, oil was not even mentioned in the plenary sessions. Oil may not have been on the conference agenda but it cast a mighty shadow over the sessions, and the obvious scramble for oil leases made the Russians, in the words of Wickham Steed of the *Times*, "the arbiters of the conference."

The Soviets had thrown the conference off balance at the opening by announcing, with a flourish of propaganda, the conclusion of an agreement with Germany—the Treaty of Rapallo. It was a heady triumph for the defeated sides in the war, the two pariahs finding common ground to upset the victors.

What the conference hoped to settle was the fusing of Russian nationalization with the rights of property owners and leaseholders, a difficult task for the Bolsheviks, who had refused to pay compensation for nationalized properties. Prime Minister Lloyd George of Britain was the first to acknowledge the facts. He suggested that the Russians pay reparations to leaseholders and property owners by giving them ninety-year leases on their former territories, an arrangement that would have sanctified the confiscations. It would also have given Royal Dutch–Shell the inside track for they now held shadowy legal rights to a vast amount of the oil-producing territory. This proposal provoked an impassioned outburst from French and Belgian delegates (reasonably suspected of having been prompted by the delegateless U.S. observer) about the rights of private property.

Boyle's obviously friendly and frequent meetings with Krassin and Rakovsky gave rise to rumours that Shell had made an advance deal with the Soviets, a story that Boyle finally thought necessary to deny in a public statement.

The British, working to establish a position they believed had been privately accepted by the Russianss and would be publicly accepted by them, introduced a motion to define a former owner as one holding property or rights prior to 1918 nationalization, a condition that would have negated Standard Oil's purchase of half of the Nobel properties. At this juncture the U.S. government temporarily abandoned isolationism and instructed Italian ambassador Richard Washburn Child to negotiate for his country. He immediately urged a complete re-examination of the situation, a delaying device to put everything back to square one.

It was alleged that this speech followed a long strategy session with Standard Oil representatives. One observer wrote that the Russians were being stalled by U.S. interests, who were convinced that the Bolshevik regime was doomed to failure. "Standard's policy," wrote Glyn Roberts, "was to wait and watch, and perhaps to partake in a little boycotting and freezing-up of sources of trade. At the right moment, when the starving Bolsheviks, cap in hand, humbly admitting their error, begged for any terms, Standard would step in." He recognized the conference for what it was: a battle between oil giants involving the international interests of Britain and America. It was a struggle that would continue until after the Second World War, when Britain would be forced to cash in what few oil chips she had left.

Boyle's health prevented him from playing more than a spasmodic role in the sessions, for he was confined to his bed part of the time, and to a wheelchair when he was able to get around. He had lost upwards of sixty pounds, and his hair was greyed and silvered. Only his mind functioned as well as ever.

After a month of fruitless negotiations the conference suddenly ended, but the Soviets, almost certainly at Boyle's urging, suggested that the conference be reconvened at The Hague in August. Boyle was demonstrating his belief in the Churchillian observation, uttered much later, that it is better to

Jaw, Jaw, Jaw than War, War, War. As long as the parties could talk, there remained the possibility of a compromise. Boyle had learned much in those days with the Rumcherod in Odessa.

Following the end of the sessions Boyle held a meeting with Walter Samuel, the future Lord Bearsted and future head of Shell, in which it was agreed Boyle should return immediately to London for medical treatment. Hill recounts that Boyle consulted a leading heart specialist named Parkinson, whose first word was for Boyle to get his affairs in order at once. Providing his patient abstained from worry and gave up travel, he might live for several years, said Parkinson, but otherwise he could not hope to survive for very long. "Go to a nursing home immediately," he advised. "Never mind going back to your hotel." For once the Klondiker did as he was told, entering a nursing home near Paddington Station. His medical adviser expected him to stay there until he was well enough to leave, but Boyle intended to stay there only long enough to permit to him recover enough to get to Holland for the conference at The Hague.

Joe Boyle Junior was on hand; he had come to London some two years before and had briefly visited his father in Rumania. Young Joe's own affairs were in disorder, for he had separated from the Dawson bride he had married six years earlier and was intent on following the law, which he had always preferred to the engineering studies his father had insisted he take.

Boyle was no easy patient. He was attended by an efficient and kindly nurse, Dorothy Wilkie, who became more agitated than Boyle when she found him holding board meetings with Shell officials and his own staff members. His recuperative abilities were remarkable. Hill found him much improved after only a few days, fully expecting to take part in the next conference. He still held Shell's power-of-attorney and was intent on conducting and finally bringing to a successful conclusion his long negotiations with the Russians. Deterding and his senior associates felt it was unlikely that Boyle would attend the meetings although they did not say so, possibly out of kindness or respect for his feelings.

Boyle told his doctor that he would be leaving London on 14 June to attend the opening session the next day, and nothing the doctor could say would alter that decision. In any event he must not walk, the doctor insisted. Boyle grudgingly accepted that verdict. He was wheeled to Liverpool Station in an invalid's chair and placed aboard the train by Hill and Junior Boyle, en route to a sea passage from Harwich to the Hook of Holland.

Because of the location of the new meeting the Hague staff of the consortium had been placed in charge of things, under the direction of Deterding himself and Captain Samuel. They were mightily surprised, and more than a little upset, when Boyle was wheeled into the company's Scheveningen offices. In the painful meeting that followed, Shell's wide-ranging agent learned that there had been policy changes as well as staff changes. Boyle insisted that his agreement with Shell made him the negotiating head for the company. Deterding agreed that this was so, but said Boyle would have to act in concert with him.

One proposal that Boyle discovered was being considered was a Russian suggestion that Shell receive a block concession in Russia but accept the responsibility of settling the claims of others who were in the running by buying them out or sharing production. It was a comfortable deal for the Soviets, who would have their share of the revenues without any of the headaches implicit in ownership and leasehold claims by rivals. It would, however, have left Shell in command of the field, a condition unacceptable to the United States, France, Belgium, and a few others involved in the matter.

As predicted by the sceptics, the second conference settled nothing although it dragged on until 22 July, with the dogged Shell negotiator fighting valiantly to save it. Standard Oil was the villain and the victor, pressuring other European interests to oppose the Shell case. Russia's delegates, insisting on unacceptable conditions of long-term credit, finally made sure that nothing would be agreed upon.

In the opinion of Shell's Canadian negotiator the game had

been lost because the company had altered its tactics. This belief disrupted his easy-going relationship with Deterding, and it became even more difficult when Boyle spent a few weeks as Deterding's guest after the conference. They were now at odds on many things, and their inability to be reconciled very likely stemmed at least in part from Boyle's declining health. Although his first major breakdown, in Kishinev, had been a paralytic stroke, his problems now were a failing heart and a general breakdown in functions involving his kidneys, resulting in a dropsical condition in his legs. His condition made it imperative that he seek treatment; he was soon installed in a Sunningdale rest home, still battling and taking his fight to friends in the British government.

It was a futile struggle that merely incensed Deterding to the point that on 1 September 1922 Boyle's power-of-attorney was cancelled and he was left in the muddle of his shattered hopes and dreams. Withdrawal of his negotiating rights—he had in effect been fired—found him bitter, charging that Shell had not reimbursed him as promised. The company for its part made a fuss about some £8,000 it claimed Boyle had not accounted for. The sharpest blow to his pride was a Shell claim that he never had been more than a contractor, and not the associate he had understood he was, in the great design for Caucasian oil development.

Very quickly Boyle decided to go to the courts. By mid-September he was warning the former members of his staff of his projected course of action, asking them not to reveal the confidential intelligence work on which he and they had been engaged. September was to be a heavy month for all who hoped to bring Russia back into the comity of nations by the international development of her oil resources. Standard Oil assumed the lead during a third conference in Paris that month, persuading almost a score of companies, including Royal Dutch–Shell, to boycott purchase of Russian oil until all the previously existing rights and leases and properties had been restored to their foreign owners. It was a cut-throat business, for Shell returned to secret negotiations with Russia little more than six months later.

Boyle's break with Shell seemed irreparable. The company charged that he had refused to carry out policy instructions to safeguard its Russian interests. Boyle charged that Shell had broken its agreement with him. "Col. Boyle," Shell says today, "considered the severance of relations had been brought about by the Group and claimed 50,000 pounds, the agreed 'minimum' ... [and] a further sum of 50,000 pounds was claimed by way of damages for breach of contract in respect of which he was to be remunerated by a commission."

In many ways it was the termination of his association with Deterding for, as Shell admits, "from the tone of the correspondence between Sir Henry Deterding and Col. Boyle there was undoubtedly a good relationship but from the time the Group revoked all his powers of attorney there was a good deal of bitterness."

Boyle's health made it difficult for him to move, but he still got underway more quickly than the law courts, where his writ against Royal Dutch–Shell and associated firms could not be issued until 6 March 1923.

There was enough time left for one more adventure in the grand manner, perhaps the most courageous of his life, considering Boyle's physical condition.

In the autumn of 1922 Boyle and Hill had noticed a strange item in the newspapers reporting that the S.S. Claude A. Solly had been arrested in Batum. They realized that it was not a vessel being held for non-payment of port charges but their oil business associate of the same name. Boyle, who had been confined to bed, arose at once. He went to see Krassin in the Russian offices in London, paid a call to the Foreign Office, and alerted Tzegintzov in Constantinople, where he was still on the Shell payroll.

From private sources he learned that Solly was being held by the dreaded OGPU. Krassin professed to know nothing of the case and pointed out, untruthfully, that Georgia was an independent republic and could do as it pleased. There was no stopping the stricken giant, who announced his determination to proceed to Russia and free his man. The Orient Express would have him as a passenger one more time. His companions were George Hill and stout-hearted nurse Dorothy Wilkie, who insisted on going along with him. Boyle was game but weary when he met Tzegintzov in Constantinople, only to be told that Solly was not in Batum but had been locked up in Tiflis. Russian officials in Constantinople refused to issue him a visa to visit the "independent" Republic of Georgia. Boyle fired off cables to all and sundry, notifying Moscow officials among others that Solly must be freed.

The British embassy urged him to wait. The caution of the British officials didn't arise from a lack of interest; they knew that the Foreign Office was working hard in Moscow to resolve the matter and end a crisis that it appeared had been created not by the Georgians but by Moscow itself.

Boyle said he was going with or without a visa, told the Russians as much, and laid his plans. Finding berths on a coastal steamer proceeding to Batum, the fiery crusader set out on his final mission. The ship called first at Sochi on the Russian side of the Black Sea, and the Russians refused to let Boyle go ashore. They agreed, however, to send the telegrams of protest he had directed to London, Moscow, Tiflis, and Batum, telling the world he was on his way and would insist on landing at Batum unless Solly and his staff were freed.

Whatever the reasons—Boyle's clamour, British representations, or a change of heart—there was a message at the next port of call: Solly and two of his staff had been released, moved to Batum, and placed on an Italian steamer headed for Constantinople. "Wait for us," the message concluded. "We will pick you up and take you back to Constantinople." The name of their courteous host and his ship was not recorded in the joy of the reunion with Solly and his staff. They had a memorable party on the ship and Hill took a picture of them, one of the last ever made of his old commander.

On his way back to London he stopped in Athens and visited Marie's eldest daughter, Elizabeth, now the queen of Greece. He wrote Marie to tell of his visit but made no attempt to go to Rumania. He did not want his queen to see him in his present condition.

Boyle reached England early in November, stopping briefly in London before proceeding to Scotland and Ireland to visit relatives. Cousin Charlotte sadly recalled the last six-week visit to his ancestral home. Cousin Joe was so ill that he spent most of the morning in bed. But he got out to walk slowly to visit the neighbours and drink the tea that was always waiting for visitors. They all said he looked on the verge of death, but marvelled that he never spoke of his bad health. One day he said quietly to Charlotte that he would like to return to Canada, even visit the Klondike, though he realized it would hasten his death.

In the homey warmth of the Boyle home his spirits and interests revived enough for him to engage Alec in a lively argument about remodelling and enlarging The Burnside. It was something he could grasp, and back in London on 6 February 1923, concluding a residence at the Rembrandt Hotel, he sent an architect's drawing of what he had in mind with instructions to start the work. In his letter he said he might be making another trip to Constantinople in the near future.

A few days later he took up residence at Wayside, St. John's Road, Hampton Hill, in the home of his old and dear Klondike friend Edward (Teddy) Bredenberg. He wrote to tell his Irish kin of the new address and promised to visit Buckna once more when the tulips were blooming. Alec was sternly counselled to consider the virtues of raising pigs, an art that in England "was hopeless, no breed, no systematized care, no price.... Buy your sow and tell me what she costs, but get her and feed up your potatoes," he commanded. It was a lengthy letter, full of other instruction and advice, and warning that he would soon be over to see that his instructions were being followed. Brave words, but the truth was in the final lines: "For me I am doing quite all right, sometimes a bit better, sometimes not so good, but one way and another God is very good to me, and I can see the brightness in the sun when it shines."

In his small room he had his bed arranged so that he could sit up and enjoy the sunshine and look at the spire of St. James Church, just across the road. His life with the Bredenbergs was as happy as it could be made. His relationship with his only son, who came but rarely, had not improved, although Junior Boyle knew his father was dying. The Bredenberg sons, Thorvold, Anthony, and Chris, were a delight to the ailing guest. He and Teddy spent many hours yarning of the old days. He continued to write letters, some pursuing his court action against Shell, others to the love of his life in Bucharest who, like others, realized he was dying.

As he sank he found himself unable to write. Tony Bredenberg was enlisted to handle his correspondence. He told later of Boyle's frequent letters to Marie. He sent a few of his own to put her properly in the picture, and as a friend of Joe Boyle he too became a friend of the queen.

Some time on 13 April Joe Boyle wrote two letters and placed them under his pillow. Nurse Wilkie, tenderly caring for him, noted he had had a peaceful night but had not slept. Saturday morning, 14 April, dawned bright, clear, and warm, the sort of day that poets write about. About 10 A.M. Joe Boyle asked his nurse to draw back the curtains. She turned to do so as he spoke of getting up. When she looked back she realized he was dead.

Teddy Bredenberg took charge of the letters. One was addressed to him and thanked him for all the love and comradeship of their long association. The other was addressed to Queen Marie. He mailed it immediately. Soon afterwards Tony Bredenberg penned a telegram for Buckna. "Col. Boyle passed away at 10 to ten this morning," it read. "Please accept my sincerest sympathy."

Joe Boyle's death, in his fifty-sixth year, stirred a flood of obituaries. The *New York Times* took notice of his colourful career. In Woodstock the *Sentinel-Review* reported, wrongly, that Joe Boyle Junior was with his father when he died. His sister, Mrs. Susan Laperriere, told reporters that her brother's last wish had been to return to Canada and that he had just written instructing her to reopen The Firs and make ready to welcome him.

The truth was that Junior Boyle was in London, but miles from his dying father. When Teddy Bredenberg telephoned to inform him that his father was dead, the son instructed the Bredenbergs to arrange the funeral, saying that it would not be necessary for him to go to Hampton Hill until the day of the funeral, Tuesday, 16 April. This left Bredenberg in a quandary. He had planned to have George Hill make the arrangements in an emergency, but Hill was away for the weekend. Fortunately he managed to reach Tzegintzov, who came at once to plan this last service for his erstwhile commander.

So it was Tzegintzov who wrote to Marie with the full story of Boyle's passing. Six weeks later he received an acknowledgment in an emotional, twelve-page letter that Lord Beaverbrook, who read it years later, told Flora Boyle was one of the most remarkable and affecting he had ever read.

There was a special understanding between us, something deep, real, strong, I may say holy, based upon a perfect belief, faith and respect ... there was something straight in us both, straight and simple and uncritical, which made it seem that fate had meant us to come together....

He was all strength and honor, and he had given me his faith and I had given him my trust. We had clasped hands at the hour of deepest distress and humiliation and nothing could part us in understanding.... No one knew his heart better than I. Women played but little part in his life and he had a wealth of love unspent. I came to him at the end of a long, stormy road. I was in distress. He recognized at the same time some of his own spirit in me. I was something of a miracle in his life and when he had his stroke I was the haven in which he anchored for a while.

For me he is not dead. He was so big, he belonged absolutely to nature. For me he is in the trees, in the sky, in the sea, in the sun and in the wind that sweeps round my house. He is in the freshness of the early morning and the silence of the night—and the stars seem to watch me with his eyes and the clouds seem to bring me messages from that great heart that was mine.

By any standards this outpouring was the heartfelt cry of a woman in distress, of a woman who had been in love.

Hill was back in time for the funeral and placed a large, signed portrait of the queen above the casket. "Podge" recalled something else and put a spray of special orange lilies on the casket as well, flowers he knew had a private significance for Marie and Joe. Among other floral tributes was one from that indomitable little lady whose hand Boyle had been proud to shake in the distant Crimea—Dowager Empress Marie Feodorovna of Russia.

Several hundred attended the simple service, following the coffin, conveyed from Wayside on a hand cart to the grave in St. James Churchyard. They were from many walks of life: politicians, soldiers, and just plain friends.

Not all of them had left when two vans drew up at the Bredenberg home. Their drivers marched into the residence and the room in which Joe Boyle had died seventy-two hours earlier, and removed all his personal effects. They had been ordered to handle the task by Junior Boyle. Into the vans went all of Boyle's books, his correspondence, clothing, uniforms, pictures—everything that had been his. What became of them is a mystery, because in the years to come Junior Boyle seldom spoke of his father or of their days in the Klondike. He said later that he had destroyed all the rubbish and placed the rest in storage.*

---

*Recent events have shed some light on this account. On 30 June 1983 Flora Boyle Frisch told the author that in late 1926 she and her brother

In time a white stone cross appeared in the cemetery, with a white stone border on the rectangular sides of the plot, placed there by Lord Beaverbrook. It remained for some months, until Queen Marie herself came one day to Wayside. Bredenberg showed her the room in which Boyle had spent his final hours and was astonished when she walked up to the fireplace, dropped her head on her arms, and softly began to weep. There were some minutes of complete silence, after which she turned and remarked, "It's all right now, Teddy. He knows we're here. The Big Man knows we're here." It was then that Bredenberg realized that the queen was a spiritualist and a believer in psychic phenomena. He brought her to the cemetery where she looked at the grave, and said that she was not impressed by it. She had him measure the grave, and announced that she was arranging for its perpetual care and that he would be hearing more from her.

Bredenberg was warned that some large crates would be delivered to his home. In due course they came, followed not long afterwards by the queen herself. Once again she held her private communion with Boyle in his former bedroom, emerging refreshed to superintend the placement of a large stone slab on top of the grave. Some six feet in length, it was engraved in the lower right corner with the insignia of the Order of Maria Regina. On it had been engraved:

Joe had examined the Boyle effects in their London storage locker, where they had been placed by Joe Junior in 1923. They found some old uniforms, a sweat-stained forage cap Joe Junior would not let her have, and Queen Marie's private letters to Boyle. Together, following a request made to them by the queen, they destroyed the letters and a parchment in Rumanian writing that appeared to declare Boyle the Duke of Dawson. In response to Flora's questions about the medals, pictures, and other gifts from the queen, her brother told her he had them in safekeeping in a vault and would show them to her later. This he refused to do, and what happened to the medals and orders, the pictures and gifts, remains a mystery.

Lt-Col. Joseph Whiteside Boyle, CBE, DSO
November 6, 1867, April 14, 1923

At the foot of the slab were words from one of Boyle's favourite
Service poems, selected by Marie as his eternal epitaph:

... man with the heart of a Viking
and the simple faith of a child.

Subsequently the white stone cross disappeared, to be
replaced with an ancient, rough-surfaced gravestone, crudely
carved with a cross. It had been shipped from Rumania, from a
plot where Marie had shared her thoughts with her beloved.
They had talked of death, and she had suggested that Boyle
should be buried at Bran, and that her heart would be entombed
near him. The cross is said to be one of those planted on
Rumanian soil hundreds of years ago to mark the burial place of
some traveller in the ancient land. It may well have been such a
cross that Marie and Joe noted one late summer's day.

A less unfortunate addition soon appeared, a heavy concrete
urn in which the queen could place the flowers she brought to
the grave. She came as often as she visited her royal relatives in
England, which for a time was every year. In the urn she placed
those special lilies she and Boyle had so admired, and which they
considered a secret link between them. Around the grave she
planted tendrils of ivy, carried from the Rumanian countryside.
They flourished and at one time half-covered the stone.

Periodically, Bredenberg told friends, the queen appeared,
heavily veiled for her vigil in the Wayside room and a lonely
return to the grave. She maintained her anonymity, although
one of these visits attracted the notice of a London columnist
speculating on the identity of the lady in black who appeared
from time to time at this suburban cemetery.

In New York, during her 1926 North American visit, she told
Flora that the grave would be maintained forever, and decorated
from time to time with the lilies of remembrance. She was
convinced, she said, with simple and obvious conviction, that
Boyle was with her, for "he is beside me in death as I was always
beside him in life." Unhappily for the best-intended promises,

the perpetual care was temporary—cancelled, it is said, by Carol upon his accession to the Rumanian throne. The queen died before the Second World War, and thereafter the appearance of the grave declined. It became overrun with weeds and tall grass, the stone half-visible and the slab covered with dead leaves, soil, and weeds.

It was briefly cleared in 1954 with a promise, kept for several years, that it would never again be permitted to fall back into its weed-covered muddle. But by 1971 it was obvious the promise had been unfulfilled, for once more it was almost lost, along with the other graves, in the green grass and vegetation.

The cross assumed a slight tilt, but remained something distinctly foreign, much different from any other marker in the cemetery. In her book, *My Country*, the queen seems to speak of this very stone:

One was especially dear to my heart. It stood alone in dignified solitude upon a barren field, frowning down upon a tangle of thistles that twisted their thorny stems beneath its arms.... It appeared to have been there from the beginning of time. Tired of its useless vigil it was leaning slightly to one side, and at dusk its shadow strangely resembled the shadow of a man.

❧ THIRTY-TWO ❧

Aftermath

Settlement of Boyle's estate was long delayed. For one thing there was little left to distribute: fewer than £3,000, and whatever might be realized in Boyle's action against Royal Dutch–Shell.

Final distribution came in October 1929, after Boyle's will was found in a trunk full of oddments sent from Rumania. The will confirmed Junior Boyle as executor. The net estate was divided with one-third to Elma Boyle, one-sixth each to Joe Junior and daughter Flora, and one-ninth each to sister Susan and brothers David and Charles.

There was nothing to recover from Boyle's fabled gold lands in the Klondike. After the Canadian Klondike Mining Company and its various subsidiaries had been forced into bankruptcy, the creditors settled for about fifty cents on the dollar. The properties, acquired by Yukon Consolidated, became part of the single corporation that had always been the dream of Arthur Newton Christian Treadgold, and for a time he was in charge of the consolidated operations.

Junior Boyle had arrived alone in London. He was jobless but always seemed to have resources, arousing some family suspicions that he retained something from the wreck of the mining ship. One of his tasks was to pursue the action his father had launched against Deterding and his consortium. This claim went to arbitration instead of trial and finally was settled on payment of £25,000, about $125,000 in those days, comprising almost all the assets there were to distribute. Arbitration commenced 21 November 1924. The settlement disappointed and angered some of the heirs, particularly when they learned that Joe Junior had been given a good position with Royal Dutch–Shell that led, eventually, to a directorship and made him head of the firm's large legal department, which he helped to set up.

Shell's view is that Boyle was fairly dealt with. He had, the company points out, been advanced and spent £40,000. There is no occasion to challenge this; it is impossible to verify, since Shell records are not open to public inspection. How much of the amount was salary and how much expenses is not made clear. Boyle had an unlimited expense account, and he claimed he had never received any of the promised £50,000 minimum. Much of the settlement failed to get into the final disbursement, for both Shell and Deterding made claims and other levies to which the executor agreed, reducing the payment to £15,543. Included in the deductions was a payment for £1,566 to Deterding for the gift horses presented to Ferdinand, Marie, and Ileanna. The cost of the arbitration was minimal, a mere £210, split between the two principals of the settlement.

The deed of release of the estate, signed in 1929, tells us that Boyle's death notice in the *Times* cost 25*s*., and that when he died he owed Teddy Bredenberg £12 13*s*. 4*d*. for board and lodging. His simple funeral cost £410, the equivalent of about $2,000 today.

Some of the entries cannot be explained, such as the £2,375 paid "for services rendered in connection with Russia and England, 1922." And who, one must wonder, were the two Russian refugee children whose tuition fees of £50 were paid to A. L. Clarke of Beverly School, London? Most likely those of Tzegintzov, who had been reunited with his wife and children in

England. Revillion Frères of Paris were paid £117 for furs, and the architect who redesigned the Buckna ancestral home collected some £52.

Boyle's first wife, Mildred, was awarded $19,573 in back-alimony. Later she told Flora that she only collected about $11,000 and never got an accounting for the rest from her oldest child, the executor. His second wife, Elma, received $12,000 after seven years of separation.

Indicative of the light hand of the tax collector was a levy of £417 in death duties, including accrued interest. It all melted down to £7,097, about $35,000, in the net estate. As one critic remarked: "Whatever Joe Boyle was guilty of in the way of mismanagement, he had not feathered his own nest." Contrary to some opinions, he did not die penniless, but he passed away far from rich by the standards he had achieved in the prime of his success.

In this he differed from many of the gold rush winners, who died penniless losers. Treadgold, who outlived most of his Klondike contemporaries, was adjudged a bankrupt in 1920 and remained undischarged at the time of his death in 1950, a condition that hardly bothered him at all. He became, in fact, president of Yukon Consoilidated from 1925 to 1932, until his associates joined forces to remove him from a post he fought to the last to retain. Treadgold, like his friend and rival Joe Boyle, was much in the courts. He fought for the last seventeen years of his life, trying to overturn an adverse judgment in the Supreme Court of Canada that cost him control of the many leases he had squirrelled away, and which even Boyle had not been able to get from him. The Treader was still battling away in the courts at the age of eighty-seven, when he was struck and fatally injured by a London bus.

There are mysteries in the Boyle story, one of the most intriguing the presence on his grave stone of the CBE designation (Commander of the Order of the British Empire). Marie had some reason for inserting the inscription, and Shell correspondence refers to him with that distinction. Was the queen wrong when she had his CBE inscribed? Is there any truth to the legend that the order had been granted but withdrawn or, as one account has it, rejected by Boyle because of the disasters at Genoa and The Hague? There is another legend: that Marie wanted to write "Duke of Jassy" on the marker, but was dissuaded by her British relatives and advised that a posthumous CBE would be issued.

As far as the official record is concerned, "there is no record held in the Central Chancery [of the orders of knighthood] that Lt-Colonel Joseph Whiteside Boyle DSO was ever appointed an Officer of the Order of the British Empire." Flora Boyle says she knows the secret, but the story was told to her in strictest confidence by Queen Marie and she is unable to relate it. Unless she does so, the secret will die with her.

The irony is that a Joe Boyle did win the CBE—Joe Boyle Junior was decorated for services to the Allied cause in the Second World War. This surviving Joe Boyle had grown in the shadow of the great oak that was his father, but managed to rise above the shackles that such an upbringing can impose. He became a person of stature in London, active in social, theatrical, and sporting life, as well as in business. He had studied law under a tutor, cramming hard in the evenings, to obtain the professional qualifications of a barrister.

His sister Flora, and his secretary of many years, the late Miss Marion Braham, agree that he never was formally invested with his legal laurels because he did not take enough dinners in the Middle Temple, but his abilities in the law field impressed as stern a judge as Deterding.

All his life he was enchanted with the theatre and, lacking his father's inhibitions, was in search of lovely ladies. His early romance with Elsie Janis was terminated when his father stepped in. But in London, even as he rose in the Shell legal hierarchy, he followed the footlights and became a theatre patron and backer.

Freed from his Dawson wife, Joe Junior became involved in a tragic love affair affair that ended in a headline-writing scandal in every American yellow journal. The romance began just after he reached England. He fell in love with one of the most beautiful graduates of the Ziegfeld Follies, a former telephone operator from Erie, Pennsylvania, who won fame as the glamorous Kay Laurell, one of the most highly paid stars of the era, rewarded for her beauty, for she never spoke a line.

Dumb on the stage, Kay was anything but that elsewhere. She was an intelligent, ambitious, hard-driving young woman who wanted to become a cosmopolite so much so that she studied French, Spanish, music, dancing, deportment, and elocution. She rode horseback and played golf, which was slowly becoming fashionable with women of her class.

In 1916 this determined creature married Winfield Sheehan, secretary to the police commissioner of New York City, in a Roman Catholic church in London. A year later they quarrelled and separated under a separation agreement forbidding remarriage. Some five years later she met Joe Boyle Junior, and they fell in love. Unable to marry, they lived together. When in 1926 she discovered she was pregnant, both parties rushed to obtain divorces to legitimize the child. It was a race against time that failed. On 31 January 1927, Kay Laurell gave birth in a London hospital. Informed that it was a son she replied, "Good, that's just what I wanted," and died within a few minutes. She was thirty-seven, the same age as her lover.

A few hours before her death she signed a will making Joe Boyle Junior her sole heir and executor, a more substantial legacy than he may have realized, for she had saved her money and had been generously treated by Sheehan. The will was so worded that it did not include any assets she might have in the United States. This point seemed inconsequential until, two years later, her mother died and it was discovered that Kay had left about $100,000 in various kinds of securities and bank deposits in her mother's care.

Joe Junior's divorce came soon after Kay's death. He married three times in all, and acquired a substantial estate after the death of his second wife. He had no more children, and many thought the Boyle male line would expire with his death. They had forgotten, or never knew, of the son by Kay. Boyle raised the child and pursued a history-making lawsuit in the United States in an attempt to claim the American assets for his son. The suit provided dramatic opportunity for the Hearst Sunday supplements, for illegitimate children had consistently been refused this kind of relief.

But this was a Boyle child, and the Boyles often won. In his case, the court ignored precedent and ruled that the $125,000 now accumulated belonged to the child and would be held for him in trusteeship until his age of majority. There is, somewhere on the continent of North America, a middle-aged direct descendant of Klondike Joe Boyle, the saviour of Rumania, although he does not welcome the limelight and has refused to talk about the Joe Boyles from whom he stems.

This man's father lived adventurously, although not on the scale of the King of the Klondike who sired him. During the Second World War Joe Junior and his private secretary, Marion Braham, were seconded to Britain's Enemy Shipping Claims Committee along with another Shell executive, Leonard Astley-Bell. Their activities remain a secret, but Miss Braham admitted that they had to do with the recovery of funds from properties and industries owned by enemy firms, and with preventing enemy agents from obtaining rare, invaluable, and very necessary war materials around the world. The operation saved millions of pound sterling that might have landed in the treasury of the Axis powers and earned Boyle a very justly awarded CBE.

Boyle retired in 1950, but not before one final fling in keeping with the Boyle tradition for a last curtain. The advent of the Iranian oil crisis in 1948, with the rise to power of Mossadegh, was the forerunner of what happened in that unhappy country in the recent past. Once more Shell was imperilled by the actions of extreme nationalists, and once more it called on a Boyle to help. Joe Junior, recruited for the assignment, was dispatched incognito to Iran where, Miss Braham said, he toiled under cover for eighteen months in difficult negotiations that at least averted the crisis that came thirty years later.

Following his retirement Junior Boyle and his third wife made their home in the Bahamas. He died there in 1960, possibly by his own hand after discovering that he was the victim of terminal cancer.

In Woodstock the slow disintegration of the Boyles occurred over a period of many years. The Firs, abandoned about 1920, was lost some five years later when Ebenezer L. Sutherland of Embro sued for non-payment of $5,059 principal and interest on a mortgage taken out by Dave Boyle in 1915. Dave, who remained a bachelor, was employed as a steward on Canadian and Mexican race tracks, making his home in Woodstock between seasons and, as was the old custom, turning up once a year to pay all the family bills.

Of the Boyle children only two survive, Flora Alexander, making her home on Long Island where she was 89 years of age on 24 May 1983; and Charlotte, the sister born after the breakup of the first marriage, who resides in Rochester, New York.

Flora's interest in her father was heightened one Saturday in August 1920, when she met Prince Carol in New York and heard him pay lavish tributes to Joe Boyle, the man who was responsible for the survival of the country he one day would rule. He urged Flora to visit Rumania. She replied that she would be glad to do so if the invitation was extended jointly by the queen and her father. She was studying art in New York and living at the Brotzell Hotel in West 27th Street but lacked the means, and the invitation, to make the journey.

Six years later, happily married to art connoisseur and yachtsman C. Henry Frisch, she and her husband were invited to meet Queen Marie at the Ambassador Hotel. The queen insisted that they stay on for a private audience, at which she talked at length about Joe Boyle and what he had done for her country. They met several times more in the course of the week the queen spent in New York. Marie talked about Joe for hours and presented Flora with photos and other mementos of his life in Rumania. One of the jewels she wore, Flora noticed, was a necklace of gold nuggets, the gift of the sourdough who loved a queen.

Marie urged the Frischs to come to Rumania and take up the ducal estate that had been granted to Boyle with his title. Flora was almost persuaded but her husband, strongly republican in sentiment much as he appreciated the queen, objected that they would have to give up their American citizenship.

The queen's tour crossed the continent, touching several points in Canada; one of them was Toronto, where she met Dave Boyle in private audience. He admitted that Marie was graciousness itself. He did not refer disparagingly to his brother's dukedom any more after the meeting.

Marie's public tribute to Joe Boyle was printed in the Montreal *Family Herald and Weekly Star*, a contrived piece of work, probably fashioned with the assistance of a "ghost," which lacked the spontaneity and conviction of her letter to Tzegintzov.

Marie was called home in 1927 because of the serious illness of Ferdinand, who died the following July. Carol assumed the throne, but his relationship with the Queen Mother continued to be stormy. Marie's last years were desperately unhappy, as Carol cut off the perquisites of her position and reduced her staff, estate, and income. She died at Pelishor on 18 July 1938, after a painful illness that defied special treatment in Dresden. Rumanian rumour, among the most vicious in the world, even said that she had been shot by her son during a wild quarrel. The facts seem to be otherwise, but the story may have been acceptable to some who heard it and knew Carol's history.

Flora Boyle's married life was happy but brief. Her husband Henry lost his business and residential property in New York and Westchester in the Great Crash of 1929. She was left a widow not long afterwards when he suffered a fatal heart attack. Forced to support herself, Flora attacked the problem with all her Boyle tenacity, making a career in radio as a commentator and script writer. She worked with the Judy Canova staff when that talented entertainer was on the Paul Whiteman Hour. Fascinated by her father's story, she wrote a series for *Maclean's Magazine* in 1938 that encouraged her to think of a full-scale biography. With this in mind, she sailed to England early in 1939, intending to visit the British Isles and Rumania in search of material, and hoping to spend some time on the estate of the Duke of Jassy.

In England she and her brother met George Hill, whose book about his adventures with Boyle had just appeared. Joe Junior, rather surprisingly, is said to have been incensed at some of the things Hill had written, and threatened to knock down the former intelligence agent. Hill, contrite, admitted he had inflated his own role in the story.

Both the Boyle children were angered by the Kim Beattie book, published in Canada with its recitation of fictional exploits of a hero who hardly needed imaginary deeds to augment the genuine. Hill, in his turn, charged that Beattie was guilty of plagiarism, and the anger of all of them was heightened when it was announced that Beattie was selling film rights for the book, the film to be made in California.

Flora, trapped in England by the war, determined to return and halt the film project. She had written several articles about her father for Lord Beaverbrook's *Daily Express*; it was that old friend of her family who came to her rescue once more. Thanks to Beaverbrook, whose political star was rising as the war worsened, Flora was able to find a way home through neutral Ireland. She went directly to Hollywood, breathing literary fire and legal destruction, and put the quietus on the proposed film story of her father's life.

The Canadian Army had a brief, final look at Boyle in 1927. Forty years later the army headquarters library in Ottawa had no publication that even referred to him.

After more than half a century, it is possible to make some estimates of Joe Boyle's career and to pronounce more firmly on one of the most remarkable Canadians in the nation's history.

We now know that Klondike Joe Boyle was much more than the doughty adventurer that some of his contemporaries had labelled him. He was a thruster, of course, but a talented one. Like most of the men who sought their fortunes in the Klondike he was forceful, and at times domineering and overbearing. He was either admired or disliked, but he was never ignored.

He was a simple man in many ways. But his actions were complicated at times, and his depths hard to plumb. His feeling for his family ran deep, and the way in which he responded in the environment of the Boyle home in Ireland was genuine and affecting. But he could be cold and uncaring, as witness the treatment of his second wife, Elma, the woman from Detroit who might better have, as some said, been married comfortably to a middle-class businessman.

Queen Marie rightly diagnosed that until she entered his life, women had played but a secondary role in Joe Boyle's considerations. His dealings with his first wife were strict but open, which is probably more than could have been said for her dealings with Joe.

Children adored him, and looked up to their Uncle Joe, and he had the capacity of making each one of them feel special. A child's instinct in these things is more often than not a reliable guide to the character of an adult. From the Klondike through the years until he became a hero to the children of the royal family of Rumania, Joe Boyle could relate to youngsters and they could enjoy his company.

One of the children Joe Boyle charmed is Mrs. Molly Crickmay, of Morro Bay, California, who met Joe Boyle at the turn of the century in London. She then was Molly Boyle, a sister of English Joe Boyle, who was eventually a member of the Bear Creek office staff in the Klondike.

He came to our house with a letter of introduction to my father who was a newspaper publisher at the time. Although our surnames were the same we were not related, but "Uncle Joe" as we called him, soon became a family friend.

He stayed at our house in London and to my four younger brothers and me he was a hero. He was so big and strong he could carry two or three of the boys on his back. He told us stories of adventure, all thrilling to us, somewhat sheltered children in Victorian London.

Mrs. Crickmay remembers the excitement of the day when Uncle Joe gave the children a golden sovereign to be equally divided among them. She spent her share on an autograph book and the first name in it, with an original verse in his hand, is that of Joe Boyle. It is dated 14 January 1902 and that young admirer has never surrendered her gift.

In 1907 she spent a holiday at The Firs in Woodstock, the year after her family moved to the United States. Uncle Joe, she remembers with delight, took her, his mother, and Flora on a boat trip through the Thousand Islands. "I am in my nineties," Mrs. Crickmay concludes in a letter recalling her experiences, "but I am glad that I can still remember Uncle Joe, our hero of long ago."

The magnitude of Joe Boyle's achievements are relatively unknown, perhaps because some of them crumbled to dust almost within his relatively brief lifespan. The scope of his activities in Eastern Europe, now demonstrated in his own documents, has not previously been realized. Furnished often with inadequate tools, human and otherwise, he attained far more than any man had a right to expect, as he fought his country's enemies and those of the Rumania with which he became so closely associated. When he succeeded it was through force of character and indomitable courage, linked to foresight and daring. Joe Boyle did not suffer fools gladly or take No for an answer. His documents are proof of how his capacities expanded in the crisis of a world war.

Essentially, he liked people, regardless of rank or station. It irked some that he had the common touch coupled with the ability to live comfortably with the more exalted. Even his most resolute business enemies found him a lifelong friend. His solid virtues, as much as his pugnacity and tenacity in argument, upset those who disliked him.

He had his share of disaster. Sometimes it was the product of his own impetuosity; on other occasions he was overcome by forces he could not control. His Rumanian-Russian peace treaty foundered on the greed of Rumanian politicians to hold Bessarabia. His work to consolidate Shell properties in the Caucasus and establish a working relationship with the Bolshevik government of Russia was undone by politicians and the rivalry of global oil consortiums. Regardless of his successes and failures it cannot be said of him that his reach was less than his grasp.

It may be fairly said of him that he could have been more tolerant at times. He demanded much of people, but asked none for more than he would himself attempt. His combativeness frequently led him to excess, particularly in the Yukon where his resort to courts, and his persistence in pushing his cases, sometimes went to extremes. This aggressiveness, so useful in wartime, was a peacetime burden that led to unnecessary problems domestically and in the wider world of human relations. Joe Boyle, it is likely, suffered from an abundant masculinity that made it difficult at times to express the emotions he so obviously felt.

His qualities were magnificent, and sometimes his faults matched them. But had he been all of the things in which his critics found him at fault, he would not have been Joseph Whiteside Boyle DSO, King of the Klondike, Duke of Jassy, and Saviour of Rumania. The world, for its part, would have been much the poorer.

Bibliography

A NOTE ON THE BOYLE PAPERS

Much of this account of the life of Joseph Whiteside Boyle is based on previously unpublished information derived from people who knew him and, primarily, from a treasure trove of Boyle documents somewhat miraculously preserved in Northern Ireland. These Boyle Papers, as I prefer to refer to them, are foundation material for any story of the fascinating Canadian hero. They comprise scores of documents, reports, letters, memoranda, notes, photographs, receipts, and papers of many kinds, having to do with his career overseas, and to a lesser extent with the collapse of his mining empire in the overwhelming distraction of a world war in which Boyle became totally immersed. My interviews with upwards of a dozen people who lived near his ancestral home in Ulster were timely but not by a great deal, for they all are now dead, including his favourite cousin Charlotte. Between them they sketched "Cousin Joe" in his most human moments, demonstrating the simple, very attractive side of a still very complex character.

A major source of information has been his daughter Flora of Long Island, New York, with whom I spent some ten days writing down and taping her story of her life at the family home in Woodstock, Ontario, in the Klondike, and in sundry other cities in North America and England. It was Flora who insisted that there were many important Boyle documents extant, despite general opinion that none had survived, and that they could be found in Ireland.

This certainty led the author overseas, first to England and Hampton Hill, where Boyle had been buried in 1923, and then to Upper Buckna, Broughshane, Ballymena, County Antrim, where James A. Boyle, present occupant of what had been the Boyle ancestral home since 1720, was able to provide the clinching evidence. Only a few weeks earlier, he said, he had taken a small trunkful of papers left in Ireland by Colonel Joe to the Public Records Office of Northern Ireland in Belfast.

James Boyle, a high school teacher, realized there was something unusual about this mass of material, some of it in Russian and French, that had been kept under the stairs for more than half a century. His sister Mary, the wife of British Foreign Office employee Ian Soutar, recalls that as a child the contents of the trunk were examined by the Boyle children, who found them strange and fascinating but unenlightening.

So in 1970, the Boyle Papers came to my attention while still being processed in the Public Records Office. The extent of their information is exciting, including letters, reports, and memoranda to senior Russian officials of the Kerensky government with whom Boyle dealt, to the military leaders of a nation in its last gasp, and to the revolutionary leaders who succeeded them. It is possible, through them, to trace Boyle's steps on an almost daily basis for two years, and to share his personal hopes and fears through correspondence with ambassadors, Rumanian political leaders, and royalty. Reports in his own handwriting verify the almost unbelievable stories that were spread abroad about this remarkable Canadian. One of the unique photos was not in the box. It is a cardboard-mounted group picture, found in the home during my visit, of Joe Boyle and the Rumanian hostages, taken while they were held captive in Theodosia in the Crimea, whence Boyle finally carried them off to safety—one of his most remarkable exploits.

The scope of his imagination may be seen in plans for hydro works he hoped to see built in Rumania. His interest in weapons is clear in documents and drawings of quick-firing guns that he may have hoped to use with his Yukon machine gun company.

Flora Boyle, who had come into possession of a small amount of Boyle material during a visit to England, was found to be the possessor of a number of loose pages of text that could be married-up with partial letters or reports found in Ireland.

It is impossible to know how Boyle felt about the collection of documents having to do with the court action through which, in his absence, his Klondike gold mines were put into receivership and eventually lost. Boyle, deep in the heart of revolutionary Russia, did not get most of the letters he might have answered, and when he did, he ignored pleas to come home and defend himself.

The Boyle Papers should be a national treasure. It is the author's hope that the National Archives open negotiations with Flora Boyle and the Public Records Office of Northern Ireland to have them permanently deposited in Ottawa.

Meanwhile, Canadians owe the Public Records Office a vote of thanks for cataloguing and preserving the documents.

A NOTE ON OTHER SOURCES

The Dawson newspapers are one of the best sources of information about Boyle's career in the Klondike. Lewis Green, in his book centring on A. N. C. Treadgold, covers the concessions disputes in detail. Professor William Rodney's scholarly book about Boyle includes valuable material from British official records. Researchers can benefit from a close look at Ethel Greening-Pantazzi's story of the rescue of the Rumanian hostages.

This book has been aided by an opportunity to study excerpts from his personal diary provided to Flora Boyle by Colonel Dmitri Tzegintzov. Although it is flamboyant, the Kim Beattie story is untrustworthy, and pure fiction in many places. There is reason to accept the accounts of Captain George A. Hill, DSO, of his experiences working with Boyle. Many of the sources, however, perpetuate misconceptions and legends developed in the first instance around 1920 in *Chambers* and other British publications.

There is little completely reliable evidence of Boyle's early years, including his three years at sea. I have used, in large measure, stories told by Boyle to his Irish kinfolk and friends, which parallel some told by Beattie.

Articles

BOYLE, FLORA ALEXANDER. "They Knew Joe Boyle." *Maclean's Magazine,* 1 November 1938.

————. "Who Was Joe Boyle?" *Maclean's Magazine,* 1 June, 15 June, and 1 July, 1938.

HUNTER, T. MURRAY. "Sir George Bury and the Russian Revolution." A paper presented to the Canadian Historical Association in Vancouver, B.C., 10 June 1965.

Bibliography

WATSON, DOUGLAS. "The Exploits of Lieutenant-Colonel 'Klondike' Boyle." *Chambers Journal,* January 1920.

Newspapers

Dawson Daily News
London *Sunday Express*
Montreal *Family Herald and Weekly Star*
New York Times
Ottawa *Evening Citizen*
Ottawa *Free Press*
Ottawa *Journal*
Saint John *Daily News*
Toronto *Daily Star*

Toronto *Globe*
Toronto *Globe and Mail*
Toronto *Mail and Empire*
Toronto *Star Weekly*
Vancouver *News Advertiser*
Vancouver *Sunday Province*
Victoria *Daily Colonist*
Victoria *Times*
Windsor *Daily Star*
Woodstock *Sentinel-Review*

Books

ABRAMOVITCH, RAPHAEL R. *The Soviet Revolution.* London: George Allen and Unwin, 1962.

ADNEY, EDWIN TAPPAN. *The Klondike Stampede.* Fairfield, Wash.: Ye Galleon Press, 1968.

ALEXANDER, GRAND DUKE. *Once a Grand Duke.* Long Island, N.Y.: Garden City Press, 1932.

BAIRD, ANDREW. *60 Years on the Klondike.* Vancouver: Black, 1965.

BANDHOLTZ, MAJOR-GENERAL HARVEY HALL. *An Undiplomatic Diary.* New York: Columbia University Press, 1932.

BEATTIE, KIM. *Brother, Here's a Man.* Toronto: Macmillan, 1940.

BERCOVICI, KONRAD. *That Royal Lover.* New York: Brewer and Warren, 1931.

BERTON, PIERRE. *Klondike.* Toronto: McClelland and Stewart, 1958.

BLACK, MARTHA. *My Seventy Years.* London: Nelson, 1939.

BOLITHO, HECTOR. *Biographer's Notebook.* London: Macmillan, 1950.

BONCH-BRUYEVITCH, M.D. *From Tsarist General to Red Army Commander.* Moscow: Progress Publishers, 1966.

BRINKLEY, GEORGE A. *The Volunteer Army and Allied Intervention in South Russia, 1917-1921.* South Bend, Ind.: Notre Dame University Press, 1966.

CHAMBERLIN, W.H. *The Russian Revolution.* New York: Macmillan, 1935.

CUNYNGHAME, FRANCIS. *Lost Trail.* London: Faber and Faber, 1953.

DAFOE, J.W. *Clifford Sifton in Relation to His Times.* Toronto: Macmillan, 1931.

DE ARMOND, R.N., ed. *"Stroller" White: Tales of a Klondike Newsman.* Vancouver: Mitchell Press, 1969.

DAGGETT, MABEL POTTER. *Marie of Rumania.* New York: Doran, 1926.

Dominion Law Reports. Toronto: Canada Law Book, 1912-.

FISCHER, LOUIS. *The Life of Lenin.* New York: Harper and Row, 1964.

GREEN, LEWIS. *The Gold Hustlers.* Anchorage, Alaska: Alaska Northwest Publishing Company, 1977.

GREENING-PANTAZZI, ETHEL. *Rumania in Light and Shadow.* Toronto: Ryerson, 1920.

GUINN, PAUL. *British Strategy and Politics.* London: Clarendon Press, 1965.

HAMILL, JOHN. *The Strange Career of Mr. Hoover Under Two Flags.* New York: Fargo, 1931.

HAMILTON, WALTER R. *The Yukon Story.* Vancouver: Mitchell Press, 1964.

HARD, WILLIAM. *Raymond Robins' Own Story.* New York: Harper, 1920.

HARRISON, MICHAEL. *Clarence: The Story of Edward (Eddy) First-Born of Edward VII and Alexandra.* London: W.H. Allen, 1972.

HILL, CAPT. GEORGE A. DSO. *Go Spy The Land.* London: Cassell, 1932.

———. *Dreaded Hour.* London: Cassell, 1936.

INNIS, HAROLD A. "Settlement on the Mining Frontier." In W.A. MacIntosh and W.L.G. Jeorg, eds., *Canadian Frontier Settlement.* Toronto: Macmillan, 1936.

KERENSKY, ALEXANDER. *Russia and History's Turning Point.* New York: Duell, Sloan and Pearce, 1965.

KING-HALL, STEPHEN. *My Naval Life.* London: Faber and Faber, 1952.

LEE, ARTHUR GOULD. *Helen, Queen Mother of Rumania.* London: Faber and Faber, 1956.

LEESTON, ALFRED M. *Magic Oil, Servant of the World.* Dallas: Juan Pablos Books, 1951.

Bibliography

LOCKHART, SIR ROBERT BRUCE. *The Diaries of Sir Robert Bruce Lockhart.* London: Macmillan, 1973.

MARIE, GRAND DUCHESS OF RUSSIA. *A Princess in Exile.* New York: Viking, 1932.

———. *The Education of a Princess.* New York: Viking, 1931.

MARIE, QUEEN OF RUMANIA. *Ordeal: The Story of My Life.* New York: Scribner's, 1935.

MORGAN, MURRAY. *A Klondike Album.* Seattle: University of Washington Press, 1967.

MORRELL, W.P. *The Gold Rushes.* London: Adams and Black, 1968.

MORRISON, DAVID R. *The Politics of the Yukon Territory, 1898-1909.* Toronto: University of Toronto Press, 1968.

MYER, ARNO J. *Politics and the Diplomacy of Peacemaking.* New York: Alfred A. Knopf, 1967.

O'BRIEN, JAMES J. *Hoover's Millions and How He Made Them.* New York: privately published, 1932.

O'CONOR, JOHN F. *The Sokolov Investigation.* New York: Robert Speller and Sons, 1971.

Ontario Weekly Reporter. Toronto: Carswell, 1902-16.

POPE, ARTHUR UPHAM. *Maxim Litvinoff.* New York: Fischer, 1943.

ROCHE, INTERIOR MINISTER W.J. *The Yukon Territory.* Ottawa: Government of Canada, 1916.

RODNEY, WILLIAM. *Joe Boyle: King of the Klondike.* Toronto: McGraw-Hill Ryerson, 1974.

ROBERTS, GLYN. *The Most Powerful Man in the World.* New York: Covici-Friede, 1938.

SETON-WATSON, HUGH. *The Russian Empire, 1801-1917.* Oxford: Clarendon Press, 1967.

STEELE, HARWOOD. *Policing the Arctic.* Toronto: Ryerson, 1936.

SUKHANOV, N.H. *The Russian Revolution.* London: Oxford University Press, 1955.

TCHEBOTARIOFF, GREGORY P. *Russia, My Native Land.* New York: McGraw-Hill, 1964.

WHEELER-BENNETT, SIR J.W. *Brest-Litovsk: The Forgotten Peace, March 1918.* London: Macmillan, 1956.

WILSON, COLIN. *Rasputin and the Fall of the Romanovs.* London: Barker, 1964.

WOLFF, ROBERT LEE. *The Balkans in Our Time.* Cambridge, Mass.: Harvard University Press, 1956.

Woodstock College Memorial Book, 1951. Woodstock, Ont., 1951.